Off the Books

Off the Books

The Underground Economy
of the Urban Poor

Sudhir Alladi Venkatesh

HARVARD UNIVERSITY PRESS
Cambridge, Massachusetts
London, England

First Harvard University Press paperback edition, 2008.

Library of Congress Cataloging-in-Publication Data

Venkatesh, Sudhir Alladi.

Off the books : the underground economy of the urban poor / Sudhir Alladi Venkatesh.

   p. cm.

Includes bibliographical references and index.

ISBN 978-0-674-02355-0 (cloth: alk. paper)

ISBN 978-0-674-03071-8 (pbk.)

   1. Informal sector (Economics)—Illinois—Chicago.   2. Poor—Illinois—Chicago.   I. Title.

HD2346.U52C535 2006

330—dc22   2006046213

To the barmen at Jimmy's Woodlawn Tap, for an ear and a pint, no questions asked

Contents

Prologue

In the early nineties, when I was a graduate student at the University of Chicago, I spent much of my time with families in the Robert Taylor Homes, a poor public housing development on the city's Southside, gathering research material for my dissertation. That research culminated in a book, *American Project: The Rise and Fall of a Modern American Ghetto,* that documented everyday living conditions in these high-rises, which are now being demolished in the effort to deconcentrate poverty and revitalize inner cities.

Along the way, I was hanging out in the working-poor communities surrounding the housing development. These streets were the epitome of the ghetto—that fabled place in American culture that countless journalists have lamented, almost as many academics have analyzed, and more than a few politicians have promised to fix. These neighborhoods conformed to, but also showed the gross oversimplification of, our stereotypes about the ghetto. They were predominantly African American, but they had a heady mix of homeowners, working- and middle-class residents, the down-and-out, and a few gentrifiers looking for a cheap brownstone to rehab. The region reflected class diversity. A beautiful stretch of rehabbed homes filled with bourgeois families would look across the street at a low-income housing complex, where families lived on less than $10,000 per year, and nearby there could be an entire block of empty, litter-strewn lots where homeless people built small shanties. Commercial corridors filled with low-income retail outlets—currency exchanges, liquor and "dollar" stores, fast-food chains—were slowly attracting the attention of real estate speculators who envisioned large shopping malls and who were resting their bets on rising incomes (or an influx of wealthier families). But in the early and mid nineties, much of Chicago's Southside was still primarily a working-poor black community. Families had been there for generations, living modestly and in a near-continuous state of economic vulnerability.

I was drawn to a community of roughly ten square blocks in Chicago's Southside that I will call "Maquis Park" (most of the names for places and people in this book are pseudonyms). I was particularly interested in Chicago's rich African American history, and Maquis Park was a place where blacks developed much of their social and cultural traditions. It sat at the heart of a "Black Metropolis," a term coined by sociologists in the mid-twentieth century to capture the pulsating spirit of Chicago's Southside black urban region. Entrenched discrimination in real estate and labor markets prevented blacks from moving into, and building their lives in, many of the city's neighborhoods—particularly the predominantly white communities; consequently, diverse African Americans, from elites to poor southern migrants, shared a common set of neighborhoods and built their lives close to one another, in crowded homes and busy streets. Theirs was a "city within a city."

I came to Maquis Park in the nineties, after many of the middle- and upper-class families had taken advantage of decreasing segregation and moved to other parts of the city. Although there were still some greystones and brownstones, there were also stretches of empty lots and shabby homes, and signs of municipal neglect such as irregular trash pickup and streets in disrepair. Yet even in a compromised physical landscape, there were people everywhere, and I was intrigued by the constant movement. In the early morning or late afternoon, you'd find bus stops and subway stations filled with people on their way to work, just as in any other neighborhood, and cars double-parked outside of schools as parents rushed to drop off their children. In the middle of the day, and late at night, the streets bustled with another group—a mix of those too old to work and those who worked irregularly, if at all. Men and women sat on street corners, in the park, near liquor stores, and they talked, slept, played cards, shared a beer and the day's paper. Some of their faces showed the weariness of a life in poverty. Others seemed to hide it well with laughter and a ceaseless banter with passersby.

I had a burgeoning interest in young people, especially those at the margins, and I was particularly curious about the economic activities of the local gangs in Maquis Park. Chicago's street gangs had been a part of the black community for decades, and Maquis Park was one of the mythic centers of gangland. I was interested in one small part of this history—namely, how the organization came to develop and manage its lucrative drug-trafficking enterprise. I hoped to understand why young people chose this risky path (compared with other, mainstream avenues that might have been available); how they invested, saved, and spent the money they earned; and how a gang dealt with all the conflicts and problems that arose while running a business that was entirely illegal.

The "Black Kings" were the gang that inhabited the streets of Maquis Park. Each day the gang's members went to work. They sold drugs on corners, spent money in stores, held meetings or loitered in parks, and so on. And much of this activity was confined to Maquis Park because gang members generally avoided crossing turf boundaries for fear of being shot or harassed by members of enemy gangs (or unfamiliar residents and police officers). Notwithstanding the powerful images of crime and violence that are often tied to drug trafficking and gang activity, the life of these rank-and-file gang members was actually not so glamorous. They spent much of the day just hanging out together. And much of my time with them involved sitting, hour after hour, inside cars, in alleyways, and on commercial thoroughfares, listening to their conversations or gauging their perceptions of others who passed by.

Perhaps out of the same boredom that my subjects often felt, I found myself walking about and meeting people in the area. I did this for several years and became a familiar face with store owners, restaurant managers, street hustlers, police officers, block club presidents, fathers and mothers, and many others who lived and worked in Maquis Park. With these people I had no scholarly agenda: I was not interviewing them, and I had no interest in observing their activities. When they asked about my presence, I explained that I was writing a book on public housing and, secondarily, making note of gang activity and the broader challenges for troubled youth in Chicago's poor neighborhoods.

My peripatetic behavior drew me to several constellations of people who worked off the books to make money. I found myself returning to several places each week: an alley where an underground car mechanic and his hired hands fixed cars and replaced tires; a restaurant where pimps, prostitutes, independent clothiers, construction foremen, and others passed their days and nights soliciting customers; and a park where local residents tried to shoo away pimps, prostitutes, freelance carpenters, and others who solicited customers there. None of these people lived in the nearby public housing, so they were not officially part of my research at the time. However, I treasured their stories, their histories of life in Maquis Park, their views on the O. J. Simpson criminal trial, and their tales of lauded black politicos, from shady local politicians to national figures like Fred Hampton. And so I came back often, sometimes with a question but mostly with a need to sit and listen.

I soon discovered that the seemingly random collection of men and women in the community—young and old, professional and destitute—were nearly all linked together in a vast, often invisible web that girded their neighborhood. This web was the underground economy. Through it the local doctors received home-cooked meals from a stay-at-home down the block; a prostitute got free groceries by offering her services to the local grocer; a willing police officer overlooked minor transgressions in exchange for information from a gang member; and a store owner might hire a local homeless person to sleep in his store at night, in part because a security guard was too costly. In one way or another, everyone here was living underground.

Once in a while an underground economic transaction went awry. The first one I witnessed took place on a cold December morning. A police officer brought his personal car to the alleyway shop of the local mechanic, James Arleander. The officer was a young white man who told me he had just been assigned to Maquis Park. He seemed quite sincere in his desire to ingratiate himself with residents. "I need an oil change," he said matter-of-factly. "I heard this guy is a good man, so why not give my money to him." James finished the work and told the officer that the charge for the oil change was $20. The police officer, however, said he had heard James say earlier that it would be $15. It was not a huge discrepancy, but the two haggled for a bit. Their voices grew louder, their hands and bodies inched toward each other. "I don't cheat people," James kept saying. The officer, staring out past others and carefully watching to see how the situation was developing, said above a whisper, "I'm not saying you are [cheating me], but I *did* hear $15." There was an impasse. And there was cause for concern: a police officer was involved, which made everyone nervous because the entire operation was by definition illegal; the officer was white and, given Chicago's polarized black/white political geography, people probably expected that the interaction would become acrimonious at some point.

To break the silence, Larry, one of James's hired hands, turned to me and said, "Okay, Sudhir, you were here, you heard what was going on. Who's right?" I replied almost instinctively and quickly, perhaps because it was cold and nobody wanted to linger. "James has never charged $20 for an oil change since I've been here, that's true," I said. "So how about this: this time it costs $15, but you," gesturing to the policeman, "have to agree to bring your car back at least two more times for an oil change, and it will cost you $20 each time. That fair to both of you?" Both found the proposal reasonable, and they shook hands, smiled—out of relief no doubt—and completed their transaction. I made little of the exchange, no one else mentioned it, James moved on to the next customer, and everyone else returned to warming their hands around a makeshift trash-can fire.

As I made more acquaintances, I played this kind of mediating role more often. A store owner would yell at a street hustler who did not clean up his store as promised, and the hustler would argue that the work was completed; they needed an arbiter, and I agreed to be one. A squeegee man at a gas station filled gas and washed windows, even though car owners often didn't ask for his services; I brokered payments. None of the disputes involved princely sums, but times were (perpetually) tough in this poor community, and no one took a few dollars for granted. I had observed many seemingly minor disputes escalate into verbal and physical fights, and became extremely sensitive to the need to prevent miscommunication from spiraling out of control.

Providing this mediation was revelatory. Quite literally I saw a world open in front of me that I had never before paid any mind, a world whose significance I couldn't have imagined. The innumerable economic exchanges that took place every hour, every day, no longer seemed random or happenstance. There was a vast structure in place, a set of rules that defined who traded with whom, who could work on a street corner or park bench, and what prices could be set and what revenue could be earned. There were codes in place for settling disputes and adjudicating conflicts, unwritten standards that tried to ensure that haggling did not get out of hand. The young man or woman on a commercial strip, sitting outside a store, no longer seemed to me an idle soul, but one who might be in the employ of that store manager, chasing away drug dealers or attracting customers. The homeless person sleeping outside a place of business was certainly down on his luck, but he might similarly be working off the books for the owner as a relatively inexpensive nightwatchman.

Even my work with the gangs was altered irrevocably. I could no longer understand how gangs managed the drug trade—how its members spent, invested, and hid their cash—without documenting their interaction with local residents and stakeholders. The gang's daily movements kept leading me to other local businesses that helped the gang launder money. Nor was the gang's capacity to earn illegal income unbeknownst to the social service and law enforcement agencies in the community that were ostensibly concerned with preventing violence and youth delinquency.

Indeed, out of a need to prevent street-based violence, or because they were being paid off, some agency staff allowed gangs to meet inside their facilities.

Even the most banal exchange, sometimes for little more than pennies, had to be rethought, I realized, because the transaction might weave together local parties in myriad and complex ways. But with a dissertation to finish, I had to defer my interest.

After 1996 I sought to renew my relationships in Maquis Park. I directed my attention to many different kinds of underground economic activities and the various persons, groups, and organizations involved. I observed the work of the gang, but I also cast my net wider and tried to follow gypsy cab drivers, off-the-books accountants, psychics, house burglars, car thieves, painters, musicians, gun traders, and mechanics. I met with members of block clubs, economic development boards, law enforcement organizations, ward political organizations, and other associations that either were involved directly in underground pursuits or inevitably responded to the consequences of living in the shady world. At times I used formal interview techniques, but most of the time I simply listened and chatted casually with people. I listened to their tales and learned how their lives were constructed. I observed the myriad ways the men and women of Maquis Park made their money and coped with the challenges of living underground.

Unlike before, I tried to minimize my direct involvement in underground affairs. But truth be told, I found it impossible to refuse all requests for mediation. Moreover, my finely honed Socratic technique—trying to help participants use reason to arrive at a mutually agreeable solution—was unacceptable. If I was going to stand in that world, I had to wear something other than observer's attire. So, on occasion and with considerable protestation, I brokered disputes and settled pricing disagreements. I avoided anything that I determined "serious"—which tended to be cases involving drugs, prostitution, and stolen goods. Although most people laughed when I argued that fixing cars and prostitution were not the same thing, they were willing to accept my limitation of my participation to a small number of public exchanges among street-based vendors.

Even as I write these pages, I am not entirely comfortable with the role I adopted. In my own small way, I contributed some stability to a world born of poverty and desperation. No matter how skilled, resourceful, and creative those involved may be, the world of hustling is fundamentally exploitative. It is premised on, or exists because of, the neglect of outside actors—from local and national politicians to business interests to philanthropic foundations—who refuse to allocate enough resources to black inner cities to create true economic security there. I had no illusion that I could transform this community into a stable, crime-free area. Yet no matter how I use my sociological tools to undermine stereotypes, craft better public policies, and so on, I was still complicit in helping to perpetuate these conditions.

Simultaneously, I must admit that I benefited greatly from my involvement as a broker in underground dealings. Many people perceived me as a disinterested mediator—a characterization that helped open doors and allay concerns. For example, some people told me that they were hesitant to speak with me until they saw me settle a dispute and realized I was not a police officer or a friend of any particular hustler in the neighborhood. As important, I was neither white nor black, so I was not immediately identified with the police (white) or as a resident of the community (black) who might have a reason to monitor the behavior of others in public space. My South Asian identity gave me an indeterminate and unthreatening presence, and I was known more for my status as a university student interested in the historical experiences of black Chicagoans. Over time and in this way, even though I tried to limit my direct involvement, I came to be like those residents who tended to perform similar adjudicative and diplomatic functions. Many people viewed me as part of a class of brokers and mediators who could solve a problem.

Residents still viewed me skeptically, however, when I would not accept payment for helping to mediate a conflict. And rumors expectedly followed: I was working with gangs to move drugs in Asian neighborhoods; I was bringing college students to local prostitutes for a fee; I was a police informant. In other words, despite my claims to the contrary, many felt that I was like the local mediators who carried a brokerage fee and that I was also a hustler. And if I, an absolute outsider and utter anomaly to the world of Maquis Park, could become a part of that shady world, we can see how enormous, and ever-growing, this world truly is.

The underground economy is known to mainstream America—when we acknowledge it at all—as a criminal sphere, the den of drug dealers and prostitutes, of pimps and con artists, of welfare mothers and indigents, of those who are unable, or unwilling, to work as "normal" Americans do. Most of us would be shocked to find that many local preachers are often intricately involved in this world. Or that the local gang leader may hold the respect of many residents, even as they decry the drugs he brings into the neighborhood. Or that a member of the underground economy is as likely to be a middle-aged mother who cooks lunches for the local hospital staff as to be a teenage criminal. Indeed, figuring out exactly what is and isn't "criminal" can be very hard in the ghetto, because it is difficult to find much in people's day-to-day lives that does not involve the underground economy.

I have been fortunate to get to know people who labor clandestinely and, thus, to come to understand a social world that, until I entered Maquis Park, had been all but invisible to me. Indeed, most people outside of this country's ghettos have little awareness that the underground economies exist at all, except perhaps when we fail to report some cash we received on our taxes. But in the inner city, this shady world weaves together residents, families, businesses, even politicians and police. The result is a dense, remarkable, and intricate web. It is very difficult to see, unless you know where to look. And it is constantly changing. Indeed, the only thing constant about it is change, as it is a product of perpetual negotiations, of collusion and compromise, of the constant struggle to survive—to find a purpose for your life, to fulfill your desires, to feed your family.

I am humbled that the residents of Maquis Park took me into their affairs and enabled me to see a life under the radar. This book is an attempt to provide a faithful rendition of a life that others allowed me to see, a set of experiences that others allowed me to have. It is about living and working underground.

Off the Books

Chapter One
Living Underground

Marlene Matteson was the person least likely to mourn the death of Johnnie "Big Cat" Williams, leader of the Maquis Park Kings, the local neighborhood gang. Marlene knew firsthand the destruction that gang activity could bring upon families. A mother of three, she was also a widower as a result of the gangland slaying of her own husband. "My husband died like [Big Cat] did," she said, noting the similarities of Billy Matteson's murder in 1992 and Big Cat's fall on a cold, blustery morning in 2003. "Big Cat never knew what hit him. Just like my Billy. Came up on his back, shot him when he wasn't looking. Probably didn't feel nothing." Both Billy Matteson and Big Cat were slain late at night, in the presence of their bodyguards, who were also injured. The killers were never found.

Marlene Matteson accepted the news of Big Cat's murder with a mixture of relief and apprehension. As the president of the 1700

South Maryland Avenue Block Club, she knew that gang activity created persistent safety problems in her area. She saw in Big Cat's death a sign of difficult times ahead. Life was going to change, sharply and perhaps for the worse, in Maquis Park. She could no longer call on Big Cat to keep rank-and-file members out of parks in the afternoon, when kids came back from school. She could no longer wake him and demand that he put an end to the late-night carousing of younger gang members on her block. With little help from law enforcement, she wondered who would help her police the gang members who overtook public spaces with abandon and whose rhythms and inner clocks did not match those of the residents, like Marlene, who woke each morning to go to work or take children to school.

On that December 2003 morning, a week after Big Cat's death, Marlene Matteson sat with her thoughts and with a dozen other residents of the community in the back room of the Maquis Park Prayer and Revival Center, a small storefront church on Indiana Avenue in Chicago's historic Southside black community. She was not the only person in the room struggling to make sense of Big Cat's death. The others in attendance were unlikely to express great sadness for a gang leader who peddled drugs and brought violence and instability to the neighborhood; but they, too, were touched by sadness, anger, and an uncertainty about what lay ahead.

> "You know they're going to be after each other now," said Jeremiah Wilkins, a local pastor, referring to the inevitable internecine battles among local gang members to fill Big Cat's void. "No one knows yet who's taking [Big Cat's] place."
>
> "Yeah, well, it ain't gonna be pretty, but we been there before," said Ola Sanders, the proprietor of Ola's Hair Salon on 16th Street.

"Someone's going to be the leader, but it don't matter who. We got to stay together. That's what's really important, okay?"

"Look, whatever these brothers do, we can't stop them," chimed in James Arleander, a local handyman who for twenty years had been repairing cars off the books for local residents in the parking lot behind the church. "Let's not pretend we're sad or nothing. I mean the man was a killer! You all are acting like he's your friend. Don't make any sense to sit here crying. Man was a killer." James's voice trailed off.

"I agree," said Dr. J. T. Watkins, director of Paths Ahead, a small social service center that ran programs for Maquis Park's youth. "Look, we got to go ahead. We all know why we're here. I mean no offense, Pastor. We're mourning, but we got to make our money. Do you all agree? Well, am I right or not?"

There was silence. The room was still except for Pastor Wilkins's finger tapping the wooden table in time with the clock on the wall. For nearly five minutes, no one responded to Dr. Watkins's question, in part because no one could justifiably dispute his contention—money *was* the chief reason for the group's convening that morning. The livelihood of these community leaders was at stake. Yes, they were all concerned about the escalation in violence that was certain to result with Big Cat's passing: other local gangs would be battling to control the Kings' drug-trafficking territories in the neighborhood. They were all aware of the chaos that could come as a new hierarchy was chosen. But Big Cat's death placed in sharp relief their own reliance on dangerous and illegal ways of making ends meet. They were forced to confront their own deep involvement in an outlaw economy.

Although some found it difficult to admit, everyone in the room that morning had benefited materially from Big Cat's presence. Their motive could have been personal financial gain, political power, or a desire to do their own work more effectively, whether that be preaching or changing a tire. Big Cat not only helped Marlene to police younger gang members; he also gave money to her block club for kids' parties, and members of his gang patrolled the neighborhood late at night because police presence was a rarity. Dr. Watkins and Pastor Wilkins would need to find a new source of philanthropy, now that Big Cat's monthly donations to their respective organizations had ended. Big Cat's gang ensured James Arleander a near monopoly on local off-the-books car repair by intimidating other mechanics who tried to cut into James's business. Ola probably would not receive $500 each weekend for letting the gang turn her salon into a thriving nightclub—the weekly "Maquis Park Dee-Jay" contest had been one of Big Cat's favorite social activities. And others in the room that morning were no different: some received money from Big Cat, others benefited from the customers he sent their way—for everything from homemade meals to fake social security cards—and still others were hoping to use Big Cat's influence over two thousand young men and women to win electoral office or organize downtown protests. All of them allowed Big Cat's gang to operate fluidly, whether that meant tolerating drug selling, presiding over funerals of deceased gang members, participating in citywide gang basketball tournaments, or "cleaning" the gang's profits through their own businesses.

Such is the bizarre reality of life in Maquis Park. The demands of the ghetto require an economy utterly different from what most of America can imagine. The barber may rent his back room to a prostitute; the mechanic works out of an alley; the preacher gets donations from a gang leader; and everyone has a hand in keeping the streets tolerable and keeping the goods and services flowing. The economy brings together an assortment of actors who may otherwise have little reason or interest in exchanging—let alone communicating—with one another. This mix is dangerous, but it is part of living underground in Maquis Park.

Big Cat's prominent position was the visible tip of the iceberg that is Maquis Park's shadow economy. He represented a very small part of the innumerable financial exchanges that are not reported to the government. From off-the-books day care and domestic work to pimping and prostitution, unreported earnings wove together the social fabric in Maquis Park and surrounding poor neighborhoods. Big Cat was just one of many traders, brokers, hustlers, hawkers, and, of course, customers, who moved about in the streets, homes, and alleyways selling inexpensive labor and goods—or searching for them. He was certainly one of its most famous—and infamous—but he was just one of many who performed functions most Americans associate with the mainstream economy and the government agencies that regulate legitimate exchange. He was only one of many local stakeholders who resolved economic disputes because the state had no formal authority. Many other local people enforced contracts, or resolved disputes, or, for a fee, could find you a gun, a social security card, or even a job as a day laborer or a nanny for a wealthy family. Others may have claimed control over parks, alleyways, and street corners; these people would have to be paid if one wanted to fix a car, sell drugs, or panhandle at that spot. And there were many local loan sharks, besides Big Cat, who could loan you cash, or who could find you customers—for stolen stereos or drugs, for prostitutes or home-cooked lunches—in a matter of a few hours.

The individuals who offer these services and goods in Maquis

Park are not always notorious, like Big Cat, nor do they operate solely in the clandestine world. Some move with ease between underground and legitimate economies. And in Maquis Park they may be the pillars of the community. Some, like Ola Sanders, are well-known proprietors whose businesses have suffered in recent years. They cannot resist the opportunity for immediate cash to supplement their legitimate earnings. So they rent out their space to a gang or another underground trader. They develop creative hustling schemes and do not report their income. They might even exchange services with each other off the books, letting barter replace taxable income altogether. Others, like Pastor Wilkins, are religious leaders who do not boast a wealthy congregation that commutes from the suburbs, and who instead counsel and console those near to them: the poor, the delinquent, the marginal, the disadvantaged, and the criminal. They offer solace and consolation and favors to the forgotten while asking few questions about the source of donations. With only one local bank, anyone with access to cash is a potential lender and creditor, although the exorbitant interest rates they charge make these loan sharks less pillars of the community and more a necessary evil. And there are police officers and officials who themselves understand and accept that residents live outside of the formal economy. They let James Arleander fix cars without threat of arrest; they resolve disputes secretly between entrepreneurs rather than confiscating their goods; and at times they use a "scared straight" approach with a teenage drug dealer rather than dump the youngster into the criminal justice system. Whether as traders, dealers, customers, or mediators, it would be difficult to find anyone in Maquis Park not somehow involved in the underground economy.

With such overlap of people and goods and services, it is difficult to say where the underground economy begins and ends in Maquis Park. Despite the moralizing of some, we cannot truly understand the "shady" economy if we see it as a dirty, lawless world of violence and disrepute, one that tarnishes an otherwise pristine sphere where everyone pays their taxes, obeys the laws, and turns to the government to solve disputes and maintain order.[1] Life underground is dangerous, and conventional morality is flouted there, to be sure. But its boundaries are not so clear. Nor, for that matter, is the underground economy inhabited by a single, distinct class of citizens. Anyone could be entrepreneur, client, or broker in this world. With few well-paying full-time jobs available in the neighborhood and with access only to the most menial jobs elsewhere in the city, any Maquis Park resident may turn to hustling as a temporary means to keep food on the table, clothes on a child's back, and rent paid up. Anyone might parlay their meager savings into a clandestine source of loans for neighbors and friends, sometimes at severe interest rates. And even the most religious persons might make themselves available, for a few dollars under the table, as a third party who can settle a pricing dispute or enforce a shady contract. Some may just dip and dabble in the shady world, while for a few others it becomes the sole means of survival. But even these distinctions oversimplify, because in Maquis Park nearly everyone lives underground.

Just as the shady world exists in many shades of gray, not all who participate are criminals and not all activities are heinous. If we look beyond the surface, we find an element of necessity, of pragmatic logic, even while laws are broken and even while the standards of a just life are constantly changing. How does one judge the police officer who mediates a violent contractual dispute with backroom diplomacy, where otherwise a formal attempted murder or assault charge might have been levied on one or both parties? Is the officer in question displaying care for the community by settling the incident and enabling the two individuals to keep their livelihoods intact? Or is he a rogue cop taking the law into his own hands and further depriving residents of the useful services of the criminal justice system? In this and every other case of shady behavior, residents must relentlessly define and redefine what is acceptable and what is destructive to family and community. Perhaps like any community with people working outside the legitimate economy, residents of Maquis Park will make moral and ethical distinctions—although for inner-city residents the choices may include not only relatively innocuous activities, like sales of homemade clothing, but also dangerous trades like narcotics sales. The Southside residents must differentiate between those who harm and those who annoy, between those who make a little money on the side and those who jeopardize the community, recognizing all the while that they may be the trader one day and the one passing judgment the next. The judgments are not easy, nor made lightly, for dollars are scarce, times are hard, and compromises must be made if life is to go on.

This book is about the underground economy. It explores how people work beneath the radar, earning a living and providing for themselves and their families. It examines how people cope with the attendant risks and consequences, and ultimately it tries to understand how a community lives and breathes—how it continues to function—within a very different set of rules. At its core, the underground economy is a widespread set of activities, usually scattered and not well integrated, through which people earn money that is not reported to the government and that, in some cases, may entail criminal behavior. In other words, the unreported income can derive from *licit* exchange, such as selling homemade food or mowing a neighbor's lawn, and *illicit* practices, such as advertising sexual favors or selling secondhand guns without a permit.

Most underground exchanges are short-term efforts to make a buck, but they can nevertheless follow strict patterns. Individuals know where to meet one another to trade off the books; there are usually particular places where this trading occurs and particular people who are known to be involved. People will have a rough idea of prices or rates of barter and trade before initiating the exchange. And it is not difficult to predict when conflicts may arise; nor are people entirely unaware of the means for addressing disputes over quality, pricing, and service. In other words, while there are endless reasons to participate in the underground (or to stop doing so), there are always rules to be obeyed, codes to be followed, and likely consequences of actions.

Gangs and mafias anchor our popular imagination of underground trading, but the reality is far more complicated. In urban neighborhoods of all races and ethnicities one will find not only gangs, but networks of personal tailors and clothiers, burglary and gambling outfits, stolen car rings, livery services, and other organizations that develop clandestine entrepreneurial schemes. But these organized groups are more a notable exception than the norm. Fundamentally, underground exchange is a transaction between individuals. Other parties—not only the buyer and seller—may be involved if regulation is necessary, be it third-party arbitration, holding cash or goods in escrow, or to deal with unforeseen consequences, like a threat to household security or public safety that ensues because a conflict has gotten out of hand. Thus, the underground can provide ample opportunity to make money for individuals interested in offering a variety of services and playing many roles.[2]

Underground transactions are so varied and commonplace that they escape any attempt at systematic documentation. It would be nearly impossible to gather accurate information on, let alone uncover, every type of earning that is not reported to the government. Even for a particular activity, like home tailoring, informal tax preparation, or drug trafficking, it is doubtful that one could put together an exhaustive accounting on how many goods are being traded or how much money is being earned in a given neighborhood. These exchanges are hidden from the state and not necessarily publicly advertised, which is one kind of barrier. A second is that some activities, like snow shoveling or weekend poker games, are so ingrained that they are not really perceived as "underground economic activity" even though participants can make substantial earnings from them and they might produce some financial gain for a wider circle of families, friends, and neighbors. These kinds of taken-for-granted practices might never be recorded, even in the most systematic effort to document the shady side of economic life.

Perhaps most important, the interpenetration of outlawed and legitimate ways of making money makes it difficult to establish accurate information on underground economies. This is not a novel problem, and it affects how we can understand shady activities in Maquis Park. Since the early seventies, when the first studies emerged, there has been continuous and lively debate among social scientists over what constitutes an underground economy. In fact, the disagreements begin with the very terms that are used to reference unreported earnings. The terms *informal, parallel, alternative, illegal,* and *black market* appear as frequently in the scholarly writings as the term *underground.*[3] At the heart of the debates, there is the question whether one should distinguish between licit and illicit behavior. Some researchers hold that activities, such as drug trafficking and prostitution, that are outlawed and whose earnings are unreported to government agencies, should be kept distinct from licit practices that are illegal only because there is no official government regulation of them. These scholars designate the former as "criminal" in order to isolate the latter realm of economic exchange, which they hold is quite similar to legitimate economic activity—and indeed, could be legitimate if the manager or proprietor followed workplace restrictions, paid a minimum wage, declared the income to the Internal Revenue Service, and otherwise adhered to the conventional forms of government oversight and monitoring.[4]

But attempts to separate so-called illicit goods and services from licit ones are not always successful. The distinctions are often fuzzy and the demarcations seem arbitrary. Peyote, for example, is legal for religious use by Native Americans, but federal law is unclear whether non-Native Americans can claim it as a medicinal substance if they claim adherence to Native American religious precepts. So too with prostitution and marijuana use, which are permissible in some states and not in others. Sodomy laws also vary. And all of these laws can vary over time; indeed, where referendums are in place, they can be overturned or put back into effect every few years by the electorate, thereby making substantive distinctions even more difficult. As a consequence, attempting *a priori* to remove criminal behavior in discussions of underground economies will necessarily appear somewhat arbitrary and *ad hoc*.[5]

One consequence of the lack of consensus is that one can find markedly different estimates of the size of America's underground economy.[6] One study concluded that the federal government lost $83 to $93 billion annually in taxes by failing to monitor effectively underground economic activity. Another agency report that focused only on drugs and gambling found that roughly $26 billion was being traded from this realm alone, which would put the overall federal tax gap much higher. (The drug and gambling estimate is also disputed—a recent report claimed that $50 billion is traded annually.[7]) One study focuses on individual participants, rather than sector of trade, and finds that each year four out of five Americans purchase something in the informal economy; this could lead to estimations of over-all size that dwarf the IRS estimates. Another report indicated that 25 percent of the labor force (in 1983) was working under-ground, while yet another puts this number at around 17 percent of all workers. And when income is the focus, some report that $70 to $100 billion is being earned off the books annually. All of these studies employ different definitions of the underground and therefore differ in what kinds of activities they take into ac-count. So, although one can conclude with some confidence that the underground economy is significant for Americans, one is hard-pressed to have confidence in exact estimations of its size or dollar flow, the number of businesses dealing off the books, and so on.

There are practical consequences to this indeterminacy. City, state, and federal governments are always struggling to ensure that tax coffers are filled and that there is enough money to pro-vide public services. Even by the smallest estimates of under-ground revenue, effective taxation of that income could dra-matically increase the resources at hand for law enforcement, sanitation, public transportation, and other municipal services. Thus every few years we see a flurry of public wrangling by fed-eral legislators, taxing authorities, mayors, and other officials over how big America's underground economy has become and what remedial steps need to be taken to realign taxation and policing to recover lost revenue.[8] Politicians are also concerned with unregulated trading because they must respond to the social impact of underground economies on individuals and neighborhoods. Any economic exchange that is not under state auspices could be exposing people to unsafe working conditions or exploitation. Even if the work conditions are not the problem, underground trading can be dangerous to the public and thus commands the attention of politicians and police.[9]

Given all of these variations, it is futile to attempt to give an exhaustive accounting of the underground economy—whether for the country as a whole or for a small urban neighborhood. So, scholars find it is necessary to make adjustments in their work and settle on approximations. As a consequence, research on the underground tends to take a broad, national view, or it looks at earnings in one place, like an organization or neighborhood. Some studies end up focusing on the "criminal side," while others prefer to follow the licit goods and services that are exchanged. A researcher will often find it more manageable not to look at the shady economy as whole, but instead focus on one constituent sphere such as drug trafficking or unreported domestic work. No strategy is foolproof and unsusceptible to challenge, just as no investigator can expect to have full knowledge of what takes place off the books in someone else's home, or on a street corner, or in a business. But scholarly priorities can also be a distraction or a hindrance when the objective is to look inside our neighborhoods at the real people negotiating real situations that are shaped by living underground.

Like most of the existing research on the underground, this book is also an approximation. It is about the underground activity in one urban community, Maquis Park. And it is set in a particular historical period, roughly from 1995 to 2003. I did not witness all—or even most—hidden exchanges in Maquis Park during these years. I did not speak with every person toiling secretively to make a buck, nor did I document each and every place where exchanges occurred. Even though I spent many days and nights observing illegal economic activity in the area, I cannot offer an omniscient view. This neighborhood has been around for more than a hundred years, and its underground economy has likely existed for all those years. My work dissects just a small slice of this rich history, but what we unearth is revealing indeed.

Though you wouldn't know it by looking at the dilapidated streets and empty lots, Maquis Park has a storied history. From the neighborhood's beginnings in the mid-nineteenth century until the early 1900s, working-class Irish immigrants populated the community. The region as a whole changed in the mid-twentieth century. African Americans pushed southward from areas near the central business district in search of cheaper rents and better neighborhood conditions. They moved into communities like Maquis Park that had been largely closed off due to segregation, real estate discrimination, and redlining by banks. Migrants also came from the sharecropping American South, and their arrival by the thousands in Chicago meant that the ghetto was always on the verge of bursting at its seams. Maquis Park's white homeowners had used restrictive covenants to prevent the sale of homes to blacks, but such resistance was futile in the face of overwhelming population growth and the expansion of the black community.

As their numbers grew, black Chicagoans built a "Black Metropolis." Maquis Park became part of a broad area of black Southside settlement where migrants and native black Chicagoans could find comfort, opportunity, and a place of their own in the bustling city. But largely they were shunted off from much of that city due to the racism of their white neighbors and the ruling white machine. While they lobbied, protested, and struggled for their share, as a partial response they turned their energies inward. Maquis Park and its neighboring areas became a parallel urban world, integrated into Chicago yet set off because its inhabitants developed institutions that mirrored those of the larger metropolis but served mostly black Chicagoans. They forged what at the time was called a city within a city.[10]

The Southside Black Metropolis would be alternatively celebrated and criticized. It held a thriving black press, prominent black businesses, healthy and active civic associations, and the kind of diversity and spontaneity one would expect to find in an urban milieu. It was known as "Bronzeville," a term that honored the unrelenting spirit and commitment of black Americans to forge the good life. On the other hand, its residents were cut off from many political and economic resources, and they were largely unable to acquire homes or run businesses in white neighborhoods. Thus the Southside suffered overcrowding and inadequate housing, limited commercial development, high unemployment, and severe blight. A mansion might adjoin a transient hotel, and a row of shacks might sit opposite a thriving entertainment district. The most prosperous black Americans were reminded daily of the ceiling on social mobility that kept them segregated and that forced them to fend for themselves when the city's institutions failed them. For this, they shouted at both the ruling political elites and their own black political representatives who worked in the city machine.

In their drive to provide for themselves, black Chicagoans developed an alternate, "underground" economy—one interrelated to, but distinct from, the wider urban political economy. Even though black laborers were a significant part of the city's industrial and service sector labor force, there were not enough jobs available for black job seekers. So they worked for menial, off-the-books wages, often in their own community, as janitors and cleaners, waiters and entertainers, shoe shiners, tailors, housepainters, and general laborers. Whites would not hire black contractors for home repair, but they would turn to black women for domestic help, housecleaning, and child care, and they typically paid them under the table. Although black businesses flourished, there was inadequate financial assistance available from white-owned banks. So those starting businesses and those needing cash to survive a downturn went to unregulated creditors, loan sharks, and political bosses for a loan—for which they faced not only high interest rates but also physical harm if they were unable to repay. A significant share of this parallel economy involved criminal work, like numbers running and vice, in which not only were the earnings unreported but the activities themselves were illegal.

The outcome of all these practices was the emergence of a vibrant "shady" economy in Chicago's Southside. Well into the postwar era, the Black Metropolis boasted a vibrant alternate sphere of exchange and trading that supplanted the mainstream commercial sphere. It was not only a necessity, it was also a core part of the cultural life of the region. Politicians grew famous by dispensing patronage in the form of city contracts and off-the-books work—sometimes for a kickback and always for a vote on election day. In entertainment and gambling, unreported income was always available if one had connections to the ward boss, madam, or loan shark who controlled numbers, betting, local lotteries, brothels, and gambling parlors. Storied films like *Uptown Saturday Night* and *Cotton Comes to Harlem* spoke to the flattering view that many people, not just in black America but the country as a whole, held of the shady aspirant. For centuries, the outlaw, fighting both government and the entrenched powers to rise above the fray and accumulate wealth, has been an American hero, and in the mid-twentieth city this figure found an avatar in the black ghetto hustler.

After the civil rights era, Maquis Park suffered the fate of many American inner cities. Its wealthier classes left and moved into previously segregated areas, while its working and poor households remained. The area lost whatever mitigating effect on poverty the better-off households once contributed—to ensure that some streets were cleaned, that some parks were maintained, that some schools were kept in decent condition—and blight overwhelmed the physical landscape. Many of the beautiful brownstones reached a level of disrepair that required attention beyond the financial resources of their owners. Apartment buildings became abandoned due to neglectful landlords and the out-migration of the middle- and upper-class families. Sanitation services grew insufficient, and one saw litter and refuse everywhere. The homeless set up camp in the abandoned buildings but also in shanties alongside roads and in parks. People sat idle and out of work nearly everywhere.

But the alternate economy continued to thrive. Indeed, the underground economy was fast becoming a primary economy for black ghetto dwellers. Buying goods cheaply, whether on the street or in the alley, behind closed doors or outside of the neglectful state, was still part of their recipe for household survival. Off-the-books services, from tax preparation and general labor to security and entertainment, were plentiful.[11]

Hustling was the word coined in popular discourse to refer to the indefatigable and creative attempts by the down-and-out to find work, make a buck, and make ends meet. But importantly, hustling included not only the labor to find illicit earnings, but also the work entailed in dealing with the consequences of living by shady means.[12] Hustling meant insecurity, crime, and exploitative behavior, to which people had to respond. And in a time period when policing was inadequate and law enforcement relations with inner-city neighborhoods throughout black urban America were colored by neglect and distrust, it meant people sometimes had to take matters into their own hands. Thus, the hustle also involved a diverse set of strategies to make sure that the shady world did not completely ruin the social fabric. These strategies were often as creative as the illegal activities themselves. Whether they settled disputes or enforced underground contracts, people hustled not only to put food on the table, but also to maintain order in their streets and communities.

In time, the coexistence of despair and the outlaw lifestyle would draw the attention of those in the wider world. A wellspring of public scrutiny arrived at the doorstep of communities like Maquis Park in the eighties, after nearly two decades of poverty, unemployment, business failure, and high crime had swept through and ravaged the social and physical landscape. In academic and press reportage, critics and scholars tried to make sense of the apparently marked remove of the black ghetto from the mainstream. In *The Truly Disadvantaged*, sociologist William Julius Wilson diagnosed the presence of a subclass of black Americans living not only in conditions of extreme impoverishment, but also in relative remoteness from their surrounding city. More than their inability to find work marked their "social isolation," Wilson argued. They suffered inadequate integration into many urban institutions, from the police and schools to philanthropy and the press. And, he pointed out, unlike the mid-twentieth century there were no middle-class persons to serve as role models or provide social controls over unruly and delinquent behavior that was now growing out of control.[13]

Following Wilson's essay, a flurry of critical assessment arose over the black ghetto. Scholars focused on the household as the root cause of isolation, deploying all sorts of statistical data—such as the alarming rate of teenage pregnancy, high rates of welfare dependency, absentee fathers and mother-led families—in an effort to isolate the role of black family formation in the reproduction of poverty. Detailed press reports, like Ken Auletta's *The Underclass,* spoke of the cultural pathologies, such as a lack of work ethic and a predilection for unruly behavior, that had been spawned in areas seemingly forgotten by time and morality. Human interest reportage, like Alex Kotlowitz's *There Are No Children Here,* pointed out the limited mental horizons of inner-city youth and young adults; few of these young people could envision a life for themselves beyond the ghetto, in marked contrast to the yuppies who were defining the renewed American spirit in the era of globalization. By the beginning of the eighties, when cities initiated revitalization programs to attract middle- and upper-class residents, the ghetto was pitied for what it lacked (normal families, good schools, working adults) and criticized for what it boasted (gangs, drugs, and crime).

In a way, this kind of attention to the urban underclass was nothing new. From the late nineteenth century onward, Chicago's black communities (and those in other major industrialized cities) were the repositories for public indignation and, eventually, some type of social reform. The clarion call of distress over a population living outside the social mainstream occurred every two or three decades. Depending on the political climate (conservative or progressive), policies like mass arrest and incarceration, urban renewal and housing construction, philanthropic investment and community development, would follow to integrate the disenfranchised. America's concern in the nineties for the dispossessed black inner city, seeing in it a form of existence that must be razed and then restored, is really part of a long history of inveighing against and expressing moral outrage at how the minority poor live.

In the midst of this public clamor and sometimes self-righteous inspection, Maquis Park and many other alienated and poor black communities perdure. Though not always in full measure and in comfort and security, households manage. Parents feed and clothe children, chaos does not rule, and people experience joy and see beauty. Residents deal with problems, like crime and delinquency, even if their ways of coping and maintaining social order do not receive much attention. And, as this book contends, an important dimension of their daily struggle to create a habitable place to live and work has occurred behind the scenes. Their labor takes place with resources amassed in the underground economy. Their work to restore order and keep Maquis Park safe and secure takes place often outside government agencies that can be, at varying times, neglectful and begrudging in allocating resources, yet spiteful in the drive to police and punish. Their collective labors have coalesced largely outside the watchful eye of media and scholars, for whom the tragedies of poverty have perhaps justifiably attracted more attention than the simple and remarkable ways in which people actually tend to their affairs in such environs. This book is about making visible these everyday "shady" efforts by Maquis Park residents to maintain their community.

Chapter Two
Home at Work

Marlene Matteson, Eunice Williams, and Baby "Bird" Harris are Maquis Park's "soccer moms." The three live on the 1700 block of South Maryland Avenue, each renting a small three-bedroom house that requires rehabilitation and repair that they cannot afford and that their landlord refuses to provide. On a cold, clammy April morning, they gather in a nearby empty lot to clear debris. In a few hours, their children will be there playing games and climbing trees. As they pick up bottles, condoms, crack cocaine receptacles, newspaper, and used car parts, they talk about their children, the week that has passed, and the spring that is dawning.

The three women often remark on how different they are. Bird, for example, earns her living as a prostitute, plying her trade along Maquis Park's main thoroughfare as well as on busy downtown streets. Eunice works in the formal economy, cleaning offices at minimum wage, and supplements her income by selling homemade soul food to the local lunchtime crowd. Marlene has various off-the-books jobs in the service sector; she earns most of her underground money as a $9 per hour nanny for a white family in the neighboring upper-class university district. When it comes to religion, Eunice believes that "Jesus is the answer, it don't matter what the question is." Bird, having slept with "most of the preachers in this community," feels the church is no longer a place where one can find salvation. And Marlene spends much of her time ensuring that religion is not a subject of conversation when the three women are together. Talking about crime, Eunice believes that the "gang and drug problem" is a moral cancer eating at the heart of the community; Marlene perceives the root causes as "the police not getting enough kickbacks and our politicians not taking care of the problem"; Bird thinks the gangs are poor managers and need to "let the pimps show them how to run a business."

As mothers, workers, and neighbors, however, Marlene, Eunice, and Bird share the same basic struggle. Each has children whose fathers live elsewhere and fail to provide any material support. Each works sixty to seventy hours a week. They are all concerned about crime, gang activity, and lackadaisical teachers in the local schools. With a roof over their heads, they have become magnets for friends and relatives who, facing hard times or uninterested in paying rent of their own, eat their food and stay in their homes. They all see themselves as future homeowners, on the verge of accumulating joy in the form of leisure and grandchildren. Spending Saturday mornings together, as their children sleep or watch TV, provides an occasion to acknowledge the likeness of their predicaments and their parallel dreams.

Their waking lives are an unending effort to provide the simplest of things: food, clothing, and shelter for their families, and a neighborhood that is safe. These are hardly chores that separate them from the majority of American women who, through discrimination, custom, and preference, have assumed domestic leadership. However, unlike most women, Marlene, Bird, and Eunice keep house and home in a poor community where joblessness and poverty are entrenched. Like many of their neighbors and friends, they muddle along by pooling together income from various sources, bartering for goods, and developing intricate schemes to exchange services. The source of their household income varies and may include, at any one time, some combination of legitimate permanent work, irregular unreported labor, and illicit secretive trading. In other words, they are part of both the mainstream economy and the shady world.

Jobs

The employment experiences of Marlene, Bird, Eunice and the other women on their street block are similar to other blocks in Maquis Park, where women take a leading role in making ends meet for those in their household. A closer look at Marlene and her neighbors on the 1700 block of South Maryland Avenue shows some of the ways the underground economy plays a role in these day-to-day efforts. Most of these women will move back and forth between the legitimate economy and the shady world over the course of their lives. Households can have income coming in from both sectors. The norm is for women to change their earning profile by alternating between the underground and legitimate economic sectors, taking advantage of different opportunities that arise to generate income. For example, just as Eunice held jobs in various service sector firms before and during her soul food delivery service, other women who work clandestinely for unreported wages take up work as cleaners, clerks, cashiers, and cooks in the mainstream economy.

Some of the fluidity of these women's earning lives is a by-product of the world they inhabit. Conditions in neighborhoods of concentrated poverty can change quickly and in ways that can leave families unprepared and without much recourse. A good day might yield a particularly strong expectation of impending good luck or improved social welfare, whether this relates to one's lottery pick or earnings, or the assurance that a decent lover will remain so. A bad day might force even the most religious devotee to question the tolerance of her Lord. Today's prostitute might become tomorrow's janitor, and vice versa. This does not invalidate the need to understand differences in work or differential aspirations for women in one or another illegal trade. But it does mean that there may be important links between the development of moral and ethical systems and the material world that supports them. Taking a close look at the ways these women draw on the shady economic world is useful for understanding how they keep order at home and in their community.

For the three women, underground work is an ever-changing combination of unreported wages from employment at a legitimate business, petty entrepreneurial activity in the home, and spontaneous opportunities to earn money around the neighborhood. Eunice represents the most common use of underground economic revenue. At 53 years of age, Eunice wants to work less, if at all. In the late seventies she began working full-time for her uncle's janitorial firm. She earned several hundred dollars per month under the table to supplement her welfare benefits. In 1991 she was caught by a government caseworker and became ineligible for public assistance income. She found a full-time minimum-wage job at Drexel Cleaning, where she now works part-time—usually twenty to thirty hours per week, depending on availability. Each morning before leaving for work, she wakes at 5 a.m. to help her daughter make soul food, which is either purchased by customers at her door or delivered to customers by her children and grandchildren. (She pays a teacher $20 per week so that her grandchildren can leave school at lunchtime and assist with deliveries.) On occasion, Eunice and her daughter cater weddings, baptisms, and other events. Her daughter and all the other adult boarders are expected to help her with the $700 per month rent and the utilities payment. Only her daughter and nephew—who work at the car wash—regularly provide this assistance. The remaining adults who live with her—a brother, a family friend, and her son—do not contribute monetarily; neither do the six grandchildren who live there. (It is also common to find another friend or relative, usually with children of his or her own, to be living with Eunice for short periods of time.)

Eunice's street block, like other blocks nearby, has a disproportionate number of female heads of household. Of the twenty-one inhabited housing units on her block, in sixteen one can find a woman who plays this role or who shares the responsibility of paying the rent, managing bills, attending to the educational needs of their children, putting food on the table, and otherwise taking a leadership role in the decisions that affect the home. Thirteen of these women work in the underground economy. Some sell legal goods and services like Eunice and receive their wages under the table. This work is underground, but it is *licit.* Two work as lunchroom cooks off the books at local elementary schools. Four work irregularly as nannies and babysitters—Marlene manages to find full-time jobs, but typically only part-time work is available. And two use their cars as "gypsy cabs," charging a few dollars to help local residents run errands. Some of these women also work as psychics, tax preparers, wedding consultants, and hairstylists.

The remaining underground workers are in the *illicit* sectors. One is a local conduit for welfare recipients wishing to sell their food stamps to businesses for cash. Along with Bird, another neighbor, Cotton, is a prostitute. Unlike Bird, however, who came to prostitution from low-wage but legal service sector work (and plans to return someday), Cotton has not had work experience in the legal economy and has no desire to leave her street trade. Cotton says, "I'm fine where I am. My next job is taking care of my man, not serving no burgers or cleaning no toilets." Two women help traffic in narcotics—one "rents" her apartment to gang members and drug dealers as a place where they can process and package cocaine and heroin, the other is a lookout for the local gang.

Not all underground labors are the same, either in terms of the income that can be earned, the risks involved, or the personal consequences and effects on quality of life in one's home. While there are many different ways to make money off the books, women tend to have several types of opportunities to make money illegally. Perhaps the most common is *homework.* Women who work for unreported wages in day care and domestic work will have a stable client pool for 12 months on average. African American women must compete with a labor pool that includes not only other African American women, but various immigrants from Mexico, Puerto Rico, and other Caribbean nations, and, on occasion, young adults from Europe who work as au pairs. There is an upper stratum, including Marlene, composed of those working as full-time nannies for white middle-

and upper-income employers, sometimes for years at a time. Marlene says, "I'm lucky because I have a family that pays me for 30 hours; since they trust me, I always find other people I could work for like that." The vast majority of women cannot find full-time domestic work so easily, however, because they have not developed relations with families who can provide references to other potential employers. In a workforce lacking protections of unions and government regulations, job security, to the degree it exists, is a reliable reference.

Women who lack these resources draw on personal and highly localized connections when seeking work. There is usually somebody on the block who needs a babysitter and will pay cash. A relative may also need day care, but here the payment may be in-kind— such as use of a car, some food, or drugs. Cash payments may be as little as $10 for a day's work.

The clergy are important brokers of jobs for domestic workers. The midsize and larger churches in Maquis Park cater to commuters from upper-income residential areas. A local pastor helps Marlene and other domestic workers find families to work for, but he charges 10 percent for each successful placement. In Maquis Park alone, there are nineteen pastors who provide this service. Most have one or two families that express a need for some type of household help each Sunday. It is worth noting that these clergy typically move women around from family to family. In this way, the pastor is guaranteed a pool of job seekers who must rely on his brokerage service. As one woman explained to me,

"I had this real nice black family up there in the Loop. I was
with them for a month, they liked me and they were going to let
me move in, you know, be full-time with them. I'm old. That

would have been fine. But Johnnie [her pastor] got to them, moved me to somewhere out Hyde Park. See, he just wants his money, so he likes to stay in control."

"Why don't you just go back to the family? Why do you need Johnnie?"

"And what if that family gets rid of me? Where am I going next? See, I can't take that chance, you know. You just never know. I've been doing this too long to know that you can't be relying on those kinds of families. They may get angry with you, say you stole something, the man could lose his job, move out of town. All I got is Johnnie and it took me the longest just to get him on my side."

Women who have no relationship to a pastor or another such broker often look for work in one of the three day-care centers near their block, and in five others dispersed throughout Maquis Park. None provides them with more than 10 to 15 hours of work per week, and all pay menial wages under the table, with no benefits. Even if they find work, women cannot easily cite these employers as references—the day-care providers refuse to admit hiring the women, for legal reasons—and they have limited time for job searches outside their neighborhood. Mary, one of the women, explains:

It's not like I get a call each morning that they got some work for me. I run down to the church and have to wait, and maybe I clean something for free. Then Pastor Owens tells me, "Oh yeah, so and so, she need you today." See, he gets his free work out of me and I got to give him my 10 percent! . . . [Or] I go down to Missy's center, and maybe I just take care of those kids, cook them breakfast, and then Missy say, ok, we got a lot of kids, so I'll pay you $30 today. So, I just waste my whole day, sometimes, and I don't get nothing.

Homework is not always available, and because the pay is off the books, the women are not always able to draw on legal protections or recourse when they suffer poor work conditions, indiscriminate firing, or discrimination or harassment at work. Nevertheless, they tend to prefer this kind of underground labor because the work can be steady, there is relatively little personal risk, and the middle- and upper-income families who hire them can be understanding and tolerant of their unstable lives.

In contrast, vice is another option for women living underground and it has a markedly different earnings and risk profile. In fact, the existence of a large client pool may be one of the only identifiable benefits for women in the vice industry. Bird and her neighbor Sandra, both sex workers, do cite other advantages, including the capacity to set their own hours and be with their children after school, and, occasionally, the opportunity to remain at a single job for two or three years, sometimes longer—this extended job tenure requires that they form a relationship with a pimp or secure access to a particular spot (a public housing building, a street corner, a truck stop). Neither is easy. Pimps take on new workers only after they build some basic level of trust, which can take time; and because there are many people fighting for good sales spots, only sex workers with a pimp or other individual who will guard the spot are able to secure a place for the long term. Cotton has been a prostitute for five years, changing her pimp only twice in that time. Bird, a ten-year veteran, has worked only for her pimp—whose father pimped Bird's mother. Their johns, however, change often.[1]

In general, however, sex work is not reliable or safe employment for most participants. Bird and Cotton have developed stable arrangements with their respective pimps, which distinguishes them from the many young women who experiment with vice work for short durations. Roughly 40 percent of the approximately 150 prostitutes in Maquis Park work for individuals who find them johns, provide them the rudiments of security (read: occasional vengeance on johns who abuse them), and serve as a source of credit. Rarely do gangs operate as pimps, unless they control a drug den where prostitution is sold alongside drugs—three of these exist in Maquis Park. Typically pimps are lone wolfs who pay an agent, like a gang and/or a police officer, for the right to place their workers in streets, buildings, and alleyways; almost all are men, as the age of the madam has long since passed in Chicago. Not all pimps are alike. The men Bird and Cotton work for make sure their workplaces are hidden from the police and try to find nonabusive johns, but most pimps do not seem always to take the needs of their sex workers into account.

The supply of johns does not differ markedly for prostitutes who work for pimps and those who work alone. Both draw on men in the neighborhood, residents of the nearby white working-class areas, and drivers who stop at the local truck stops. The challenge for the self-employed prostitute arises in the moment of circulation: they do not have pimps who can provide them with valuable information such as the location of safe alleys and street corners, house parties where they may ply their trade, and spaces where police are likely to patrol.

Wages and work conditions can also vary. Women working on their own earn, on average, $50 per evening for 4 to 6 hours' work. A trick can pay as little as $10, which seems about the norm; once in a while, they may find a man who wants to spend a few hours drinking and carousing before soliciting sex, and in this case they can earn $25 or more. But the work is irregular, and there may be many evenings when clients are hard to find. So these self-employed sex workers must expend time and energy finding a place to greet their johns and a space to provide their services. These logistical difficulties are exacerbated by the fact that many self-employed women sporadically turn to prostitution. These might be young mothers in need of income, women who have lost family support, or drug users turning to the vice economy to support their addiction. Compared to their counterparts who work for pimps, prostitutes working on their own have a higher rate of physical assault by johns and a higher rate of arrest. In the five years I observed vice in Maquis Park, there was only one fatality for a prostitute who was managed by a pimp. In contrast, thirteen self-employed prostitutes died during the night hours at work. Of these, ten died at the hands of either an abusive john, a spouse or partner jealous of their work, or a pimp trying to clear them away from a spot; the other three died of drug overdoses, although they too may have been dealing with some type of harassment.

Sex workers with pimps can earn more money, and their work is more steady. Bird and Sandra, for example, have a pimp who tells them where to wait and sets up appointments for them. Cotton knows that her pimp will find enough work for her to earn $500 to $600 per month, but depending on the number of days and hours per day she works, this may not be much better than the $50-per-evening statistic mentioned earlier. It is the reliability of an income stream—relative to those who do not have a manager—that is critical. Cotton relies on her mother, who babysits her five children (none of whom come from a john, she proudly says), and draws on disability insurance to round out her monthly rent payments. "On a good month," says Bird, "I make about $750, but that means I'm working all the time, which I just can't do no more." These women do not escape all of the dangers of their profession. Numerous job hazards effectively reduce their work time. Cotton estimates that she is beaten up, by either a john or her pimp, at least once a year, for which she loses two to three weeks of work. She finds this tolerable because, she says, "If you don't have a pimp, you're getting hurt all the time, I mean each week." She and Bird also face capricious pimps who steal from them, force them to pay fines for mistreating johns or for getting arrested, and occasionally make them work for free. At least twice each year, police activity disrupts their work schedule by forcing them to find new locations or alter their work hours, which reduces their earnings.

There is a much wider set of goods and services, beyond sexual favors, that women sell off the books in Maquis Park. Some entrepreneurial women sell foodstuffs, homemade clothing, counseling and psychic services, social security cards, hairstyling and hair-care products, pirated movies, and kitchen supplies (what Eunice calls "ghettoware"). Some have computers and prepare résumés, others offer tax preparation or basic accounting services, and a few, like Marlene, make money by hosting gambling venues and parties. Several women either have owned businesses in the past or have worked in them for extended periods. Most, however, are self-employed and occasionally may do temporary, off-the-books work for a local business, such as a hairstyling salon or bar. In general these women are in their late thirties and forties. They prefer to live with their children, take care of their grandchildren, and work as necessary to bring income to the home. The hairstylists estimate earning $200 to $250 per month; the gypsy cab drivers earn $200 to $300 in a busy week; the six local psychics and "spiritualists" make, on average, $4,000 per year; homemade clothiers can take in $350 to $400 per month but the work is never steady enough to ensure this income stream for an entire year.

It is a popular custom for women to sell handicrafts and artistic products that they have made or designed in collaboration with other producers. At subway and bus stops, public parks, street corners, and special events like parades and block club parties, there will usually be a slew of women offering African-inspired jewelry and clothing, books and "how to" manuals, paintings, and remedies to heal disease and mental-health problems. Most women say that the work is irregular and driven by their own inspiration and need for supplemental income. Few rely on such exchange to support themselves.

Eunice's homemade soul food enterprise is unique in its longevity. She has sold home-cooked meals for over a decade. Until 1996 she catered small events like family gatherings and church functions. She then asked her daughter to help her expand the business to daily sales. Her customer base includes neighbors, local police officers and security personnel, several hundred employees at a local bread factory, staff at the local schools, delivery crews (UPS drivers, mail carriers, and so on), local construction workers, and employees at the local hospital and university. Her success may be partly attributed to two monthly payments she makes. One is to the local gang, which prevents others from competing with her by selling foodstuffs in the immediate area. Another is to a local police commander, who, says Eunice, "sends a car to my house in front at lunchtime, so I don't have to worry about getting robbed until I can get that money to the bank." She revealed that she paid $50 cash each week to both the policeman and the gang, but she would not tell me her personal income. My own estimate, based only on observation, is that a typical month brings $1,000 (net) into her home. In the last six years, her business has closed down for one month each year due to a variety of circumstances, including family trips to Arkansas, hospitalization, arrest and conviction of a relative or family member, a daughter "flying off and disappearing with some man," and exhaustion.

Women who sell handicrafts and homemade goods and those who offer some type of skilled service like tax preparation should be categorized separately from their counterparts who work in unpredictable, dangerous, and poorly paying underground spheres. They fall under the catch-all category of general labor, which includes a range of off-the-books menial work in both licit and illicit sectors. Women who sell drugs, perform services for the local gangs and drug dealers, or participate in larceny rackets are rarely employed longer than a few months. They may earn upward of $50 to $75 per day for serving as a police lookout, or $100 per week for allowing drugs, guns, or stolen goods to be made, sold, or stored in their home. But the work is fleeting. Their employers are distrustful and continually find reasons not to employ them or, worse, not to pay them. Typically the workers are fired for accusations of embezzlement, and they suffer tremendous physical abuse. Their male employers inevitably demand sexual favors and colonize their apartments to hide their own guns, drugs, and stolen goods inside and to gamble and host parties.

Then there are any number of not legal, but less harmful, jobs. On Eunice's block, for example, two women work in a school cafeteria, performing odd jobs that can range from food preparation to cleaning, and earn $50 under the table each week for ten to fifteen hours of work. They have worked in their respective schools for three years; over that time, they have increased their work from five days per month to fifteen days, on average. They also wash cars for school employees, run errands for teachers who cannot leave school during the day, and work at special events such as basketball games and dances. They rarely make more than $300 per month, but their meager income, which is both steady and more than what many of their counterparts earn, places them at the top end of this *lumpen* stratum. They have each established a monopoly on such opportunities at their respective schools, so that teachers will not hire others without consulting the two women.

Others are not so lucky. Numerous women walk the streets, entering businesses and organizations daily to seek whatever work may be available. Oceana, a thirty-three-year-old mother of six, rises each morning to walk through Maquis Park and drum up employment. She lists her own work over the previous six-month period:

> I picked up garbage for a guy who worked in the city and who was fucking some lady in the van and needed some time off one day. I bought some kids some beer. I always have someone who can't leave work but who needs a bag [of pot or crack cocaine]. The lady at the library lets me put the books back on the shelves. That minister likes me to walk on his back, or sometimes do a little more, but I'm not talking about that. Unless you paying [she laughs]! I also wash cars down at the police station. I bake cakes at the church on Sundays in the morning. I painted that house over there for a week. Eunice was sick a couple of times, so I cooked with her daughter [and helped her sell the meals]. That Arab al-

> ways getting a blowjob from that girl, so I watch the store for a lit-
> tle while, while he does his thing. Yeah, I do just about anything
> and everything, baby.

In no month did she earn more than $200. Usually she is satisfied if she can find $25 per week.

It is easy, and all too common, to draw a binary distinction between illicit underground economic activities—often seen as "criminal" as opposed to economic per se—and licit exchanges. Following this line of thought, Marlene and Eunice, who merely hide their income, should be categorized separately from Bird, who earns by providing an outlawed good—sexual favors. There *are* some important differences between women who sell illicit goods and services and those whose work is illegal because the income is not reported to the government. For example, levels of personal danger vary. Prostitutes, drug sellers, participants in stolen car rackets, and shoplifters experience more jail time and physical abuse than people who are just ducking the IRS. Women whose work is illegal only because it is unreported to the government may still have recourse to the law in a way that prostitutes and car thieves do not. For example, a woman who sold clothing in a park without a permit nevertheless reported an incident of theft to the police, who then helped her retrieve the stolen items. Similarly, when Eunice's house was burglarized, she reported the theft of the kitchen equipment she used to make her soul food lunches; she did not find the merchandise, but she claimed to have received adequate compensation from her renter's insurance policy. Bird cannot call the police to help her when abused or robbed by a john—unless an officer will act informally by finding the john; however, on occasion she does pay the gang for protection and will call on them to exact revenge. The personal dangers women experience in the illicit sectors can affect their own outlooks, perceptions of security, and relationship to their families.

These distinctions are important, but from the perspective of the women's efforts to keep house and home, the lines between different kinds of underground economic activity begin to blur. Household income for a poor family can come from many different sources; it is not always possible to keep the revenue streams separate, using money derived from off-the-books tax preparation for one purpose, money from drug selling for another, and so on. In fact, it is often easier emotionally to combine these so that one does not have to be reminded of the origin of the income. For example, a head of household desperate to make rent might not ask many questions regarding the money given to her by boarders. Just as important, there is no societal consensus regarding the illegality of certain behaviors, such as narcotics use, gun possession, and prostitution, so we should not expect that the residents of Maquis Park are uniform in their opinion or that their ethical distinctions necessarily conform to those of Americans living in other kinds of communities. How their decision making emerges in the context of illegal activity is best understood in the context of the overall strategies by which they manage their households and struggle to keep their communities habitable.

Homework

It is easy to believe that today's inner cities are inhabited by two distinct groups, a view readily accepted by the mainstream social science community. Elijah Anderson summarizes this belief in terms of "value orientation," defining these two groups by how they cope with crime and delinquent behavior. One, schooled in older African American traditions, attends church, participates in social institutions like schools and labor markets, and in general accepts the laws and ethical codes of conduct of mainstream society. They are oriented toward "decent" values, as Anderson writes. The other group, he says, adheres to the "law of the jungle" as opposed to the mainstream social standards; they possess a "holier than thou" attitude toward conventional social mobility, seeing education and hard work as futile; and they are willing to use violence to settle disputes. Anderson labels this group, to no one's surprise, as "street."[2]

With respect to underground activity in Maquis Park and the women whose lives are affected by it, it is only partially instructive to categorize people in the abstract as "decent" or "street." In fact, pointing to their expressed moral or political views does little to advance our understanding of their lives, because such opinions are always in flux, adapting to the needs of the moment, and they may never be articulated precisely enough to create a comprehensive worldview. For no other reason than to exercise caution in disclosing one's own receipt of illegal resources, people will be motivated to lie or, at the least, be circumspect in disclosing their behavior. The staple tool of sociologists, the interview, thus gives only part of the picture. A more illuminating way to proceed is to explore the relations that bring the women together, both conflictually and cooperatively, across social settings, including the ways in which they must respond to a local underground economy that shapes the quality of life in their neighborhood. Their decisions may be based on their own direct involvement in the shady world, their need to work with others so involved, or their indirect receipt of illicit goods and services via another member of their household. But whatever the type and degree of their complicity, individuals base their actions on their own sense of right and wrong. By documenting the everyday way in which their lives unfold, in their households and with their friends and associates, navigating between worlds legal and illegal, we get a rich understanding of this ethical sensibility.

Marlene, Bird, and Eunice dream of the "good life." They point to a time in the distant and unspecified future when they will have accumulated wealth and security, when today's hardships will be alleviated. Marlene and Bird want someday to hold well-paying jobs with benefits, and Eunice would like to see her daughter turn their homemade food sales into a successful Southside Chicago restaurant. All three imagine a Maquis Park free of street crime and shoddy schools. Each sees leisure-filled retirement in the offing, whether made possible by grandchildren, who Marlene says "are going to take care of me like I do for them," or by a higher power, who, in Eunice's words, "has me a home waiting that no man can build."

But there is a more immediate future for these women, one more concrete and unavoidable, involving a specific set of tasks that are rooted in the home. Any day brings the urgent need to make rent payments and put food on the table, ensure that winter clothes are purchased and that children reach school. There are other adults who live with them and who depend on them to make good decisions in the home, which reaffirms their need to provide refuge. And for a few women like Marlene who take a greater role in public affairs, such as pressuring police to patrol parks or close down abandoned buildings where drugs are sold, stabilizing the home environment reaches beyond the domicile.

This shorter temporal horizon is organized around pure pragmatism and relies on the underground economy. Opportunities to stabilize the household must be sought via off-the-books income. The women exchange labor for services, obtain loans from local credit sources, and purchase goods and services on the street, from cleaning supplies and underwear, to even household furniture and electronic equipment. There is almost always someone on one of the major Southside thoroughfares hawking such items. From the outside it is tempting to label their daily life as focused on a set of "survival strategies," an endless number of decisions and adaptations chosen in the hope of "making ends meet." But survival is not their goal. Neither Marlene, Bird, nor Eunice believes that her life is driven by poverty and constraint, void of an imagined future. They make sense of their present conditions in terms of their potential for social mobility. They use the phrases "hustling," "getting by," "just taking it day by day," to describe their contemporary actions, but these clichéd renditions of *la vie quotidienne* in the ghetto do not fully describe who they are or how they live. Marlene and her peers plan, weigh options and envision alternate paths, entertain investment and accumulation strategies, opine on thrift and sacrifice. Mobility, for them, is organized around needs and visions, urgencies and dreams. Their decisions to attend to their present predicaments are wrapped up in their thirst for a future in which some of their present predicaments will disappear. By understanding their orientation to time and the home, to immediate needs and hoped-for futures, we can appreciate their calculus for making the decisions that shape their days.

Is this space between "ought" and "is," between what exists and what is possible, the one in which most Americans live? Perhaps. But for the women in Maquis Park this navigation occurs underground. It is the shady world that shapes how they singularly aspire amid hope and reality, deferring one or the other as needs dictate. It is the underground marketplace that lies at their front door, in the form of a vendor, a customer, a nuisance, or a job opportunity. Of course, this vehicle for improvement is limited by the amount of money they are able to earn off the books and by the laws and codes of conduct they may transgress while doing so. Predictably, menial wages and the possibility of arrest and perhaps incarceration have a dampening effect on people's faith in the hustle as a panacea. And yet, even small amounts of money go a long way for a poor family. Individuals will undertake considerable risks to accumulate the most meager of sums. Some of the exchanges and income may appear so miniscule that they hardly constitute an economic enterprise. Yet, for a poor family $20 can open up a range of possibilities: ten pairs of socks can be purchased for $5 from the man at the corner gas station; another $5 buys enough low-priced meat at the local food store for five people; with the remaining $10 the household might take a gypsy cab to the welfare office and then buy a small cake for the kids and beer for the parents. In this way, the ability to supplement one's income by even small amounts through underground labors can alter the parameters of what's possible, especially for the head of household who needs to support herself and those living in her care.

Underground economic activity is important in their present and future lives not simply by affording them cost savings. The shady world plays a critical role in their work to create a stable household. Most of these women do not have career prospects. They do not, and arguably cannot, rely on the security blankets of social insurance available to others—for the most part, social security, unemployment insurance, and pensions are not commonplace for these households. So these women make that abstract notion of obtaining the "the good life" concrete as they build, manage, and support their households by other means. They weave their lives beginning with their extended family, that loose congregation of people who reside in their home, and moving outward, creating ties in the home, on the block, and through the neighborhood.[3] They also follow personal networks by creating alliances with trusted persons in the home and with more distant friends, kin, associates, gang members, social and political allies, and so on.

In the household the women see potential sources of support. The people coming in and out of their home are other poor individuals—whether friends or kin—who are likely also to be oriented toward the underground as a venue for work, goods, and services. All such persons could help the household make ends meet. Indeed, friends, grandchildren, ex-lovers, and such are not necessarily burdens, but people to whom these women may turn someday as times get tough and as aging knocks at their own door. Imagining the future translates into envisioning stability in and around their homes. And so understanding the underground economy from the perspective of these women must involve looking at the ways they stabilize their households.

It would be incorrect to suggest that men do not play an active role in domestic affairs.[4] Several structural factors shape how men participate in the households on Eunice's block. It is well known that poor families' reliance on public subsidies has placed many restrictions on the types of household arrangements that the poor may form.[5] To remain eligible for many government subsidies, parents and guardians adhere to restrictions that limit the residence of other income earners in the household. Historically, in poor households, black and white, women have disproportionately assumed the publicly recognized role of primary guardian.[6] They tend to be the recipients of public welfare, including nutritional subsidies, medical care, and housing assistance, on behalf of their children. As they manage the receipt of these subsidies, they must also be careful to hide other sources of income from government authorities, social workers, and other bureaucrats who could report their unlawful activity and jeopardize their eligibility in the program. Thus, one finds that women hide the men who live with them. This does not mean that men must live in a totally surreptitious manner; however, it does mean that men tend to possess diminished profiles—whether at the home or in civic spaces such as schools and social service providers—and limited roles inside the home. Whether in practice they are active or not, they are less often associated with the care of the children and the management of the home environment.

Not all families receive public subsidies and have to hide male income earners. Even in welfare households, part of the diminished male involvement is a product of men simply refusing to contribute to child rearing and child care, cleaning, and other domestic labors.[7] Eliot Liebow's study of "streetcorner men," for example, described the views of men in poor communities toward marriage, work, and child rearing. His analysis suggested that the absence of full-time work made it difficult for men to fulfill the role of "provider."[8] Leaving aside the merits of Liebow's argument, this view of women on Eunice's block is undertaken to complement his analysis. If men do not choose to participate in domestic affairs, how do women sustain their leadership role over time, what are the effects on their own short- and long-term outlooks, and what role does the underground economy play in this process?

The composition of households is fluid for most of the women on Eunice's block. At any particular time, a head of household may be faced with differing boarders who provide income (or not), who share her bed, and who use her home for shelter and sustenance. Two of the twenty-one households on the block have a nuclear family arrangement. Both are thirty-something professional couples, with one and three children, respectively, who moved to Maquis Park because homes were cheap and because they wanted to return to the neighborhood of their youth. One couple plans on eventually incorporating a grandmother and uncle into the home; the other has no plans for expansion beyond additional children. Both participate in the underground economy primarily as consumers—one hires a local youth to mow their lawn, the other pays a neighbor under the table for home repair. There are five other houses with married heads of households, where the husband lives full-time.

In the remaining fourteen households, there may be husbands, male partners, or lovers present, but they move out and return often.[9] With the exception of the two professional couples, households on Eunice's block display shifting arrangements of friends, partners, and extended family, what the anthropologist Carol Stack called "domestic kin networks." For the summers of 2000 and 2001, several changes occurred to households on Eunice's block. In some households the overall number of residents remained the same but the boarders had changed. In other households the number of boarders increased or decreased. In each year that I observed patterns on the block, there were similar changes. The 2000–2001 period was not so different from other years, and there is no reason to suspect that the households on the block differ significantly from others in the community.

The households on Eunice's block change for many reasons; nevertheless, household composition is driven fundamentally by economic necessity. Most obviously, in all households, members consume, thereby adding a cost that must be met. Moreover, women expend considerable energy managing the household, a form of work that usually is not recognized—and less often re- munerated; nor is it taken into account in conventional economic estimations. In the ghetto, managing one's home means attending to generic chores like cleaning, cooking, and child rearing, but in ways that are woven into the local underground economy. For example, barter and in-kind payments are an integral means through which women acquire services for the household. Eunice cannot always pay the local handyman with cash; instead, she offers him a week or more of free lunches, depending on the work he performs. In the afternoon, Marlene babysits children of mothers who return the payment by shuttling her kids to school or cleaning her house. Fifty dollars in food stamps enables Laetitia to purchase $75 worth of car repairs or $30 worth of beer at a local store. Friends and relatives come into the women's homes because they cannot pay rent themselves. They are likely to be working in some underground trade, and they also rou- tinely form arrangements with heads of households based on barter, exchanges of labor for rent, and promises of future pay- ment. For Eunice and her neighbors, the source of money is sometimes secondary to the need to obtain services and money from their boarders, even if it is "drug money" or "gambling money."

It is worth mentioning the three different types of boarders who move in and out of households—any household may con- tain a combination of the three. The first are members of the ex- tended family (and, less often, friends) who are relatively perma- nent boarders. They have negotiated with the head of household to live in the home, and this negotiation differentiates them from others, like a husband or children, who live there permanently without negotiating an arrangement. Eunice's mother has lived with her for nearly twenty years; Bird's grandfather lives with her permanently; Marlene's cousin has lived with her for a decade. Although these relationships are more than simply economic in nature, in all three cases material factors were at play in the head of household's decision to allow the individual into the home. Discussions among the household head and prospective boarders are usually quite explicit in terms of the monetary and in-kind support the boarder must provide: the two most common obligations are to pay monthly rent and/or utilities and to provide day care; however, monetary payments are rare, so providing day care to the kids in the household is the norm. After his wife's death, for example, Bird's grandfather approached Bird with promises to provide after-school day care for the children in exchange for taking up residence in a spare bedroom. Eunice's mother agreed to contribute toward the rent each month and occasionally help with the soul food preparation. Marlene's cousin's car was made the common property of all household members in lieu of rent.

A second and more common boarder is one who resides for extended periods of time, from a few months to a year. A seasonal employment opportunity may bring this individual into the home for a short duration; or the person may move in and out for various reasons, the most common being loss of income, inability to pay rent on another unit, domestic disputes, exit from jail, or renewed intimate relationships. In almost all such cases the head of household explicitly requests a monetary contribution; if the payment cannot be made, then there are attendant requests for payment via food stamps, periodic purchases of groceries, and in-kind services like cleaning, babysitting, and use of car. Mary, for example, allows a male friend to live with her. However, he agrees to leave his own job and take care of the kids whenever Mary finds work—alternatively, he must pay for a babysitter. Sandra's mother babysits the children during summers, living rent-free, because Sandra cannot afford day care. Both Mary and Sandra have kicked the boarders out of their respective homes when promises to help were not kept.

A third kind of resident comes into the household unpredictably, often for only a few days or weeks. This person may arrive because a domestic dispute forced them to leave their own home. Before Bird's grandfather moved in permanently, he was living with Bird on and off because his wife repeatedly threw him out of the house for running midday gambling parties. Sandra's sister is repeatedly abused by her own boyfriend and, with no battered women's clinics in the neighborhood, she takes her children and moves in with Sandra for several weeks so that she can be close to her work; she has always returned with her children to the home of the man who abuses her. The other common scenarios include persons leaving jail or prison who need immediate shelter, and heavy drug users who move between many different households, testing the patience of each.

Looking again at the units on Eunice's block, in a one-year period there were almost two dozen changes in household composition due to the exit or entrée of at least one of the three types of boarders (permanent, part-time, temporary). In 60 percent of the cases, an underground economic issue motivated the change: most commonly, the household head demanded that the incoming member contribute a portion of his unreported wages; or the boarder was found to be making money off the books in the house (for instance, hosting gambling and prostitution, or selling homemade items, guns, or drugs) and did not turn over part of the revenue.

All such dealings with boarders have their consequences. In terms of energy expended on household stabilization, the head of household must display ongoing vigilance and diplomacy. Particularly when their homes are a safe haven for numerous friends and relatives, these women must provide assistance to others in ways that do not jeopardize themselves and their children. If the prospective boarder offers to contribute money and the source of that money is illegal, it presents a difficult decision for the household head. Marlene spoke with me about a situation in her own household that illuminates the challenges of balancing the need for material and social support from others with safety and welfare for those in her home:

> "When my husband died, I was getting a little money [from his street gang], but then they lost [a street war to another gang], so I wasn't getting nothing. That's when my brother [-in-law], Teetie, moved in. Teetie [a drug dealer] was paying half my rent, so you know, I wasn't working and that helped. But he started sleeping with my sister, buying her drugs, and I wasn't having that. But if he left, shit, I'd have to find that money and ain't nobody else living with me was working. So I was just trying, for months, to get him to stop beating her, feeding her that bad dope, making her sick. But that's when she ended up in the hospital, so I told him to get out . . . I borrowed money from Otis for rent until I found my job, but I'm still paying that back and he charged 30 percent interest."
>
> "Did Teetie ever sell drugs in your house?"
>
> "Well, I won't lie to you. I was so desperate for rent, I let him do it. Big mistake. He was selling out the back and it just made things worse. But I needed the money. So I decided paying a loan shark and getting beaten up [if she didn't make her payments] was better than letting Teetie kill my sister."

As Marlene's observation suggests, conflicts must be prevented, but also resolved if they arise. Marlene's kind of situation is a recurrent challenge for women who must maintain a secure household while providing a refuge for others who request to stay in their home. The overriding dilemma concerns whether, and how, to obtain the monetary or in-kind support from the boarder. Even an ailing grandparent is not immune from explicit negotiations concerning contribution to the home. The need to extract payment or services from household members is not an issue that can easily be addressed through good-faith contractual discussions before the individual enters the home. It is an ongoing struggle for the head of household. Bird, for example, told her grandfather to leave her home because he was bringing in prostitutes during the day and hosting daytime gambling while Bird's children were present. He also refused to devote part of his gambling revenue, and disability and social security payments, to household rent. Asking her grandfather to leave was a difficult decision for Bird. He ended up homeless for nearly a month, staying on the streets, in shelters, and in the local hospital. Bird explained her decision to me one day while her grandfather watched TV in the next room:

> "You and Pops [your grandfather] been together for a long time?" I asked Bird, as she fixed me a plate of food.
>
> "Too long, but he just came back. He was gone for a while," Bird answered, with little emotion in her voice.
>
> "Yeah, 'cause she kicked my ass out, the bitch," Pops chimed from the other room, referring to Bird. "And I got diabetes. She didn't care, I was living on the streets. Bitch does what she wants, to her own kin even. It's all about Bird." His voice trailed off.
>
> "Don't listen to him," Bird instructed me. "He was fucking crack-whores up in here, making money on these poker parties. I don't care if he had died. And around my kids! No one does that to my kids."

"Your kids?" Pops yelled. "They was learning about life. Shit, you can't keep hiding them from this shit."

"Yeah, and you can't keep sitting around," quipped Bird, who then began to whisper. "It was hard, you know, it's your grandfather and he's sick. I just gave up, though. Nigger wouldn't pay me no money. Now, if he ain't making any, then I would've said do something else, clean up or something. But he was making all this cash, and he tore up my mattress upstairs and hid it there. Now, I should get some of that, you know, I'm the one putting a roof over his head."

"Mattress was tore up before I got here," Pops cried out. "Don't go lying to the nigger, now."

In a five-year period, Bird kicked her grandfather out of the house eight times. He never spent more than a month away. Usually he stays with another daughter (unrelated to Bird) until they reach a compromise. When he returns, Bird demands a deposit of several hundred dollars and a promise to help with rent and household duties. Although not every household may be dealing directly with prostitution and gambling, Bird's situation is representative of the difficult choices that heads of households must make, recurring issues that force households to remain fluid and adjust their composition, and the way in which the underground affects their decision making.

It is tempting to employ concepts from conventional economics when analyzing the decision making of Maquis Park's heads of households. In this view, the women are rational calculators, weighing the costs and benefits of any action that might expel an individual and remove that source of income from their home. Bird, for example, must simultaneously eliminate the cost of a household member who is endangering her children, retain the benefits her grandfather provides (he babysits), while searching for ways to secure a portion of his income. To some degree, her own reflections suggest that she is thinking about the decision by lining up costs, tallying benefits, and assigning probabilities to future outcomes. Like Bird, most women on her block seem to be mindful of each month's bills and work to meet these costs by calculating actual income, potential sources, and the costs that accompany each. But there are other factors at play, often nebulous but deeply significant. Bird's decisions are inflected by perceptions of her own life as a shady laborer and the exposure of her kids to the instabilities of living underground. Needless to say, her own emotions and desires affect her decision making:

> If I die, what happens? What happens to [my kids]? I leave this house every day, and you know, he's a son of a bitch, but he loves my kids. Until I, you know, win on the numbers or get something real big, that's just what I have to deal with. He's all I got. See, you keep asking me "Why I don't kick him out of my house?" Yeah, the nigger ain't paid, he ain't done his part. But if something happened to me out there, and the kids ended up alone? . . .

Bird believes that expelling her grandfather once and for all from the home would be the best decision for her family. But she both feels an attachment to him and worries about the risks accompanying her employment as a sex worker. Both shape how she lines up costs and benefits.

Candice is a thirty-five-year-old, high-school-educated "runner" who distributes drugs for the local gang. She lives in a second-story apartment with her three children and mother. Her comments mirror those of Bird; namely, she thinks about her household composition in light of the hazards of her vocation:

"I understand that I'm doing something that, well, could get me killed. I know someday, when I stop this, when I just get old, I may have nobody."

"What do you mean nobody?" I asked.

"You know, my kids are around this shit, what if they go to jail. They already been taken away from me, and I had to work with DCFS to get them back. Shit, you know, they see their momma as somebody who makes their life harder. They may not see what I got to do to keep food on this table. If they don't they could just get all this hate inside them, and when I need them, shit, they may not be around. I know that, but what can I do, it's the life I live, it's the choice I'm making right now."

"It must be tough to feel they're okay," I said, "when your work is so dangerous."

"Autry helps. He ain't my man or nothing, I mean he was and he is trying to be again, but he stays with my kids. One of them is his. I mean, I don't want him living here, you know? But I got to think about what happens if I'm not around. At least my kids, they got him and they got my momma. I just have to live with that until things change and I can be on my own."

It is commonplace to hear women like Candice and Bird say that their work in illicit sectors places their families in jeopardy. They remark, both when exhausted and when coldly analytic, that they may not live long enough to receive love and support of other persons. Alternatively, they see their actions as endangering their family, thereby alienating and angering these potential sources of long-term assistance. They are not only eliminating their opportunities to meet their prince or savior—Cotton says, "You meet the most fucked-up men when you whoring, ain't no Denzel [Washington] out there"—but they experience diminished hopes that they are creating the conditions for children, relatives, and partners to aid, comfort, and provide for them as they age.

It is not surprising that living underground can affect one's general outlook. In general, those who define their primary work as being in the illicit underground trades, like theft, robbery, vice, narcotics, and weapons trading, express less confidence that they will have someone to provide for their welfare as they grow older. This heightened sense of personal danger and insecurity, in both the short and the long run, is one way to differentiate women who work in the illicit trades from those who, like Eunice, sell licit goods under the table or who, like Marlene, live illegally simply because of failure to report income. Nevertheless, the illicit traders' perceptions of insecurity are only a more cathected version of a concern that can exist for all women. Most of the women whose lives are unfolding in the shady world are pessimistic about the long-term stability of their households. And it is in terms of the household, and the fragility therein, that women express their vulnerability. They are concerned not only for the well-being of their children and spouse, but also for their capacity to maintain a private space where sharing and support can exist—a space in which, one day, the women hope to be on the receiving end.

Even the youngest mothers acquire this sensibility. They focus their attention on crafting their own roles as heads of households, which means more than simply being mother to their children. They are betting that a good future will come through the terrain of the household, and so they work toward security by learning their home-based role in a domestic network of close friends and relatives.[10] Not all young mothers have their own households to manage—in fact, most poor women who cannot support themselves through employment or government subsidies will live as permanent and part-time boarders of other friends or relatives. Eunice's sixteen-year-old pregnant niece, Sheila, who lives in her house, speaks for these young aspirants: "I want to be like momma, with a big family, being there for people, always kids around, my own place, but where a whole lot of people feel like it's their home. My momma's in jail, she ain't had that, but I want that for her when she gets out." As these young adults become heads of households, they promptly orient themselves to bridging long- and short-term horizons through their capacity to stabilize their household for others in their social network. Below are two statements, one by Laetitia, a mother of two and recipient of rent subsidies who lives on Marlene's block, the other by Renee, a twenty-two-year-old mother of three, who lives a few blocks away:

> I just moved here, I was living with my momma. I know I can always live with her, but she needs to see that she can live with me too. And she's going to move in soon, which is good 'cause she is a [gypsy cab] driver and I can get a little money, and somebody to help me . . . It's like, I'm already thinking about getting old, can you believe it? But I got to find a school for my kid next year, and you just wonder sometimes who's going to be there for you when you grow old. I think my kids probably will take care of me. My momma taught me that. That you always got each other, you always keep your place where you can live and you know someone else going to give you that place when you need it, someday when you old and can't work.

> It's not like I always sold dope. You know, I used to wash cars, and I was begging when things got bad. But now, once I sell just a little

more, I'm going to quit, cause Mr. Ahmad [who owns the local liquor store], he say he'll pay me and teach me how to work the front . . . But I got to let my brother and his friend stay here, 'cause they got the dope. But my brother's cool, you know, before he was in jail, I was living him, my momma, my auntie, all my sisters, we all stayed with him. So I'm helping him out now I guess, that's just the way it is. You only got your family.

Laetitia and Renee point to the role of "family" in shaping a vision of the future. This is perhaps the most common way women in Maquis Park resolve the conflict between the short-term decisions that must be made reluctantly in order to stabilize the household, including acceptance of underground income from the boarder or participating in an illegal scheme themselves, and the long-term perception that a stable home environment is necessary. With no career or social security, it is the family that will provide at the end of the day. Even though some of their immediate decisions may jeopardize their ability to secure a protective and nurturing domicile, as long as they make their home available to others, then they can count on other kindred spirits when times are tough. The perception is strongly held that just as other family members are turning to them and moving into their household, so too will they need such help at an unknown date. Sending away otherwise close friends and relatives because their income is not always legitimately derived—or sufficient—may be folly. As long as that income does not drastically undermine the security of their own household, which is a decision that the women make repeatedly and in the context of their overall needs and resources, then the benefits of receiving additional monetary support will outweigh the risks.

But while "family" is preeminent in these women's concepts of their future, the clarity of their visions varies greatly. Most noticeable is a marked generational difference among these women in terms of their perceptions of the relationship between short-term instability and future development. Most of the adolescent and twenty-something parents and heads of household speak in a vague and secular language. For them, security is an equation based on adequate income, home ownership, employed children, and responsible spouses, and they seldom explicitly say how long in the future they will need to wait or the precise steps they must take to reach their goals—jobs, retirement planning, investments, education, and so forth. This is partly understandable, given their age, limited experience with savings, and the lack of decent opportunities for work and training.

By contrast, the older residents make the links between today and tomorrow differently. Some will invoke religious rhetoric. For Eunice, "refinding the church" is the best explanation for her ability to remain optimistic despite the weight of her hardships. Seeing the future out of an unstable present involves embracing transcendent notions of personal development and salvation. It is a classic and common tale of Christian redemption, flavored with the spice of ghetto life, and it enables her to cope with "liv[ing] an illegal life in the eyes of God."

> "Now, I wouldn't say this usually, but God knows all anyway, so I must live honest. I used to do anything to put food on that table, I mean anything. I was on welfare for the longest and it was like one long party that you just wanted to end, you know? [laughs] Selling a little dope, maybe stealing. You had to do this if you had a family. I mean everyone just—"
>
> "Now, I'm lost. You always talk about these women who pimp

themselves, and that they have no respect for themselves and
should see Christ. Now, you say it's okay?"

"Not okay. I'm just saying before I got back together with the
Lord, I was desperate, doing anything to take care of myself."

"And now?" I questioned. "How do you explain the fact you
don't report your income from the food you sell?"

"Oh, the Lord sees that. Yes, I do live an illegal life in the eyes of
God. But he also sees I ain't selling no drugs, I take care of my
grandchildren. All that money? It goes to my babies, keeps them in
school. I mean, you always going to take care of your children.
That's the bottom line, sugar. But you can't hide that it ain't the
same if you pimping or cooking."

"But what happens if the Lord takes it all away?"

"If that happens, it's for the best. He knows why he does what
he does. All *I* know is that I've been blessed with the ability to
keep myself alive and my family alive. My family will not suffer as
long as I'm on the earth. All this money I'm making? I got bank
accounts, my babies have money for their college. I don't roll over.
That's what the Lord taught me."

Where Eunice turns to her innate entrepreneurial drive and di-
vine dispensation, Marlene rests her hopes for salvation on activism. She strives to be part of a social group that collectively
assumes the mantle of responsibility for community improvement. Her vision is equally utopian, a future of security and
care—but the resting place that motivates her daily behavior and
that meaningfully ties together her short- and long-term horizons is collective social action. Heaven is a political El Dorado,
not the Lord's pasture, and her place there may be secured by
building relations with others who will support her in her time of

need. For her, the household is also at the center of this activity because she is placing her loved ones in a broader network of allies who may teach, support, comfort, and otherwise act as a safety net. And, as with Eunice, the underground economy colors her vision.

"I'll always have the gang. See, they been here for thirty years. They take care of their own. Now, people 'round here see the gang as these niggers on the street. No, sir. What you seen, Sudhir, when we get together at the church, when we hold those rallies for kids, see, all that's the gang. All them brothers was in it back in the day. They were all [in the same gang]."

"But I don't get how that makes you so secure about life," I asked. "You're resting your fate on drug dealers. You think that you're going to be safe and provided for by these people? That really doesn't make sense. I mean you're putting your kids in jeopardy, no?"

"I didn't say nothing about drug dealers. Lionel [the police officer], Pastor Prentiss, they were in the gang, too. They know my kids, and that's why I work with all of them. You have to be part of the community, something bigger, see. I know my brother will always be there for me, just like I'm there for him right now, helping him out. But there are lot of folk out there [in Maquis Park] that help me too, and I help them . . . Don't matter in some ways if it's the gang or the church. You just got to depend on people who been with you through thick and thin, and that's what I'm looking for."

"And you feel like you'll be taken care of?"

"I don't have a choice, I have to believe that. You see what we deal with, you see what we have to do to survive. It's not always pretty, I'm no angel, and for that matter neither are you. We all got a shady side. Around here, it's that you do what you have to do to survive. But the other thing is that you do what you can to make sure you don't need to live always desperate, you know, looking to make a buck and doing whatever it takes. That gets tiring, that's a life of danger, so I think you start building something with other people around you."

That Marlene and Eunice link personal and family welfare with the resources in the wider community is not surprising; neither is their turn to activism and religion. For that matter, Maquis Park is really not much different from other American communities in this regard. However, whereas taking refuge in the church or in activism to deal ethically with social problems may not be the province of the urban poor, the necessity of coping continuously—morally and practically—with shady economic activities may be. Whether the overriding sense of comfort is rooted in extended family, one's own innate capacities, or a faith in the Lord, all such foundations are tested by the shady activities that help households make ends meet.

The Battle over Homans Park

The women of Maquis Park work in a huge variety of industries, often self-made, often at least partly illegal, in order to support themselves and their loved ones. Some off-the-books work is legal and women simply choose not to report the income, but some spheres, like prostitution, can pose dangers and great risks not only for the women but for others in their household who depend on them. Working underground is not always the preferred option, but a socially legitimate job can be a luxury. A shady job affords them flexibility and, since much of it is locally based, it is easier for them to take on work while managing their household affairs.

Given the risks that living and working underground entail, the women face moral quandaries: nearly all of the women on Eunice's block expressed concern at one point in time about their unlawful behavior. Even if they were only preparing taxes for a friend off the books, they worried about the illegal nature of their activity and whether their children and other household members might suffer for it. According to the current popular and scholarly fashion of looking at American inner cities as consisting of "decent" and "street" families with differing value orientations, the former obeying the law and the other flouting it, the neighborhood is made up of two competing networks, with the law-abiding ("decent") families staying close to one another and either actively resisting or hiding from the other ("street") group. This is an inadequate basis for understanding the experiences and worldviews of families who live in urban poverty.[11] It is true that Eunice and her neighbors will talk about other people on their block and in their neighborhood as criminal and contributing to the lack of public safety. Like parents in any neighborhood, they will decry the behavior of marauding gangs and street hustlers who make it difficult to walk about the community securely. They will at times express their opinions as values: involvement in crime is wrong, young people should not join street gangs, people must be attentive to the needs of their neighbors.

But the households on Marlene's block do not exist in isolation from one another, such that their opinions are generally being offered about people with whom they have no practical connection. Nor is the underground economy only a matter that falls between head of household and boarder. Household management in the shady world also has a neighborhood character, one that is not encapsulated in the values that people may hold and offer to the researcher. Their household management strategies and their visions of future improvement are made in the context of living with other people who share similar circumstances. And by observing how they work to keep their overall communities habitable, one can see in practice how their ethical designations of right and wrong, proper and unjust, began to take shape.

Importantly, residents on Eunice's block are connected in some way to the people who may be compromising public safety. Moreover, they may not have the luxury of offering a criticism about a perpetrator and leaving it at that. This means that one will see not only expressions of disgust or disdain, but potentially practical relationships in which different people must work alongside one another to keep some stability in and around the home. Thus, one must temper an assessment of their expressed values with an acknowledgment of the practical circumstances that forge social relationships among a diverse group of people. One must, in other words, take into consideration that there is a material foundation to the development of a moral framework. Because the underground economy plays such a key role in bringing resources into the home, household members are often caught between their desires to live a just life and their needs to make ends meet as best they can. Deciding what is right and wrong is made complicated because any household could potentially be turning to the shady side of the economic fence to put food on the table. Thus, instead of a value dichotomy, there may be shades of gray, such that residents tolerate some kinds of off-the-books work, but not others. They may empathize with some kinds of hustlers and shady entrepreneurs, but hold others in low regard. And these viewpoints may not be universally shared or kept consistent over time. Just as household circumstances shift and opportunities to earn money (legitimately and off the books) can change, so too are views of permissible and questionable behavior likely to adjust. This does not mean that there is no moral core, only that moral righteousness in the form of absolute lines of demarcation between right and wrong are not possible—nor advisable if the point is to keep meeting the needs of the household.

In 1999, Marlene, Eunice, Bird and the other residents on their street block had to confront Big Cat, the leader of the local gang in Maquis Park, the "Black Kings." Big Cat's gang had been increasing its activities in Homans Park, the nearby recreational space that Marlene and her neighbors allowed their children to use. Marlene and her neighbors were worried about the consequences for public safety. It was not simply that there were gang members milling about. There was an escalation in public underground activity, both by the gang and its drug-trafficking operations as well as by the many individual shady entrepreneurs who worked in the neighborhood selling clothes, fixing cars, offering sexual services, and so on. There were rumors that Big Cat had recruited some non-gang-affiliated merchants to the park, in hopes of offering them a space to ply their trade while, in return, imposing a street tax on their revenue. By doing so, Big Cat was claiming a say in the use of the park that for many years had also been the domain of Marlene and other residents who worked in "neighborhood watches" and block clubs, and for whom park access was important for family stability, not just personal gain.

When Big Cat increased the levels of shady activity in Homans Park, this pitted residents' own needs to maintain safety in their homes and streets against their own appreciation for the need for households to make ends meet by earning money off the books. It brought together two stakeholders, the gang and residents, who had differing interests and for whom a usable public space meant different things. The Homans Park incident captures the struggle over safety and security in poor communities. And it shows that underground jobs—from prostitution to child care to selling merchandise on the streets and in parks—are fundamental to the functioning of households and communities, and reveals why the debates over how their park should be run caused such strife.

As in other densely populated urban areas, Maquis Park residents feel great attachment to their local park. Homans Park is small, a block square, and is the principal recreational site for those on Marlene's street. The park is not directly adjacent to major thoroughfares in the community, where trucks and cars pass by sometimes at high speeds. In fact, two of the streets that pass by the park are dead ends, further limiting car traffic. Homans Park is tucked away, a few blocks to the south of the main thoroughfares, which gives the parents some relief that cars will not endanger their children. The park's relative inaccessibility keeps away not only drivers, but also other residents of the city who are not likely to come into the area unless they live nearby. Indeed, the park's modest offerings rarely attract the wider residential population. There is a swing set, but it is broken and has lain unrepaired for five years, despite numerous resident petitions and pleas to the alderman. There are a dozen benches, some bent out of shape and exposing dangerous steel edges. An unattractive, undulating concrete play area doubles as a handball and basketball court, depending on whether young or old are playing. And a large grassy patch is available for families to barbecue or throw a baseball; a winding asphalt path, littered with glass, refuse, and the occasional cardboard tent of a homeless person, encircles it. (More serious endeavors, like an organized baseball game or a family reunion, require families to walk several miles to Washington Park, one of the city's most beautiful recreational areas, which offers baseball diamonds, fully functioning basketball courts, a historic field house and swimming pool, and miles of ponds and pathways.) If one were to drive by Homans Park quickly, there would not be much to distinguish it from the other block-long stretches of weedy ground that litter the neighborhood. Its state of disrepair makes it almost as unsuitable for children as the nearby empty lots filled with broken glass and abandoned cars.

The fact that residents are able to keep Homans Park available for recreation and leisure is no small feat, and it testifies to the dedication of local residents to fight for usable public space. There are four major periods of activity in the park. In the mornings, children meet and greet one another, as the park is directly on the path to a local day-care center, elementary school, and a high school. The kids congregate again from 3 p.m. until 6 p.m., as they make their way home. In between, from 11 a.m. until 3 p.m., the children are replaced by adult men and women— gamblers, cardplayers, gossipers, book readers, Bible thumpers, snoozers, and, on occasion, a local historian who seems to remember most of the residents and nearly all of the important events that have taken place in and around the park. Judging from the bottles of beer and cheap wine around the concrete square and in the lone trash can, the site is particularly amenable to public drinking. The local historian explained:

> You have two streets that almost dead-end, nowhere to go. You have the other streets that are filled with potholes, so there's no need for people to be driving through here. Which means, ain't no need for police to be around either. It is a very nice place to get your drink on, particularly in that early morning hour when

you're just getting up. Don't have to worry about getting hit by a car if you stagger on the street. That's very important to some of these cats.

Although it is set off from the thoroughfares enough to limit car traffic, Homans Park is isolated enough to be well suited for gang activity. It is proximate to some of the busier streets so that customers can quickly come by and purchase drugs from the local gang. Indeed, because of the generally limited car and pedestrian traffic, those who come to the park expressly to purchase the gang's crack and marijuana are easy to detect. Big Cat and his local gang depend on places such as Homans Park that are close to the main thoroughfares and that can attract customers. They meet customers there, and they conduct group meetings in the open basketball court. Given the lack of facilities in the area that welcome gang members, Homans Park has become for them a prized possession. For as long as residents can remember, the gang has tried to occupy the park day and night. There have always been arguments and fights between gangs and the nongang public for use of the site. For Big Cat, the park is not only a significant sales spot, but a historic symbol of the gang's long-standing presence in Maquis Park. As he said, "I was initiated into the gang here, my brother was initiated here; I got shot here for the first time. This was the park that had the riots with the police in the seventies. It is part of who we are [as a gang]. We fight to keep it in the family." Until the late nineties it was the second most profitable outdoor sales spot for Big Cat.

Big Cat's gang and other street gangs in the city had gone through several important changes by the time Marlene and her neighbors faced them in Homans Park. These changes are addressed in greater detail in Chapter 6. For now, it is worth noting simply that after the seventies, gangs became entrepreneurial actors. For much of the twentieth century, the gang was primarily a social network for marginalized or at-risk youth who were having troubles with school, who could not find work, and who otherwise gravitated toward like-minded peers. Yet most would leave the gang in their late teens and early twenties, as they found jobs and became bored with hanging out on street corners. To be sure, some gangs did traffic in narcotics, rob stores, and direct criminal activities. But this was not the rule. Only after the seventies did young people—teenagers and adults in their twenties and beyond—begin looking to the gang to make money; in part, this was an expected response, given unemployment rates for youth that hovered around 50 percent in Chicago's ghettos. As gangs began moving into underground economies—drugs, larceny, extortion—they became "corporate" entities, organized to support the material as well as the social needs of young people.

Throughout the gang's history, from its *petty delinquent* period to its *corporate* stage, the wider community had to ward off the gang's threats to safety and public access. As the gang became corporate, residents' struggles shifted to reflect not only the gang's changes but also the residents' increasing reliance on the underground economy. All of this can be seen in the matters surrounding security and access in Homans Park.

Eunice and Marlene have fought for many years to ensure a minimal level of safety in Homans Park. "Sometime in the late eighties," Marlene recalls, their labors produced a quasi détente between the neighborhood's two opposing factions: the residents and the gang. Negotiations between the two parties have resulted in a range of agreements, which work and then fail, and the terms are renegotiated. In general, Big Cat agreed to limitations on drug selling, such as preventing rank-and-file members from selling narcotics immediately before and after school as well as during planned activities, such as a family reunion. In exceptional cases, the gang leaders pay cash to Marlene (or her counterpart) in exchange for their help in reducing police presence (Marlene has considerable sway with the local beat officers, who respect her own agreements with the gang). Their agreements break down every six months or so, but the lines of communication have long been open and clear enough that Marlene, Eunice, or another neighbor might call the gang and rekindle negotiations. Their influence with the gang, however, does little to resolve the many other activities that have made Homans Park inhospitable for families. Local residents have still had to contend with inadequate policing, harassment and sexual abuse of young women, poor upkeep by the Department of Parks and Recreation, prostitution, episodic drive-by shootings by enemy gangs, non-gang-affiliated youth violence stemming from high school disputes, and a stream of homeless persons and squatters who sleep, defecate, and leave their refuse there.

But around 1999, Marlene says, "everything changed." The gang's presence shifted, the relationships between residents and the gang also changed, the people in the park were no longer the same, and there were new annoyances that plagued local families. Marlene describes the situation before and after.

> "Used to be," Marlene reflected, "the worst thing was Big Cat's boys slanging [selling drugs] on the corner. Not good. But, okay, we could deal with it. Then, no one was buying the crack, remember? Big Cat changed things around, remember that? See, he started losing money and that's when he, that's when he, what's the word I'm looking for?
>
> "Diversified?" I offered.

"Yes, you could say that," she laughed. "He had a lot of new ideas for how to make money. The park was the first place, basically, where we all had to deal with the new thing going on."

"The new thing?" I asked.

"Well, I guess a gang is always a gang, don't nothing change about that. But the things a gang does are different. And he was doing some new things, which means we [the residents] had to *react* to what he was doing. It wasn't like we could just talk to him and it would be safe; we had a new kind of relationship. We had to agree and disagree all over again."

Marlene's language is telling. Rarely does she see the gang as the "enemy within." As a longtime resident, perhaps her history of diplomacy with the gang has made local gang members appear less threatening; they are, after all, kids in the neighborhood whom she remembers as part of her own youth. But the gang's natural, integral place in the neighborhood fabric is what created the challenge for her neighbors when the organization of underground activity in the neighborhood began to change, at least with respect to the gang and its involvement in the shady world.

Maquis Park's residents had been familiar with an entrepreneurial street gang whose efforts centered around a lucrative crack cocaine operation. With that economic base withering by the late nineties, Big Cat sought other investment and income opportunities, which took some people by surprise. He began to extort businesses, sex workers and pimps, gypsy cab drivers, homeless persons selling socks or offering to wipe windshields. Almost anyone whom he determined to be earning money illegally was susceptible. One evening, in a drunken stupor, he stumbled upon a card game in a local park and demanded that the winners give him 10 percent of their profits. "We were laughing," said Bird, "but we all wondered what's this boy been smoking? I mean if he starts asking old men playing cards for five bucks, who's next?" In transforming Homans Park into an underground economic bazaar, Big Cat came directly into contact with Bird, Marlene, and their neighbors on the 1700 block of South Maryland Avenue.

Big Cat turned his attention to both Homans Park and the immediately surrounding areas, which included abandoned buildings, empty lots, and alleyways. He started by consolidating his drug-dealing operations. Drug trafficking would no longer be restricted to a few hours per day, but could take place around the clock. In addition, he recruited other underground entrepreneurs to the park. He called the local gun traders and asked if they wanted a secure space in an abandoned building where they could meet customers and showcase their weapons. In general, he aimed to skim off the profits of other traders by providing them a relatively secure place to conduct their business and warding off competitors; in turn, he would charge them for protection services.

Big Cat did not expect to make thousands of dollars at Homans Park. But the crack cocaine trade was declining. The gang leader feared that his organization would lose its stature and its ability to recruit young people, if he did not quickly find other sources of revenue. The Homans Park venture was an experiment in economic regulation that Big Cat hoped to replicate in other local public areas. As important as the money to be made, however, were the relationships the gang had with other community players.[12] If Big Cat ran a small outfit—a dozen or so members who hung out on the corner—his need to work with residents and local organizations would not be so pressing. But in his own words, he was a "businessman" who depended to some degree on residents' tolerance and, to a greater extent, on their purchasing power. And he had ambitions to rise to a more prominent position of power in Maquis Park. So the Homans Park initiative was about far more than increasing gang revenues; it was the start of Big Cat's personal upward-mobility path.

"I know it may not be easy to be a politician, or even get respect around here, but that's what's important to me. I grew up here, I know the ghetto, I know Maquis Park and I love my people."

"Are you kidding me?" I said, disbelievingly. "*Your* people. Correct me if I'm wrong, but *your* people are pretty upset at you for taking over this park. I'm not exactly seeing how they're going to elect you to public office."

"It takes a while for people to come around."

"Come around?" I laughed. "Come around to what? What exactly do you want them to open their eyes and see?"

"You think it's all about me making money, don't you?" he said, leaning over to me as if speaking to a child. "How do you think Marlene got the power she got? You know what she will charge you if you want her to call the police or find your stolen car? Lot more than I charge you. Everyone who's got power around here got money. Legit, illegit, it don't really matter. Now, I need to be able to control something, and here, I'm talking about helping people make money, helping them to feed their families. The park is the place where you can sell something, buy something, maybe find something you need, a television from Jimmy or a microwave. Maybe buy some shirts and socks. Maybe Marsha will suck your dick. Without having to worry about [the police], without having to worry about getting robbed by bringing your money to some nigger at night."

"You're going to guarantee that police won't bother you? That's a tall order."

"You see any around here? You've been counting. How many police did you see in the last week patrol?"

"Two cars," I answered.

"Now, you tell me whether I got something that people need or not!"

Like Big Cat, Marlene Matteson also understood that a gang cannot run an economic operation without some consent from the local residents. Even if that consent takes the form of turning the other way when illegal activity takes place. As president of the 1700 South Maryland Avenue Block Club, Marlene had watched Big Cat alter the gang's presence in the park from December 1999 to May 2000. Pimps brought their sex workers to an abandoned building near the park. Carliss, a car mechanic, moved his outdoor "Oil and Tire Change" operation to the alley next to the park's basketball court. Two gun brokers came to a nearby abandoned building once a week to sell handguns and pistols. A few men sold stolen car stereos, guns, and other electronic equipment from the back of two beat-up beige vans that were always stationed at the park's entrance. Mo-Town, the local hot dog vendor, and Charlie, who sold stolen cigarettes and beauty products, set up their respective carts at the edge of the park. And now the drug sales were, as Big Cat had promised, round the clock. All of this was secured by placement of Big Cat's rank and file around the area: all were armed, they physically searched and harassed passersby, and they drank and smoked marijuana until the early morning hours with loud music blaring from their stereos. They also charged a fee to each entrepreneur based in and around the park.

By the end of May, Marlene had readied herself to take on Big Cat, determined that the neighborhood children would be able to use the park over the coming summer. She weighed her options carefully. The nominal protector, the local police, had never provided enough help to make the park safe. Marlene had discovered early on that the official "community policing" meetings at which law enforcement officials invited residents to air their concerns, tended to favor those who had greater conventional social clout—which, in Maquis Park, meant homeowners who were in good standing with the local alderman. Marlene did have her own friends on the police force whom she could call, but she preferred to solicit their assistance for timely response to domestic violence incidents. She didn't want to risk diminishing this capacity by asking police to put pressure on Big Cat. Marlene also had contacts with grassroots clergy, with whom she had worked with in the past on political campaigns and who had shown their effectiveness in mediation between local residents and the gang. However, it had been a few years since she had partnered with Pastor Wilkins, a leader in gang intervention, so she thought she would wait before enlisting his assistance. She knew of several ministers who had accepted gang donations in return for hosting funerals of slain gang members, but she was unsure exactly who benefited and whether they would support her or lean toward the source of their largesse. She knew of other block club leaders, staff at social service agencies, parole officers, and so on, whom she could call, but she did not know whether Big Cat had formed similar quasi-charitable relationships with them. She worried that they might not help her for fear of jeopardizing their own under-the-table revenue, not to mention their capacity to win concessions from the gang.

Marlene's situation that summer put into relief several aspects of social control within poor communities. And it showed how the underground economy alters residents' capacities to work practically on issues that threaten their overall welfare. First, as a goal, public safety can mean different things. Most urbanites would probably conceive of safety in terms of the absence of criminality, at least those forms of deviant behavior that inhibit safe passage and that jeopardize the health and welfare of families.[13] For Marlene and her neighbors, "absence" was not the primary criterion, either in terms of the nonexistence of perpetrators or the lack of shady activity. Absence was not even considered a possibility. Residents detested Carliss's underground car repair service because of the oil slicks and dangerous metal parts he sometimes left behind, but they understood that this was his source of income. And for that matter, although many did not approve of sex work around the park, they similarly understood it to be a form of work, which like any other labor in the community was instrumental in supporting households. Witness two comments made that May, at an impromptu block club meeting Marlene convened to discuss the changing landscape of Homans Park. The first is by Arlene Danielle, a seventy-year-old grandmother; the second is by a forty-year-old man, Timothy Carter, who drives a school bus part-time:

> Why did [Big Cat] chose *our* park? And why ain't we calling the police? I mean let the brother [Carliss] stay, shit, he fixed my car real good, but the boy [Big Cat] needs to go. I mean you can't be charging people tax if they selling a box of candy or some socks. Good Lord. I mean I knew [Big Cat's] mother; she would have never allowed him to do that. She would have said to get his boys out of there. That's what we need to be doing, [we] can't even go [to the park] no more. Like I said, don't mind the young man sell-

ing his dashikis or nothing like that. Heck, you know I feel safer when there's more people there . . . But I can't have drug dealing and we have to have some police, somebody.

Why can't we be doing what Big Cat is doing? I mean if he gets 10 percent from those bitches [prostitutes], why can't we take that money and put it in our club? Now, I know you all ain't going to be with me on this, but I'm just saying, we should be the ones who say what happens [in Homans Park] and who does what. I mean we live here, most of them gangbangers don't even live here. Like Michael—I know his momma, they live on 78th and Ashland, boy just come around to make his money. Ain't fair. Call the police, Marlene, shit, tell them I'll control the place, ain't like I got nothing else to do, the damn Board of Ed[ucation] ain't giving me no hours.

Here we see two basic visions of how to create public safety. The first is that residents may weigh delinquent activity that has an economic dimension differently than, say, crimes of passion like domestic violence and assault. This does not mean that all underground activity is tolerated. But if the activity generates income, any ethical dilemmas it creates must also be judged in terms of how the activity supports a household and even the wider community. Given that poverty and desperation drive much of the illegal economic activity and many households receive some kind of unreported income, the options for curbing such behavior may be limited. Complete eradication may not be a realistic option. It is unlikely that pimps, gang members, car mechanics, or hot dog vendors are going to stop selling their goods and services without either a new source of income, the threat of apprehension by law enforcement, or the fear of reprisal from another entrepreneur, like a gang, that has the capacity to inflict physical harm. Marlene and her neighbors felt that even if the local traders were threatened with police detection or gang beatings, they would probably just move their operations temporarily, only to return to Homans Park if the other location proved unsuitable.

Consequently, requests to stop the activity had to be replaced by a second vision of diplomacy and intervention. Timothy's suggestion became more and more popular during that month, namely, to intervene by creaming off some of the revenue that Big Cat received through the gang's imposed tax on the underground entrepreneurs in the park. Timothy understood that he was effectively intending to replace the gang as an extorter of street merchants. He received little support from his neighbors, the majority of whom suggested that it would be immoral to take money directly from the street traders. But they did agree that it might be worth regulating underground activity themselves, thereby limiting their overall vulnerability to Big Cat and reducing the attraction of the Park for shady merchants. Marlene spoke to her neighbors about what regulation might mean. She put forth social control strategies that did not necessarily involve taking cash receipts from the street traders, but that might instead be organized around restrictions on use of the park at certain times— much like the historic agreements over times of drug sales that had been in place with the gang. She suggested that some of the people in the block club who were making clothes or selling homemade food might even benefit from the customers now congregating in the area. The block club agreed to accept some kinds of underground activity in the park, at least provisionally until they could find another place for some of the traders. They recognized the need for people to earn income. Timothy explained the consensus opinion to me after another block club meeting:

> "We just went over all the kinds of things happening in the park and we made a strategy for what we could accept, you know what we could live with and what we don't want in our park."

"What you could live with?" I said. "I don't understand, it's your park, why do you have to live with anything you don't want? Just call [Police] Commander Calabria, he'll understand."

"Commander ain't going to do shit. I don't care if he's new around here. Ain't nobody done shit in the past, ain't nobody doing shit tomorrow. Like I was saying: nobody can sell nothing when the kids is in school and there ain't no selling on weekends. Well, maybe lemonade, but no pimping or nothing like that. And we want all the pimps and whores and drug dealers gone. We'll have to deal with people selling shirts and shit like that, I mean that's cool. Carliss can stay there, but we're going to make sure he cleans up after he fixes the cars. And he can't fix the cars *in* the park, just next to it. I mean he has a whole parking lot across the street."

"Where are you going to put the whores?"

"Marlon [the pimp] has to take his women at least a block away, away from the kids. Plenty of places over there. And Big Cat, well, that nigger can't be selling drugs here no more, no way."

"Hmm," I said. "Never going to happen. Nice try though."

"Fuck that, it'll happen."

"Are you kidding me?" I interrupted. "Big Cat is never giving up money, not now, not with summer coming around, not that kind of *tall* money that we're talking about."

"Well, maybe not, but we've got a few months to make his life hell, and that's what Marlene is going to do. By time, we'll figure out someplace else he can go. Pastor Wilkins is going to help us, too, so that'll be a big help."

"Oh, really? That's something new. You're going back to the church?"

"Ain't never left the church, my man. Remember and don't take this the wrong way. But you don't live here. We always had a good relationship with the church, we all go to church, we never strayed. We may not be doing things in public, but Pastor said he'll talk with Big Cat, help us. He did it before, he'll do it again. He'll get some of these people out of here."

The block club members grappled with one another to determine an adequate level of economic activity in the park. Because summer was around the corner and kids would be playing outside at all hours, they had to make the park safe soon. Only then could they contemplate more permanent solutions. But their available means of response did not give them cause for optimism. They initially supported mobilizing *en masse* and attending the "community policing" meetings organized by the local district commander, at which residents could speak about their concerns. They thought that a large group of protesting residents might bring about nightly patrols, which would scare off the gang and the other shady entrepreneurs. And a few of them actually met with several officers and explained their work and their need for police assistance. They hoped to convince the local police officers to station a car during the afternoon, when children tended to gather. Paralleling these efforts, they sought help from several social service agencies that ran recreational programs for children; they believed that a small arts-and-crafts service or other summer school program might help dissuade the shady entrepreneurs intent on distributing their wares in

Homans Park. Their work did not yield much fruit: the police failed to provide any meaningful protection, either in the way of intervention or increased patrols in the park, and no social service agency would invest the resources to begin a new program for kids on such short notice. As a consequence, Marlene and her neighbors did not place much hope in law enforcement's capacity to provide aid, either now or in the future. After her two-hour meeting with neighbors, Marlene explained their collective decision to consider other, non-law-enforcement options:

> We all figured out what was going to happen. Police would come three or four nights, then later it would go down to one or two nights, then we never see them again and we're going to have to deal with it after that. So, why not just deal with it ourselves right now? That's when we said we can't be wasting our time with the police. At least not at the meetings. We all have people we know who are officers, we can call them if we need to, if things really get bad.

Marlene's assessment of their prospects of receiving help from the police was based on years of protesting and fighting for better law enforcement services. Along with her neighbors, she had grown frustrated that the typical response would likely be a brief, almost token increase in officers assigned to the park, followed by a return to the status quo. In the short term, a few nights of police patrols were viewed as grossly insufficient; additionally, the residents on the block could not see how police could provide longer-term assistance without an overall commitment by law enforcement officials to ensuring their safety—which they felt would take a long time to bring about. So, while they still would consider pressuring the local commander to ask for support, they decided to consider other strategies.

Why the need to think in terms of short and long term? In urban black communities that suffer police neglect and that have historically been alienated from the police, one finds little faith among the populous that officers intend to provide meaningful preventative enforcement, such as walking the streets, meeting with residents and store owners, and developing trust through outreach and effective communication. Chicago's Southside neighborhoods are a prime example. Residents routinely protest for better policing. They request greater police presence around parks and abandoned areas as well as on children's routes to schools. Such requests may result in modest and temporary increases in local police presence, but there is widespread opinion, based on decades of experience, that this will not last longer than a few days or weeks. So, few rest their hopes on the police for long-term guarantees of security. Having said this, the character of the public safety problems—often rooted in shady activities that bring resources into the household—make it difficult for police to respond effectively. Even Marlene and her neighbors are quick to point out that a restructured police profile, built on a regular, more engaged relationship with the community, may still not be sufficient to deal with those issues that have a material component, particularly given that there are so many people who depend on underground income.

Thus, residents must adopt a logic in which social control strategies are linked to the longevity of their impact, as well as to the substantive nature of the problem. Even though the police are only one resource and their perceived contribution to public safety may be limited, they are still residents' first point of call for much of the violent crime and property-based crime in the area. For rapes, assaults, robberies, and homicides, Marlene and her neighbors do not think twice before calling the police. However, they might have to make more than one phone call, particularly when there are underground economic issues at play, and when the activities involve public safety, property-based crimes such as car theft and shoplifting, contractual disputes over street trading, and generic nuisance and loitering problems.

So while the short-term goal is to restore security and order—to which the police can haltingly contribute—over time, maintaining safety requires a sustained capacity to influence both the actor and the activity in a particular space. It may mean more than kicking the gang member off the street corner, finding the shoplifter, or removing the sex worker from the park. It may entail preventing the gang member (or prostitute) from returning, or working with the gang leader (or pimp) to help him find an alternate sales spot. It may mean developing relations with people who can retrieve stolen goods. In other words, the longer-term interest is in part preventative. Residents understand that underground traders move about the community and may return to their immediate locale; because police do not often have intimate connections with these actors, residents may need to enlist the involvement of those who do.

There were still people living on Marlene's block who felt that all moneymaking in the park was unacceptable. But this was a small minority compared to those who believed that underground activities differed in terms of their associated dangers. Some behaviors (drug sales, gun trading, prostitution) carried greater hazards than others (food sales, hairstyling), and the dangerous ones required outright expulsion from the park. Even among such moderate voices, there was not unanimity regarding distinctions—while some would not tolerate prostitution, for example, others felt that it was an individual choice and not necessarily a public hazard. Nevertheless, proponents tended to adopt what Timothy called the "realist" position: people in the community were going to continue making money illegally, and the block club needed to take this fact into account. Nearly everyone agreed that it was not irresponsible to look for others beside the police who could help provide for the welfare of families; however, small minority felt that any usurpation of public safety functions from the police constituted a dangerous position in the long run.

It was the view toward the long term that animated residents' discussions. They were understandably nervous about what might happen after the summer, when the agreements with Big Cat expired. Nevertheless, three months felt like a long time to many of Marlene's neighbors. They adopted a strategy for local social control that mirrored household management. That is, apart from their activism in political campaigns, they rarely thought about solutions to local problems that might yield benefits beyond a few months. They spoke often of the lack of trust in basic institutions, like the mayoral administration, police, elected officials, and social service agencies, that might enable them to think about longer-term initiatives. (Indeed, at times it appeared that they were less angry about a social transgression than about the lack of a timely response by agencies in the wider city.) Just as people came in and out of their house based on personal problems as well uncontrollable circumstances, so too did neighborhood life wax and wane in ways that did not always point to a source of immediate blame. Recognizing this, residents acted as if it were fanciful to think about a solution to the Homans Park issue that would be effective beyond the summer. One should enjoy the park now, because it may not even be there in a few months. Marlene, attempting to assuage Arlene's concerns about making a "deal with the Devil," made the point that the future was fragile, even illusory. "Look, as far as we know," Marlene said, [Mayor] Daley might just tear the damn thing [Homans Park] down, like he did with the school and the pool. Don't worry about what you can't control. And don't start believing that you know what's coming down the road. We have a park, right now. That's all we know. So, let's use the damn thing."

Notwithstanding their differing opinions on strategy, the members of the 1700 South Maryland Avenue Block Club were far more cohesive than divisive that spring when the need arose to recover access to the park. Bird's concerns over the fate of her children were no different from Carrie's, though the former was a prostitute and the latter worked as a salesperson in a technology firm. Both wanted safe public spaces. Moreover, both knew that their need to act collectively, one of the only sources of strength that they possessed, outweighed their differing moral views. Carrie said, "I don't approve of what Bird does, but I do approve of her being a good mother and watching out for her kids and mine. I can't change the world, at least not by myself, and I guess I realized that after moving in, I can't change my own neighborhood by myself either." What the block club seemed to provide was a relatively safe, informal space to air shared fears and discover the possibilities of working alongside one another. In private, the neighbors expressed their disdain for Bird's involvement in sex work, and they spoke critically of those on her block who harbored guns and drugs for the gang. Eunice expressed the prevailing attitude when she said, "What you do in your household, that's up to you. What you do outside your door, that involves me. Knowing the difference is what makes a good neighbor."

During that spring, when they needed to fight Big Cat, Carrie, Eunice, and their like-minded neighbors did not often speak to me about the difficulties involved in working with persons who they felt had disreputable work habits. Yet it was easy to tell that it still took considerable energy and patience for them to reach out to those who flouted their own moral boundaries. One indication that their collaborations were not the preferred mode of neighborliness was that there was little discussion about lasting approaches to gang intervention and public safety beyond the summer period. There were few concrete long-term proposals put forward at the block club meetings. The sense of relief at having halted Big Cat's entrepreneurial advance was no small victory. Marlene and her neighbors often said that they wanted to enjoy a few days in the park that spring before taking on the more difficult challenge of finding a permanent solution to the newest underground bazaar in their community.

There was also a bad taste left in residents' mouths after they started talking with one together about strategies to produce safety in Maquis Park. Those who supported underground activity in the park—as long as the block club could regulate the trading—found themselves at odds with their neighbors who wanted to make no such moral concessions. In general, Marlene's neighbors would privately empathize with the secretive and illegal actions that households must take to survive. Discussing these publicly, however, meant acknowledging their support for such questionable practices in full view of their neighbors.

As summer neared, Marlene and her neighbors admitted that a distance was growing among them as a result of their differing opinions about the appropriateness of shady behavior. Having to acknowledge a need for hidden income supplementation—indeed, some individuals voluntarily admitted their own involvement in shady trading—produced some collective discomfort. Many told Marlene that they preferred not to meet with one another, unless it was for purely social gatherings intended to provide food and recreation for their children. So discussions of shady trading and gang mediation now took place in private conversations with Marlene, rather than in public group settings.

Marlene and others on her block debated acting on their own, without the police. A representative faction—likely Marlene and Bird—would confront Big Cat and work out a solution. They believed this could be a feasible short-term strategy, but knew it could backfire in the long run. Bird explained:

> You never do these things without somebody, somebody like a church or a cop, somebody else who is legitimate. Well, not legitimate, that's not the word I'm looking for, but you know, like an organization that is part of the community, who you can call and who can be on your side. Especially, when things go wrong, and they *always* do when you working with these niggers [in the gang].

Bird understood that her neighbors must work with people who often have greater familiarity with shady matters. Families must be able to call on people who have the capacity to deal with perpetrators, not just one time, but over the course of weeks and months as problems recur. A police officer may scare the gang leader into leaving a public area for a few weeks, but residents need someone who can monitor the leader's whereabouts, maintain open communication with him, and otherwise be retained over time both to prevent problems and to respond quickly once they occur. This means locating people who have the trust of those they watch over. Indeed, without some support from an intermediary, residents seeking assistance can quite easily be rebuffed, neglected, or even physically harmed by merchants who are protecting their source of income. All the more reason that long-term safety involves protecting oneself from future retaliation as well as securing immediate comfort. When underground economies are concerned, occasionally the right person to provide such protection may herself be benefiting from shady activity.

There are several kinds of persons who may function as intermediaries. In Maquis Park, the options are typically clergy, social service staff (such as outreach workers, school counselors), select law enforcement and parole officers, precinct captains, store owners, and residents like Marlene who are active in social clubs, political organizations, and neighborhood associations. Essential characteristics include one or more of the following: the broker can influence police behavior outside of formal channels; she can retrieve stolen property; she is embedded herself in an underground trade; she receives indirect revenue from a trader, like hush money from a pimp or a "finder's fee" from a loan shark; and she can influence the delivery of city services (street cleaning, speedy permit processing, and so on) through connections with the alderman or her staff.

For the Homans Park matter, Marlene needed an intermediary who had secured the trust of Big Cat, who had positive relations with the police officers assigned to the park, and who understood what safety might mean in the context of people reliant on hidden economic activity. The natural choice was Pastor Wilkins at the Maquis Park Prayer and Revival Center. Wilkins had been working to reduce street gang violence and had two decades' experience with conflict resolution over underground economic issues. Much of his work with the local gang had occurred in the late eighties and early nineties, before Big Cat assumed leadership, but he worked with Big Cat and other gang members on a 1993–1995 campaign in which the Southside gangs had sponsored a candidate for elected office. And perhaps most importantly, Wilkins grasped the stakes, both for neighbors and the gang: he had observed the gang's rise as an economic actor, its fall downward, and its most recent attempt to change direction. Excited about his first meeting with Marlene and some of her neighbors, Wilkins told me that the Homans Park issue presented an opportunity to return to grassroots "missionizing and organizing" that he had done a few years back with more fervor:

> "We are, all of us in the clergy, at the whim of our Lord. Who has asked us to be in service of our flock. To lead, guide, and of course, to heal. Big Cat is not a bad young man. I've been around his type for forty years. Somewhat led astray by temptation, a little bit guilty, wants to be there for the community. Like many of us. So, yes, I think that this is a real opportunity to heal the wounds between the young people and those like Eunice and Marlene who have kids and who want what all of us want: safety and a good place to live."

> "And what about the drug dealing, the illegal activity?" I asked. "How do you deal with that."

> "Well, young man," he said pensively. "I'm a realist and I'm a man of faith. Let's take one thing at a time. Let's get the people together in a room, figure out how to get them to talk to one another. People have to eat, they have to do what all of us do: work, save, be there for their family. But they can't be making life miserable for each other. And the park for me is just a symbol. It's a

symbol of being responsive to the needs of everyone. And who knows, maybe if Big Cat can see things from the parents' perspective, he'll change. I mean, he is also a parent. Let's not forget that. He's got kids."

"You said this was something you had been doing all your life. What exactly is it that you do?"

"It's a little bit of missionizing and organizing. Spreading the word to the people, letting God speak through you and then using the Good Lord to bring people together. When all these so-called 'gangbangers' was brought together a few years back—remember, when we almost got one of our own leaders in [aldermanic] office? It was the so-called criminals, the drug dealers, that were out there marching for change. They called me crazy. Why? Why can't it happen again? That's what I'm seeking to accomplish."

As the summer of 2000 approached and Pastor Wilkins formally agreed to come on board and help Marlene's neighbors, there was cautious optimism among households on the block. Pastor Wilkins was a familiar figure, in no small part to his decades of service to the community and his help with households. But no one underestimated how resistant Big Cat and his gang might be, especially when there was money at stake. Most just hoped that the ensuing negotiations would not make things worse than they already were.

The struggles of the residents on the 1700 block of South Maryland Avenue are day-to-day, and success in maintaining public safety depends on a group of committed stakeholders willing to confront problems head on, quickly and effectively. But Maquis Park is a poor community, which means that the style of maintaining social order has constraints that likely do not exist in wealthier communities. How they act in a collectively efficacious manner is rooted in attributes particular to poor, *African American* communities.[14] To begin with, law enforcement's involvement in matters of public safety cannot be relied upon, so relative to other kinds of communities, the residents' own initiatives play a larger role than the police in keeping law and order. Maquis Park's residents do not necessarily prefer to act on their own, but while they fight to procure effective support from law enforcement, they cannot sit back and wait for safety-related problems to take care of themselves. This means acting on their own, perhaps more often than they want to.

The costs and benefits of working on their own would begin to surface after the summer of 2000, as Big Cat and his gang made even more attempts to supplement their illegal revenue in the community. The park, as some residents feared, was just the gang's first assault on usable public spaces in the neighborhood. There were signs that Big Cat's outfit was interested in finding other such places to congregate and anchor their drug trafficking. Moreover, rumors were circulating that Big Cat was expanding his shady interests in the community by finding stores to extort and self-made entrepreneurs (like Eunice) to tax. People feared not only gang reprisal but also that their own underground attempts to support their households would soon be threatened. And they would have to find efficacious ways to stave off the gang, maintain social order, and ensure that their own livelihoods were not threatened.

Just as the women of Maquis Park must make difficult decisions about accepting illegally obtained money to support their households, they are also faced with a complex scenario when it comes to underground economic activity in and around their streets, sidewalks, and public areas. In this regard, they are not alone; in American inner cities, women are a bridge between private and public spaces.[15] That poverty is feminized does not mean that men are not poor. Rather, women have historically been the recipients of public benefits (such as welfare, health care, food stamps) for their families. In the absence of responsible male involvement in the home, and given the difficulties they face in trying to enter the labor force, they have taken the lead in domestic and local affairs, including assuming the burden of child rearing and volunteering for the many clubs, associations, and organizations that deal with neighborhood matters. In suburban and middle- and upper-income communities, the boundaries between the home and the outside world can be maintained intact. Police service is better, there are fewer people per capita in and around the home, sanitation and street cleaning tend to be performed regularly, households are not crowded together, and therefore people do not infringe on each other as much. The home can be a stable refuge. In Maquis Park, in contrast, private space is at a premium, if not a luxury. Relatives and friends who cannot afford rent are always coming in and out of a crowded home, there may be more people and cars on the street, and property-based crimes, as well as rape and various forms of assault, compromise the safety of public space. This means that female heads of households are busy attending to the welfare of their households. They are also at the front lines of public safety maintenance. For all these reasons, it is not surprising that women in Maquis Park move between the home and the wider community, or that they are at the forefront of dealing with the negative consequences that underground economic activity can have on quality of life. It is that particular struggle for African American women that bell hooks calls "homeplace resistance."[16]

There are different forms of shady activity that weigh upon the minds of Maquis Park residents. A steady stream of peddlers and independent contractors, like car mechanics and gypsy cab drivers, loiter in public space seeking customers. Their presence effectively turns recreational spaces, alleys, and other thoroughfares into workplaces. Some of this work, such as automotive repair, can be hazardous for children and passersby. There are also myriad illegal activities, ranging from gun trading to drug trafficking to sex work, that can become violent and make it difficult for parents to take their children safely about the neighborhood. An abandoned building can provide storage for stolen equipment, a public park is an advantageous spot for narcotics sales, and the couches that litter alleyways are makeshift bedrooms for local prostitutes.

Eunice, Marlene, Bird, and their immediate neighbors on South Maryland Avenue are not exceptional in terms of their need to cope with neighborhood-based underground activity. Their struggles exemplify how women in poor communities assume the mantle of community safety. And importantly, their work with one another illustrates the not-uncommon ways in which individuals of different backgrounds, tastes, and preferences must come together to realize common interests.

Chapter Three
The Entrepreneur

There is no cash register at Leroy's Auto. Leroy removed it six months ago to make room for a microwave. There are cars being fixed in the two garage spaces and customers come and go. There are berths for two cars—usually only one vehicle is being worked on at any given time—and the room smells of grease, dust, and cigarettes. Leroy's two mechanics mill about, repairing motors and transmissions, and fielding questions about O. J. Simpson's innocence from an interested ethnographer. Despite these quite normal signs of a small car-repair business, cash transactions are rare in Leroy's Auto, and payment by credit card or check is not allowed.

On one not altogether unique day, Leroy's Auto completed seven repairs. One person paid in full ($10 for a tire change). Two made partial payments for more expensive work; both promised to pay the balance within a week. Another offered to paint the office, which Leroy accepted. Two paid Leroy with used televisions and cell phones. And one shouted a promise of payment, slapped Leroy on the back, and sped off with his car. Leroy gave the TV and phones to the two mechanics in lieu of cash wages. He gave $10 to his son to fetch some parts at the local junkyard, and he asked me for $20 to buy everyone lunch. I agreed, but asked that he change my oil in return.

"If I had a dollar for every dollar I don't get paid . . ." Leroy likes to say. Leroy gave up his register not only to make room for a kitchen appliance but also because his customers seemed unable to pay with our nation's legal tender. His own records suggest that 20 to 25 percent of his customers bring cash with them when they pick up their cars—although some of these people pay for only part of their repair at a time. The others offer in-kind payments: some pay with electronic equipment or clothes, a few have an installment plan, and some remunerate Leroy with products or services from their own businesses (hence the used microwave). Each month will be the last for his auto business, Leroy predicts, although he has now been saying that for five years. "One day, we'll be out of here. But I've been saying that for a while now. Maybe this is just how it is."

If one were to canvass the entrepreneurs in Maquis Park, a rich and busy portrait would emerge, contradicting the area's stark physical decimation. Beneath the closed storefronts, burned-out buildings, potholed boulevards, and empty lots, there is an intricate, fertile web of exchange, tied together by people with tremendous human capital and craftsmanship. Electricians, mechanics, glassmakers and welders, accountants and lenders, carpenters and painters, sculptors, clothing designers, hairstylists and barbers, cooks, musicians and entertainers. The list seems endless. In Maquis Park, these traders, brokers, and craftspeople move between socially legitimate and underground venues. Only a few are listed in the yellow pages, and only a few—such as Mandee Wilson, who runs "Mandee's Late Night" nightclub, and Ola Sanders, the proprietor of "Ola's Hair Salon"—can boast small businesses. But any resident of Maquis Park knows where to find these services. These entrepreneurs are foundations of the community, operating in a very different public sphere, exempt from yellow pages listings and business cards: they can be found in homes, on designated alleyways and street corners, and in bars and restaurants.

Whether one is starting or sustaining a business, "underground" institutions provide a backbone for all aspects of local enterprise, from loans and credit to advertisement. The cash economy abuts a world where trading and payment occur through verbal promises, in-kind payments, and barter. Laborers and entrepreneurs, including small business owners, general workers, equipment renters, and creditors, participate in highly intimate exchange networks, where personal connections and impersonal contractual exchanges coexist. In the ghetto, advertising and marketing, credit and capital acquisition, enforcement and regulation, and other aspects of commerce seem as easily conducted via informal channels and outside the government's eye as through legitimate venues where the state is the arbiter and lawmaker.

Attending to business matters off the books is not the sole province of gangs and criminals. In Maquis Park, the underground economy also impacts socially legitimate businesses. Here we focus on one segment of ghetto-based entrepreneurs, those who own or manage a small business in Maquis Park as opposed to those who "freelance" by offering housepainting, personal therapy, tax preparation, or other individualized service. These store owners and managers can give us the deepest understanding of the interplay between underground and legitimate economies. (Those who run a small business became the target of the street gang's ascension in the shady world after the summer of 2000, after the Homans Park incident occurred. Big Cat, leader of the Maquis Park Kings gang, redirected some of his energy from use of park and public areas to local stores that might equally serve his aspirations to expand underground economic revenue for the gang. Beginning with the autumn of 2000, Big Cat and local proprietors fought one another for control over shady opportunities.)

In recent years most attention has been to the upper stratum of inner-city businesspersons, namely, those who direct empowerment zone boards and chambers of commerce, whose lives are often tales of rags-to-riches success. This chapter focuses on far less prominent individuals, most of whom live in Maquis Park and who have staked their own hopes in a small commercial establishment within the community. They are men like Leroy Otis Patterson Jr., who took over the family's car repair business after his father passed away in 1996. Leroy is of a class of local proprietors who own, co-own, or manage modest businesses, like hair-styling salons, restaurants and take-out food establishments, barbershops, dollar stores and convenience shops, shoe and clothing outlets, and electronic stores.

These otherwise legitimate businesspersons find themselves drawing on the underground economy extensively. Whether they patronize a loan shark or pay for cheap labor under the table, they participate in a common system of exchange that integrates state-regulated entrepreneurship and off-the-books commerce. Some businesspeople are wealthier and more stable than others, but irrespective of their commercial acumen, the shady economy lends them flexibility and quick access to resources, thereby enabling them to develop and sustain both modest and meager ventures in an entrepreneurial landscape that changes quickly and unexpectedly. At the same time, however, working underground means that these *petit* capitalists must tolerate insecurity and risk beyond the normal thresholds of proprietorship. And when they draw on off-the-books resources, there may not be a government agent whom they can call to protect their assets and enforce their contracts. So, while underground resources help grease the economic engine, they can also be a constraint and a barrier to real economic growth. These businesses live in both the legitimate and the unregulated economic spheres.

Webs of Exchange

Two notable characteristics of today's urban ghettos are the entrenched "joblessness" of the local population and the evisceration of the community's physical infrastructure: they are brought together in the image of young adult men and women moving about vacant lots and burned-out buildings, with little in the way of work and employment that might anchor a daily routine. It is a portrait of "social isolation," to borrow the sociologist William Julius Wilson's phrasing, that is evident in both the physical and social remove of the inner city from the societal mainstream.[1]

Contributing to the alienation of the inner city is the lack of adequate support for commercial activity for residents and outside parties seeking to make investments there. One hears every so often of gentrification initiatives that promise to revitalize, but these exceptional cases of development activity typically do not provide support for local development in a way that might directly benefit the indigenous population.

There are many factors that shape commercial prospects for

urban poor communities. Perhaps most important, aspiring business people often are stopped by the persistent barriers to credit and financial services. In 1977 the federal Community Reinvestment Act (CRA) mandated that federally insured financial institutions meet the needs of all borrowers, particularly historically disadvantaged groups. In general, banks have been willing to adhere to these obligations only when there is consistent and strong pressure from organizations that monitor their behavior. And most urban poor communities have not been suffused with mainstream lending institutions. So, it is not too surprising that banks and savings and loans that have followed CRA mandates and entered inner cities have not been able to quickly establish necessary levels of trust and relations with residents and local businesspeople. It is common to find skeptical and disbelieving attitudes among residents toward the larger financial institutions: for instance, some believe that their money will not be safe there; others feel that banks will pick up and leave as quickly as they came, taking deposits with them. Although a bank's remaining in the community does help ease these fears, the basic tasks of outreach and community relations continue to stymie financial institutions establishing an inner-city presence.[2]

Empowerment zones (EZ) and tax increment financing (TIF) have been the two leading development initiatives in urban areas during the last three decades. Driven by bond and debt issues, "EZ" grants and "TIF" initiatives are a public good. They are a form of government subsidy intended to help spur business growth in a geographically bounded area. Any future tax revenue generated by that subsidized economic activity must be used to further develop commercial development in that region, as opposed to leaving the community by contributing to the city or state's general tax coffers. The notion that local revenue should fund additional locally based commerce is interesting in principal; however, certain sectors of the public have experienced relatively little benefit when their area is "TIF'd." Nationally, TIFs have generally had minimal benefits for poor, working-class, and middle-class minorities, whether they are residents or aspiring businesspersons.[3] Moreover, cities without TIF-style economic development fare better in terms of active commercial development.[4] In Chicago, minority and poor businesspeople have been shut out of development when their area is subject to TIF initiatives. Typically, the TIF designation ends up as a form of urban renewal in which the government exercises domain powers to amass large parcels of land and turns them over to private corporate entities that have no previous relationship to the area and that are not always minority-run.

Where entry into inner-city markets has been successful, city governments have not cultivated local entrepreneurship but have instead recruited outsiders—typically upper-income professionals with established credit histories and a track record of business development—to take advantage of cheap rents and low-wage labor pools in the ghetto. This has been one of the primary achievements of the Empowerment Zone initiative.[5]

It is worth pointing out that, as any ghetto dweller knows, one of the most visible symbols of business success is the "ethnic" entrepreneur. Persons of East Asian, South Asian, and Middle Eastern descent who draw on family relations to both start and take over existing businesses in the inner city have become the subject of considerable public and scholarly attention.[6] In many contemporary ghettos, the bulk of retailing and "mom and pop" establishments that were once managed or owned by blacks are now under foreign-born management. For the most part, this is seen as ethnic success and black failure, but as Timothy Bates persuasively argues, since the sixties blacks have pursued self-employment in other, more lucrative areas, such as entertainment and technology. College-educated African Americans no longer pursue inner-city retail opportunities, Bates argues, because "running a retail store in the ghetto, bluntly, is a waste of their time."[7] But for the ethnic entrepreneur whose communicative difficulties and cultural distance may close off other occupational sectors, the inner city became an attractive space for economic growth.[8]

It may be true that college-educated black Americans can better enhance their income and social capital by leaving the ghetto. However, there are still many who remain rooted inside the inner city, within traditional spheres of black self-employment like retailing, personal care, and funeral services.[9] And there is very little understanding of the social context of black business practices and the ways in which merchants, traders, shopkeepers, and others navigate their inner-city environment.[10] Even less understood—or even acknowledged—are the roles of informal, underground, and illegal economies in the lives of these businesses. Unlike the wealth of existing literature on informal economic behavior in American immigrant populations, there is little to draw on for an appreciation of in-group lending, credit and loan-shark services, informal and unreported hiring, and so on among black ghetto merchants. Alas, the most enriching studies to date have focused on drug dealers and economically oriented gangs.[11]

One point that scholars agree on is that commercial pursuits in ghettos add risks beyond those that one normally finds in small business development.[12] Owning a restaurant or hardware store offers no guarantees in any neighborhood, but decisions to both operate and sustain these businesses are made even more cautiously for those in inner cities. If only for heuristic purposes, it may be worthwhile to consider business development in the ghetto to be an entrepreneurial activity—that is, borrowing a standard dictionary definition, one in which a person "organizes, operates, and assumes a risk for a business venture." This is certainly not standard practice. Students of modern business tend to separate out the entrepreneur from the small business owner: entrepreneurs are seers and risk-takers, and studies of their mental strategies often have the quality of hero worship; writings about small businesses, on the other hand, are less dramatic and focus on the practical dimensions of commerce. If, however, "organizing, operating, and assuming a risk" for future commercial pursuits is a hallmark of entrepreneurship, then in the ghetto, local residents may work for years, if not decades, simply preparing to assume such a risk. Some understand the steps along the way; others have little knowledge or opportunity to learn. Moreover, saving small sums of money for equipment or a rental deposit can take inordinate amounts of time, and one repeatedly sees men and women dissolving their accumulated savings on medical treatment, food, household rent, and personal pleasure—only to begin again.

Compared to other ethnic groups, African Americans have not had great experience owning and operating businesses in America. Centuries of discrimination by governments, financial institutions, and customers have limited their opportunities for commercial startup and advancement.[13] Today's commercially successful black businesspersons most probably do not live and work in places like Maquis Park. But just as the success stories vary in their details, so to do the paths of the struggling unknown businesses of the ghetto. There is great variance within Maquis Park's merchant class. One can categorize the businesspersons by industry, tenure in the community, number of employees, revenues per month, race/ethnicity of owner, and so on.

One such group is the African American businesspersons who offer goods and services in a single establishment, with relatively few employees (typically fewer than ten), and who live in and around the community in which they conduct business.[14] These community-based entrepreneurs do expand on occasion, owning multiple stores or capitalizing on business activity outside their own area; and, as will be apparent, they experience insolvency and spend months or years working as wage labors and accumulating the necessary capital to begin anew. Thus, the definition should not be so rigid as to preclude social and geographic mobility or—equally significant—failure. Nevertheless, from a sociological standpoint, the African American proprietor who is geographically based in the ghetto (both as a businessperson and resident) is a distinctive social actor. These individuals may be distinguished through a combination of their personal attributes and social relations. Importantly, they are the most visible signs that urban poor communities do contain a heady spirit of work and entrepreneurship. They receive far less attention than their counterparts who have left the ghetto and formed successful businesses elsewhere. And so they should remind us that the inner city's entrepreneurial capacity is not restricted to its potential as a space of development for outside parties—which is typically the view of civic and government leaders who support urban renewal and gentrification.

Perhaps the most illuminating study of work in American ghettos was written nearly a half century ago, in the sixties. In *Tally's Corner,* Eliot Liebow studied inner-city streetcorner men, not small business owners, but his writings are still instructive. Unlike the middle-class bureaucrat, made popular in William H. Whyte's postwar depiction of the "organization man," inner-city dwellers define their relationship to work less in terms of their present occupation and lifestyle, and more in terms of their future vocation and unrealized lifestyle.[15] Like the aspiring actor who happens to be waiting tables, Liebow's subjects see themselves as men in-the-making, specifically in terms of imagined futures as successful businessmen and family providers. In contemporary Maquis Park, one may also find a cook who fancies himself an inventor or a school-bus driver playing music on the subway after work to maintain his musical "chops." Some have owned a business in the past and they plan on reclaiming their vocational spirit in the future.[16]

For these "don't work and don't want to work minori[ties]," Liebow notes that work is rarely a "stepping stone to something better. It is a dead end."[17] And although they appear, "from the middle class perspective," to be void of future-time orientation, Liebow suggests that these men are simply oriented to a different future, one with few prospects for stable employment and one that their fathers and grandfathers before them faced.[18] So the men tend ultimately to prefer the comfort of like-minded, streetcorner souls, and to shun—or castigate—those demonstrating modest optimism and pragmatic attitudes toward mobility and family. The men in *Tally's Corner* did search for jobs on their own, but they were never far from the voices and opinions of their peers: their decisions to look for and accept a job, to stay working, to spend or save money, all were born out of their relationships and exchanges with one another. Over time, the notable achievers gradually separate off. For the rest, the group becomes a source of familiarity, comfort, and support as well as a tie that binds and that depresses their own motivation to pursue opportunities or alter their lifestyle.

Liebow's analysis of the "man–job" relationship strikes a chord not only for streetcorner men, but also for the wide lot of men and women in the inner city who move through the world of commerce. Individuals' pasts shape their response to their present material situations and their aspirations for the future. How people come to their jobs dictates the directions they may eventually take. For businesspeople in Maquis Park, one must examine how, over the course of his life, the individual has created the conditions to "assume a risk for a business venture" and how he might have assumed these risks in the past or watched others do so. Liebow's critical observation, that "each man comes to the job with a long job history," might be more accurately written: *each man comes to the job with a long history forged out of his deep set of ties to others who have faced, and will likely continue to face, similar circumstances.*

The working lives of Leroy Patterson and other local businesspeople are molded both by their individual initiatives but also by the context in which their labors occur. While these pages do not contain their complete life histories, we can see the broad contours of the ways in which the group reproduces itself over time, and the tension between a person's particular aspirations and the collective weight of the neighborhood's past.

Businesspeople in Maquis Park—and many in the broader residential population—speak of the local economy in terms of individuals who are linked together by formal contracts as well as myriad informal bonds. Their capacity to undertake commercial pursuits is a consequence of their own place in the local network of economic relations. They describe themselves as being woven together in a web of exchange based on highly personal connections. The implication is that any other such networks, namely, beyond the ghetto's borders or those of another racial or ethnic group, are difficult to penetrate. From their perspective, the broader economic landscape looks like a set of loosely overlapping guilds and business associations. This portrait of exchange weighs heavily on the minds of local merchants. Commerce becomes an activity wherein one must continuously secure a position in a network of social interaction and transaction. Risk taking means leaving one's present network in hopes of entering another one.[19]

At a quick glance, the legitimate entrepreneurs of Maquis Park look as if stuck in a rut or, at best, economically immobile due to the sameness of their associations. A few may expand their business, move to middle-class neighborhoods, and so on, but this is rare. Over time, most do not seem to leave the physical area and its residents, irrespective of their stability and solvency. Their webs of exchange, composed largely of other local, ghetto-bound individuals and businesses struggling to survive, do not seem to afford much room for entrepreneurial growth. So, for the entrepreneur, commerce is not as the textbooks read, namely, the continuous pursuit of opportunities to improve one's economic position. Instead, much of these entrepreneurs' energy is devoted to anchoring themselves within their respective commercial relations, which in the ghetto can mean simply living day-to-day and remaining solvent.

From an outside vantage point, their relationships appear to dampen mobility; nevertheless, the businesspersons display a clear preference to remain with their current peers. This preference can lead them away from new entrepreneurial waters. In particular, in reinforcing their current position, the men sometimes forgo opportunities to expand, particularly when this would necessitate severing local ties—for instance, they might decide against accepting contract work that involves a move into another community or opening a store outside of Maquis Park. Protecting one's *present* position is viewed as exigent, particularly when there are signs, in alleys and along main thoroughfares, that enterprise is failing. More than just economic survival is at stake. The loosely formed group of legitimate businesses becomes the basis of a shared identity. The group functions much like the cafeteria meeting place Mitchell Duneier described in his study of black working-class men. "Social life at the cafeteria functions to bring about a conception of the collectivity as a means to the possession of higher self-worth . . . What is true of them is true of him."[20]

Thus, the businesspersons make decisions that are motivated by a desire to secure what little they have, which effectively means never straying too far afield from others in their economic circle. Expansions, moving into new commercial areas, shifting their vocation, or other decisions are mediated by the ability to ensure that their current relationships are not jeopardized. Their entrepreneurial spirit reverses the conventional "bootstrap" thesis that is so often applied to inner-city black Americans: namely, that the urban poor should learn to pull themselves up without others' help. Instead, in Maquis Park, men and women see their own chances of success as predicated on their capacity to bring others along with them.

The turn inward, toward others in one's immediate network, is not surprising when one considers the nature of commerce in Maquis Park. Impermanence rules as entrepreneurs react to new opportunities. A catering company quickly decides to shift gears and build affordable housing; the owner of a "dollar store" opens a church where his store once stood; and a "tire change" shop will aid an ex-barbershop store owner by allowing him to style hair on the premises—eventually the store might become a barbershop if demand is high. These realignments may not occur with great fanfare, and only a highly localized client base may be aware of them. It is rare to find systematic commercial expansion, as firms are likely to *decrease* activity and alter their products in swift response to a slowdown in demand or a shift in opportunity. Similarly, individuals are likely to shift their personal vocation frequently and easily: preachers become barbers, singers become school counselors, painters turn to preaching to supplement income, bartenders operate as car mechanics.

In this manner, businesses come and go, and can change orientation sometimes radically. To outsiders, these shifts appear as signs of instability in the business environment, but in fact they are also a sign of strength. That is, these entrepreneurs are changing their businesses quickly and choosing to stay within their own social and geographically limited networks, rather than take chances by leaving the area or their peers. Making adjustments in order to continue working with existing friends and associates seems a rational decision, given their belief that they need to remain in these local support networks to have any chance of staying afloat.

In a commercial climate organized around limited resources, unrelenting insolvency, and a sentiment that makes participants nervous to cut off social ties, the underground economy asserts itself. It permits a clearer understanding both of the ways the entrepreneurs forge their webs of exchange and the long-term consequences of this for personal stability and achievement. Consider the turnover and fluidity in local shops. The capacity to make these moves, from, say, cutting hair to changing oil, is premised on a certain level of economic activity not being subject to high levels of bureaucratic regulation and state sanction. This does not imply an absence of regulation or enforcement or codes of conduct, only that underground institutions rather than government agencies may be facilitating the changes. Obtaining a government permit before making every change would be cumbersome and cost-prohibitive, if not impossible.

Many basic economic services along Maquis Park's commercial thoroughfares are fulfilled off the books. For example, there is a socially accepted interchange between small (legitimate) businesses and underground entrepreneurs. A small business in Maquis Park might hire quickly and for short tenures to address an opportunity, and all such hiring and firing might be conducted off the books. Verbal agreements among parties familiar with each other will rule. Because the labor relations are informal and secretive, they may go unprotected by OSHA, the EEOC, and other government bodies who set rules for proper and safe working conditions. Similarly, if a small business has a problem, the owner might call the police, but just as often one will find merchants working in backroom negotiations with local leaders to address issues like shoplifters or clients who have not paid their bills on time. Instead of bringing their grievances to a government venue like small claims court, the merchant may call a friend or another merchant to mediate the dispute. In this way, various people in the entrepreneur's network will be drawn into the activity in informal and underground ways. Many standard business exigencies, from advertising to credit acquisition and contract enforcement, will all be fulfilled without formal connection to the state. And the individuals who perform the work—like accounting, tax preparation, and lending—may not have any formal training, nor will they be licensed by any regulatory body.

The surreptitious and perhaps questionable practices at times become public knowledge and hence subject to critical inquiry. Those shopkeepers not actively participating in the underground do judge their colleagues who hire labor off the books, deal with loan sharks, host gambling parties, and so on. Sometimes proprietors who are new to the community and cannot easily draw on personal social relations to conduct business off the books will complain. Immigrant entrepreneurs who have their own informal credit and lending networks may try to limit their involvement in the local underground economy. Such persons may say publicly that they do prefer not to work underground, but their assessments are modified by their own value orientations of good and bad, legal and illegal, "street" and "decent." Outright public criticism certainly does occur, and one can find shopkeepers taking the moral high ground by denying that they work in an illicit or unregulated manner. But sharply worded denunciation is very muted in the constant chorus of discussion about doing business in Maquis Park.

Fish Tank Merchants

As a longtime resident and entrepreneur in Maquis Park, Josiah Pegues knows well the crests and troughs of ghetto-based commerce and the importance of the underground economy in shaping one's financial future. Now a local clothier offering the latest fashions as well as throwbacks to the seventies (sports jerseys, Fedora hats, and the like), Josiah was once a fiery preacher who ran one of Maquis Park's oldest churches. On a quiet spring day, while waiting in Leroy Patterson's office while his car received its weekly washing and service, Josiah puffed on a pipe contemplatively and offered his own theory of "business in the ghetto."

> "Business in the ghetto is like a fish tank. You got all kinds of fish and they get these crumbs from outside that they all fighting for, but only a few get them, so some die. Then, the big fish eat the small fish, so some more die . . . And more crumbs coming in, but

only crumbs. And once in a while you get a big fish who says, 'Man, I'm going to see what life is like outside this tank, here.' So, he jumps out the tank thinking he'll get treated good outside, be one of these guys throwing the crumbs in the tank! But, he finds nobody who gives a shit about him, and he sits on the ground, looking into the fish tank, thinking, 'Man, I sure had it good back in the ghetto.' And he dies."

"So, what's the moral of the story?" I asked Josiah.

"First, my son, don't ever forget that even if you're a big fish around here, it's only because someone is feeding you from the outside. So, you are one crumb away from that small fish. And don't forget you can't be who you are unless you got small fish to eat. That's what it's like around here. Today's big fish may not be tomorrow's [big fish]."

Josiah Pegues has been both a big and a small fish in Maquis Park. He has owned stores, directed churches, and worked out of his house. With two Cadillacs and a palatial house on the historic Southside boulevard Martin Luther King Jr. Drive, Josiah now sees himself as a big fish. But he knows that his luck may not last. "I don't care who you are around here," he says. "We ain't like those white folk who just own the same store they have been owning all their life. Nice and quiet, doing their thing. You don't know what's going to happen around here when you wake up. Your place could be burned down, your customers could die or move out, you may go to jail. Nobody knows."

Uncertainty is characteristic of small business ownership in general. The perception of impermanence weighs heavily on the minds of Josiah and the other businesspersons in Maquis Park who own businesses and who sell their services. Local entrepreneurs must be attentive to life in and out of the fish tank. They must be flexible enough to handle neighborhood problems as well as challenges from the wider world. A short list of the challenges they face would include security and safety; widespread dissatisfaction with city services such as sanitation, transportation, policing, and physical maintenance; sustained poverty and an unpredictable local consumer base; ensuring a stable clientele, which is important for businesses like barbershops, clothiers, and restaurants; meager support from financial institutions, public and private; and a public stigma as stakeholders in a high-crime community that is viewed as unsuitable for commercial investment and development (a fact that can impact entrepreneurs indirectly by limiting investment from others around the city).

In this context, entrepreneurs like Josiah Pegues command respect locally for having established and sustained commercial ventures. A few have personal earnings that place them in the middle- and upper-income tax brackets. They can afford to live elsewhere, and some do. But some of the more successful businesspersons, like Josiah, are longtime Maquis Park residents who prefer the beautiful early-twentieth-century brownstone homes that pepper Maquis Park's otherwise blighted streets. As Josiah pointed out, small fish become big fish—and vice versa. Moreover, since they share the same fish tank, feeding off some of the same commercial opportunities, resources, and customers, the modest proprietors, like Leroy Patterson, can really be understood only in relation to some of their more successful counterparts.

In Maquis Park, one of the most important schools of "big fish" is the Maquis Park Development Board (MAPAD), an association of successful local proprietors and financiers. MAPAD is an organized pro-business lobby of eight to twelve men, including Josiah Pegues, that was formed in 1981 to procure wider government and civic resources. MAPAD promotes real estate growth, lobbies for municipal contracts, and sponsors forums on economic development opportunities. These men are a conduit for job-training programs, they award substantial funds obtained from governmental and philanthropic bodies for social services, and they have alliances with the cultural workers who want to turn the broad Southside of Chicago into the "Black Metropolis"—a gentrified space of entertainment and recreation that would cater to those interested in the black American urban experience.

The membership of the MAPAD board does change on occasion, although most members have remained on the board for at least a decade. What they have in common is a solid tie to the local economy and political clout. They appear on the news, in gossip columns, at society functions, and they are for the most part the spokespersons for the Maquis Park community. They participate in government-sponsored economic programs, they advise on empowerment zone and TIF development, and they routinely sponsor philanthropic community-building initiatives. When a local foundation or the mayor wants to direct money to Maquis Park, invariably the MAPAD board helps manage the receipt and distribution of contracts and funds.

The work and personal histories of the MAPAD board of directors provide a fairly representative portrait of an elite business tier in Maquis Park. These individuals would be classified as middle and upper middle class. They report that three-quarters of their business is based in the black community. Few have successfully established a client base in white, Latino, and Asian communities, which they admit with some frustration.[21] The MAPAD board is keenly aware that reliance on the black community is both a source of strength and a precarious economic foundation. They orient themselves to traditional African American economic sectors, like funeral and insurance services, hairstyling, real estate development and speculation, fashion, and the provision of social services. While some own stores, others provide supplies, such as food or cleaning services, and day laborers. Some have commercial interests in "human service" enterprises, like day-care centers, community development organizations that build housing, and social service agencies. Nonprofit organizations are not usually thought of in the same breath as for-profit businesses. However, in Maquis Park the two are deeply intertwined and must be considered as a single field of entrepreneurship. This is apparent when one views the biographies of the men on MAPAD.[22]

Samuel Wilson, chair of MAPAD, was a prominent real estate developer in Maquis Park during the late seventies and early eighties. He purchased several large properties from city "tax sales" and built multipurpose facilities on each site. He rented office space in these buildings, but he realized that developing community-based social service agencies could generate greater revenue. So he used his political connections to win city and state contracts for day-care provision, job training, and development. He continues to run these five agencies and is a central figure in promoting economic development in the broader Southside region of Chicago. His closest friend, MAPAD secretary Jesse Jefferson, once operated a local branch of a national fast-food franchise but also saw the opportunities emerging in community development. He saved up money, sold his franchise to his son, who changed it into a soul food restaurant, and then founded a prominent nonprofit real estate development corporation that builds affordable housing in and around Maquis Park. His business combines government funding with private-market investment.

The business histories of other MAPAD board members show movement between nonprofit and commercial worlds. In the ghetto, where profit-based economic growth is stunted and unpredictable, nonprofit commercial opportunities are a significant revenue stream. So it is not surprising that successful entrepreneurs can have a foot in both worlds: Reverend Josiah Pegues gave his son control of his church and the youth center it administered, then opened a clothing business along one of Maquis Park's commercial strips. John Brooks purchased a barbershop, bought the bar next door, became a developer of affordable housing, and is looking to purchase the adjacent properties to take advantage of available tax credits for low-income housing construction. Alford Davis is a consultant who helps churches and social service providers procure lucrative state funding. His father was a prominent judge, and his mother worked in the State of Illinois Department of Children and Family Services, where Alford worked for a decade before starting his consulting company. Over a period of ten years, Orlando Allison has been a (nonprofit) affordable housing developer, funeral parlor co-owner, manager of a barbershop, and most recently, co-owner of a small cleaning firm. Among MAPAD members, the profit–nonprofit link is accentuated by the practice of supplying goods and services to each other. Jesse Jefferson's son provides food for all of Samuel Wilson's day-care centers; Orlando Allison's janitors clean many of the local restaurants, shelters, and single-room-occupancy dwellings; Samuel Wilson's day-care providers now have satellite offices in local schools, where they provide adult education and tutoring.

The men recognize and embrace the need to redirect their skills and energies from one economic sector to another. As Samuel Wilson states, "None of us will be doing the same thing ten years from now. Okay, we may own the same business, but if you look at what that business does, today it's a barbershop, tomorrow it's a night club, then it's a housing developer, then back to a barbershop." Other MAPAD board members share the belief that impermanence is opportunity, a view that does not always hold for the struggling proprietors for whom impermanence can threaten business solvency altogether.

The flashy Josiah Pegues does not represent the majority of African Americans who own and manage businesses in Maquis Park. Most are far closer to Leroy Patterson, whose auto shop has been around for years but who struggles to ensure that his business will be solvent tomorrow. Patterson is one of several small business owners in the community for whom expansion and ownership of multiple establishments are nothing short of dreams. Based on my own survey of the neighborhood, out of 157 operators of small businesses in the area, 115 were African Americans, including Josiah and Leroy. The black proprietors typically own or rent a single establishment; nearly all live in Maquis Park or an adjacent neighborhood; and most manage ten or fewer full- and part-time employees—a few have between fifteen and thirty staff members.

In a poor community, owning a business places one in fairly elite company. Nevertheless, there are distinctions among the local shopkeepers that are worth mentioning. A small class of persons whose work is based in Maquis Park do not live there. This elite group includes a candy maker, several real estate developers, a savings and loan president, two funeral parlor owners, and a handful of people who run social service agencies (day care, foster care, vocational training centers, and the like). They are in a distinguished class because of their demonstrated capacity to work in and outside of Chicago with clients and customers of all races and backgrounds. They are not geographically tied to the community, apart from property ownership and family life. They are part of the city's black elite, active in social and philanthropic circles, and they just happen to have a significant commercial presence in Maquis Park. On occasion they participate in parades and charitable drives, but in their philanthropy they are not self-designated spokespersons for Maquis Park nor are they actively sought out to weigh in on local affairs.

Ethnic entrepreneurs are another class of merchants in Maquis Park. They have capitalized on the general disinterest in inner-city business development by claiming a significant share of the local retail sector. Koreans and Chinese, whites, Lebanese, South Asians, and a few people of Dominican ancestry run their businesses out of local establishments. Like black owners of small businesses, they face the challenges of running a business in the ghetto, but they differ because they transfer business deeds through extended family lines, they reside outside of the black community, they are not active in local issues, and they have fairly stable internal revolving credit systems, which makes them less dependent on banks. They certainly do not work in isolation, but they are not embedded in the same webs of exchange as the local black proprietors. And just as significant, in Maquis Park the majority of ethnic entrepreneurs do not see themselves as part of the community. This typically means they avoid participation in philanthropy and economic development initiatives. They will remark on the difficulties of conducting business there, but they do not see active civic involvement in local affairs as a means by which to ease their challenges.

Indeed, at times their observations of their African American counterparts are colored with prejudice, typically imbued with the time-tested and empirically unsubstantiated myth—one that also conveniently ignores the history of discrimination faced by black Americans—that immigrants have a work ethic and blacks do not.[23] Many attribute black business failures to a lack of support among black shopkeepers. A South Indian shopkeeper whose liquor store stood adjacent to Marlon's Kitchen had watched as Marlon, the proprietor, began organizing shady activities that inevitably spiraled out of control. On the morning when Marlon was packing up his belongings and closing down his store, this shopkeeper said to me, "You know our people would never do these illegal things, that's why we'll always do better and blacks will always die hungry. Some are okay, some know how to make money, most are just dogs." Another remarked that blacks should adopt the respect for family that supposedly is a part of Asian culture. "These blacks don't stay together, don't respect the family like we do. How are they ever going to deal with their problems and get ahead?"

The ethnic store owners are not intricately wrapped up in Maquis Park's underground economy, although like other merchants they must respond to public drug trafficking, vandalism, shoplifting and robbery, and inadequate policing. However, this does not mean that they lack unreported income or clandestine economic relations. When I asked several foreign-born business owners how they could open up a store so soon after arriving in the country, they offered elaborate schemes of revolving credit that were flavored with their own underground, from loan sharks to extortion, from illegal accounting to illegal labor practices, including not paying family members and improper use of children as employees. In other words, the capacity of foreign-born persons to succeed in inner cities has to do with numerous informal and hidden "in-group" activities. From credit extensions to hiring, they rely on interpersonal relations in order to avert bureaucratic and governmental regulations, as well as the established credit histories that financial institutions routinely demand. Most of these activities are not rooted in Maquis Park, but I still managed to find many instances of ethnic shopkeepers in the community hiring local residents off the books, and for menial wages. When I asked Big Cat if he was extorting ethnic store owners in the community, he replied, "Shit, why do you think I began doing it to everyone else? I started with them Arabs and Chinks, they were the first that had to pay." Only one of the ethnic merchants in the community admitted to paying Big Cat; a handful of others, however, readily described other illegal activities, such as offering residents cash for food stamps—50¢ on the dollar—paying local teenage women for sex, and selling diapers and food to mothers for sexual favors.

There have been a variety of scholarly comparisons of ethnic and African American businesspersons. Factors often associated with the foreign-born, like respect for family and the presence of a work ethic, are portrayed as cultural and rooted in tradition.[24] These are usually singled out by conservatives intent on promulgating the immigrant's homeland as holding the key to America's race problem. That is, American blacks should work hard, like the immigrants who build businesses in their neighborhood. But liberals have also been quick to make comparisons, although they tend to point to the historic influence of racism on black business development—an influence that is not as prevalent for ethnic merchants—and to limited educational opportunities, financial services, and training for inner-city black populations.[25] There are, however, also commonalities. For example, in addition to limited relations with financial institutions, ethnic and black shop-keepers also share a highly personalized social capital.[26] That is, just as shopkeepers of Arab, South Asian, and Korean origin rely on others in their ethnic network for credit, transfer of business titles, and dispute resolution, black business practice also is rooted in social networks. In fact, the myth that ethnic entrepreneurs are more likely than blacks to rely on each other for credit to start up businesses (instead of using financial institutions) is precisely that—a myth. Black Americans use internal lending and informal credit to a greater degree than their ethnic counterparts, particularly Asians, for whom banks are far more willing to (and do) offer loans for business development—in a tragic twist of fate, since the eighties, the federal government's small business loan program has primarily benefited ethnic entrepreneurs, not black Americans.[27]

Where there may be a point of contrast, however, is that for black Americans the peer networks of support and resource exchange are more likely geographically, not ethnically, bound. For example, the perceptual horizon of commerce for many of Maquis Park's African American merchants does not extend beyond their immediate area. They do not expect to serve white clientele, nor do they actively pursue opportunities to advertise their stores outside of predominantly black areas in and around the Southside. This is in sharp contrast with ethnic commercial relationships in which networks of foreign-born persons (whether based on kin, peer, or another meaningful tie) span the metropolitan region.

There do seem to be parallels to inner-city black business in white urban areas, particularly in places with little residential turnover in which one ethnic group dominates—such as Greektown, Little Italy, and the Polish Quarter. But such areas typically are not very large, in terms of either physical space or population served. Moreover, even in these places, success is dependent on the kinds of non-ethnic-based resources that one finds to be lacking in Maquis Park. Namely, commercial success is a product a stable local customer base and sustained levels of consumer capacity in the surrounding area; safe, hospitable, and attractive business climates that have active police surveillance and decent city services; and a municipal commitment to make sure trash is picked up, cars are towed, and city development and economic funds are allocated to community businesses.

Not only do predominantly African American inner-city neighborhoods lack these amenities, but African Americans differ from whites because they have never had the luxury of moving out of their community to develop new business opportunities when the local area runs dry. The high levels of hostility they have faced when trying to outreach to white neighborhoods, win citywide contracts, enter white-dominated union trades, and participate generally in mainstream economies is staggering.[28] And this discrimination still exists, despite the great strides African Americans have made. In this historic context, we should not find it surprising that the merchants of Maquis Park embrace their locally based social networks and turn primarily to each other to support their respective commercial pursuits. From their perspective, economic activity is at its core a group phenomenon, so much so that their language sometimes downplays individual achievement in place of emphasizing the survival of everyone in their network of exchange. We turn now to these networks in order to understand the intersection of legitimate and underground economies for small business owners.

West Street is one of the three commercial strips in Maquis Park. Its place in the community is similar to that of commercial districts in other economically depressed inner cities. Retail stores predominate, particularly those offering goods and services specific to African Americans' tastes (beauty products, hairstyling, cuisine) and to poor people (outlets, dollar stores, currency exchanges). West Street is a long commercial thoroughfare that crisscrosses the community and is filled with numerous small business owners. The dynamics on West Street vis-à-vis underground and legitimate economies are no different from those in other commercial districts in Maquis Park, which has five major centers of retail and light industrial activity. Maquis Park's merchants face many of the same gang members, street hustlers, and prostitutes, and they complain about the same potholes and poorly maintained sidewalks; conversely, the underground activities on the street bring proximate actors together. By focusing on the West Street thoroughfare it is possible to understand in greater detail something of the experiences of proprietors throughout the community.

At one end of West Street, Leroy's Auto Shop sits next to an abandoned lot and across from a drug store. To the west, there are small mom-and-pop stores, a health clinic, a gas station, several beauty salons, a barbershop, a few small fast-food outlets, a hardware store, several dollar stores, a Laundromat, two liquor stores, a shoe and clothing outlet, a community social service center, a "fix it" tire and battery replacement shop, and a real estate management company. In between the stores, there are burned-out and abandoned buildings, and empty lots that function as parking lots and spaces for street vending. Most of the stores are owned by individuals or small families—the wealthier commercial owners, like the members of MAPAD, may have a financial stake in a local business. At seemingly all hours of the day and night, there are throngs of passersby inhabiting the street corner and colonizing the vacant properties. The commerce in the open-air spaces is all underground; in the busy-ness of its vendors and its significance to the community, it rivals the business taking place inside establishments: drug dealers stand in front of stores and on street corners receiving orders; prostitutes take their clients to the alley (or to the back of a store, if they have such an arrangement); painters and handymen drum up business by stopping pedestrians or customers at the hardware store; vendors sell fake social security cards at the liquor stores; gypsy cabs are available along the street, as are shoes, pens and paper, and homemade clothing and food.

A single individual owns 75 percent of the stores on West Street, 10 percent are owned by a married couple, and the rest are owned by three or more people. Of the black-owned establishments along the West Street commercial corridor, roughly two thirds of the proprietors have owned more than one store in the past. They are all over the age of 35. The majority live and work in Maquis Park or in an adjoining neighborhood, and their stores have generally been located within a two- or three-mile radius of Maquis Park, in other equally impoverished black neighborhoods. These store owners have tended to remain modest retailers, offering a fairly circumscribed range of goods and services, be it clothing, take-out food, liquor, hairstyling, real estate brokerage, social services, or car maintenance. The majority are, not surprisingly, men. The "glass ceiling" that has prevented women from entering the halls of corporate America and that has limited their mobility within that arena can also be found in the small business world. Although on West Street there are a few women who own and manage retail stores—such as Ola's Hair Salon—they are few in number.

Roughly 60 percent began their careers by pooling resources from friends and relatives, not by soliciting loans from banks or savings and loan institutions. Only 42 percent have ever received a bank loan to open or sustain a business; and only 6 percent have ever benefited from a government program intended to aid minority and/or small business owners. A small minority (10 percent) of the current proprietors either have a secure line of credit from a financial institution or feel that they have the credit history required to obtain a loan. The prevailing wisdom, however, is that loan applications will be rejected. K. C., the co-owner of a Laundromat, puts it succinctly when he says, "We all try, time to time, to get to a bank, but a dog just don't want to go back if all they do is get beat. I guess we need a year or so to forget that last beating, and then maybe we'll go back. But most of us can't get no money. Shit, *I wouldn't lend myself no money,* knowing what kind of credit I got and how much I owe!"

The store owners' weak political ties exacerbate their poor relations with mainstream financial institutions. Although Leroy and his peers speak with political officials regularly, they have limited influence within the black political machine, particularly the local elected alderman.[29] The alderman can ensure that permits and easements, essential to any building or shift in land use, are distributed in a timely fashion without bureaucratic delay; the alderman also has some power over regulatory and enforcement bodies that give penalties for a seemingly endless list of business practices, from inadequate financial reporting, to work conditions and hiring practices, to improper use of physical space. Informally, the proprietors concede that the local alderman can also prevent trash from being picked up outside their stores, direct police and city inspectors to their stores at a minute's notice, and harass them with fines and warnings. It is commonplace to hear proprietors complain that they must continually contribute money to the alderman's campaign in order to ensure that the city government works for them and that the government does not target them unfavorably. A common way in which this complaint is expressed is the store owners' suggestion that the local elite proprietors—the members of MAPAD—usurp the relationships with the local alderman and other elected officials. Autry Vincent, the owner of a local dollar store, states,

> I know [Alderman] Mattie hears what we all [on West street] are saying. But she likes the big dogs, like Samuel, Josiah Pegues, and them. They are the ones who get the first crack at the empty city lots that go for sale. They never have any inspectors harassing them. So I guess I just got to wait until I'm the big dog! But that ain't gonna happen anytime soon and, shit, I'm 58 years old, I can't be doing this forever. It's just that, once in a while, we'd like to see her give us something for all the money we give her: just fix the pothole in front of our store, get the police out here when things happen. Anything!

It is true that the elite entrepreneurs affiliated with MAPAD do liaise with social institutions outside of Maquis Park in order to promote business or address concerns. But the MAPAD members themselves profess to only limited influence outside the community. Jesse Jefferson offered a job to the son of a municipal agency supervisor, which he believes was critical in helping him win city funds for housing construction—he stops short of saying that the agency head requested him to hire her son. Samuel Wilson says that the MAPAD board's capacity to behave in this fashion is not as strong as that of "white folks, like the Irish," but he admits that his colleagues are nevertheless better connected than most of the other local African American entrepreneurs. MAPAD board members claim to use their clout as best they can to ensure that police protect their property, that political officials provide sanitation and street repairs near their homes and businesses, and that city planners place bus and subway stops near their facilities. They argue that the benefits are community-wide: "Look, when we get trash picked up, we get *everyone's* trash picked up. Shit, I mean, they should stop complaining. We trying to do things for the community, not just us," said Alford Davis, a MAPAD member.

But regardless of whatever cooperation exists between elite MAPAD board members and struggling store owners, the fact remains that it is tough to do business in the ghetto. Maquis Park, like many other inner-city neighborhoods, simply suffers from the lack of a community that consistently spends money. Few store owners claim that demand is sufficient enough to create a steady, reliable business climate. Only the (Korean and Middle Eastern) managers of the two respective liquor stores suggest that they are not overly concerned about the general loss of demand. As one said, "We're busy day and night. Our problem is not enough people, but too many people. Look at all these people in here not buying anything, just hanging around." For the rest, however, the customer base wavers, usually declining over time. These shifts lead to expected outcomes for businesses that cater to local populations. Insolvency is always on the horizon, if not at the front door. The histories of many of the retail businesses on the street show a cycle of bankruptcy, sale of property to a friend or relative, and subsequent revival of commercial activity under a new name. There is considerable turnover at the level of small businesses, particularly retail establishments. Only 9 percent of the stores on the street have been in existence for longer than ten years. The average tenure appears to be three to five years, at which point the owner declares bankruptcy or sells the store.

For all of the small businesses (including those affiliated with MAPAD), the underground economy shapes the business climate. Not surprisingly, underground economic activity most often appears to these businesspeople as a set of activities over which they have limited direct control and that jeopardize public safety. Prostitutes, drug dealers, handymen, and other underground traders who loiter in front of their stores are a nuisance. These underground workers harass customers and compromise safety. They enter the stores to beg for money and food, and they urinate in the alley. Proprietors and managers must ward off drug dealers, addicts, gang members, and street vendors who hang out in their stores and sleep in their alleyways. Various criminal activities, from robbery and assault to vandalism and loitering, command their personal time and energy as well as that of their business. In other words, the underground economy is one of many ecological factors to which they must respond.

Yet despite the attitudes of small business owners, in reality it is impossible to clearly separate public and private business activity along the thoroughfare. Street-based and storefront entrepreneurial activities are inevitably intertwined. Across the threshold of public and private commercial spaces, the underground economy provides an important link by connecting persons, goods, and resources in the shady unregulated world to the modest world of single-owner and family-owned commercial establishments. At times there are even cooperative—and productive—arrangements between those in and outside of stores that temper the irritation caused by life on the street.

One sign of the linkage between legitimate and underground work is that local proprietors tend to interpret the shady operators as people with limited means, like themselves, who are trying to make a living. From their perspective, illicit income generation may be a sign of poor morals or values, but it is at root an action by an individual struggling to "make a buck." Jesse Jefferson explains:

> Yes, it's a desperate group out there that disrupts what we're doing, coming in here and begging or maybe stealing right outside our door. Stealing cars or bikes or robbing people, maybe selling drugs, they all make a buck and do what they have to. But these people are also our customers. That's what's hard about doing business here. You got people who you don't want around here, but who you depend on. And if you are committed to Maquis Park, you are always trying to help them, even though they may be hurting you in some ways . . . Our business is never just about making money, it's about community relations at the same time.

Samuel Wilson also points out that some underground activity may be better thought of as entrepreneurial. He cities a parallel between his use of political connections that may not be completely proper and a street hustler's work at a demolition site:

> See this suit I got on? I used to steal these, sell them to people like me, you know aldermen and folks like that in the '60s. Right outside this office, people still doing what I was doing to get [where I am]. Seeing something open up, find a way to get in there, make a buck. Now, what we do is just a bigger, fancier version, you know, buying that abandoned building before others get it, low-bidding that contract 'cause we got the money to take the hit. But ain't no different than the guy who comes here after work. Jordan used to pick up cans and walk over to that recycling truck. Now, he got his brother's car—which he sleeps in—and, for five bucks, he drives other folks over the truck. He says he got twenty guys he does that

for and now he's going to take those guys over to that CHA site where they are demolishing the building. [He's trying] to get all the copper and wire. The demolition company lets the men sleep there and [in return] they get a security force! See, this man got himself a business! That's how it works around here. Pretty soon, I'm sure he'll be one of us [on MAPAD]. It's just that we do this kind of stuff all the time and we got a phone and office. That man on the street only got what's around him.

There is a generosity of spirit in Samuel's attitude, a vision born of personal experience and shared by many of his colleagues who manage small businesses. Even as they grumble about the troubles caused by the underground, they recognize themselves in the men and women on the corner, in the hustlers in the alley. Their response to these people has a certain benevolence. When the shady world causes trouble, as it inevitably does, the entrepreneurs know that just calling the police is inadequate and not wholly beneficial for anyone involved.

They characterize their own, alternate approach as "community relations," which involves three critical activities: (1) protecting private property; (2) minimally alienating residents when adopting policing and other preventative security measures, such as dogs, night patrols, and calls to officers when absolutely necessary; and (3) incorporating the "desperate group" into one's business informally in order to reduce the potential for conflict, theft, and vandalism.[30]

The framework of community relations includes a set of strategies for coping with underground trading in and around one's place of business. Business owners achieve this balance between self-protection and benevolence in several key ways; two of the most important techniques are hiring employees off the books and being flexible in their line of work. Fairly common is the shopkeeper's use of the local residents for part-time labor, with wages paid off the books. It is difficult to discern how much of the local hiring is unreported to the government; however, the stores along West Street have quite minimal staff, so even the presence of one or two individuals performing work under the table is significant. Over a three-year period of activity along the street, approximately 70 percent of the stores reported that they employed one or more individuals informally. Cash was the most common means of payment, but on occasion the proprietor would pay the individual in-kind, with a specified amount of food, liquor, or other store product. Although a few stores reported that all of their labor costs are under the table, the majority said that their full-time employees are legitimate and that they use part-time unreported work flexibly, in response to a particular need.

One recurring need is security, particularly for those MAPAD-affiliated businesspersons who have expensive equipment or who own multiple establishments. Many will hire local men and women under the table to provide security in their stores. For example, although a security guard is on patrol during the evening in his day-care centers, Samuel Wilson pays homeless persons to sit in the rear of the property and hand out food to others in need. This might be a token display of generosity, but he believes that this symbolic gesture helps deter people from taking out their frustration by vandalizing his property. He explains, "I got a guard that I pay, that's for the insurance. But I have people who I pay who sit in the back, make sure nobody vandalizes my place. It's not a full-time job with benefits. I know that. But it's something. And you always have to find something to help people who are trying to make a buck." Other MAPAD members also hire street vendors, homeless persons, gang members, and other underground entrepreneurs. Some have modified the arrangement by permitting street entrepreneurs to use their place of business after hours. In exchange, they receive services that might be loosely categorized under the "security" umbrella: by virtue of their presence around the stores after hours, the off-the-books workers deter would-be thieves. Josiah Pegues narrates a common bargain struck by shopkeepers:

> You know James [Arleander]. He's like a lot of folks that needs a place to work. But they can't pay rent, 'cause they don't make enough. So Leroy [Patterson] lets him come in the shop late at night to fix a car . . . Sometimes I let [Brandi] bring her people in [my place] 'cause she needs a place to cut hair. Jesse [Jefferson] lets folks play bingo or play dice up in his place. And don't get me wrong. We get a lot out of it. We look real good around here when we spread the wealth, you know. Folks love us 'cause they see us helping the little man.

These are not token gestures, Josiah argues. The proprietors estimate that they can save several hundred dollars a month, sometimes more, by hiring off the books. His colleagues view permitting the use of their facility by local homeless persons and street merchants not only as crime prevention, but as a means to improve their public image, ensure a loyal customer supply, and root out competitors. The elite proprietors, such as those affiliated with MAPAD, typically do not charge individuals for use of their space; this differs from the more modest shopkeepers for whom subleasing can be an important means of supplementing income.

Those who are hired off the books will work in one of several ways: stocking shelves, cleaning, providing security, finding goods for customers, and performing minor repair and errands. If payment is in cash, there is typically a fixed fee for a day's or a week's work. For example, Charles Teele pays $350 per month rent to live in an hotel for transient persons, and he receives monthly disability payments; he supplements his earnings with $75 per week under the table that he earns by working five hours per day, five days per week, helping customers at a shoe store. Mark Matthews makes $10 per day off the books, for three hours' work, watching over potential shoplifters who come into a West Street grocery store after school. He is homeless and squats in the local abandoned buildings. He will receive greater remuneration if he is willing to accept food instead of cash. When his son is not available, Leroy Patterson usually hires someone for $10 per day to find parts at the local junkyard—the person in question usually makes two trips per day, the total workday being six hours. The two beauty salon owners each have a woman on hand—at $15 and $20 per day, respectively—whom they send out on errands for beauty products or to purchase drinks for customers; the women also clean the store at day's end. The owner of the barbershop has a lunchtime "runner" who takes the day's bets to a local gang leader and who earns $5 to make two such trips.

Store owners and managers pay $5 or $10, or something in-kind, for someone to distribute signs, posters, and flyers around the community—on billboards and buildings, and to churches, social clubs, schools, libraries, and restaurants. More commonly, they ask that these casual employees canvass the area and find potential customers. Leroy and the owner of the tire repair store both hire men to walk local streets during the day and search for people with flat tires or cars in need of repair. Both men also hire the sons of the local pastors as part-time workers under the table;

in exchange, the pastors advertise their services to the congregation. The beauty salon owners send people to stand outside the local subway stop to pass out coupons for discounts, with an occasional modest commission for each client that comes into the store.

Such hiring arrangements can foster intimate ties among managers or owners and those they hire. Unless the workers steal, fight on the premises, harass customers, or otherwise antagonize the staff, they can usually work as long as they are physically able to. Some owners prefer to replace their hires continuously. Most do not because they desire stability and because they often have to leave the individual alone in the store with customers. One local shopkeeper states: "In some ways, even if you just paying people cash, you know under the table, you can't be too careful, because these folk are representing you. They are putting out an image to people and you want to know what they doing, what they are saying."

By hiring off the books, the proprietors see themselves as local philanthropists, helping people down on their luck. The black business owners cite their hiring as a means to differentiate themselves from the "foreigners" who, in the words of one of the beauty salon owners, do not "give back anything to the community and who just suck our blood like leeches." In fact, however, nearly all of the foreign-owned stores hire local residents off the books or legitimately, and a few sponsor recreational activities and programs for children.

The use of casual, off-the-books hiring is indispensable for many of shopkeepers because the demands of business can shift at a moment's notice. A surge in demand might last only a month; a contract may require extra labor for only a few weeks. Hiring through formal channels, which could necessitate paying employment insurance and social security taxes, is difficult and expensive, and the recruitment process can take time. The use of local residents also enables the merchants to advertise their stores and publicize sales and events. One proprietor noted the "side benefits" that come with employing local residents:

> Let me explain something to you. I take Jimmy in[to my store] once a month or so, he makes good money, maybe enough to pay a bill or something, or pay someone to sleep on their floor. You know, fifty bucks, and he hauls the stuff for me from the distributor. Now, when Jimmy needs to buy something, or hears that others want to buy a tool, then he sends them to me. All these niggers fixing cars buy their shit from me. Why? Because Jimmy spreads the word, says I'm a good man. Which I am. So, you got a lot of side benefits, you could say, when you take people in like that.

These under-the-table work opportunities certainly do not provide much, if anything, in the way of social mobility opportunities or long-term stability for the street persons being hired—even though a street hustler or homeless person can establish trustworthy relationships with a local entrepreneur and ensure part-time employment as long as the store stays solvent. Perhaps one could also argue that they take time and energy away from persons who might apply himself more productively to finding work with better pay, benefits, opportunities for growth, and mobility prospects.

But the persons who are hired are often desperate for cash, so they are eager to get these under-the-table work opportunities. Many of them are down on their luck, and some suffer mental and physical disabilities, as well as alcohol and drug addiction; for them, the work is really about survival, and it is doubtful that they are prepared to work full-time and pursue conventional employment paths. However, for others such work might be less beneficial; not only are they being taken advantage of—being paid below-minimum wages in exchange for their labor—but as long as they work clandestinely, they are not motivated to find more stable employment. However, these individuals, like the proprietors who hire them, perceive themselves as tied to the local economy—they are not ready or willing to float about the city looking for work. They have strong personal networks of family, friends, and business associates who are often near them and who are helping them make ends meet. Leaving the geographic area might make rational sense, from the perspective of improving their material condition, but it may feel risky and isolating, hence inadvisable.

Employing local residents without reporting wages is one of several ways in which proprietors work underground to remain flexible and respond to changes in the local business climate. Another significant venture for West Street merchants entails surreptitiously changing the goods and services they offer. The shifts can be dramatic—a "fix it" tire repair shop offered hairstyling as the demand for car repair declined—or they can be modest, as in the case of a restaurant owner who began selling pirated CDs and movie videos next to his cash register.

Store owners frequently stumble upon an opportunity to make extra income by selling goods they have recently acquired. They set aside a small area in the store for this purpose. Sometimes they capitalize on a neighbor whose business has become insolvent and who needs to liquidate their supplies. Ola, for example, bought nearly $2,000 worth of skin care and hair treatment products from a friend whose store had gone out of business; she paid for the goods under the table and instructed her employees to notify customers that the goods were available upon request. (She claimed to have sold the items for $5,000 and, after paying back a loan shark from whom she borrowed $2,000, she was left with a $1,500 profit). After discovering that customers could not pay for their car repairs in cash, Leroy asked them to pay with used electronic equipment, which he sells clandestinely out of the back room of his store. After having been caught at this by a police officer, he sold the equipment to a neighboring tavern owner who distributed both electronic equipment and used microwaves and refrigerators out of his store. In all of these cases, the revenue is not reported as income to the government.

Sometimes a merchant will work with a local resident who has goods or a service to offer but lacks a physical space in which to operate. These individuals hope to capitalize on their personal relationships with the shopkeepers by selling their goods and services in and around the store. Subleasing one's store to local vendors is a widespread practice that can supplement the income of the proprietor or manager. Managers might engage in this behavior secretly to avoid detection by their supervisors.

A few shopkeepers have extensive subleasing arrangements with local street entrepreneurs. On weekday evenings, Leroy Patterson permits local car mechanics to use his facility. He instituted this practice after realizing that many of his local customers began patronizing repairmen, like James Arleander, who carried their equipment with them and worked in public spaces like alleys and parking lots. Whereas Leroy charged $10 to $20 for an oil change and $50 for a tune-up, James would charge half as much money for the same work. Given that Maquis Park is a poor community, Leroy felt he was losing many potential customers and so began recruiting mechanics, including James, to his store to conduct minor repairs after hours. Leroy gets a small percentage of the mechanics' receipts, and he has been able to increase his customer base—particularly those who may need more expensive repairs and who would have previously gone elsewhere:

> I get a little change, a few hundred a month, so it's not bad. It's also great because lot of people now start bringing their cars in, you know, for body work or fixing an engine. James can't do those kinds of things because he don't have the right equipment, but sometimes he brings a customer in and I tell him that if [James] can get the guy to get a bigger repair, I'll kick back a little something to [James]. Hey, I know it's a little strange, but you got to do this to survive around here.

Sellers of goods and services typically either pay a small fee outright for the use of the space or, like those who work out of Leroy's Auto Shop, they pay a fixed percentage of their own revenue. On rare occasion, merchants accept in-kind payments—for instance, James might work for Leroy in exchange for use of the store after hours. The use of a fixed percentages often leads to disputes among the involved parties, because the sellers have an incentive to misrepresent their actual sales. Thus, proprietors generally prefer a fixed fee. In addition to Leroy, several other stores have subleasing arrangements on West Street. A restaurant allows the gang to gamble on Saturday and Sunday evenings for $300 per weekend. The prostitutes use the back room of a dollar store; the store manager charges the pimp $500 to $750 per month but hides the activity from the proprietor. The manager of a currency exchange sells fake social security cards on site that are obtained by a local pastor, earning roughly $500 per month.

In addition to the activities described above, two soul food cooks have made an arrangement with Ola to sell homemade lunches at her beauty salon. Felix offers psychic services at his hardware store, including palm and tarot card reading and hypnosis. Organized gambling games (dice, poker, sports betting) are open to the public in the back areas of several stores, and one can find self-employed hairstylists who wait inside several establishments, paying a small percentage of their daily receipts to the store manager. Homeless persons who sell beauty products, socks, T-shirts, laundry supplies, and diapers usually hang out in front of the subway station or outside several dollar stores along West Street. Electronic equipment and other typically stolen goods are easy to find, as are individuals who can find state ID cards, guns, knives, ammunition, and other relatively inaccessible goods. In one of the liquor stores, a man sitting in the corner specializes in inexpensive business cards and customized stationary (his brother works in the printing services office of a downtown corporation and allows him to use machines after hours); gypsy cab drivers are also in waiting at the local restaurant; and there are many places to find drugs and prostitutes.

Just as off-the-books hiring creates mutually beneficial bonds between business owners and the struggling members of the community, money lending ties the owners to one another. Local businesspersons speak continuously of the need to ensure liquidity—in Josiah's phrase, to have "cold, hard cash you can get in an hour"—with which to purchase property or a service, hire someone, buy supplies, make a political donation to a local official, or hire a consultant. Remember John Brooks, who says his last-minute donation to the local alderman was critical in outbidding a competitor for purchase of a commercial property. The majority of entrepreneurs report highly unstable relations with the city's financial institutions and so do not rely on bank loans or a line of credit. As we have seen, few have successfully used banks to help them start a business or undertake other commercial initiatives, such as expansion, franchising, or advertising. Entrepreneurs commonly complain that financial institutions "redline" the community, making it impossible for them acquire capital and credit on demand and in a timely manner.[31]

Instead, it is common to find the merchants relying on each other and local underground creditors. Even the more successful affiliates of MAPAD at times cannot obtain credit with banks and savings and loans. So they, too, use each other informally for loans, whether for as little as $50 or as much as $5,000. Samuel Wilson explains how this system works:

> Let's say I give Jesse [Jefferson] $5,000 for something. First, for me to do that means I'm jeopardizing myself because I'm removing cash from my business and hiding it—although, a lot of times it may come out of my pocket, but that's also shady if I don't report it later on, especially if I make money. Then, Jesse and I have to trust one another. Now, what happens if he doesn't pay me or we fight about something? Well, we have to find someone to come in between, you know, settle it. Who do we trust? Not a lot of folks. Ok, now, let's say he makes his money, let's say he turns the $5,000 into $10,000. Well, I want some of that. Does he report the profit? Does he put it in his bank? He's got all that to worry about. Maybe he pays me, says he has no profit, and gives the extra $5K to a friend to hide the profit for a while because he can't deposit large money in a bank without explaining it. Now, that friend may be lending money to someone else and that other person may be doing the same . . . So, you see? It's a small group of us that are really helping each other, but it's very hard because if one person gets screwed, a lot of other people might. And a lot of this is on trust. I don't care if it's the guy on the street or in here. All of us got a

group of people we work with. It's what you do in the inner city, and you can't lose that. Who's going to trust you next?

As Wilson points out, the use of credit fulfills several functions. It is an adaptation to the lack of credit and the perceived barriers that have been erected by financial institutions to black businesspersons. It also cements relationships within existing social networks. Ties that bind are effectively ties of debt, such that people who know and owe one another can call on each other for favors with greater ease. And with this peonage comes comfort and familiarity. Even if one is turned down by a friend or a local loan shark, Leroy Patterson says, "at least it's not cause we're black and living in the ghetto." In this manner, illicit credit and investment schemes reinforce their interpersonal networks and promote group solidarity. "We know each other's secrets," says Alford Davis, a member of MAPAD. "That's what happens when you lend money to each other. You always got something on somebody." In this way, the merchants look at their mutual indebtedness not necessarily as a hindrance, but as a means of strengthening a business association. As Alford Davis went on to say, "When you owe somebody, you're less likely to say 'no' to something they want because they can tell your secrets."

Marion, who owns a dollar store on West Street, says there are seven stores from whom he solicits small loans. He also suggests that there are ties forged through internal lending among the local shopkeepers, and emphasizes the vulnerability of those who do not participate:

> "You know who's in and who's out." Marion said assuredly.
> "What does that mean, 'in' what?" I asked.
> "If you not trying to help me by giving me change when I need

it, then I don't help you and we don't have that bond. Everyone knows the [stores] in the community who feel they are too good for us."

"Maybe it's not that they feel superior," I retorted. "Maybe they realize it may not be smart to lend to each other, I mean it could be illegal too, especially if it's income or used illegally."

"This is the ghetto, Sudhir. This ain't the suburbs. We need to rely on each other way more than most folks do. I mean look around: where are the customers? Where are the nice streets and with people driving nice cars? You need to know who's watching your back. And you can't forget that, not for a minute. You lend me your hand—or your money—I lend mine to you. It's a real easy way to know who's in and who's out."

But beneath the bonds that may be forged and the significance of one's willingness to lend, elite merchants occasionally draw on one another to take advantage of a commercial opportunity. In such cases, nontrivial sums of money are exchanged and the stores may end up using the funds to undertake fairly significant shifts in their commercial orientation. For example, among the more successful, like the MAPAD affiliates, loans of $5,000 to $10,000 enable the members to place a down payment on a tax-delinquent property, purchase a large quantity of goods whole-sale, or hire laborers and expand their hours of operation. When Samuel Wilson wanted to help his son start a job-training pro-gram and take advantage of available government funding, he pooled $15,000 from his fellow MAPAD members: "I owned a business, but no bank would give me the money that quick; they can take months and months with us, and sometimes we can't wait that long." And when Orlando Allison noticed that a foster-care agency was opening up on his block, he borrowed $7,500 from a MAPAD colleague to purchase a tax-delinquent property at a city auction; he then borrowed $5,000 from Samuel Wilson to clear the building and open up a social service agency that would provide services to the newly arriving foster-care clients. In lieu of interest, the creditors asked to have priority for any outsourcing opportunities that arise.[32]

Most of the business owners who participate in internal lending do so for much smaller sums of money than $5,000. For them, informal credit rarely functions as a means to play the stock market or capitalize on an investment opportunity. There is little glamour in the need to obtain quickly small amounts of cash. For example, shopkeepers on West Street may draw on one another to pay a utility bill, buy a tool, or hire a laborer. There may be less than $100 that changes hands, and such loans are sometimes repaid in-kind. (Leroy's loans to Marlon, the restaurant owner, are sometimes repaid with free lunches.) Over a one-year period, among the non-elites the most common reasons for borrowing money (almost always less than $1,000) were to pay utility bills and rent; to replace or fix broken equipment; to purchase supplies; to hire a local resident under the table; to pay an official, such as a police officer, precinct captain, or city worker, for a service; to hire a van or truck; and to repay an outstanding debt or loan.

As with elite proprietors, the smaller merchants on West Street also turn to off-the-books credit in order to remain flexible, should opportunities arise. But for these merchants, the pursuits are more modest. Fifty dollars helps meet a rent payment, $25 can buy needed supplies, and so on. Occasionally larger amounts are borrowed. The local gang leader approached Ola Sanders to turn her hair salon into a dance floor at night. She decided to borrow $2,500 from a local creditor (at 30 percent interest) to buy lights and a speaker system so that the gangs could host weekend parties. Leroy borrowed $500 from Ola to purchase ten used microwaves, which he then sold in the back of his store for $750; he continues to buy used electronic equipment (some of which is stolen), including refrigerators, car stereos, computers, and televisions, and estimates that this business accounts for 30 to 40 percent of his total revenues. Persius, the manager of a dollar store, asked a creditor for $3,000 so that he could buy the unsold cell phones from a neighboring merchant; he sold cell phones on one side of the store, and, two years later, removed the dollar items and sold only phones and phone-related accessories. Six months after that, as demand lagged, he borrowed $5,000 from the same creditor, sold his cell phones, and restocked his store with dollar items. A year later, with slackening local demand, he had to borrow an additional $2,500 to pay rent and utility bills, but ultimately he declared bankruptcy—suffering both bad credit and physical abuse from the creditor, who broke his arms and sent him to the hospital.

The creditor is a specialized underground vendor who plays a critical role in the local economy, particularly for shopkeepers and residents who may not have bank accounts or access to lines of credit.[33] In general, the leading owners and MAPAD members do not involve themselves with creditors. But for the typical non-elite store owner, creditors offer immediate access to small sums of cash. And in some cases individuals prefer the loan sharks to friends and others in their social network because they can borrow secretly without great risk of public exposure. It is common for Leroy and his peers on West Street to use local creditors, for both personal and business purposes, although they are loath to patronize them because of the exorbitant interest rates. As Leroy says,

It's not just that these niggers charge you that high interest, you know 20 or 30 percent, but they got you by the balls. They start coming in your store, at least the worst ones, think they own the place 'cause they lent you fifty bucks or something. And once you start with them, they just keep coming back . . . You got two types, you got the gangs and them that harass you, then you got some that leave you alone, the professional types. But you never can tell how these niggers going to act, so you can't really trust them. It's just not good to get involved with these people, but we all do, we have to, we don't have money and sometimes, at the end of the month, you need it.

Local creditors lend varying sums of money (from twenty-five to several thousand dollars) and demand different forms of payment depending on their relationship to the client and the sum of money being lent. As Leroy noted above, there are two types of creditors: "part-time" lenders are kingpins in economies of contraband, such as stolen car parts, drugs, and weapons, and they actively seek out lending as a way to store and "clean" their illegally obtained cash. The second type, the "professional" creditor, has no other underground economic role other than that of a lender. The interest rates do not differ greatly among the professionals and part-timers—sums are exchanged for 20 to 30 percent unless the client has a poor history of payment, in which case the rate is higher. However, there are differing payment plans offered. Part-timers will accept weekly payments, and they do not hesitate to inflict physical punishment if money is not paid on time; they are always seeking to use a business for money laundering, thus their overriding interest is to push the proprietor into larger and larger sums of debt. The "professional" lenders want to earn an investment on their loan; they usually do not inflict physical harm, but they will repossess business equipment or personal items (cars, household appliances, electronic equipment) if payment is not made, and they usually prefer payment in full at a specified date.

Elite businesspersons will occasionally loan money to the smaller shopkeepers and street vendors in Maquis Park. Their loans typically range from $25 to $500, but unlike creditors they do not always seek (or expect) to recoup their loans. Indeed, they are rarely paid back, says Samuel Wilson, who views these disbursements as part charity and part sound business practice.

> I always keep $100 in my pocket. Now, if I give it out, I'm getting back something. If they can't pay it back, they have to work it off. But we [who are successful in Maquis Park] understand that you have to give something back . . . There's not a lot of banks around here, and for guys on the street or, you know, even someone who owns a store, a hundred bucks may get them over the hump. Buy some equipment, pay that light bill, I mean, you will never believe how far I can make fifty bucks go around here.

Over a three-month period one summer, Samuel Wilson, Josiah Pegues, and Jesse Jefferson kept track of the money they lent or gave away for business purposes. Each parted with approximately $2,000 to $2,500 during those ninety days. Small grants from $25 to $250 were typical and went to men and women who performed various off-the-books labor. The money was used for the following: equipment purchases, rent, utility bill payment, gas and personal car repair, transportation out of town, a permit or city license, state identification cards, food, medical care, funeral services. Fifty percent of the money was given as free grants, for which the elites did not expect repayment. The remainder was given as no-interest loans that they thought would be repaid within six months. However, six months after making the initial loans, only 25 percent of the money had been repaid to Samuel. Josiah received only 10 percent of the money he had lent, and Jesse was still waiting for 95 percent of outstanding debt to be recovered.

Realizing that the loans might never be repaid, the three men demanded that the borrowers perform in-kind services, which included cleaning their homes and businesses, repairing their cars, running errands, performing night security, escorting elderly clients to and from their businesses, delivering goods and documents, and picking up lunch and dinner. "Yup, it's a lot cheaper than hiring somebody," said Josiah. "I may be out some money, but I always got someone to help me around here and I don't have to pay no union wages. There's a lot we get out of the deal so don't think just 'cause we giving away money we're not getting anything in return."

Most of the store owners understand that they are not working actively to build up a credit history when they lend to one another. They are quick to suggest that if banks would offer them credit, they would probably dispense with off-the-books lending—if not immediately, then over time. As Josiah Pegues notes, if they had relationships with financial institutions such that they relied on them for resources, they would fight harder than they now do against institutional discrimination in the financial sector: "You get tired, tired of fighting them banks, the white-run creditors. Sometimes, you just feel better when you're with your own. So, I guess most of us would like to have more available sources of cash, but some of us have been fighting for thirty years! I mean at some point you just take your loss. Maybe our sons will be able to do it the right way, get the loans, get the mayor to support local businesses in the community. But we have to do this ourselves."[34]

Through credit, hiring, and subleasing, the underground economy becomes a rope that ties merchants together. The rope can be either a lifeline or a noose. For those who draw on loans and off-the-books labor, the shady world provides a resource and helps them survive a generally inhospitable business climate. But it can also wring their financial necks and drive them into bankruptcy—or, worse, physical harm.

Underground modes of conducting business play an important role in reproducing the black shopkeepers' tight-knit webs of exchange and their overall perception of geographically confined commercial opportunities. Drawing on one another (as opposed to banks) for credit, hiring friends and local inhabitants off the books, and subleasing are three prominent examples of how unreported economic behavior can reinforce local merchants' social networks. Although the community is a source of strength when adapting to immediate challenges, the strength is fleeting because everyone is relying on others who, like themselves, share limited capacities and who are often on the precipice of default. Thus, these ties afford them few opportunities for growth and development, particularly when times are tough and people need an infusion of capital from outside.

When Leroy and his colleagues—or, for that matter, Josiah Pegues and the elite members of MAPAD—weigh opportunities to move outside their peer network and pursue new business opportunities, expand their social ties, and so on, they can experience fear and doubt. Lacking an established credit history and relationships outside their community, the men feel that they could be left on their own, without a safety net, if they strayed far from

Maquis Park. So an underground commercial venture that is close to home appears more attractive to them than a socially legitimate opportunity that takes them outside of familiar geographic and peer spaces. Allison Davis, a member of the elite MAPAD board, explains:

"It's a mental thing, really. And a lot of us get stopped by our fear. Say you got the mayor asking if we want a job out somewhere in Winnetka, you know, some white community. Yeah, there's money, but we don't trust it."

"What do you mean you don't trust it?"

"I mean it never happens. So, when we do get a bone, we don't believe it. And you get out there, you cleaning homes or doing construction or whatever. And you're outside your own home, your community. If the mayor all of a sudden say he don't like you, then what next? You don't know nobody, you can't just start looking for clients. White folk will never come to you."

"Okay, so then, you just come back to the Southside," I said. "I don't see the problem. You made some money and you come back."

"Well ain't that easy. Maybe the job you got means you got to go out of pocket. Where you going to get that money? A bank? Hell no, most of us got no credit or it's just hard to get it. Friends? Well, they ain't gonna lend it to you 'cause they see you out there, far away, doing your thing. And then, you left the Southside. So, folks around here wonder what your loyalty is. 'Ain't down with the community, no more?' That's what they be saying."

"But, c'mon, there's got to be some people who get out?"

"Yeah, I ain't saying it don't happen. I'm just telling you what goes through a man's mind when he gets these chances. It ain't

> just getting that job. It's about what you might give up. You are
> out there on your own, man. That's a scary thing for a lot of these
> folk who always just been getting the crumbs all their lives."

This is not an attitude restricted to the smaller merchants on West Street who experience bouts of insolvency. The same is true for elite businesspersons, including Davis's peers on the MAPAD board, who had chances for significant economic gain that would have taken them out of Maquis Park—to new communities or new clients. Their own disinclination suggests that they are apprehensive about entering unfamiliar commercial territory. At a quick glance, this certainly seems irrational and deeply counterproductive. These men look as if they are trying to improve not only their own lot, but that of the entire network to which they belong. One cannot help but predict failure for an individual who seems not to want to move unless an entire ghetto apparatus of businesspersons and resources move with him. Yet the entrepreneurs in the community place tremendous value on their current relationships with their associates. These ties seem enduring and reliable even if limited in terms of resources and ties to the wider world.

In this structure, whether by design or by accident, connected individuals appear to move in lockstep. As one actor makes a change, others are affected. Absent is anything resembling career development. It is rare to see individuals moving "up the ladder," whether in terms of wage work to equity ownership, steady salary augmentation, or increasing responsibilities, duties, and supervisory powers that typically come with job promotions. Instead, individuals move about from one commercial arena to another, responding less to their own developmental growth (be it education or widening social contacts) than to associates who may offer them a "quick money" opportunity or a "sure thing." People coax and drag one another into the next big thing. As such, the majority have come to anticipate that their business will change within three to five years. If they are lucky, someone will surprise them with a moneymaking scheme, and so they must be ready to respond. "Everyone around here is a handyman," says a prominent Maquis Park business leader. "Whatever the work, the answer is always 'I'll do it.'"

From the perspective of formal economic logic, this guarded outlook produces behavior that can appear strange at times. Seemingly not bothered by the fact that his customers do not pay in cash, Leroy Patterson feels he cannot turn these patrons away who come to his auto shop. He is well aware that it is risky to extend payment plans and bartering arrangements to customers, instead of demanding cash, but it is a way for him to secure a customer base and compete locally. After accepting appliances and electrical equipment in lieu of cash for one year, he directed his mechanics to repair those goods so that he could resell them from his store. One day I saw Leroy fastening a large wood plank on the garage, immediately next to the "Auto Shop" sign, that read "Fridges, TVs, Microwaves for Sale." Like his peers, Leroy displays great discomfort and hesitancy when confronted with opportunities to move to greater heights, where profits are larger and where all manner of status and power could follow. In his view these rare beneficences are offered by officials at government and financial service agencies who have otherwise ignored the community for decades. So even if the rewards are great, if taking an opportunity means putting into jeopardy an existing network of alliances, clients, creditors, and suppliers, Leroy will likely stay put and remain with other like-minded and likeable colleagues in the neighborhood.

In fact, for the local black merchants, other business climates are really just other examples of informal and highly personalized economic relations—like those in Maquis Park—to which they are not privy. They interpret economic spheres outside the community as also possessing an infrastructure of unreported exchange that makes any legitimate economic venture feasible. In their minds, Chicago is a set of commercial associations of individuals woven together by off-the-books and legitimate commerce. As the successful businessperson Orlando Allison says:

> I've noticed business all over the city and it's all about hand-shaking, promises, lot of things going on behind closed doors. See, the mayor just comes in here thinking that we're going to jump. Banks think that too. But you don't just do that. Whenever you do something, you are building up new relationships with people and you have to do things shady—well, maybe not shady like committing a crime, but shady like you depend on each other. You need to do little things that may not always be right—hire somebody, switch some money around, pay somebody to get a permit. I mean you need money for this, but you need people to watch your back. And that's everywhere in Chicago. So why would I just pack up and start moving around the city? There's still racism here.

Those expressing this theory of commerce recognize that underground commerce is not the same everywhere, but they argue that one will find merchants in every neighborhood drawing on income and economic exchanges that go unreported—that this is the backbone of small business growth. This perception shapes their understanding of why businesses in Maquis Park fail. In their eyes, bankruptcy and insolvency are frequent in Maquis

Park, not because people are bad businesspersons, which they may be, but because actors have limited political and economic capital—both legitimate and underground. Their white counterparts have clandestine connections that are useful in times of distress and that can be parlayed into formal business growth. Black merchants do not have cozy relationships that help stave off foreclosure, or that lead to a city contract, loan, or a lucrative investment opportunity.[35] They do not have much recourse to mainstream institutions when problems arise, and their underground relations are composed of other similarly challenged businesspersons. As Manning Marable so often points out, the capitalist state is also a racist state, so we should not be surprised that these merchants' view of business is racially organized.[36] Theirs is a saga of ghetto capitalism.

Notwithstanding this limiting economic gestalt, there are elite merchants in Maquis Park who do exhibit mobility and who collect contracts and secure financing that enables them to work outside their own ghetto community. Sometimes they manage to open another store or secure entrée into a citywide political-economic circle. Yet, in the minds of those staying behind in Maquis Park, the successful businesspersons will not come back and use their connections to help others in Maquis Park. Thus, Leroy, Ola, Josiah, and others more often speak about those risk takers who *could not* compete outside the area and so return to Maquis Park with tales of discrimination, bankruptcy, and exclusion. With such a skewed perspective, it should not come as a surprise that many of them believe that real mobility—as touted in mainstream myths of entrepreneurship—simply does not happen for black entrepreneurs in Maquis Park. The combination of minimal exposure to those who manage to conduct business outside the area combined with the frequent exposure to those who have failed to do so reinforces the belief that, as Josiah Pegues opines, business in the ghetto is a fish tank.[37]

Many of us are likely to see something familiar in the experiences of businesspersons in Maquis Park. Their informal work with one another is not so out of the ordinary, and it is likely that personal connections probably mean as much in the economies of other communities as they do inside the ghetto. Hiring off the books and lending under the table are by no means the sole provenance of the ghetto entrepreneur. But the ecological features of the ghetto can make even the most mundane, generic economic exchange something extraordinary. When the stores on West Street lend a few dollars to one another, when they barter, and when they exchange in secret, they do so in a social context of deep instability and limited resources. Their expectations of one another are colored by impermanence and uncertainty. Professional associations are disproportionately composed of people who are strapped and who are struggling day-to-day to stay solvent. These are individuals who may be involved in somewhat questionable commercial practices—not always heinous, but clandestine, creative, and perhaps even embarrassing.

Knowing that others must be inventive and work underground to remain viable, businesspersons can thus form complicated relationships with one another. They are all in the same boat, so they may rely on their neighbors for material and emotional support, and for help in remaining flexible and capable of adjusting to an unpredictable business climate. In the short term, such networks seem useful in helping people stave off crises and avoid insolvency. But they can also be limiting. Importantly, the ties forged out of shady economic dealings often do not provide a solid foundation either for long-term personal mobility or for the viability of the group or the community. One may argue that the life span of small business ownership is short by nature. But U.S. businesses generally do not fail because of an inability to confront extortion, the need to visit a loan shark because of the lack of a line of credit, or the need to fight off hustlers and vagrants who make customers feel unsafe when entering the store. These are not the common problems identified in studies on small business practice. But they are examples of ghetto-specific challenges that must be added on to the normal exigencies of entrepreneurship.

Marlon's Saga

Marlon DeBreaux began operating small businesses in Maquis Park in 1980. He is a fixture on West Street. His story reveals the myriad ways that the underground economy functions in the lives of Maquis Park's businesspeople. Marlon inherited his passion, cooking, from his father and his grandfather, both of whom owned small restaurants in Chicago's Southside. He has owned, managed, and worked in many fast-food restaurants and diners in the community. In 1989 he bought his restaurant when the previous owner retired. Since that time, he has experienced bankruptcy and the general ups and downs of small business ownership. But the variety of his previous struggles did not necessarily prepare him for the downturn at the end of the nineties when his restaurant, Marlon's Kitchen, began losing business like never before. The demolition of nearly ten thousand public housing units in the area drastically reduced demand along West Street, and competition arose in the form of new fast-food franchises that opened a few blocks away. In addition, two fast-food franchises also opened nearby, further diluting his customer base. "Kids stopped coming, so their families stopped coming," he recalled.

"Used to be, that we had everyone coming in after school, it was like a nice hangout. But, then, everyone wanted the Big Mac, not the Marlon Burger."

Unlike most merchants, Marlon had built up a line of credit with a local savings and loan. He did not have a stellar credit history—two bankruptcies, a history of personal and commercial default—but unlike his peers who similarly suffered, at times Marlon could persuade two local loan officers to came to his aid. Now, however, his luck with the bank seemed on the verge of running out. Marlon was having trouble paying his outstanding bank loans. He received a warning from his loan officer around the summer of 1999 that he would soon ruin his credit rating and that foreclosure of his business might be in the offing.

Adding to these constraints, in the autumn of 2000, Big Cat, the leader of the local Maquis Park Kings street gang, began extorting West Street businesses. Big Cat worked with another member of his gang, Ellis Clearwater, to solicit payoffs from commercial establishments—in time they would make these demands not only on West Street, but on all of the local commercial thoroughfares in the community. The fee they charged varied. For foreign-born shopkeepers, they would demand several hundred dollars or more each month. They levied the highest fees on stores selling liquor and sporting goods. For black-owned stores, they were slightly more forgiving: some reported having to pay $50 or $100 a month, although the amounts could change and for no discernible reason. Eventually Big Cat would demand that stores hire his rank and file, and launder his money, but that was still down the road. For all of the stores, Big Cat promised to find stolen goods, prevent vandalism, and monitor the homeless persons and squatters who sometimes harassed customers and urinated in the shops.

Marlon figured that he would need to supplement his monthly

income by $500 to make the payments to his bank. To earn extra income, he decided to allow various off-the-books economic activity in his restaurant—and in the alleyways and adjoining parking lot. "Nothing illegal," he explained:

> Just that I let Theotis cut hair inside—I'd get about $150 to $200 a month from that 'cause that nigger was good, really good. James and them would come through and get some business changing oil or something. I'd get a little from that. Little Johnnie watched the cars for me at night for free, and he'd put flyers from the [night]club on the cars, sells customers gum and hair products, things like that. I'd get about $50 a month. My girlfriend was selling shirts or clothes—that brought in some change. You know, just little things, helping to pay the bills, that's all.

These extracurricular activities did not bring in the extra $500 every month, but Marlon earned enough to make his bank payments for a few months. He understood that these schemes were tenuous at best. He just needed some time to think about more permanent solutions.

In time, his attraction to shady enterprise grew and he expanded the off-the-books side of his business even further. He looked for other hairstylists to cut hair in his restaurant during the day. He asked James Arleander if he wanted to move his open-air car repair service from the alley next to the barbershop to his own alleyway. Marlon started delivering food to businesses and homes, but did not report the sales revenues or the wages of the high-school-age boys who delivered his food.

In the eyes of some West Street shopkeepers, Marlon's response to business decline was only a more developed version of their own business management strategy. Leroy Patterson, a longtime friend of Marlon, explains:

See, we all do things [like Marlon did]. You got the business you
see when you walk in, then you got what you need to do to survive. Like, I sell microwaves and fridges sometimes, but I'm supposed to be fixing cars, right? Ms. Olson runs that center for kids,
but she got soul food for lunch she sells and she got dusties [music
parties] and bingo at night. I mean, you already know all this. For
us folks, sometimes we call it working at the shack, 'cause that's
what it feels like. Like we got a little space that we fill up with anything and everything. That's what Marlon tried to do, until the big
cats got pissed.

As Leroy notes, there are other business owners who supplement
income by allowing other people to covertly sell goods and services inside their store. None of them report the income to the
government. A typical case involves Ms. Olson's Youth Center:
several times a month, her center hosts bingo and dance parties,
events patronized mostly by the local senior citizens. She also sells
soul food lunches on Thursdays and Fridays in the back of her
store. She receives a small fee from those who host the parties and
from the lunchtime cooks. These activities are widely known, but
they are also irregular: two months may pass without dances and
lunchtime sales, only to resume again without much notice.

Not every store owner supplements income illegally in this
manner. However, it is no secret which merchants are creatively
using their physical space for shady dealing. In fact, there is a
code of conduct among merchants that regulates the amount of
underground sales that can occur within a particular store. The
shared guiding principle is not to earn as much as possible. Instead, everyone should ideally have an opportunity to supplement
his or her income. The store owners understand that their own
ability to make money off the books is dependent on their capac-

ity to evade detection by law enforcement and to ensure that their own ventures do not cause great disturbances, such as fights or shootings. In part this means securing the support of others engaged in similar activities. Specifically, this means working with other proprietors who could call the police or who may report that their own commercial activity is being hindered as a result of another person's illicit activities. Thus, the prevailing attitude is mutual recognition: In a challenging business climate, people should assist one another as much as possible while remaining competitive; illicit income generation will only work if everyone respects the needs of each other to earn under the table.

Marlon's attempts to earn income transgressed this code of conduct that placed the group's interest in sharing underground opportunities ahead of the individual's wish to monopolize them. Leroy Patterson states,

> Marlon got greedy, that's what did him in. See, you got to be careful because if you start trying to get all this kind of business yourself, then other folks are not going to look out for you. They see you hogging all the slop. You got to take what you need, and people will understand. But remember, everyone else needs to make some money too. Marlon forgot that. And when he tried to get James over to his place, that was it, they told the alderman and the gangs, and they both came down on him. That was when it was too late. We [the other store owners] tried to tell him, but the cat was so desperate, he wouldn't listen.

Ms. Olson offered a similar explanation:

> We all looked out for Marlon. Don't think that just 'cause we were angry at him doesn't mean we didn't help him. No sir. He just

lost his mind. He could have just asked us for a little money. We could have gotten it to him until he got on his feet. He's a good man, a family man. He helped me when I needed money.

After six months of earning extra money off the books, Leroy and Ms. Olson both told Marlon that he had to sell his business and take a minimal loss. They warned him not to rely on illegal income generation to pay his bank loans. His creative schemes were threatening the capacity of other merchants to supplement their own respective earnings. Most importantly, Marlon was trying to usurp their own arrangements with hairstylists, prostitutes, gamblers, tarot card readers, and other merchants who worked out of their respective facilities. Most of the street vendors working on or near West Street, like James Arleander, already had contracts with other store owners or with the local gang (who taxed their ventures in exchange for providing "security" patrols or a safe space to work). By recruiting them into his restaurant, Marlon violated the rule specifying that such opportunities needed to be spread out among the group.

In addition, Marlon's attempts to commandeer shady activity around West Street could have attracted attention to the schemes. Most notably, the residents were hearing rumors that the gang leader, Big Cat, was extorting businesses in Maquis Park. Although the shopkeepers were still trying to confirm the rumors, many felt assured that Big Cat and his subordinate, Ellis Clearwater, would turn to extortion of commercial establishments to meet the drop in demand for the drugs they sold. With Big Cat and Ellis seeking new ways to bring revenue into the gang, the merchants did not want to let word leak out about their own illegal moneymaking ventures. They worried that the gang might try to tax them. So they asked Marlon repeatedly to stop expanding his underground economic profile, particularly when it threatened other merchants' arrangements that were in place.

Marlon ignored the advice of his peers. He advertised his restaurant (and its adjoining public spaces) to the local street vendors with even greater ferocity. One night he became drunk and wandered into Mandee's Late Night bar, where he met Autry Vincent, the owner of a local dollar store. Leroy says Autry confronted Marlon about his new entrepreneurial zest:

"Autry walked up to Marlon and asked why [Marlon was] so interested in pulling business away from everybody else. See, Autry had a few women who braided hair in his store and he also controlled all them psychics—you know who read your fortune, or read the cards, shit like that. He made good money that way, probably a few hundred a month, and he thought Marlon was going to take it away. He and Marlon started shouting and Marlon said, 'First I'm going to fuck that bitch [Arlene Dennis, one of the ladies who reads tarot cards], and then when I take her over to my place, I'm going to ask her to read my fortune and you know what she going to tell me, Vincent? That your old lady going to be walking out from my house on Sunday morning.' Autry just hit him, just like that, and said 'Marlon, you do that and none of us going to be with you anymore.'"

"What did he mean by that?"

"What he meant was that all the other people who got a little business, you know, folks like me, we wouldn't support Marlon no more if he got in trouble. And well, I have to say that even though I'm [Marlon's] friend, Autry was right. I just thought Marlon was getting greedy and I had to look out for myself first."

Even though his overtures to local street vendors were earning him several hundred dollars per month, Marlon was growing desperate. He faced a new set of problems with the shady traders now working out of his store. The hairstylists who worked in the back of his restaurant fought with each other over who could solicit diners during the busiest hours. Outside the store, there were shouting matches and interminable haggling between vendors and customers. Pimps challenged one another over the right to place their prostitutes inside Marlon's Kitchen—a prime location, given the traffic of blue-collar workers and truck drivers from the neighboring white communities. Things hit rock bottom when the gang caught wind of Marlon's affairs: they demanded that he pay a street tax. Ellis demanded that in addition to the free lunches, Marlon pay a 20 percent fee on all illegal receipts. When Marlon refused, a gang member came to his apartment late one evening, beat him severely, and threatened to inflict an even worse thrashing if he did not accede to the tax.

It was at this time that Alderman Mattie Carson took notice. "Carson wanted her take and so did Ellis," Marlon recounted several years later. "That's when I was dead in the water, man. I realized I made a mistake." On a late night visit, Carson told Marlon that the shady dealings were causing disturbances for the other store owners and jeopardizing public safety. "She kept telling me it was unsafe, but I knew she just wanted me to kick in a little something to her own [campaign] pot. But, man I couldn't afford that." Ellis Clearwater appeared a week later and threatened to physically assault Marlon again. Ellis was concerned because Marlon had attracted street traders and vendors away from other stores—some of these stores were paying the gang a street tax for the right to have traders (who also paid off the gang) work in their store.

Marlon approached Leroy Patterson, Autry Vincent, and other local black proprietors in Maquis Park. He pleaded with them to speak with Alderman Carson and persuade Ellis to lower his 20 percent gang tax to 5 percent. "None of us would help him," says Leroy, describing their collective displeasure at Marlon. Marlon had "crossed the line" by encroaching on the right of everyone to modestly supplement their income. He put his own interests ahead of the group. "How could I defend [Marlon]?" Leroy asked:

> The brother had pissed us all off. There was plenty to go around and he just wanted it all. Now, I'm not saying he could've kept his joint open. But he knows how these things go. We're all in the same boat. You just sell your store, and wait a while, open a new one. Everyone does that, all the time. But I don't know, maybe he was drinking or his girlfriend was telling him shit and he didn't listen to us. We all told him, "You hurt us and we ain't gonna help you." We would've talked to [Alderman] Mattie, she would've listened. We could've gotten Ellis to take nothing for three months, but Marlon just crossed the line, man, he just tried to get too much and didn't want to leave nothing for us. Wasn't right what he did. And worse, I'm not sure if the nigger can ever come back 'round here. That's the worst thing. He lost all of the trust we had for him.

In the past, both shopkeepers, Autry and Leroy, had worked with Alderman Carson, as well as with Big Cat and Ellis Clearwater, when such problems arose. Autry and Leroy would give free goods and services to the alderman and her friends. In return they received expedited treatment on building permit requests, their family members were relieved of jury duty, the potholes outside their store were repaired in a timely manner, and police looked the other way when they became creative with their businesses—Leroy, for example, once sold refrigerators on the street, outside his auto shop, and police and the alderman simply ignored it. Similarly, Leroy provided the street gang members with free auto repairs; in return the gang watched over his store at night with their street patrols. For his part, Autry gave Big Cat and Ellis's girlfriends free diapers and toys. On occasion, he helped the two men to launder money through the store. Marlon knew that both Autry and Leroy could have helped him, but he underestimated the damage he had done by drawing shady business away from them and other merchants on West Street. By the time he called upon Autry, Leroy, and others for help, it was too late. His colleagues had already decided to withdraw support.

Having lost the backing of his peers and unable to fend off both the gang and Alderman Carson, he turned to Ajay, a local loan shark. But the 30 percent interest rates Ajay charged increased Marlon's debt, pitching him toward bankruptcy. Marlon could not make his weekly payments to Ajay. To erase Marlon's debt, Ajay demanded a 51 percent ownership share and the right to attach his name to the store—which reopened under co-ownership as "Ajay's Chicken Shack." Soon afterward, he gave Ajay's brother Asaara his remaining ownership shares and left Maquis Park entirely. A year later, Marlon recalled the saga. It was the shame he felt in the eyes of other proprietors that led him to cut his ties with Maquis Park. The rebuke of political officials was fleeting, working relationships could be reestablished, and gang members did not remain in power long enough to be of concern, but he could not face Leroy, Autry, Ms. Olson, and other longtime associates and friends. A proud man who saw himself first and foremost as a proprietor, Marlon now felt as though he lost his identity in Maquis Park. He had to leave the community in order to regain his self-esteem and start another commercial enterprise.

After Marlon's Kitchen went out of business, Big Cat began to fulfill his promises by extorting more stores along West Street. He taxed them and solicited periodic "protection" payments. He demanded free merchandise and money laundering. Proprietors were outraged at the gang's attempt to colonize underground activity, which historically had been outside the gang's purview. But under the threat of destruction to person and property, they felt there was little they could do to resist. They continued to pursue a third party, and eventually Pastor Wilkins, as we will see, would step in to provide mediation. But all of this was months away. For now, in Marlon's Kitchen, West Street had lost a historic place of business. Marlon would, in fact, return about two years later, having saved up his money and reestablished some of the connections to Leroy, Ola, and others. Time healed some of the wounds and allowed him to return two blocks off of West Street, where Marlon's Eats now serves fried chicken, ribs, and other fare.

The risks of being a business owner in Maquis Park are great; generally, the rewards are not. The underground economy offers, or at least seems to offer, a means of navigating the pressures of ownership. So even though the choice to participate in the shady world may be tough, we must acknowledge that the decision is made in a social context shaped by concentrated poverty, low consumer demand and high commercial insolvency, pervasive institutional discrimination, and neglect by the city. In other words, those at the bottom of the economic ladder in Maquis Park include not only the down-and-out folks on the street who struggle to live in a world of limited means. The bottom rungs also include the fraught store owner who struggles to stay above water and who sometimes draws on resources and techniques that are unpleasant, questionable, or, at times, downright criminal. On West Street and other streets like it, it is widely believed that the economic deck is stacked against local entrepreneurs. And so it is accepted wisdom among the local merchants that they must work creatively, and sometimes illegally, to ensure the survival of their business.

Although the entrepreneurial spirit in Maquis Park blends off-the-books and legitimate economic behaviors, by no means is every store oriented toward the shady. Nor does every store hide income, hire laborers secretly, or obtain credit via loan sharks. For many business owners, the underground economy does not involve their bookkeeping, but it inevitably involves their space; it manifests in those who trade illicitly in public, and who loiter, deal drugs, and compromise public safety by harassing passersby. For them, the shady world is just another ecological factor that impacts business in the ghetto. They too must respond to streetcorner persons and drug dealers who bother customers and block their entrances. But even if they eschew involvement in shady enterprise, they may still benefit from their neighbors who do attend to problems off the books and help ensure habitable public spaces.

Rather than seeing themselves as a separate law-abiding group criticizing a criminally oriented counterpart, the usual judgment of most of these shopkeepers toward shady entrepreneurs is like that of Marlon's peers toward Marlon, who understand his plight and will look the other way until a local threshold of ethical behavior is crossed. Marlon's usurpation of more than his fair share of unreported income transgressed an important code of conduct—one that probably is quite specific to communities like Maquis Park. There are other codes, although enumerating them is difficult, and partly deceiving, because they often manifest as timely responses to situations that can arise unpredictably.[38]

Despite their accommodations and tolerance of one another's

shady behavior, the local businesspeople do demand some propriety of one another. They expect that questionable behavior, if it is to take place, should occur at certain times and in particular places. Drug dealing, prostitution and pimping, and "hustling" are activities to which residents and merchants have grown accustomed and made adjustments. There are some places where no drugs will ever be sold, some parks where one will not be hustled, some alleyways where pimps will not ply their trade, some parking lots where no illegal car repair will be offered and no gypsy cab vendor will set up shop. Understanding the geography of illegal commerce in the entire area, as well as the distinctions along particular thoroughfares like West Street, is useful for residents and shopkeepers looking for, or looking to avoid, underground activity.

People who live and work in Maquis Park are generally aware of underground activity occurring around them, and they adjust their schedules accordingly. They know what corners at "hot" because the local gang has assigned drug dealers there; they know where to find employable street hustlers who will run a quick errand or watch over customers in their store. They know which local loan sharks should be avoided because of their capricious interest rate alterations and their unforgiving payment schedules.

To carry out business with any chance of success, the merchants must carry themselves responsibly in terms of the *local* standards for public conduct and social behavior. This requires a knowledge of the social geography of shady activity, including the awareness that one may be encroaching on a neighbor's shady dealings. It also requires knowing how to resolve conflicts and respond to problems. For example, one may call the police to report shoplifting, a burglary, or extortion, but enlisting other shopkeepers behind the scenes and organizing a collective response without the police may be as effective. Similarly, soon after the dissolution of Marlon's Kitchen, the clergy made themselves available as a viable avenue for redress for shopkeepers needing to fend off the gang's coercion.

On several occasions, I watched a group of store owners rebuke a pimp who sent his prostitutes to West Street during the after-school hours. They found him to be morally licentious in a way that a pimp who abstains from this behavior is not. After pleading for several months (including failing to acquire help from the police), they beat up the contemptuous pimp and told him not to return to West Street. In this case, the local standards of ethical business practice do not coincide perfectly with those of so-called mainstream society. Some of these practices are simply offshoots of a local "Don't ask, don't tell" principle. Merchants have learned to look the other way when their neighbors run afoul of conventional business practices, most explaining this mindful ignorance as the only way not to get caught up in another's drama. Such is the metric of morality in the social context of Maquis Park.

But what *should* one make of the fact that some shopkeepers will tolerate, for example, fellow merchants who allow sex workers to sublease their facilities? "As long as them whores don't hurt my customers," says Agnes, a beauty salon owner, "I don't care what they do in there." Is this negligence? pragmatism? Or worse, is Agnes an accessory even if she does not benefit from these arrangements herself? To this, we can add the thorny question, What are the long-term consequences of such activity—and such ignorance—for creating a legitimate and safe business climate? If shopkeepers continue to distrust the police and fail to call upon them as other citizens would likely do, whether out of cynicism or because they are also operating shadily, the distance and distrust between Maquis Park and municipal institutions may only worsen. Certainly, as this continues over time, there may not be an effective civic voice that pressures police to be responsive. For that matter, neither are the necessary ingredients in place that would foster residents' trust and willingness to use the police instead of suffering quietly or taking matters into their own hands.

This does not mean that there is no respect for the law among West Street merchants. They spend much time as residents and local stakeholders trying to acquire adequate police support and intervention. They attend town hall gatherings and "community policing" meetings. They march in anger to speak with the local district commander. They write letters to their elected representatives. Not surprisingly, failing to gain a satisfactory improvement in local security, they sometimes deal with public safety themselves. Most of their self-policing does not involve vigilante justice or corporal punishment, but is of the sort described above, in which they develop creative prevention techniques, such as hiring local street hustlers off the books to provide security inside the stores. This is in part adaptive, but it is also a practice historically conditioned by unreliable government services that other communities take for granted. And as shown above, it is a means for shopkeepers to reach out into their communities and maintain a good public image, recruit potential customers, and advertise their goods and services.[39] It is the life of business in the fish tank.

Chapter Four
The Street Hustler

James Arleander has been fixing cars off the books in Maquis Park for over a decade. At the height of his entrepreneurship, in the early and mid-1990s, he saved several thousand dollars and nearly convinced a real estate company to offer him a storefront lease. Doing so required years of diligence and patience. James also had to find innovative ways to store his money because he did not trust banks: "I kept it in trees, I dug holes in the park, had it in my underwear, man it was crazy!" In the end, neither the real estate company nor the bank deemed James creditworthy. He languished in depression for six months: "I spent all that money on booze, just drank it away 'cause I was so upset I couldn't get nobody to help me."

Eventually James returned to his tried-and-true ways of entrepreneurship. But fixing a car in a public space, he says, is not easy.

He lists the obstacles that an underground worker must overcome.

First, you are doing something illegal, which means police must be involved. You have to deal with them, and you can either hide [from them] or pay [them]. Now, you can pay with money or favors—wash your back, I'll wash yours. Then, if you're hanging out making noise, getting oil on the ground, you are pissing off other folks. And you are probably upsetting people like Leroy [the owner of Leroy's Auto] who got a real business fixing cars. So, not just police, but the entire community is a problem. Again, you can hide or pay, and you pay in *many* kinds of ways. Then, you have to get your parts. That takes money. And where are you going to keep your tools at night? You can't be bringing that shit along with you. So, you need to hide it, store it somewhere. See what I mean, it's not just me asking somebody if they want their carburetor fixed, you dig? It's a whole operation you're dealing with.

Any businessperson will recognize the challenges James outlines, even if there are some questionable features: James deals with the government, he manages public relations, he must locate inexpensive tools and car parts, and he must store equipment safely. He continued by listing additional tasks, such as ensuring that customers pay, finding ways to store his daily receipts, hiring people to run errands, and advertising his services.

Securing a physical space to work is at the top of James's daily concerns. It is a luxury for him to use a place for longer than six months—most hustlers are not as successful, he says, and move every few days or weeks to another location. Over the course of his life, James has worked in alleyways, empty lots, homeowners' garages, abandoned building sites, church parking lots, parking lanes, even under expressways.[1] He prefers back roads and alleyways, as well as church parking lots where ministers safeguard his shop. He usually pays a neighboring resident a few dollars per month to store his equipment, or a percentage of the daily take if he stores them with a minister, but James has also hidden tools in abandoned buildings and park bathrooms.

The public character of James's work shapes all aspects of his trade. When he scouts a location, his first task is to secure his personal safety and welfare by building relationships with those who control access to the space. In the last few years, he has relied on three places—an empty lot and two alleys. The lot is under the watchful eye of a block club president; a local barber owns one alley, while the other alley abuts a tax-delinquent abandoned building controlled by a ward precinct captain. With each of these regulators, James has developed a business relationship: he pays the barber and the block club president for use of the lot and the first alley; in return for use of the second alley, he does personal favors for the precinct captain, such as auto and home repairs. These individuals help James by keeping police away and by preventing other car mechanics from stealing his clients or offering their services nearby. On occasion they help James settle disputes with customers.

James Arleander is one of the oldest hustlers in the area. Men and women like James tend to prefer the title *squatter* or *hustler* to either *homeless person* or *streetcorner man*. Whatever the appellation, several attributes distinguish these individuals. First, they lack a stable residence. They sleep on the streets, in shelters, in vacant public housing apartments, or, if they're lucky, they pay a few dollars per month to stay with a friend or relative. They are vagabonds who move through short periods of homelessness, squatting, and temporary stays in rental units.[2] They are also laboring nomads. James and his peers work in short stints. They do not focus on long-term employment, but instead pursue short-term opportunities to gain income, whether legal or illegal. Because they do not look for work at employment and job-training centers, they do not show up in conventional measures of unemployment and labor force participation. Finally, their physical movements span fairly limited geographic areas. Those in Maquis Park rarely leave the city's Southside, and most are recognizable figures—the exceptions being the small migratory population that travels regionally to find seasonal and temporary work in the steel mills, minor league baseball stadiums, and agricultural farms and plants.

All street hustlers interact to varying degrees with city agencies, most notably the police but also the local elected officials who tolerate their commerce, sanitation workers who permit them to sift through collected trash, and Chicago Parks and Recreation employees who look past their makeshift shelters. Over time, street hustlers can develop fairly intimate relationships with the many actors assigned to keeping public spaces safe and accessible. But, remarkably, hustlers are not at the mercy of these stakeholders. In the tight web of the underground economy, there is a structure of codependence in which information, goods, and services pass between the two.

This inner-city nomad population is a public concern, both for conservatives tired of "squeegee men" and panhandlers, and for progressives interested in reducing homelessness and mentally ill street inhabitants. Our social-scientific understanding of this population has been shaped by public policies interested in reducing homelessness and ensuring public safety. Thus, research has been guided primarily by the need to estimate the size of this vagabond population and to develop effective but humane policing strategies, such as enforcement of laws against public panhandling or sleeping on the street. The discussion below complements and complicates the standard policy perspective by examining how hustlers weave themselves into the social fabric of a community. The community character of this population does not make news nor is it well understood.[3] In Maquis Park there is always a steady stream of men and women who hustle, but it does not take long to notice similar faces in the crowd. Their neighborhood involvement coalesces around the underground economy; it is through hidden earnings that they support themselves, build social relations with the wider public, and play a part in the daily life of a poor community. And without a business, or often a home, to call their own, hustlers create their world, and make their opportunities, on the street and in the public eye.

Underground entrepreneurs possess skill, business acumen, and tremendous potential for innovative skills and strategies. What most lack is a physical space to ply their trade. There are exceptions, like women who sell cooked meals from their homes and businesses that host gambling, but the vast majority of hustlers have no such place of work. Their needs for space vary. Some have equipment that must be housed, others need a place to sell their finished products, and still others need sites to advertise and recruit clients. These standard commercial requirements are accentuated in a poor community because of the lack of usable physical property. Unused (and often unusable) land parcels and empty tracts can stretch on for many blocks in the ghetto. Commercial establishments are interspersed with fire-strewn, barely standing properties and abandoned buildings. Private, sheltered, decent space is at a premium, and those in possession of it guard their property carefully, as the threat of theft, arson, and vandalism is always near.

Although inhibiting legitimate economic development, Maquis Park's dilapidated physical ecology does enable *illegal* economic activity to flourish. The abandoned buildings and lots beckon sex workers, gangs, and car mechanics. Businesses and churches allow traders to use their rear lots for a fee. Chicago's alleyways, sheltered from the main street, are another prize commodity because they provide ample space to sell clothes, fix electronic equipment, offer a sexual favor, sell dope, read a tarot card, or advertise one's services. Similarly, parks are more than purely recreational centers; street corners are more than pedestrian stopovers; an overgrown tree is more than comfort from an unforgiving sun. They all possess economic value to the vigilant and creative hustler.[4]

To hustle, one does not simply set up shop in an alleyway or on a street corner. Chances are that others have already claimed that spot. Moreover, it is likely that any claim to use turf and earn revenue will be contested by other entrepreneurs. For example, block club presidents watch over persons who colonize abandoned buildings, sometimes charging the users a fee for protection from police; the elected alderman's precinct captains are usually aware of the more successful entrepreneurs and exact a fee or favor from them whenever they wish; even police demand obeisance when certain territories are appropriated for personal gain. At times it seems that there are as many types of persons professing control over a place as there are types of people who want to make money there. In the ghetto, one must negotiate public space before one can hustle.

When more than one person uses a building or street corner, disagreements and conflicts inevitably ensue. There are the ever-present dangers of apprehension by law enforcement, but there is also harassment by other traders and customers for which courts and police do not provide recourse. Various styles of cooperation and collaboration can arise to cope with conflicts, from lasting relationships to onetime associations that dissipate after the transaction is completed. The search for safe, usable physical space brings people together in unexpected ways and strange bedfellows are made.

What is called "public space" showcases these interactions. Public space differs from some private properties, like homes, organizations, and businesses where people are living and working—although public spaces do include some privately owned properties, like slum and abandoned dwellings where there is minimal surveillance or few attempts to curb public access. In general, those areas in the ghetto that are considered public space are the areas, such as street corners, alleyways, and sidewalks, that are typically publicly owned and maintained and to which all citizens in theory have access.[5]

Most communities take such public spaces for granted. Very few middle-class Americans see an alley as a venue for monetary gain; but in the ghetto these spaces are full of possibility. Traffic in ghetto public areas is heightened because of the lack of adequate private, personal space. People are pushed outside by overcrowding, families' "doubling up" to pay rent, and the generally inhospitable condition of apartments. What some might see as a mass of Americans lying about, and out of work, is in many cases an ensemble of persons who lack private places where they can rest. In Maquis Park, working and nonworking people will socialize in their cars, on discarded couches in alleys, on park benches, and so on, because they don't have access to a living room or dining room where they can entertain guests or read the morning paper.

The lack of private space, combined with people's needs to purchase goods and services cheaply, transforms this human ensemble into a ready consumer base and at the same time transforms their places of gathering into valued underground sales spots.

It is possible to distinguish three main types of shady entrepreneurs who challenge each other for the right to use public spaces in Maquis Park. Most are simply selling goods and services. Some "traders," like those who walk through Maquis Park hawking socks and T-shirts, may have only a very short-term interest in a space; others, such as gang members monopolizing a street corner for drug sales, have longer-term plans. A second type of participant, the "regulator," tries to control the use of a space by attending to some of the conflicts that can surround off-the-books entrepreneurial activity there or by demanding a payoff or "street tax." In return, the regulator might offer protection against the police, prosecution of nonpaying customers, or arbitration of contractual disputes. For example, one hustler may tax a homeless man who wishes to sell stolen goods at a particular location, while another might exact a fee from the same person to forestall police intervention. The trader and the regulator may be the same person. The third type of entrepreneur, the "predator," earns a living by preying on person and property in these spaces; not only do car thieves, robbers, stickup artists, and pickpockets make money in public areas, but their actions disrupt the practices of the trader and the regulator, and the arrangements between the two. If customers are afraid to park their cars or walk around, the trader loses customers and the regulator misses out on derivative income.

There can be potentially limitless relations among traders, regulators, and predators—recall that there is no government or third-party actor who ensures a fair economic use of these public areas. It would be a mistake to view the relationships among the three kinds of entrepreneurs and the customer pool as systematic or predictable. In fact, such relations are not necessarily ubiquitous—even in Maquis Park, one will find public spaces without regulation or any underground activity altogether. What must be analyzed is the process by which traders, regulators, and predators work with and challenge one another to create a climate suitable for making money illegally. Since any such claim on territory is never permanent and is routinely contested, it becomes necessary to understand how parties find ways to use a space successfully, whether through force, consensus, or a mutual détente. At the foundation of their interactions is the appropriation of public space in a way that is viewed as legitimate by the local community of actors.

Underground claims on public space involve a fundamental tension. The public aspect of that space—that it is available in theory to all citizens—is breached or at least threatened by its private use and control. This means that the socially legitimate use of that space is compromised and the citizen is pitted against the underground hustler. Now, it may be the case that a public area was already unfit for public use—think of litter-filled parks and playgrounds in disrepair. Nevertheless, once a space is appropriated for shady purposes, the public's capacity to use the area is diminished. The consequences are not insignificant in Maquis Park. Residents already have a difficult time getting the city to fix potholes, pick up trash, keep parks clean, and so on. That burden is now heightened by the need to proceed cautiously around those trying to make a buck. In other words, this public/private antagonism can jeopardize safety, exacerbate the extant difficulties of protecting property, and inhibit free communication and association.

As in any community where a problem arises, residents may use private means of response and redress, or they may contact their representatives, like the police and elected officials. Underground activity is private in that it is an exchange among individuals and corporate groups, but it is also private because participating actors give up their right to many public resources by entering into exchange. A drug purchaser cannot call the police if the narcotic falls short in quality or quantity; a purchaser of stolen equipment may haggle with the seller, but no court would adjudicate the transaction. (To be sure, not all rights are given up simply because individuals are transacting off the books. Homicides are still investigated and prosecuted, even if they occur in the context of an illegal exchange.) Given the inability of the justice system to play a formal role, it is an open question how underground economic exchanges are regulated.

The specific challenge of maintaining habitable public spaces requires some social control over the illegal exchange that takes place there. Our vantage point is that of the street hustler, people like James Arleander who fix cars, sell clothing, perform odd jobs for under-the-table wages, and otherwise hang out in public spaces looking for short-term work. These people are an important thread in the social fabric of inner cities. They can compromise public safety if others perceive them as threats or if they are involved in criminal activities and harass people who pass by. However, their material interests—as hustlers—can lead them to work on behalf of public order, because passersby are people they can solicit for business or money. Ease of access for pedestrians will increase the customer base. Because they depend on an active, bustling public theater for customers, street hustlers must be careful when inhabiting common areas. Their dual roles can lead them to be not only predators on public space but also contributors to the regulation of social behavior that threatens public access and passage. In other words, in Maquis Park, hustlers have many roles, as traders, predators, and regulators.

The "Social Vulnerables" of West Street

James Arleander is one of the most active street hustlers in Maquis Park, keeping himself busy by managing an outdoor car repair trade. Over a five-year period, I rarely saw James suffer because of lack of demand. His work never catapulted him into the ranks of small business ownership, but he was always servicing two or three cars at a time. "I've got a good thing going," he likes to say. "Enough to get me by, and that's not bad in these times." The services he typically provides include tire patches, oil changes, body work and exterior painting, carburetor and radiator repairs, minor transmission and battery servicing, and internal alterations such as replacement of a car radio, seat adjustment, window replacement and cleaning, and odometer modifications. His clientele is rooted in Maquis Park and neighboring areas and includes police officers, schoolteachers, personnel from the Parks Department and the Sanitation Department, and students in the nearby university community.

Required business acumen for James exceeds technical knowledge and a set of tools. James spends a fair amount of time developing relationships with local police officers as well as precinct captains who work for the local alderman. Both come to his aid if customers do not pay, thieves steal his tools, or the gangs harass him; conversely, the police depend on him for information on petty crimes and property theft. He has become more than simply an underground mechanic. James is a political broker in Maquis Park. Other hustlers working in Maquis Park or seeking to establish a foothold there come to James before starting their own trades. They request his assistance with police and they ask him about profitable sales spots. He charges solicitors a fee for consultation, and he may enforce a "street tax" if they remain in the area. It is common for him to use these associates to gather information on local crimes, which he then passes onto law enforcement and political officials in order to secure his own position. Conversely, he communicates to hustlers information from city officials, such as requests not to harass customers at subway stops and opportunities for "cleanup" work at special events like neighborhood parades that pay $25 to $100, depending on the work involved. In one summer period, he listed twenty-two other hustlers who worked with him in this way; in each month that summer, he earned approximately $250 through his brokerage.

By no means does James control the actions of all hustlers, nor is he the sole broker in the neighborhood. He is one of the oldest, and his sphere of influence shifts over time—always rooted in and around the alley, street corner, or empty lot where he may be working. But there are others whose social role in Maquis Park mirrors James's. They too have developed a role in community affairs. Artie Calvert is a street merchant based near the subway tracks who helps squatters find abandoned buildings where they can take up residence. Maria, who lives in a small park at the southern edge of the community, works for local store owners by finding reliable homeless persons who will work as part-time security guards. Tony sells stolen goods in James Park; he extorts small sums of money from others who perform sex work, car repair, and other underground labors there, while providing them information on free food, shelters, and sympathetic police officers. These hustlers know one another and often work together to exchange information and services.

The local character of Maquis Park's hustlers is rooted in their relationship to the underground economy. By bartering, laboring, and selling goods and services, they participate in public activities and they form a critical part of the community's effort to control behavior that compromises public safety. West Street is one of several major commercial thoroughfares that cut through Maquis Park. Traverse the strip from its eastern boundary, at the corner of James Park, over to the expressway that borders high-rise public housing developments, and a colorful use of public areas emerges. At the eastern end, Artie Monroe shines shoes for those entering the subway. Every few hours, he canvasses the block to see if other hustlers are begging or hustling in a way that might disturb his prospective customers. He does not confront each and every person, but if he finds them to be a threat, he will ask them to respect his own trade and move away; if they are not familiar faces, he may demand a tax or persuade a store owner to pressure them to leave. He works with several store managers by recruiting customers and removing loiterers. On "check day," when public assistance and social insurance payments are distributed in Chicago, Artie receives extra compensation for removing drunks and drug addicts who have celebrated that day and who have passed out in front of a store or in the back alley. Occasionally he helps proprietors find stolen goods, particularly if the value of the property is high, and he will shovel snow from driveways, sidewalks, and the parking areas in front of stores. If it rains, the managers may allow him to shine shoes inside.

Artie works with another hustler, Marion, who is twenty-one years old and disabled, and looks to Artie as "the dad I never had." Artie says he found Marion overdosed in an alley from a "bad batch of heroin. I took him to the hospital, and he came back two weeks later. He hasn't left me ever since that day." With a hint of seriousness, Artie says, "One day all this will be his!" The two help other squatters find places to live. They notify squatters about available abandoned buildings, and they make calls to landlords who will allow groups of homeless persons to live in basements during winter. Artie and Marion pay a landlord a fixed sum and then try to make a profit by recruiting people in need of shelter from the local parks and restaurants.

One landlord compared the advantages of working with Artie and Marion to that of employing trained security guards. The latter could watch over his property, but they would have no understanding of the complexities of squatting in the area.

> I used to hire this firm to drive by my buildings, check up on units where people weren't living. But the problem was that people always found a way in and my property was damaged. Artie is great because he makes sure that people stay there for only short periods of time and they really do take care of the place. You have a few people that go to the bathroom on the floor—but he cleans that up himself! I mean, I know it's not legal, but I look at it as I'm helping these people out who have nowhere to turn.

Another building owner said that working with Artie and local squatters on his property helped ensure that gangs did not store drugs in his building.

> It's just safer when you have people around. I feel sorry for the guys because they have to leave when I rent out the apartments, but when I can't find anybody to rent, I need people around. Otherwise, you got the crack users coming in, you got gangs dealing drugs, you got all sorts of people keeping their stuff there. One

time, I found about thirty car radios and stereos in a room. It was all stolen stuff, and I kept thinking I could get in trouble if I don't take care of this.

Overall, through shoe shining and landlord assistance, Artie says he earns $500 per month from May until September, $750 afterward when "shoes are dirtier and people need a place to stay because it's so cold." He is forty-seven years old and has not filed a tax return since 1986 when he left the army, could not find work, and so began to hustle. I have known Artie for over a decade and have marveled at his optimism and persistence. On only two occasions have I not found him at his assigned corner: once when he went to the hospital because a gang member assaulted him for falling asleep at a local crack den; a second time when he was asked to march in the local parade as a representative of Maquis Park.

One block to the west, a dozen men wait outside for work in an empty West Street lot. Most are general laborers who paint houses, repair plumbing, and perform landscaping for local homeowners. Some wait for general contractors in search of laborers at nearby construction sites. The composition of the group changes each week, and this lot is one of several spots in and around Maquis Park that the men rotate between, hoping to meet homeowners and potential employers. They tend to congregate early in the morning. However, the availability of work is unpredictable, and so any given day might pass with most of the assembled crowd milling about for many hours. Next to the men, a small group of homeless persons sells batteries, socks, T-shirts, videotapes, and other equipment they have stolen or bought wholesale in shopping malls at the edge of the city. They pay a hardware store owner on West Street to take them to the shopping malls once a week. They also keep unsold merchandise in the store, and in return the store owner now possesses a small security force. The hardware store manager says that since he began working with these men, he has not been robbed; previously he was robbed once every six months. An elderly woman brings hot lunches to the lot—$2 per plate. She pays off the local precinct captain for the right to sell food; the precinct captain forces other food sellers to leave the area. The men receive free coffee, donuts, and even minor medical supplies (aspirin, Band-Aids) from another store manager. The shopkeepers on the block are appreciative of this small crowd of generally well-behaved persons who stand outside. One manager, a Korean American who has been in the area for two years, described an incident in which the group came to his aid:

> Last month, this guy robbed me. With a gun, too. It was scary. But one of these guys saw it and he followed the man. I was told that he waited and brought a bunch of other guys and then walked over and got my money back. Told that guy never to come around again. I know it's not a big thing, and maybe I could have called the police. But these guys are there, they help me, and they know who's doing what. So you ask me, "Why do I give them free tools and things?" Well, business in this community isn't easy. You have to have friends. You need to have all kinds of people helping you.

One block west, Carla Henderson watches over illegally parked cars in front of the grocery store and keeps an eye out for loitering drug traffickers, while her sister Janette sells sexual services to customers inside the neighboring "Hot Time Liquors." Carla was once a beautician in Maquis Park. She quit her job because her husband was sent to jail for a murder conviction and she could not afford day care. She received public assistance for nearly a decade. After her children graduated from high school, she became a crack user. She lost her public housing lease because her sister, Janette, was using the apartment to service johns and had allowed the gang to process crack cocaine inside. With no family nearby, Carla became homeless and began working odd jobs to make a living. She has stopped using drugs, but she has a severe drinking problem. Carla and Janette work for several stores, on West Street and in local shopping malls, helping the proprietors manage drunk and disorderly customers. Carla describes her work with the stores:

> Imagine, you got this Korean couple. Lot of them own stores. Now, you think they going out there with a gun and chasing people away who ain't behaving? Hell no. That's where we come in. First, Janette and I help these poor people by making sure niggers ain't disrupting their business. You know hanging out, doing nothing . . . We also started finding lots of young women who need diapers or food or clothes, maybe for their babies and maybe for them. But they only had [food] stamps. So we get stores to pay 50¢ on the dollar for stamps. Maybe the store owner wants to get his dick sucked. We got plenty of women who'll do that! Then, we also find women who want to get their haircut or get a nice makeup thing done. We get lot of money for bringing in new business. So, yeah, we have a good thing going, but it's a lot of work.

Martin is the daytime manager of the large grocery store on West Street. He admitted to working with Carla and Janette in the food-stamp scam—whereby he pays local welfare recipients 50¢ for each food stamp dollar. However, he prefers to think of his work with Carla as partly philanthropic:

"I try to hire people to work here," said Martin. "Like kids from school, but it's very expensive. And not everyone is so reliable. Lot of people steal from me. I never thought that these homeless people would be the best people to work with."

"How do you work with them?" I asked.

"Well, a few carry groceries, you know, deliver to homes or to the cars for old people. Some will make sure people don't sit out there, playing music loudly and drinking at night. Trash doesn't get picked up, so Carla finds me somebody to make sure it's clean outside. She makes sure nobody sleeps in the alley, or sells drugs."

"What about the police, can't they help you?"

"Yes, police are good. They are very nice to me. But it takes them a long time to come and you cannot call police for every little small thing. So, these people, the homeless ones, they're quicker to help me."

"OK," I said, "but you must know these homeless people are also doing things illegally?"

Martin replied, "I know they do things, like Janette: she makes her money by selling her body. OK, so, I ask that she not do that too much inside the store, and she doesn't make life hard for me. If people sell their things, they know I don't want trouble, so they keep quiet, maybe do it out back."

Janette Henderson also works with Tony Terrell, a street hustler based in nearby James Park, by sending johns to him that are interested in stolen car radios or narcotics. The two are lovers and move about a network of abandoned buildings, where they store food and stolen merchandise, and sleep with other squatters. They are relentless, working early in the morning until the early evening, when a bottle of beer or a narcotic helps them find sleep. In a typical week, Carla earns $75 to $125. Janette and Tony can make at most $100 to $150.

Down the road from the Henderson sisters, the Jackson brothers sit outside a cheap blue nylon tent, replete with a cooler of beer and soda and food donated by the local stores. They welcome "welfare mommas" who are hoping to find a store owner who will work with them on a food-stamp scam or who are looking for fake social security cards. Bill Jackson says, "These welfare mommas are our lifeblood, but now they got rid of [public assistance], we got to diversify, so we're going into real estate." By that, the brothers are alluding to their newfound venture: they receive $5 per night from a rental agency to prevent homeless persons and sex workers from sleeping and using drugs in several unused properties on the block. They earn additional money by sending prospective renters of single-room-occupancy apartments to local real estate brokers. Both Jackson brothers, Bill and "Babycake," weigh 350 pounds and receive a monthly disability check ($200 each). In their youth, Bill and Babycake were the heart of a popular singing group in Maquis Park. In the eighties, they were local *wunderkinder,* well on their way to recording a popular R&B album, with stardom not far away. They suffered a setback: Bill joined a street gang and began trafficking guns to Maquis Park from the suburbs. Babycake joined him—reluctantly, he says—because he had no other options at the time. "I was young at the time, needed cash, had no work. And that's a great business around here, guns. Big money, *tall* money. Good work if you can get it." Now, they sing each Saturday and Sunday at several storefront churches.

Drawing on their uncle's connections with local landlords, the Jackson brothers now rest their entrepreneurial aspirations on expanding their security services for proprietors. They have twenty-five men, almost all of them hustlers or homeless persons, that they can call on to sleep inside unused properties. Work is not steady, but there is usually a handful of persons they can find to perform these services, which nets them about $100 every two weeks:

> "Ever heard that line: 'I could've been somebody?'" Babycake asked me, one blistering hot summer day as we drank beer outside his tent.
>
> "Yes, why do you ask?"
>
> "That's how I feel about my life. Our life. Well, I guess the good thing is that we never gave up."
>
> "You guys make more money than any of these other hustlers," I interrupted.
>
> "That's true, but in the long run, where will we be? We will probably never starve. I mean it's funny because we should be in real estate. You know how we make most of our money? Just the other day, this cat from the rental agency asked me where the hot areas are around here. I told him exactly what block to buy, what to develop, where people wanted to rent. Hell, I found him renters. We got tons of people, just coming out of jail maybe, just got their first job, who need a place. Maybe we should have started our own agency."
>
> "Why don't you?" I ask.
>
> "Yeah, I don't know. Easier just sitting here. Someday, though, maybe someday."

In the last few blocks before West Street intersects a large public housing complex and an expressway a bit further along, on any given day roughly two dozen hustlers can be seen stirring up business. There are familiar faces, like James Arleander who has set up his car repair service. But others come around less frequently and contribute to the changing entrepreneurial potpourri on sidewalks, alleyways, and adjacent streets. "Madame Connie" begs people for change and will, in her words, "suck a dick, turn a trick, make your magic," for $5. "Pops" and his fellow recyclers comb through trash cans and solicit store managers for aluminum, copper wire, and other recyclable goods; occasionally they will offer to clean floors and bathrooms, or run errands for a proprietor, in exchange for the right to peruse trash before it hits the alleyway receptacles.

Throughout the busy street, there are hustlers who move about looking for work while avoiding the wrath of those who have already established right of access to specific public areas. These transient hustlers may have a relationship to a physical area like the regular hustlers on West Street, but theirs is an itinerant life, born of the need to keep moving to find garbage and construction sites that they can scour for recyclable objects. They may also have relationships with shopkeepers and elected officials, but unlike Artie and his colleagues who hustle on West Street regularly, these are not typically restricted to a geographic area. They may, for example, be on good terms with a contractor who notifies them of new construction projects where they can roam in search of material and scraps, or they may have relationships with different restaurant owners who expect them to come by and pick up cans and food. This can mean that, over a given day, they will travel far greater distances than those regular hustlers who have established themselves on West Street.

Given these hustlers' desperation and outright poverty, it is easy to imagine them constantly fighting with each other, vying for resources and moneymaking schemes. At times, there are indeed disputes and disagreements, and a squabble or physical fight ensues. From the outside world, we might picture a Hobbesian world of fierce competition for the meager monies and hustles that are available. And yet, trust and cooperation generally trump strife. Even when there are visible, and at times violent, disputes, hustlers draw on shared codes of conduct that help resolve conflicts before they get out of hand. "We never hustle each other, usually," said James Arleander, describing the relationships among the hustlers. "Everyone is struggling, we don't go for the kill with one another. We try to be compassionate." James's statement complicates the conventional view of hustlers and homeless persons as dispossessed and loners, when in fact, in a community like Maquis Park, they have an elaborate and carefully cultivated social order.[6] A closer look at their own internal relations reveals a social system that deters situations that could be dangerous (whether to one's health or one's wallet) and keeps a relative peace.

As if reciting a prepared speech, Maquis Park's hustlers are quick to extol their camaraderie. They recognize that their own capacity to generate income is contingent on a certain degree of safety and predictability in the human traffic on and around West Street. They acknowledge that their own interests match those of proprietors and police, both of whom are invested in safeguarding public access for customers. But most hustlers downplay their self-interested behavior, which they say is "survival" and a part of all entrepreneurial activity. Instead, they emphasize their individual role in a human community of "social vulnerables"—Bill Jackson's phrase to describe that mass of hustlers who inhabit public space.

> Don't you think it's strange, that the ones who ain't got nothing, not even a roof over their head, we're the ones who are caring for each other. We are the social vulnerables, the ones who really un-

derstand, I mean really understand, that you can't live alone, you always need somebody . . . If you're rich, you always can buy a hotel, a friend. But, lot of us have nothing in our pockets. We have to know how to live with each other or else we couldn't get by. See, this is what you must understand about the ghetto, about this community.

When I asked Artie Monroe, "Bill Jackson says you guys are 'social vulnerables.' Do you agree and, if so, what does that mean to you?" he responded in similar terms.

I know what B. J. [Bill Jackson] means. Yes I do. We are the ones at the bottom, the ones you all have forgotten about. We are struggling, doing whatever to make a dollar, but don't write about us like we're greedy sons of bitches, okay? Write about how we make sure we all sleep at night safe, somewhere. That we share our food. Yeah, if you come around where I'm doing business, I'll get pissed at you. Yes sir. I'm protecting my livelihood. But at night, I may try and find you to make sure you ain't sleeping in the cold. Would you do that for the people you associate with?

It is not a purely philanthropic practice that Bill and Artie describe. "Social vulnerables" share a similar labor market position (with few meaningful employment prospects), compromised housing status (characterized by squatting and homelessness), and an inability to access private spaces for more than brief periods. In the ghetto, they are brought together by their public visibility. Not only do they work outside, but they eat and sleep there. They often urinate and defecate openly, and their sexuality is similarly on display for other hustlers who stay with them in abandoned buildings and alleys. The full range of emotions they experience is well within the reach of others who choose to care. Most do not.

But they are attentive to each other's needs. Sometimes this means simply turning away while a friend relieves himself.[7] Other times the effort requires greater attention, such as helping a fellow hustler find medical care. Over the course of one bitterly cold winter stretch, I observed several hustlers bringing blankets to people sleeping in parks; some took homeless persons into their own illegal abode—however crowded it may have already been—and others canvassed the area persuading men and women to patronize the local shelters. None of them was paid for this work; none of them had a formal tie to an advocacy organization or transitional housing center. And they did not believe that the city's human service agencies would be following in their footsteps.

In Carla Henderson's opinion, people who don't live this life not only fail to pay attention to the hustler and her plight, but they are unaware of the social support that this subgroup provides one another. In an ironic twist, she says that this inattention shields the hustlers, so their shame does not end up a source of embarrassment.

> "I'm not saying we don't hear what people say about us, don't see that they look down on us," says Carla. "You just find ways to do your business and keep things from people. Look at you. You known me, now, how long? Five years?"
>
> "Yes," I replied, "and I've known your sister [Janette] longer."
>
> "Yeah, and you been with us day and night, right? Ever seen us eat? Ever seen us take a bath? Ever see us taking shit, wiping our ass?"
>
> "No," I said.

"You know I read the paper every day? Remember that weekend, you were here for the whole time, you remember? I bet you didn't see me read the paper. You probably think I can't read. You know I like crosswords."

"Okay, now you're lying." I said, shaking my head.

"Okay, well, I don't do the crosswords that good, mostly because I don't have a pen! But I try. And I'm just saying, when you out on the streets, you learn to keep things private, to yourself. Even when you can't get no privacy, even when you can't close a door behind you. You know the Jackson Brothers, the big one, "Babycake"? He has this problem where he has to shit every twenty minutes? Where do you think he goes? I bet your never noticed how he takes care of it. See, now, you're going to watch him, I know you! I know how your mind operates. But you still ain't never, ever, I mean *never* going to see me getting my groove on. And I do daily, my friend . . . You just move on, each day, God willing."

With so much of their life lived out in public, the street hustlers and the general squatting and homeless populations are attuned to one another's habits and movements. In one six-month period, November 1998 to April 1999, I documented the sleeping arrangements of area hustlers. In six abandoned buildings, four basements, seven stores, and five vacant units in and around West Street, sixty-five hustlers moved about, sharing shelter. By spring, the arrangements shifted due to many factors, including health problems that drove people into the hospital, criminal issues that sent people to jail, lack of income that motivated some to find hustles in nearby communities, and numerous arguments, conflicts, and accusations of theft, adultery, and so on that forced individuals to move. Fourteen of these sixty-five individuals distributed food and notices of available shelter—sometimes for a fee, more often for free. Three women passed out free blankets and winter clothing they had collected from local churches; two other men used a stolen cell phone to call city emergency services as they came upon distressed homeless persons in parks and alleyways.

Artie, Carla, Jay-Bird, James, and the other hustlers on West Street know one another, as well as most of the other men and women who walk by. Knowing the ins and outs of their community is what makes their livelihood possible. A good part of their lives is spent watching each other, drumming up business, and finding shelter. But "social vulnerability" requires a fine line between beneficence and self-interest. They are attuned to the desperation that pushes hustlers to take advantage of one another. They may help one another find shelter or aid in times of need, but they cannot let their guard down. Artie attributes his vigilant surveillance of other West Street hustlers to an "optimistic paranoia" that tempers his trust of fellow streetcorner persons.

> "Most of the time," Artie said, "you have a fairly peaceful situation. You help me and I help you. But it's a jungle out here. We all are looking for a place to set up, make money, but it's rough, because there are so many of us out of work. I call it optimistic paranoia. And you got the young kids now, never had work, not like me, I worked in the factories, I wasn't always out here."
>
> "So, on this block," I asked him, "how does it work? It seems like a mess of people. How can you say that you 'control' this area by the subway? There must be about fifty people out here now, and half have already asked me for money, some have asked me for drugs."
>
> "See, you see chaos, just a mess," replied Artie. "But when Mister Watson got his shoe store burned down, who did he call?

When Ishmael had that shooting inside his store . . . He called me. So, yes, you have a lot of hustlers, but there are hustlers *and then there are hustlers*. And we know which is which."

"But that still doesn't get at my question," I persisted. "Do you get money from all of these people hustling on 'your' block? And if you don't, how can you say you 'control' it?"

"Up and down West Street," Artie said as he pointed westward, "you can use the sidewalks, but at any point, there is somebody that can say, 'Get the fuck off and go somewhere else' and you have to listen. It could be me, it could be another nigger, it could be Carla, it could be a [gang member]. Now, there are just way too many people for me to worry about. The most important thing is that I keep my relations with all the people in the stores and the police. That's the first thing, you dig? Now, I also have to watch over people like James [Arleander]."

"Why? I thought each hustler had their area?"

"No. Now remember: there are niggers and then there are *niggers*. James, if he goes in and starts talking to Ishmael [the store owner], tells him he can help him keep his area clean or get these niggers out of the front area, where they hang out? Well, he may do what I can do, you see, and he may do it for cheaper, so I have to watch all the time, see if James is over here talking to people, playing me."

"How can you *possibly* keep track of all of that?" I asked, incredulously. "That's impossible to watch over."

"You learn a lot of skills when you live on the street. And remember, I spend my whole life here! Like I said, most of these people are just passing by, just making a few bucks day to day. That's cool. But I try to provide [store owners] more than that. I offer them a service when things go wrong. And, you know, I help out hustlers. You saw me [ten minutes ago] find that boy a shelter;

I sent him over to that [abandoned] building. Didn't charge him a penny. See, I'm not an evil person. It's complicated, and it's hard when you don't have no place to stay, no place to make money or nothing. The streets is what you need to understand, what you breathe each day."

As Artie suggests, situations change quickly and, as people adapt, old relationships dissolve and new ones form. At any one time there may be established understandings among street hustlers, and between street hustlers and the wider citizenry, over the use of public spaces. But the same restless energy, born of impoverishment and spiraling toward appropriation of public areas, can also foster impermanence and the need to manage tensions arising in one's relationships.

Crucial to a hustler's success is a vigilant eye, to survey the ever-shifting scene, and the flexibility to change one's situation to fit new circumstances—because in the ghetto, competition can come from anywhere. There are two basic kinds of competitive behavior, each of which provokes a different reaction among street hustlers. The first is competition between hustlers who have an established presence on a street (in a park, at a shopping center). These can occur daily. How hustlers react is shaped by the fact that these individuals need one another for support. In particular the temptation for vengeance is muted. If they were to respond strongly to every encroachment, they would have little time left to earn a living and find a secure place to rest. Sometimes these networks are based on geographical features, such as major thoroughfares like West Street, where hustlers have known one other for months, if not years. In Chicago's Southside, one can also find many small hustling clusters that are not rooted in any particular locale. Up to a dozen persons might migrate together, moving about the neighborhoods, colonizing abandoned buildings together, stealing and selling merchandise cooperatively, and otherwise devising schemes with one another.

In the second form of competition, someone outside the familiar social group is the predator. On West Street, nearly every day newcomers develop relationships with merchants or peddle their wares on the street. The local hustlers continually fend off such threats to their livelihood. Artie, James, and their West Street counterparts vigilantly watch over the transient hustlers who might set up shop in an alleyway, street corner, or other accessible region near West Street. They may not ask the person in question to leave, but they will be sure to monitor the newcomer's behavior. Their greatest fear is that the individual might eventually try to take over their own hustle or bring in other hustlers and saturate the area.

On one day in autumn—typically the season in which hustlers strengthen their connection with merchants in order to secure a stable relationship for the upcoming winter—the Jackson brothers watched Cornelius "Bird" McKinley pull his aging brown van in behind them, in an empty lot on West Street. Bird is a famous Southside hustler. He moves about the community with stolen merchandise, anything from car stereos to jewelry to wigs. He is a magnet for thrifty shoppers as well as for scandalous thieves who need to quickly rid themselves of stolen goods. He will usually buy the contraband, but if it is expensive jewelry or electronic equipment that he cannot afford to purchase outright, he will sell on consignment. I sat with the Jackson brothers, sharing a beer, and watched as they expressed concern over Bird's recent arrival.

"You better worry, nigger, when Bird rocks in town. Nigger will take over everything, leave you with nothing. That's why they call him Bird. Should call the brother Vulture, since he just leaves behind bones after he's done with you."

"I know him, I've known him for years," I countered. "Man is harmless as a crippled cat. Wouldn't hurt nobody, just sells his stuff."

Babycake broke out in laughter. "Oh, man! You are ignorant. You ain't learned shit since you been here. Bird sells his shit, yeah, but you know what he does. He takes business away from you. See, there he goes! He's going into Leon's store. I bet he'll ask Leon, 'Do you feel safe? Do you need to get rid of anything?'"

"So? Why would Leon even deal with him?" I asked.

"See, what Bird does is set up somewhere, real innocent like. Then, a month later, he's got about ten people around him, they're selling food, some are shining shoes. I mean this brother is like a little king or something. Then, if you selling food, you are run out of business, or if you cleaning cars, Bird finds you someone new who'll give you a better deal. Never trust Bird."

Later that night, Babycake and Bill Jackson, and their friend Tony Terrell, approached Bird and threatened to assault him if he did not leave West Street. At first Bird refused. Then Tony started beating on Bird's van and tried to flatten his tires. Bird quickly jumped in the van and moved on to another location, much to the relief of the West Street hustlers.

Once every few weeks, a West Street hustler will describe an incident in which an unfamiliar face arrives on West Street and challenges someone for the right to hawk goods at a particular public spot. Most of the competition from outside parties is over access to public space. Although eruptions are not common, hustlers know they are possible and so mentally prepare themselves for the need to physically defend their territory. (Alternatively, in the case of transients usurping new areas, they know they may have to use force when colonizing a new sales spot.)

Established hustlers like the West Street contingent monitor local pedestrian traffic because they might have to leave their own location from time to time. They worry that others might occupy their corner, alley, or street corner while they are gone. Given their precarious state, it is not altogether rare to hear of a local hustler who, suffering a bout of bad health, ends up in an emergency room at a hospital for a short period of time. Moreover, these men and women experience frequent run-ins with the police, who send them to jail; an officer who is in a good mood might simply require the hustler to go to a shelter and leave the area for a few weeks. Some hustlers view jail with a mix of apprehension and relief. Carla, a West Street hustler, says she "disappears" from Maquis Park for several months at a time by going to jail:

> You're going to think this is funny. But if you're poor, you *need* jail. You really do. That's where I disappear to. The food is good and it's better in the winter; the people are okay to you, except for the guards that try to get up in your kootchie. And you get some peace. I mean, you have to know when to go! You can't go right after [check day] when everyone's in there because they're drunk. No. You go middle of the week, slow time, get a few days, get rested, get warm. See, everyone around here does that. That's why we know the cops so well; we see them all the time. They're like our landlords.

As Carla states, living with unfamiliar faces in a cramped cell is not the desired option because of the chance of physical assault. But relative to shelters, for example, some hustlers prefer jail because there they do not have to leave each morning at six o'clock—as they would in a shelter. And their preferences are accommodated in other ways: Cook County Correctional officers will separate hustlers from other arrestees whom they may believe to be more dangerous. One jail attendant at Cook County Jail said, "It's not official policy, but we don't stick these homeless people who, you know, just need a night to rest. We don't put them in with the rapists, or even burglars. These guys—and some women—come in all the time. They don't mean harm; they may just need to get out of the cold. I don't know, I guess I got a lot of feeling for these people. They work their tail off, they get arrested, and I know they do things wrong, but they are just desperate, they just need to survive."

As we have seen, hustlers do not exist in a vacuum, negotiating only with each other. Their success also depends upon their ability to navigate relationships with those in the wider community. Store owners and store managers, for example, struggle to control public traffic on the sidewalk, particularly at their front door, and commonly hire homeless persons to work as sales clerks and security personnel inside their stores. Hustlers are experts on the use of public space. So it is not surprising, perhaps, that store owners and managers turn to hustlers as an immediate resource. Indeed, the two have compatible interests. Both require a base of customers who feel safe, can enter and leave stores unharmed, and know how to find what they are looking for. Unruly customers, drug dealers, and a general mass of people hanging out on sidewalks and streets make it difficult for customers to enter stores. The manager on duty must devote considerable energy to patrolling external areas. One of the most important services the hustlers provide is to help manage and coordinate the pedestrian and commercial traffic in and around the store. On occasion, street hustlers may offer the practical benefit of tracking down shoplifters, recruiting customers, and advertising services, but more often they help the manager on duty by ensuring that people do not loiter too long, that customers do not drink alcohol on site, and that street peddlers do not disturb customers or inhibit access to the store. Some stores hire security firms, but the local hustler likely has a personal knowledge of the client base and can influence local pedestrian behavior in a way that does not always escalate into conflict. A street hustler can persuade, cajole, and otherwise work with a troublemaker in a diplomatic and efficient manner. Security guards and police officers may be more forceful in their work, but they often face problems from disruptive, boisterous clientele who challenge their authority.

It bears repeating that the hustlers who offer merchants these services are not necessarily looking for additional income. They may not even be driven by the need for money. In fact, it is quite common for hustlers to instead request in-kind remuneration services from the local shopkeepers and store managers. Many have other entrepreneurial schemes that they are busy managing, whether begging or fixing cars, and so need a private sheltered space. James Arleander articulates a typical hustler viewpoint:

> You can always make money. Money can come from anywhere, if you have some kind of initiative. But getting a place is priceless. That's the hardest thing, to just have some place to keep your shit, go take a shit, rest, hide from police or people who may be upset at you. We're out in the open, we are vulnerable. Very vulnerable. So, any place we have, we really guard it. And that's why you see us hanging out around the same areas. See, the ones who have a place to go to, they look like they just doing nothing, just sitting around.

But that's not true, they have the most business going on. It's the ones who are moving, the vagrants. They're the ones who are begging, borrowing, stealing.

As James intimates, a relationship with a proprietor may lead to the use of a restroom, storage space for personal belongings, and a place to rest or sleep during inclement weather. Richard Watkins has owned a clothing store in Maquis Park for twenty years, and he has taken pains to include the hustler population in his work.

> They have this kind of know-how, it's really amazing. Like, for instance, when kids talk about what styles they like, on the bus or in the park, there is probably one of these guys around just listening, even though they look like they are sleeping or not paying attention! Michael, he's been working for me, part of the family, you know. I pay him, I don't pay him much, but he gets to sleep here, he cleans up, he stocks the floor with the new clothes. You know, he does painting and construction, don't you? So I let him pass out his little flyers to customers. He tells them he can fix their houses.

Not every proprietor provides hustlers these services. But over time, sympathies develop between the two and monetary exchanges begin to be supplemented with these in-kind offerings.

Apart from the proprietors and their staff, the police express some of the greatest support for local hustlers. This may seem contradictory since officers who patrol the streets are continuously faced with problems that arise from street hustlers working in public space. The officers find themselves responding to residents and stakeholders, like political officials and landlords, who complain about the inability to walk through streets and public parks safely. They are asked repeatedly to locate jobs for these vagrant men and women, prevent them from using parks as public restrooms, and otherwise exile them from the neighborhood. But in Maquis Park contradictions are commonplace, and the police often rely on just these hustlers to solve other problems.

Hustlers create a variety of problems in Maquis Park, and there are approximately one dozen police officers who work to navigate relationships between West Street hustlers and other members of the community. Some work solely with a small set of store owners and managers by helping them create a safe business climate. In practice, this means mediating exchanges between hustlers and those who employ them. These beat cops usually work to ensure that hustlers do not steal from the store and do not violate any underground arrangements in place between shopkeeper and hustlers in their service. Other officers help Parks Department personnel deal with hustlers who sleep in recreational areas or use park areas for economic purposes. They may forcibly remove individuals or ask that they congregate in areas away from children. This is not easy, because hustlers gravitate to playgrounds, baseball fields, and basketball courts to find customers. And on occasion one may find law enforcement assisting landlords who want to remove squatters and homeless persons from their property. Complaints rarely come from the landlords, because many live in other parts of the city; more often, residents and resident organizations like block clubs and church associations will call the police. Police officers undertake these labors cautiously, as they risk public criticism if they are discovered to be tolerant of crime and vagrancy.

"Community policing" meetings are the formal venue in which law enforcement officials hear reports of public safety problems.[8]

In Maquis Park, residents attending these discussions routinely identify incidents involving local hustlers. Such problems include harassment on streets, use of abandoned buildings for drug sales, prostitution, encampments in local parks, and urination and defecation on lawns, in alleys, and around private yards. The following exchange, at one Maquis Park Community Policing meeting, exemplifies resident complaints as well as the police response.

A forty-something woman, holding a child, stood up and asked the police official a question, her voice rising as her speech continued.

"I am a mother, I have the right to walk around. I have the right to have my children stand outside. I pay taxes, I want to use my local park. Now, that man who sells socks, he harasses me, just like all them other squatters. They smell, they come over and play with my kids. They steal things. Why are they there? Why are they allowed to sleep there?"

The police official responded, slightly exasperated, "Excuse me, Ms. Williams, do you have a particular problem that occurred? That would be more helpful."

"I got many problems. People hooting at me if I wear a short dress. People peeing on my lawn, people taking a shit right there in the park where my children are playing. People selling things! If I want to buy something, I'll go to the store."

"Yes, Ms. Williams," the police official replied, his patience being tested. "We understand. Now, we can't get all these people out, because they have the right to use the park too. And, you know, they are going to sell things somewhere, and we do try and get them not to harass people."

"Not to harass people?" Ms. Williams exclaimed, putting down her child. "Your job is not to help them do their business, but to get them out of there. This ain't a shopping mall. They're dealing drugs!"

Residents are aware of the relationships between street hustlers and local merchants. They even acknowledge that hustlers make a contribution to public safety despite turning local areas into commercial theaters. A small number also recognize the effective role of police who have developed informal techniques for dealing with hustlers. However, such concessions do not staunch their criticism of police. Nor do they downplay the belief that police should be the only guarantor of social order. Hustlers, in other words, should not be directing public traffic. Even Marlene Matteson, one of the residents who works intimately with police in informal dispute resolution and who routinely mediates problems between hustlers and residents behind the scenes, is vocal in her belief that police are abdicating their responsibility to deal effectively with what she calls "street thugs." She recently worked with a police officer to settle a dispute between a store manager who refused to pay a street hustler his $20 daily fee because the hustler failed to prevent two shoplifting incidents that day. When I asked her how she could simultaneously work alongside the police while criticizing them for partaking in the same backroom diplomacy, she replied:

> There's a difference between doing something when something bad happens, and just thinking it's okay that folks ain't doing their job. If I didn't work with [Officer] Blue and get that man his money [$20], then that store would've been robbed or burned down. So, I don't have a choice. And Officer Blue doesn't either. But if you had police up and down that street all day, doing what they're supposed, and if you had the mayor making sure these

stores ain't exploiting these street thugs, giving them $20 and making them work like dogs, well maybe me and Blue wouldn't have to be doing what we're doing.

Those police actively involved in Maquis Park, particularly those who respond to hustlers and to disputes in public areas, feel that cooperation with hustlers is inevitable and even beneficial. One officer summarized the law enforcement approach.

> Let's be real. The realistic way is the best way. Think about it. From our standpoint, you can have three kinds of people in those places: you can have a mom and her kid, you can have a gangbanger sell dope, or you can have some of these people who don't have anywhere else to go. I mean do you want a gang banger out there? No. And so these men, who don't have a job, who have a lot of problems—they're on drugs, they drink, they're going to be there everyday. You can't get rid of them. So you use these men—and the women too—to get information. You find out what's happening by getting them to tell you what they see. And believe me, they see everything. And you make sure you take care of the little things before they blow up. Somebody beat somebody up, somebody stole somebody's blanket? We try to deal with it before it gets way out of hand.

This officer's views are typical of law enforcement officials who work in Maquis Park. Namely, street hustlers are a potential threat to public space, but there is little chance of removing them from the community altogether. Thus, officers must employ an alternate strategy—other than outright removal, one grounded in a quid pro quo wherein the police tolerate some street hustling while using the street traders to gather information on crimes. In this manner, street hustlers along West Street have developed a symbiotic relationship both with merchants and with the police. All three have an interest in maintaining accessible public spaces suitable for pedestrian traffic. So, the parties have developed ways of working with one another to ensure that their personal needs are met.

The dynamics of hustling on the streets and alleyways most probably differ from the organization of commerce and daily interaction in the vast majority of American communities where the boundaries between public and private space are perceptibly defined. In the ghetto, safe and habitable public space is at a premium for households. Indeed, for that matter, one cannot always take it for granted that a private business will be accommodating for customers or that a household dwelling will be pleasurable and free of stress and strain. The presence of a large poor population, unable to afford basic rent and household expenditures, combined with a down-and-out group of men and women seeking out every opportunity to survive and make a buck, makes for constantly shifting, and sometimes unpredictable and dangerous use of all spaces where people gather and conduct their affairs. It means that ghetto residents spend an inordinate amount of time trying to find and create safe places, whether for child rearing or simply to rest after a long day's work.

Yet, in a community like Maquis Park, even though poverty is entrenched and hardship and city neglect have affected families for generations, it is important to recognize that life does not stand still. The arrangements among hustlers, police, and merchants that enable local actors to eke out some measure of safety and security are temporary and always subject to change. As with Carla (a West Street hustler), the local street-based population can face health problems that send them to the hospital or criminal problems that land them in jail. And in these cases they rely on help from police, who may ensure that they are not beaten up in jail and that their court case moves along smoothly. Today, however, the use of the "beat cop," who may have long-term relationships with local residents and businesspersons, is no longer standard law enforcement practice. There is turnover among the officers who are assigned to work in Maquis Park. So it is less frequent that hustlers and police get to know one another on a continuous basis. One officer, Matthew Naismith, had been working in Maquis Park for about a month when he offered these comments on the local hustlers:

> It's amazing; I mean, I grew up in Marquette Park. You know, white, Irish mostly. No homeless people. But here, wow. I mean I see that these people work with stores, they know who the criminals are, they know what the problems are in the community. I'm just trying to play catch-up. I see a lot of other cops, they use these [hustlers] all the time. But I'm not there yet. I'm still learning who they are. I can see they don't trust me. And, you know, I don't trust them. Not just yet. But I respect them. I got to admit that I do.

These same officers may also need to develop a discriminatory ear when residents cry out that hustlers are invading parks, loitering on streets, and otherwise making public space insecure. They may need to listen to the complaints while understanding that there are extant working relationships between shopkeepers, residents, hustlers, and police that help keep the peace. It may take some time for Officer Naismith to acquire this knowledge, and his ability to "catch up" might depend not only on his own capacity to listen and be diplomatic, but also on the existence of other police around him who can transmit their knowledge and expertise. Yet with turnover, these experienced officers—the ones who understand the shady world and the role of hustlers in it—may come and go with little opportunity to pass on their wisdom.

The merchant population is also dynamic. Shops close and proprietors relocate their businesses, and it can take a new store owner months, if not years, to feel comfortable working with local hustlers—as opposed to simply shooing them away from their shops. For those persons who were raised and continue to live in Maquis Park, comfort with hustlers may not be long in the offing, but among newly arrived merchants it is not always an inevitable consequence of their presence in the community. Here, it is important to include the voices of those shopkeepers who simply find no use for this population. One hardware store manager in Maquis Park was unyielding in his view that local street vendors and hustlers should be removed from the community.

> I've been here five years. I'm from this community. I'm tired of all these people hanging out. Now, I go to my sister's house on the North Side. I don't see people selling, I don't see no prostitutes in the back sucking dick. Why do we have to have this here? I will never accept it, and I'm very upset at all these people who give [hustlers] work. I'm not paying them, no sir. I'm not giving in to this. We could all do better to get police to fix our streets and keep things safe for people.

It would be unfair to suggest that this view is rare and that merchants are entirely uncritical of local hustlers. Even those shopkeepers who have established productive relationships with the hustling population nevertheless express frustration at having to accommodate this street presence. For these reasons, and because of the internal competition that exists over opportunities to work and make money, hustling is never secure and it takes a great deal of work for street based vendors and traders to stay in one place over time.

Jane Jacobs offered the classic theory of how public order is maintained in the city with her notion of "eyes on the street," the *ur*-concept for modernist planning in terms of creating safe urban spaces.[9] Jacobs drew on the vitality of New York City's streets—primarily the West Village neighborhood in Manhattan—to develop ideas regarding the important role that private citizens play in public space management. Her theory suggests that vibrant thoroughfares, which combine commerce and pedestrian fellowship, are an ideal type of informal social control. The "sidewalk" plays an important role, in her view, as an interstitial area that separates the private activities of inhabitants—including both domestic life and legal store-based commerce—from the rapid movements of motorized vehicles.[10] Where there is continuous activity, one has a greater chance to deter criminal and nuisance activities.

In urban ghettos, where underground activity is publicly prominent, there may still be "eyes on the street" approaches where passersby, hustlers, and other local inhabitants police each other's activities. However, the system of regulation and social control of behavior will differ from that of a largely white and bourgeois Manhattan locale. On the inner-city sidewalks and street corners, there are many kinds of entrepreneurs—shopkeepers, pedestrians, gang members, thieves, street hustlers, prostitutes, and so on. Their particular interests are not always clear and discernible, and therefore individuals must be "streetwise" and wary of each other's presence and interest.[11] Moreover, because official policing is never adequate, there may be many parties that play a role in controlling public behavior—even as they contribute to the disruption—in a way that mimics law enforcement. In the context of hustling, some of these parties may be contributing to public safety while disrupting the free use of public space.

In ghettos or in tony bourgeois enclaves, police may be formally responsible for protecting person and property, but in practice they do not necessarily fulfill this role. Jacobs's theory placed a stronger emphasis on the casual kinds of self-policing that can occur as people negotiate with one another over the use of sidewalks for right of way or access to store entrances. She paid less attention to the dynamics in the ghetto, where one finds that *non*governmental entities play a more formal, locally recognized, and legitimated role in policing, particularly when illicit activities threaten people or compromise their ability to access and utilize public areas of the community. In Maquis Park, residents and advocates do lobby police and politicians to stamp out both heinous behavior, like prostitution and drug trafficking, and nuisance activities like car repair in local parks.[12] But at the same time, they work out compromises directly with underground entrepreneurs or with informal mediators, such as the clergy. They thereby supplement official bodies in order to acquire immediate, timely solutions to security and access problems. Some of these private bodies may be vigilante in nature—street gangs, leaders of organized crime, and the like—while others may be mundane, like a block club president or a local homeless person.

It would be a mistake to suggest that law enforcement agencies are absent. Instead, they must operate in a milieu in which multiple actors effectively police public behavior and enforce codes of conduct, where many of the codes are not the rules on the books. In fact, it is not just residents who complain about regulating public space. Law enforcement and elected officials report their own dilemmas when it comes to providing effective policing for the urban poor. They hold shady types like gangs and thieves in disregard, and in official statements they are loathe to cooperate with them directly, or to employ any intermediaries, for that matter. But as we have seen, police may work informally with the local residents, merchants, and other stakeholders to acquire information, settle conflicts, and prosecute offenses. Like other public officials, their public claims to being "tough on crime" are tempered by private admissions that they are unable to adequately respond to the high levels of crime and social problems in inner cities.

As the police repeatedly point out, it is impossible for them to respond to every transgression. So they routinely adopt alternate strategies to promote collective safety, especially in an area where residents' involvement in criminality is shaped by their own need to make ends meet by deriving illegal income. These strategies may be highly informal, such as private agreements with residents and secretive mediation routines. One of the essential components of good policing strategy, identified by Jane Jacobs, is an officer's ability to develop relationships with shopkeepers and residents. It may mean making compromises, such as retaining troublemakers as sources of information rather than removing them outright from the streets. Securing reliable informants is nothing new and has always been an ingredient in good law enforcement. One might say that police are faced with irreconcilable demands: on the one hand, their responsibilities are to prevent crime and keep public areas habitable; on the other hand, doing so may mean tolerating some degree of illegal behavior and using perpetrators effectively and secretively to respond to crime.

In the nineties, Chicago gained notoriety for formalizing the old-fashioned "beat" patrols and instituting outreach strategies intended to improve relationships between law enforcement agencies and citizens.[13] Although this approach varies considerably by neighborhood, there has been an attempt by city officials to institute "community policing" in all areas. It is a favorite program of the mayor and is characterized by periodic meetings where residents express their problems and cite transgressions directly to attentive law enforcement emissaries. In theory, officers will then investigate the crimes and report back to community stakeholders. It is difficult to gauge the utility of the community policing meetings in Maquis Park, because few residents attend— except on occasion to complain directly about inadequate police services—and the issues raised there do not tend to involve underground economic matters. I have heard few, if any, expressions of support for this strategy from residents, local shopkeepers, clergy, or nonresidents who have a direct investment in safety-related issues there. The dynamics among police, hustlers, and local actors point to a suppler framework for redress and maintenance of social order, one that is so much a part of daily life that even the participants themselves do not immediately recognize it as being efficacious.

When one approaches the physical ecology from the perspective of economic regulation, one sees not only the immediate challenge of ensuring safe passage, but also the status of the inner city with respect to broader social institutions. In the ghetto the underground economy reconstitutes the character of public spaces, and residents are faced with competing demands that ultimately shape their use of common areas. Many lobby police and politicians to stamp out both heinous behavior, like prostitution and drug trafficking, and nuisance activities like car repair in local parks, but simultaneously they may work out compromises directly with underground entrepreneurs. The net effect of acting on one's own is to promote the very form of privatization of public space that makes such places uninhabitable or unsuitable for gathering. In other words, without a legitimate third-party agent, like the police, who has the consent of all parties to enforce laws and maintain order, it is difficult to see how long-term stability and security can be promoted. Thus, in the absence of legitimate and effective law enforcement and criminal justice institutions, it is entirely reasonable to see hustlers as playing a central and productive role in the life of a ghetto community.

The roles that James Arleander and his street-hustling colleagues play in Maquis Park, as partly "eyes on the street" that watch over behavior, contradict the conventional wisdom that streetcorner people make minimal social contributions—that they are criminals, a nuisance, a drain on public resources. Yet Maquis Park is in many ways not a conventional urban community. One example of this is that street hustlers occupy a central and possibly quite productive position in everyday affairs. They grease the underground economic engine and, more broadly, help the community sputter along by helping it function. James has received requests for help from Marlene, a block club president who, like most parents, is concerned about the safety of her children and her neighbors. A street gang leader has approached James, hoping to capitalize on the hustler's proven capacity to help monitor illegal activity on streets and back alleys. Other hustlers work with the clergy to settle disputes, with merchants to monitor shoplifters, and with landlords to safeguard property.

Of course, what one takes as evidence of being a "legitimate" member of the Maquis Park community may be at odds with the standards in the wider world. The help that James gives to a concerned parent might be socially valued by any urban actor, whereas his clandestine support of the gang's drug trafficking is likely to be viewed as suspect by those outside the inner city and by many living inside it.

Nevertheless, street hustlers do have some legitimacy in dilapidated areas where the local economy and the overall capacity to inhabit public and private areas are organized in relatively unique ways. The fact that the hustler plays many different roles is a testament to the constantly shifting nature of everyday life in the ghetto. At any one time, his interests may collide or fuse with those of a number of other actors, and he may be alternately perceived by his neighbors and colleagues to be predator, regulator, or prey. As predator, he raises the ire of those who want their neighborhoods to be free of street persons who hawk goods, sleep, and make their homes in public areas. In ghetto and suburb alike, these kinds of practices are a nuisance and, at times, a threat. But the hustler can also be instrumental to other actors in regulating space. His role in the community may be legitimated by his capacity to help influence how streets, alleyways, parks, and buildings are used. So he may be a resource for people like police, block club presidents, and shopkeepers. And because his own material vulnerability is not far afield from the precariousness of most other residents' lives, he can receive empathy and support even while compromising ease of movement and intercourse. James makes his livelihood one day at a time, which is not that different from the majority of residents who struggle to find work and support their households.

We should not minimize the fact that the way in which order is maintained in Maquis Park—with cops and hustlers and other actors collaborating—is not a preferred mode of collective action even for those who live in that Chicago ghetto. Maquis Park's inhabitants do not always relish having to work in backdoor ways, and many would rather have a visible police presence that is reliable and responsive. Nevertheless, the role of the hustler locally does reveal the important status of marginal public figures in a ghetto community.

Residents have empathy for James, not only because they share some of his economic vulnerability, but also because they share with him an interest in safety and security. Public space is a highly valued commodity. Overcrowding means that people value being able to stand on a street corner or sit on a park bench as a reprieve from a stressful domestic environment. Parents are constantly seeking safe open areas of recreation and refuge for their children. Though James's motives are decidedly entrepreneurial, public space is no less valued by him. He has no other place to make a living—few residents have garages he can rent to set up his auto repair shop, and he has no chance of opening up a private business. Where residents' immediate, short-term need for safety meets James's need to keep spaces safe for customers, there is a basis for cooperation that makes it possible for them to work together.

Chapter Five
The Preacher

The ubiquity of churches in Maquis Park is rivaled only by currency exchanges and liquor stores. Residents meet their maker in large auditoriums, elaborate cathedrals, converted brownstones and six-flats, and one- or two-room storefronts that are sometimes little more than concrete shacks. The clergy are a diverse lot, ranging from powerful ministers who bring out the vote for the black political machine, to soulful pastors on modest stages who never fail to remind that they too wander and stray. The congregants come from throughout the neighborhood and from as far away as the south suburbs of Chicago and Indiana. Sundays are carnivalesque, as the streets turn into theaters where parishioners showcase their faith through fellowship and fancy cars.

Sunday is without doubt the Lord's day in Maquis Park—from the morning services and church socials, to the afternoon reunions, to the evening men's prayer meetings—but for many of these churches, the six days that follow can be unsettling; the reality of the rest of the week can be harsh. There is never enough money to pay for programs, salaries, and services. Particularly for those churches that depend on the local, largely poor population for donations, the plates passed around are disappointing. Local clergy may already be supplementing their income with work outside the church; the call to serve their congregants only adds to their pressures. But many pastors will not address the stress they personally experience: their faith is strong, and they speak instead of the need to provide solace and inspiration to others in need. They weather their pain and exasperation in silence, their faith rooted in the strong community soil. And so the myriad neighborhood churches trundle on from week to week, coping with the day-to-day difficulties of staying afloat while trying to act as a source of stability and solace for those who enter their halls each Sunday.

Pastors and ministers are by no means heroes, nor do they see themselves as such. One of the oldest preachers in the community, Pastor Jeremiah Wilkins, likes to say, "Religion is religion, whether you white or black, poor or rich. You take care of people, you build communities, you serve the Lord." While they may be personally modest, their actions speak volumes to the challenges of the pastoral practice in ghetto communities. Their personal calling demands of them tremendous innovation, to find ways to sustain their churches and provide for their congregants.

Like ministers in most American communities, the Maquis Park clergy address their share of domestic problems, juvenile delinquency, and the tragedy and sadness of sickness and death. But as religious institutions of urban African Americans, the churches of Maquis Park face some challenges fundamentally different from those of most white churches. As in so many inner cities, religion here evolved as blacks dealt with their exclusion from commerce, civic life, political participation, and philanthropy. It was the church that first provided the primary institutional center for many of these activities, and its critical role continues. In Maquis Park, where social services are woefully inadequate, the clergy have become the youth counselors, the conflict mediators, the gang intervention specialists, the retrievers of stolen goods, the referral service for the unemployed and indigent, the marriage counselors, and the leaders of boycotts and protests. Some of the problems may be novel, but the civic activism of the church is not.

Alliances, lines of enmity, and a competitive spirit all inflect religious life in Maquis Park. In a community with a declining population, pastors compete for the support of local residents. They also vie for a share of limited governmental and philanthropic assistance, which funds ecumenical involvement in community development and the delivery of social services. There are trustworthy and self-interested clergy, there are clergy who attend to commuters and others who restrict themselves to local causes, and there may be deep political divisions among all of them. Nevertheless, they are the all-purpose individuals to whom residents, organizations, and outside parties turn, whether to bring out the vote or reduce gang violence.

And just as the community is inextricably linked to its clergy, so too is the preacher profoundly shaped by the underground economy. If only on a moral level, preachers must address the consequences of violating communal norms and breaking the law. African Americans have always turned to their clergy for guidance and resolution. People call on their ministers when they make necessary compromises to put food on the table; conversely, pastors inevitably raise the subject in their weekly supplication, asking sinners to pray for forgiveness for their sins. The shady world provides a place to locate goods and services for congregants, including (but not limited to) quick sums of cash, jobs, and access to credit and financing. Like their flocks, pastors must also contend with the complexities of life where the underground may be the only available resource. It should be no surprise, then, that the religious order plays some role in underground economic activity. The extent of their role, however, is perhaps unexpected.

The Community's Church

Nationally and in urban America, most African American congregants belong to protestant churches. In Chicago this is the case, although some African Americans are Catholic and a relatively small number claim other faiths. So, it is to be expected that most of the clergy in the Maquis Park community adhere to the teachings of Christ, as represented in one or another protestant denomination. Although Catholic priests and ministers in the Nation of Islam also participate in local matters and have shepherded grassroots issues, the protestant clergy overwhelmingly dominate the spiritual landscape and tend to drown out their counterparts from other faiths in terms of involvement in political issues.

The theological underpinnings of black spirituality provide the infrastructure for the church as a whole to take a civic stand on a wide range of local problems that affect Maquis Park, including domestic abuse, juvenile delinquency, and police brutality. Historically in most northern urban communities, the boundary between ministry and profane activities was always blurred and preachers were extraordinarily active in the general social life of their congregants. Indeed, in many cases, their extra-religious activities were conducted on behalf of the overall community, which included a population that could extend far beyond the limited number who entered the church. Black spirituality, thus, did not evolve in a hermeneutic vacuum, organized only around the analysis of texts and scripture. It coalesced out of the church's central role as a social and religious center, as an institution that responded to both profane and spiritual matters affecting black Americans. This deep involvement in the vital issues facing the community remains at the core of the clergy's teaching and guidance in Maquis Park.[1] But this kind of stance leads to involvement in all aspects of the community. And while many—scholars and preachers alike—may prefer to ignore the connection, the church's broad net inevitably gets caught on the many thorns of the underground economy.

Connecting the church and the shady world is not a great stretch. This vital economy cannot be reduced to the simple exchange of money and goods, because it is also a cultural activity. Through the underground economy, people build personal and collective identities, and they create moral boundaries regarding acceptable and reprehensible behavior. Though technically illegal, underground exchange still has a rich, and evolving, moral pulse, which regulates recognized codes of conduct, expectations of appropriate behavior, and patterns of conflict mediation. This morality is neither created privately nor held exclusively by individuals—no moral structure is—but is a product of the group as a whole. Likewise the ethical responsibilities that delineate how people should treat others with whom they trade are essentially shaped by the collective. Though all individuals decide for themselves how to act and what to do, they are also cognizant of how their actions look in the eyes of their peers and neighbors. The public consequences of their actions matter; and so decision making involves consultation and continual reevaluation. And the church is essential in the creation and maintenance of propriety.

The role of the church affords an insightful vantage point on how an illegal system of exchange becomes bound by and fitted with a moral dressing. The choice of the church as a point of entrée is not random. Black ministry in this country has been defined by the couplet of survival and liberation—by the need to strengthen black America's moral resolve in order to bring about social change. The church is also arguably the oldest institution in the lives of African Americans; during the American period of slavery, churches worked for social change and played a strong part in the underground railroad where slaves found passage northward to the city and freedom. Unable to marry, own businesses, form a press, or otherwise communicate and interact freely, enslaved African Americans relied on religion: in song and verse, they recorded their collective history and sent messages secretly to one another; prayer meetings were occasions to create associations and foster collective rituals; sermons soothed, counseled, and motivated the collective to persist and overcome. And the church's multiple roles in no way shrank after the Civil War. The church may have been a religious institution, but it was always also a social center, serving a "corporate and pragmatic function" by providing one of the only organizational settings available to develop collective initiatives and, in so doing, offering an avenue through which to communicate and build community.[2]

The multifaceted nature of the church meant that its congregants came to expect much from their preachers. They saw their clergy protesting on the streets as well as preaching in the pulpit. They asked their pastor as often for a meal and a job as for spiritual comfort. As the twentieth century dawned, their clergy held the ear of congressmen and mayors, union officials, and job contractors. It is now well known that the ideals of civil rights were spread through the fiery preaching and deliberate organizing of ministers; indeed, the advances made by black Americans in the last half century may have not have come so quickly had the clergy not been at the forefront. There are many reasons why the preacher occupied a leadership role in black urban communities; in particular, "he was more insulated from the power of retribution wielded by whites who vehemently disagreed with his efforts to liberate."[3] As a result, preachers, like the organizations they led, were unique, and they were able to appear in multiple and often subversive guises, from social worker and employment agent to dissenter and healer.

In the early and mid twentieth century, ghetto churches were a varied lot, with many congregations, denominations, and orientations. African Americans of diverse economic and social backgrounds lived in the same neighborhoods, and simultaneously cities were filling with newly arriving migrants drawn to churches and styles of religious practice that differed from those that attracted the native city dwellers. As the great northward migrations of southern blacks brought newcomers into already overcrowded, segregated areas, the church's purview was broad and the clergy could respond with equal passion to the call for prayer or to the call for jobs and affordable housing.[4]

After the sixties, however, the ghetto church was fundamentally changed.[5] Inner cities became choked by poverty as, for the first time, middle- and upper-income black Americans began leaving the ghetto and buying homes in formerly segregated areas. Although they left behind the squalor of the inner city, many of these families continued to commute to the areas where they had grown up in order to attend the churches of their parents and grandparents.[6] Particularly in the northeast urban corridor, well-endowed churches grew less local in orientation. They might occasionally have linked their commuters to neighborhood causes, but their own congregations often did not include neighborhood residents. Moreover, these churches tended to shy away from actively advocating for residents in the political sphere, and some more-established churches withdrew from deep engagement with local matters. Next to them, however, one could find a church whose preacher continued to be an activist and who mobilized the church membership to fight for the poor, even as the members themselves became less poor. Others ran for political office and had businesses on the side. Still others focused simply on shepherding the families who came each weekend, remaining deeply critical of those who confused the role of preacher and politician. Some preachers defined their laity widely, as including believers and nonbelievers; others presented the Bible only to those who demonstrably adhered to the faith. Some opened their doors only on Sundays; others seemed never to lock their doors.

Post-civil-rights churches cannot all be categorized as either wealthy cathedral or struggling storefront—there were many churches combining local and commuting populations that did not fit easily in either category. By no means did every member of the clergy combine social activism with private teaching. There are still many preachers today who resist public politicking, preferring instead to direct prayers, not offer breakfasts or lead sit-ins. These "traditionalists" prioritize preaching over social activism and, just as in the sixties, they conflict with "militants" who see no separation between church and community.[7]

But in today's Maquis Park all the churches share something in common—all have been redefined by the underground economy. This economy lends a distinctive character to contemporary urban religion, affecting how clergy relate to residents and how they conceive of their own pastoral function. Shady activities have altered the structure through which clergy ameliorate poverty, provide support and services, and otherwise engage in that amorphous and myriad set of activities known as "community building." It is from the vantage point of community building, as practiced by clergy, that religion and underground economic behavior intersect in Maquis Park. In a place where so many dollars, resources, goods, and services flow off the books, we should not be surprised that the church assumes some role in the underground arena. Participation in, and observation of, illegal activities raises moral questions and quandaries that preachers must address.

Of course, the church has always had some relationship to underground economic activity, particularly in the heyday of black settlement in the North. On the Southside in the mid-twentieth century, for example, businesspersons tended to their affairs not only outside the church but also inside it. Businesses routinely sought out clergy when recruiting cheap labor—which included "scab labor" to "break the backs" of unionized strikers—and the clergy were paid under the table for supplying fresh faces to stockyards, steel mills, cleaning service firms, and transportation companies.[8] There were always allegations of clergy involvement in racketeering, such as the coordination of "policy"—an unregulated urban lottery—and other forms of gambling; it was routine to hear rumors of "kickbacks" to preachers who "plugged specific stores or products" or otherwise helped influence the flow of dollars, resources, and jobs in the community.[9] The landscape of today's inner city is very different from a half-century ago. Numbers rackets and speakeasies no longer exist, and the ever-adapting black church has also shifted its role to reflect the changing character of the shady world.

In Maquis Park the relationships between shady activity, community building, and ministry may be told through a network of clergy whose ministries have been a part of the neighborhood for decades. Their individual histories, the evolution of their respective churches, and the relationships between them bring into relief the tensions enlivening African American pastoral practice. As will be apparent, labels that were once useful to delineate preaching styles, such as *traditional* or *militant,* do not offer great purchase when analyzing the underground practices of Maquis Park preachers.[10] The ubiquity of the shady economy makes it nearly impossible for a preacher to be fully beyond its reach. However, there are important distinctions among the clergy in terms of their exposure to, and willingness to engage, those who live underground. Their own struggles to come to terms with illicit, criminal, or morally reprehensible practices reveals the enormous significance of the underground, not just as a means of material survival, but as a space in which to grapple with problems of identity and belonging.

The Rise of the Black Church

When asked why he became a preacher, Pastor Jeremiah Wilkins points to the death of his younger brother in 1971.

> He was a child of God, as we all are. Walked down 59th Street one day, left our house. Was shot by a drug dealer. Crazy thing was he didn't owe no money; he never used drugs. I guess the [dealer] didn't like the way my brother cut in line in front of him at the

subway ticket booth. Imagine that: holding a grudge for that? That's when I said, black folk are living in a senseless society. That's when the Lord said, you have to turn this misery to motivation, make your grieving your gift. I began to pray and then I was called to lead.

Pastor Wilkins began by preaching at night, after working at his job as a television repairman. He hung out on street corners, in front of stores, at the subway, and anywhere else people gathered. In 1979 he founded the Maquis Park Prayer and Revival Center, taking the shell of a mom-and-pop food store and converting it into a modest storefront church. Except for a small addition to house his expanding family, the Center remains as it has always been: in continuous need of repair, hot in summer and cold in winter, too small for its many roles. Outside, bright blue walls set the building apart from the drab, grey and brown apartment buildings that line the rest of the street; inside, each wall is a different shade of lime green and each bench a darker shade of brown.

It is common for preachers to cite personal circumstances as critical factors pushing them into the clergy. Particularly for those who operate midsize and smaller churches, like storefronts, a crisis or moment of overcoming a personal difficulty was often the key motivation to pursue a calling in the ministry. Minister Hortons, a local pastor who has directed several churches in Maquis Park since the early eighties, says that a near-fatal traffic accident made him aware of the Lord's presence and he decided to quit his construction job and join a seminary. It took him several years of preaching on subways and in public areas before he saved enough money to start a church. Brother Patterson, who manages a small storefront church, says that he "was ordained by the Lord and never needed a degree to preach"; after serving as a school counselor for five years, he joined the clergy to try to offer counseling and support to local troubled youth. He also began modestly, preaching in the living room of his mother's home for three years before selling his house and living in the storefront he purchased.

In the first year, Pastor Wilkins made two critical decisions that would forever characterize his ministry. First, he welcomed into his church those he saw as the dregs of the community: "Gangs, drunks, addicts, prostitutes, hustlers, I mean what most of us would say is really the worst the community had to offer. They were all here, day and night, and we were serving them." Second, he allowed people to use the open spaces and backyard for their own mundane activities, ranging from bake sales to protest meetings.

> The first people who walked in my door was a family of a boy who got killed in a gang fight. Wanted a funeral. I said "okay" and a day later they came back with 150 kids from around the city, with those bandanas, guns, loud cars, and, of course, the crying mothers and relations who just lost a loved one. I didn't see gang members: I saw lost, lost souls and they been coming in here ever since.

In time, Wilkins's storefront became a social center, welcoming not only gang members but an array of community members who were on the margins:

> Everyday, it was something else around here that needed my attention. So-and-so got beat up and was going to kill their husband. I stepped in. Little Johnnie got shot for selling crack on Big Billy's corner; I stepped in. Officer so-and-so beat up somebody; I tried to prevent a riot. I mean every day! I had time to prepare my sermon, help ladies run their card games, and then it was back on the

street. And I never left one mile from here. There was enough to do right here.

For the first few years, Pastor Wilkins explains, in the mornings his church was inhabited by the adults and seniors who ran social meetings and Bible-study workshops, and who sold clothing and food. In the afternoons, the young men came in to iron out gang conflicts and drug disputes. In the evenings he met with families and police over domestic abuse, police harassment, and prostitution. The work at his church took up most of his time and energy. Because his congregants were neither wealthy nor able to donate substantially to the church, he could not rely on their contributions for his own livelihood. So he took up part-time work to supplement his own income. The church's other needs were met with donations, charitable contributions, and the labor of everyone "who fixed the roof, painted walls, put in a new floor, and mowed the lawns." The church quietly became a place for the marginalized members of the community to gather.

There were other such places of fellowship and assembly. Wilkins recalled a small group of preachers—about two or three dozen at any one time, according to his count—who catered to the poor and needy in Maquis Park. They would be known conventionally as "storefront preachers," although not all addressed their congregations inside halls of worship. A few possessed a separate structure whose only function was to host religious gatherings, but most of them had "one- or two-room buildings," Wilkins says, that might function as a church one day and serve another purpose the rest of the week. Some worked out of the back rooms of stores or waited until the store closed to turn an open area into a place of fellowship. Others provided ministry in their own living rooms or in the homes of their friends.

The credentials of this modest clergy set also varied. There were ministers who were ordained and part of a national network of churches. (This was a resource that they could draw on both for politicking and for their ministry, although the storefront preachers typically say that they do not have reason or motivation to utilize these broader connections.) Reverend Barnes attended African Methodist Episcopal gatherings on occasion in other parts of the Midwest; Lonnie Wilson, a self-described "old-time Baptist," had preached in Milwaukee, Cleveland, and Saint Louis before arriving in Chicago in the early eighties. Some, however, were self-taught or they were being trained either formally in a seminary or informally in an apprenticeship with an established religious leader. And still others may have eschewed any vocational path altogether, choosing instead to chart their path through proclamations of being called by the Lord to serve. All could boast a fellowship one year and, depending on material circumstances, they may dissolve their ministry and re-form at a later date.

Perhaps due to their own personal familiarity with survival in the face of material hardship, these churches relied on each other and developed joint initiatives: their preachers preached in one another's church, together they held Bible-study workshops and evening vigils, and their charitable work cleaning parks or repairing congregants' homes was also done with members of other churches. However, Wilkins says that their relationships were also forged in the face of neglect from an unresponsive city government.

> See, you have to understand, that back [in the eighties], we were really ignored by the city. Even though Harold [Washington] was mayor, it wasn't like all the black folk around here were doing

better. He really helped the big-time churches. But folks like us, we just survived day to day, helping folk who were surviving day to day. But what you have to remember is that we weren't alone. It wasn't like we were moping, with no one to help. No, we came together, we did things together, we solved problems, often with no money, or just, you know, a few hundred dollars and we could do wonderful things.

Partially as a response to the lack of municipal resources for their communities—for police, libraries, and city services, to name a few—these preachers expanded their role from personal mediator and problem solver to social service provider. What one clergy member would later call a "self-help" program was simply the ongoing, dedicated response by some preachers to meeting the needs of their congregants. Typically these self-help activities were modest ventures, such as allowing churches to be used as informal day-care facilities, providing small loans and initiating clothing drives for desperate families, sponsoring free food giveaways, and organizing parishioners to help a family with home repair and maintenance.

There were also clergy-led initiatives that reached organizations outside of Maquis Park. Together with his friend Reverend Barnes, Wilkins protested outside city agencies for more affordable housing in the early and mid-1980s. He pressured city leaders to place public library branches in poor neighborhoods. He lobbied banks to lend money to homeowners and prospective storekeepers. These efforts were not always successful, but they placed these preachers in direct encounter with citywide public and private institutions.

Such practices also brought them into contact with more powerful black clergy, namely, those who catered to the wealthier

commuters and who were directly tied into the city political machine. There were certainly imbalances in terms of resources and
influence locally and in wider social and political circles, but the
more modest clergy are adamant that these disparities were not
necessarily obstacles to working together. Wilkins worked hand
in hand with two prominent city ministers—one black and the
other white—to win construction of a new public library in Maquis Park. Reverend Barnes worked with ministers citywide on affordable housing campaigns; he held vigils for the homeless with
them, he tried to pool resources with other clergy and purchase
property for transitional housing, and he collaborated on letter-
writing campaigns with elite black ministers. Reverend Johnnie
Xavier, one of Wilkins's colleagues, provided fellowship in the
back of a grocery store, but his modest furnishings did not stand
in the way of his joint work with more established religious leaders. While recalling his work with other Chicago ministers to protest discrimination in bank practices and segregation in the real
estate market, he made the point that in the early and mid eighties much of the community building—whether this meant liaising with external actors or organizing self-help programs—was a
joint effort between small and big churches:

> In the seventies and eighties, preachers were far more together. We
> didn't all agree, but somehow we all were trying to do the same
> things, like get police to come around, get some housing built, get
> the legislators downstate to serve up some dollars to us. It's funny,
> because when I say we was "working together," I don't mean we
> was holding hands. What happened was Pastor Wilkins, myself,
> Brother Patterson, we all started getting an audience with the bank
> or with the head of the welfare office. And then, when we walked
> in the room, we saw Reverend Walters, the big dog himself, just

> sitting there! See what I mean. It was just that the big preachers, they were like advisors to all the powerful people, so we just had to be in the room with them, try to work with them 'cause we couldn't seem to do nothing without them.

In the eighties there were four large and prominent churches in Maquis Park: the Maquis Park Apostolic Church, the Covenant Church, the Maquis Park Baptist Church, and the Church of Christ. Each boasted wealthy congregants who commuted to attend the cathedral-like buildings, with spacious acreage, social and recreational facilities, and fences that insulated each compound. Each was led by a powerful preacher who could trace his political lineage to the salad days of post–World War II Chicago, when African American congressman William "Big Bill" Dawson worked with churches to make the black vote a powerful force. Most people felt that these four churches monopolized local access to jobs and resources; they distributed their patronage carefully to ensure that they could bring out the vote during elections.[11] Johnnie Xavier calls this period, which he says lasted until the early eighties, the "the Milky Way" because "inside all these black churches, you had a streak of white that was running through, controlling things and saying what was okay, what was not."

The role of the church as an intermediary between urban blacks and the controlling white political machine is not new. Beginning in the late nineteenth century, when blacks settled in the urban North in significant numbers, church leaders were respected members of the civic community who could channel public and private resources into their political districts and neighborhoods. They persuaded the mayor to hire black labor, they convinced philanthropists to fund educational programs for newly arrived southern migrants, and they successfully lobbied the state to build housing for black soldiers returning from wars. During the "Milky Way" period in the mid-twentieth century, black clergy not only lobbied for external resources but also agreed to trade-offs whose value to the black community was debatable and whose benefits for the white machine were not: in return for bringing out the black vote in support of white candidates, the clergy may have been promised patronage (jobs, contracts, services) from city leaders. Depending on one's political viewpoint, this system of brokerage could be seen as cooptation by white elites, skillful politicking, or capitulation to dominant white interests. The black vote could be the deciding vote helping a candidate to secure political victory, so the meager benefits that black constituents ended up receiving were crumbs.[12]

When Mayor Richard J. Daley died in 1976, Chicago's black leadership saw clearly an opportunity to mobilize for greater electoral power. Their hope was fulfilled in 1983, when African American congressman Harold Washington was elected mayor of Chicago. A victory for African Americans, Latinos, and progressive whites, Washington's election was also a clear indication that the political machine now dominated by whites could be effectively challenged. In the first flush of victory, churches buttressed a powerful citywide organizing initiative, built around voter education and registration and led by progressive Chicagoans, that helped defeat the machine candidates. Black clergy labored to enfranchise the black community; this "movement"—as its leaders liked to call it—spanned all levels, from the grassroots to the middle and upper class. Temporarily, at least, it appeared that Chicago's South and West Side black communities were politically unified and in line with liberal whites to successfully deflect the white vote.

A different and largely ignored outcome was the effect of Washington's political mobilization within poorer communities like Maquis Park. Johnnie Xavier's "Milky Way" description seems like an exaggeration. His view that black leadership continually capitulates to predominantly white machine bosses does not make total sense, particularly given that the city had just elected an African American to the city's highest office. However, black clergy had not been key spokespersons for African American interests. Political unity among black leaders did not necessarily mean political parity. There remained an enormous gap between the cathedrals and the storefronts in terms of their capacity to procure resources and effect social change. As with all political movements, in the efforts to elect Washington, there was a double-edged quality to the organizing initiative: namely, either join or be "cast aside." One scholar writes, "In Harold Washington black people had drafted a standard-bearer with the credentials and progressive orientation to be 'their' candidate for mayor. Community leaders from all sections of Black Chicago were forced to keep step with this new electoral upsurge or be cast aside."[13] At the least, one must conclude that Johnnie Xavier's candy bar analogy proves accurate in its allusion to the persistence of some long-standing cleavages within the black clergy.

In the campaign itself, some of the disparities among clergy could be discerned. At one point, Xavier and Wilkins met with Minister Brantley Martin, perhaps the most powerful member of the Maquis Park clergy. Martin had the capacity to mobilize thousands of voters, and it was rumored that if Washington won, Martin's success in getting out the vote would be reflected in an appointment as a high-paid city commissioner and numerous contracts for firms owned by his congregants. Xavier and Wilkins said they threatened Martin, telling him that they would take the votes of their congregants to another candidate if they were not told exactly what they would receive in return for supporting Washington. Martin recalls what happened when the two walked into his office:

> "I told them if they took their votes away, I'd see to it that they couldn't stay in the community no more," said Martin. "Simple as that. I would perceive their behavior as a destructive force, no more, no less. They were injuring the livelihood of the people who walked into their place every day for help. *That's* how important the Washington campaign was for black folk."
>
> "That's a pretty amazing statement, particularly from a member of the clergy," I said.
>
> "You wanted the truth. These guys just didn't trust anybody. I mean, I gave them hundreds of dollars. I sent my people over to fix their church, I bought them a new roof. I mean, to come in here and say I was not helping them. I had had enough."

The storefront clergy's awareness of their limits relative to the preachers with larger congregations may not always have been displayed so dramatically, in such direct confrontation. It could simply have manifested itself in differences in perceptions, with powerful people understanding fairly clearly what Washington's election could bring about and the grassroots clergy being only cautiously optimistic. A director of a storefront church in the eighties, Pastor Barnes, said, "It was just that you knew everyday that you were hoping that you would get something for what you were doing. Those guys never worried, they always knew what they were getting."

Ultimately, it would be Harold Washington's death, in 1987, that showed just how fragile political relations were among Chicago's black stakeholders. His passing shed light on who might be "cast aside" if viewpoints became too difficult to reconcile. But even as Washington came into power four years earlier, it was possible to discern signs of discord, or at least differing and perhaps irreconcilable perspectives, within the black leadership. Part of the fragility arose from the movement's having been built around Washington's charismatic power as mayor—he was famously able to quickly mend cleavages as they arose—rather than through a more deliberate attempt to inculcate leadership and participatory democracy at all levels, so that the death of a leader might be survived by the appointment of a successor. As William Grimshaw has observed,

> concern with elite self-interest points to the basis for the inability of the Washington coalition to survive his death. Washington's inclination was to "win over" opponents rather than to exclude and punish them in the machine tradition . . . Washington's reforms were not institutionalized as much as they were personalized. When he died, therefore, the reforms were put in jeopardy and promptly undermined by the very elements he had tolerated and left in place.[14]

The tenuous nature of such alliances was reflected in the black clergy. Churches that brought out the black vote for Washington were a varied lot, with differences in denomination, political orientation, size, and relationship to local residents. They may have been unified in their response to racially based discrimination, but their interests could diverge considerably. Those in poor communities struggled with unemployment, poverty, and drug addiction in a way that black middle-class churches did not; conversely, the black middle class now demanded a fair share of city patronage and contracts, two issues that were very low on the list of priorities of an unskilled, jobless population living in substandard housing.

An important subgroup within the Southside black clergy were those who felt unable to advance their concerns in the Washington administration. Pastor Wilkins's feelings represent frustrated clergy in Maquis Park who, after Washington came into power, grew at odds with him.

> We said [to him], "We need jobs, we got people with drug problems, we got people who need help, who need housing." What we got back, and I mean this is coming from black folk! We were told, "We have to be careful because we can't be seen as the poor people's mayor." On one side of their mouth, they were for the people, but they were afraid to give the people what they wanted, because they would look soft. Giving of your heart. If that's soft, then the Lord is soft. It was very frustrating not to get money for places to help people with their problems.

Father Michael Wilson, a white Southside progressive priest who supported Wilkins, remembers that eventually a segment of mostly black "grassroots and storefront" clergy began splitting off from the Washington agenda. Wilson deemed their return to servicing communities with noncity resources the embrace of a "self-help" agenda.

> I really felt for Pastor Wilkins, Brother Patterson, Minister Hortons, and those folks. See, when Washington was mobilizing, you had a real neat group of what I will call "grassroots and storefront" ministers, priests—basically preachers who were really at the roots of the African American community. Daley never gave them attention, and, for that matter, neither did their own leadership. They did things for themselves, they responded to people

with very minimal resources. Washington's election was going to change that, at least that was the public promise made to them: he was going to build housing in those poor areas, he was going to give schools better classrooms, more medical clinics. But really, none of that happened, or at least not enough. So Minister Hortons, well all those people really, they all went back to helping themselves. "Self-help" I call it, because they must be given the credit for working by themselves with very tough problems around poverty and addiction. And then, then the gangs came, and well, you know the rest. I mean after that, that's when you really had a separate, disenfranchised group. And I don't mean just the people, but also the clergy. That's when hope dissolves, when the clergy are not brought into the center.

When asked about his own view of ruling black leaders and the turn to "self-help," Pastor Wilkins recalls a pivotal meeting in 1986 that he convened with clergy who were much closer to Mayor Washington—the so-called "big preachers" who were generally thought to be the most powerful figures in the Southside black community. Along with Brother Patterson, Johnnie Xavier, Minister Hortons, Father Michael Wilson, and others, he approached the "big preachers"—Minister Kevin Ashland, Minister Brantley Martin, Pastor Harold Brusser, and Reverend Calvin Lamar—to forewarn them of increased social problems in the black community. "We asked them for specific kinds of help," Wilkins recalls. Brother Patterson, who joined in the conversation, listed the demands.

> "I can remember it like it was yesterday," said Brother Patterson. "Down in Woodlawn, at First Baptist, sitting across a long table, like we was coming to the altar! The five [big preachers] sitting there, stone-faced, look like they lost even their hearts. We said,

help us build housing, help us get medical care, help us stop police from beating on us like we were dogs, help the soup kitchens because we have homeless, meet with the gang leaders and hear what the youth are saying. What else, I can't remember?"

"Then," Pastor Wilkins continued, "They told us they were not sure what they could do. That's when I realized we had a whole new boss system in Chicago. Black preachers! It was like being down South. They got what they wanted, wasn't interested in helping everyone. Just taking care of themselves. That's when I threw up my hands. I knew then, I knew then . . ."

"What he's trying to say," Brother Patterson interrupted, "is that that's when we knew we were doing the right thing, but that we were going to be alone. Like we were before Washington came. There was nobody who was going to hear these cries. No one was really going to take that hard look, in themselves and in the community, seeing what was going on. That's when we all got back together and said, 'Okay, let's just do this, do it with our hearts and what we have. 'Cause we ain't getting no more, at least not from these so-called preachers.'"

The outcome of the meeting, according to those present, was that Wilkins and his colleagues realized that they would not be able to call on the mayor to address their constituents' needs. What Brother Patterson calls the "big-ticket items" in Maquis Park, like high unemployment, gang crime, and housing shortages, were not going to improve appreciably in the immediate future as a result of rising black power in City Hall. But it was not entirely clear that the preachers' alternative "self-help" program would be a viable means of addressing community concerns. In fact, there was no such self-help strategy in place, says Pastor Wilkins, "only a feeling that whatever was going to happen was going to be coming from us—but no one knew what to do." By the mid-1980s, the only clarity the preachers had achieved was the recognition that City Hall would provide them only limited help.

The view from City Hall did not necessarily coincide exactly with the perceptions of Wilkins, Barnes, and the other modest Maquis Park clergy. Bill Owens was a senior advisor for Mayor Washington, in charge of liaising with Southside Chicago communities. He says that many of the storefront clergy could not adequately articulate their demands; they were angry, and even when they discussed specific issues like unemployment, their demands were abstract ("Deal with youth who are unhappy and turning to gangs") rather than rooted in specific programs, and therefore were not helpful to the city administration.

> They would come into my office and start spouting on about how the community was going down the drain. Crime, gangs, drugs, people dying. And then they'd say that Harold Washington was responsible! They would just moan and never say exactly what they wanted. I'd say, okay, we'll get you each ten jobs for the summer for kids. They'd say, "Ten is nothing, we have thousands of people who are hopeless." I'd say, true, but let's reduce that by ten and then we can move on.

Owens went on to say that the smaller clergy often lacked the organization to receive assistance from the city. They did not have a staff and did not have the capacity to build affordable housing (which the city might fund). Some did not have a charter or were unincorporated, so they were unable to receive money from many external parties, like foundations, charities, and city departments that contracted with local organizations to provide social services to families.

Minister Kevin Ashland, one of the "big preachers" and a critic of Pastor Wilkins at the time, openly described the hostility of the powerful "religious bosses" toward Wilkins and other storefront clergy members. In particular, he points to one of the specific self-help initiatives the storefront clergy developed to reduce crime: instead of working with police, "around 1985" he says, the grassroots ministers worked directly with gangs and other criminals to solve crimes and restore order.

"Black people in Chicago, then and now, have only been as powerful as the preachers around them. You know what political bosses are, right? Well, we were *religious* bosses. There were probably ten of us on the Southside, maybe two or three in Maquis Park. I fought long and hard to get at the table, I could do things for my parishioners: I could call the mayor and say, 'We need more money for this school, we need a new traffic light.' These are not small things. Did the other ministers need to get our permission before they went and got in the mix with the gangs? Well, some would say no. I would have hoped that we would have been consulted, at the very least, because, well, there are consequences.

"If you're working with a beat cop, then I can't work with him—or his commander. If you're helping gangs smooth out their business, I can't get the police to get them to stop. There are consequences. The white folk downtown, all they see is that there's some crazy preacher trying to help gangs deal drugs or pimps get money from their prostitutes. Now, we were trying to control what information got out [of Maquis Park]. We didn't want to hurt our own ability to get things done. And I don't know if there weren't long-term problems. You help the gang leader, he becomes more powerful. Then what? He'll kill you."

"But what about the argument that you [religious bosses] were not doing anything to help people day to day? I mean, didn't someone have to help keep order?"

"I'd call what they did 'messing about.' And you see what happened. We grew apart for many years. A lot of the friendships? Well, they can't be repaired now. And who was hurt? The people. For many years, all these preachers, if they wanted something, it's the gangs they call, not us. Now the gangs are in jail and they're calling us. Of course, we'll help, but not all the time, and not without some recognition of what they did. So that's what I mean when I say there were consequences. There's a real divide now in the community. I'm a man of faith, but I'm not so sure it can be healed."

Ashland's link between the clergy and street gangs points to some of the long-term consequences of the kind of self-help being developed by Wilkins and other storefront clergy. Namely, in terms of the kinds of issues they were taking up, there was a chasm growing between those at the elite churches and those working at the grassroots. As a result of citywide political transformations, a social cleavage in the black clergy had risen beyond the level of backroom griping. Pastor Wilkins and his colleagues were losing hope that participation in the Washington "movement" would bring about desired improvements in quality of life for local residents.

As a consequence of the meeting, the "grassroots and storefront" ministries perceived that their work must be supported without resources from the now black-controlled city administration. Effectively, this meant they would have only limited access to city and state funds. They also could not build on patronage jobs as vehicles to increase donor contributions. And they stood little chance of reaching black middle- and upper-class supporters of religious causes; these patrons had risen in number and stature as a result of Washington's mobilization, but they typically aligned with the larger Maquis Park churches that were embedded in the Washington coalition. Consequently, in 1987, at the height of the Washington administration, the preachers' focus had grown inward. This meant that they were increasingly attentive not only to local issues, but also to local sources of manpower and funds as opposed to external resources from the municipal, civic, and philanthropic community. In an economically depressed Southside region, this meant a closer relationship with the underground economy.

Loaves and Fishes

Just as their ministry was transformed by the realignment of Chicago's African American political leadership, Pastor Wilkins and his colleagues were weathering another transformation. The texture of poverty and hardship was changing throughout Chicago's African American neighborhoods. Black Chicagoans were not unfamiliar with poverty; but for much of the early twentieth century, black poor families had lived next door to black middle- and upper-class families. Segregation had made it impossible for blacks to separate from one another on the basis of class, so they tended to inhabit the same communities. The presence of employed families meant that the poor lived in neighborhoods with resources, service organizations, and philanthropies and charitable organizations. They were not, in other words, "socially isolated."

This is the phrase William Julius Wilson used to describe Chicago's poor at the dawn of the eighties. Wilson argued that inner-city poverty in Chicago after the civil rights era was characterized by the presence of an "underclass" who were not in contact with their better-off counterparts—and the many resources that working families brought with them. Not only were underclass poor and jobless, but they worked in the underground economy, and most of their families were single-parent, run by a mother receiving welfare (the father was usually absent). The many problems of poverty—drug addiction, malnutrition, homelessness—were still around, but these were now exacerbated by the alienation of the poor from social services, philanthropic organizations, and charitable associations that often helped mitigate the effects of material hardship.[15]

By the time Washington was sworn in, the community-based problems these clergy faced had already reached grave proportions. In 1970 only two of the ten neighborhoods that made up Chicago's black communities—of which Maquis Park was one—had a poverty rate above 40 percent. By 1990, eight would have a poverty rate above 50 percent (three of them surpassed 60 percent). In the sixties, 64 percent of Maquis Park's adults were employed. By 1990 this number had dropped to 37 percent, and to make matters worse, wages declined from 1970 to 1989 and black Americans were waiting longer to find a job once they had been laid off. In addition, crime had been on the rise throughout Illinois after 1970. Minorities were in jails and prisons in greater numbers than any time in the past—the state's prison population grew by 266 percent in the eighties. Eighty-three percent of the state's black prisoners came from Chicago.

Chicago's ghetto residents had long coped with systemic problems—the plagues of alcoholism and substance abuse, the deficit of social resources—and many had used whatever tactics they could, from the unethical to the illegal, to make a dollar and get by. But in the eighties, public attention to Chicago's inner city was largely framed by the now-famous couplet "the gang and drug problem." Police and media reports focused disproportionately on the underground economy and the gangs that purportedly controlled it. The underground economy gave birth to crack cocaine. (Crack entered American cities at different dates; scholars and police officials believe that it grew to dominate Chicago's drug market in the period from 1983 to 1986.) There now appeared to be a more coordinated attempt by young adults to capitalize on the explosion of economic revenue from crack cocaine and from the rising demand for old and new drugs. Throughout black Chicago, the streets buzzed with street gangs and criminal networks in full swing, coordinating drug sales, extorting businesses, and initiating complex laundering, gambling, and racketeering schemes, all in a day's work.

This is the familiar story, the catalyst for a surge of news articles, television specials, and government wrangling. But there were also less-publicized social changes associated with the new layout of illicit entrepreneurship. Businesspersons and police officers, pimps and hustlers, block club presidents and squatters moved about the shady world, not only to generate income but to attend to the consequences of the new boom in underground activity. Parents argued directly with drug dealers, and tenants of public housing developed their own intervention strategies to reduce gang violence in their lobbies and stairwells. Store owners fought with street vendors and prostitutes for access to sidewalks and public spaces. At the same time, there was all manner of pleading by residents for effective policing, but these same people were not necessarily relying on law enforcement to address their concerns.[16] The police themselves were struggling, not only to cope with rising crime, but also to familiarize themselves with new dealers, extorters, and local stakeholders who played a role in this underground world and could be mediators or informants.

The combination of a significant increase in black electoral power, a downturn in the material status of many poor and working-class black households, the gradual withdrawal of grass-roots persons from the mainstream black political scene, and a growing reliance on underground markets were all contributing to the alienation of inner-city Chicago. Sociologist William Julius Wilson's writings dramatized the social and economic consequences of concentrated poverty and municipal neglect.[17] Less well-known, Carter Henry, a political organizer for Harold Washington who had grown up in Maquis Park, offered an alternate political analysis: black Southside Chicagoans had been stricken with "political schizophrenia."

> You got a black mayor, black middle-class people, talking about what kinds of change is taking place, how they are going to turn this city around. I saw that, I helped that along, I was proud of that. Then, I go home [to Maquis Park] and I got a whole different scene. I got Tee-Bone, the MC [gang] leader who controls the local parks, says who can hang out there. I got Pinter, the hardware store owner, who could get you out of jail for $100 'cause he knows all the cops. I got Terry, who could get you a permit if you wanted to build something or fix your house. Cost 50 bucks and he'd call someone downtown. It's like you were politically schizophrenic or something. You got one group of people who making things happen downtown, then you got other people you need to please to get things done down here. It's like the two weren't really talking with one another. Very strange, man, very strange times.

The implications of the political schizophrenia were unclear and quixotic. Poor Southside Chicagoans were turning to informal, highly personalized ways of making money and finding resources. Some methods were outright illegal, others were simply unsettling because they placed people in vulnerable situations. Hustling, barter, unreported income, and other shady practices meant that people found themselves in new relationships and, consequently, in unfamiliar circumstances. Breakdowns in trust, expectations, and reciprocity meant disagreement, conflict, and occasionally violence and death. The neighborhood witnessed things that had never happened before, like drive-by gang shootings. But even existing issues—school safety, the colonization of abandoned buildings, and so on—placed people with conflicting interests and motives in competition with one another. Minister Hortons says that with the rise of the gangs, people lost their traditional sources of help and assistance.

> Now, before the gangs came around dealing that crack, you still had a lot of precinct captains, aldermen, some police officers, even ministers, who you knew would make sure things didn't get out of hand. And this was what it was like when I was growing up, in the fifties, sixties. Then, all of a sudden, no one knew who to call. Gang shot your son? Well, there's a new [gang] leader, probably come out of jail. Anyone know him? Probably not. Somebody pimping in that abandoned building next to you? You in charge of the block club, who do you call? Police don't care; who else cares? Brother owes you $15 'cause you fixed his window [and he didn't pay you]? Used to be, you called the ward boss or somebody, but they didn't exist, or else they wasn't around here [in Maquis Park] no more. Same with schools. Principal say your son got in trouble?

> Used to be you had what was called a "youth worker" or "social worker" who knew the children, talked with the parents, took care of things. Not no more. And no social worker wants to deal with kid who got an Uzi who's making more money than he do!

The desperate circumstances of Maquis Park seemed to foster a series of ever-evolving solutions. New actors were needed, people who could address conflicts and restore the toppling social order, and it was in this role that the clergy assumed an even more important role in the underground economy. By the end of the eighties, on city blocks throughout Chicago's Southside, a decrepit, dying physical infrastructure belied a vibrant, energetic field of activist ministry in which members of the clergy— working in concert with other local stakeholders—attended to breaches in the social fabric of the community. The so-called self-help strategies assumed their most colorful character as pastors and ministers jumped directly into community affairs as mediators, arbitrators, and healers. Brother Patterson echoes Carter Henry's observation of the dichotomy that emerged in the local political field; however, he highlights the role of the clergy specifically in creating an alternate platform for addressing the neighborhood's issues that arose from underground activities.

> As a minister, a preacher, a man of the cloth, you had a responsibility to your people. The Lord really moved us to respond first, to heal, *then* think about what it might mean for the bigger picture, like what the mayor was going to think about it. If someone got shot by the police, okay, there's an issue of fairness and the courts must get involved. But myself [and other clergy], we tried first to make sure the gang didn't go after the cop; we made sure kids

could get to school on time, safely; we brought the undercover detective and the gang leader together. I mean there's a lot of work that was done that folks downtown didn't know about, or else didn't care about doing themselves. We did that. That's what it means to preach.

Pastor Wilkins, Brother Patterson, Johnnie Xavier, and other grassroots and storefront black clergy saw themselves participating in a new sphere of community building, essential for this new era. Their earliest efforts responded to those social conflicts stemming from disputes between local residents. Throughout the Southside one could find clergy meeting regularly and responding to fights between pimps and prostitutes and incidents of police abuse, domestic violence, theft, and robberies of individuals and businesses.[18] They recovered stolen goods and negotiated fair contracts between underground traders; they redirected day laborers from criminal activity by finding them off-the-books work as janitors and general laborers; and they mediated fights between domestic partners and sent addicts to rehabilitation centers.

Again, they did not work under a corporate auspice. They usually worked alone and on the streets close to their church. They also did not make divisions between faithful and secular. Minister Hortons explains:

I had my little thing going on 59th Street, just south of the projects. Pastor Wilkins was up north a bit. Brother Patterson worked in Oakland, but his brother was in Englewood so he was real good with Gangster Disciple [a street gang] issues—that was where they were located. Now, you need to understand how this worked. It worked because it was a spiritual calling: the Lord called each of us around that time; we all saw that we had to be responsive to some very ugly parts of the community. We helped each other out, you know, we provided rides for kids, maybe we got together with the police commander or principal and tried to work out a solution to getting kids to school safely. But I don't want you to think we were like a political machine. That was for the others. Back then, it was simply a matter of each of us facing the very same problems. We were so busy, so very busy with our own desperate, needy people, that it was mostly exchanging ideas, strategies, and being there for each other. Even preachers need the Lord, every day.

When pushed to consider what was novel about these efforts, Minister Hortons and others make two points. The first is to see their position within the wider field of city politics. While their labors fostered some semblance of social order in their immediate neighborhood, there were consequences; their intensely local focus meant a growing distance from important political leaders, like other black clergy who, at the start of the nineties, had already started to signal their support for Mayor Richard M. Daley and his white-dominated machine. As a result of their brand of community building, Pastor Wilkins and his colleagues found themselves with little energy to continue conventional politicking, such as addressing the directors of banks and businesses and lobbying government bureaucrats whom they had previously called on for assistance. And due perhaps to both time constraints and antagonism, they separated off from clergy who did liaison with these agencies. Instead, they found themselves more involved in the daily lives of residents whose problems and needs did not fall within the service profile of the community's "big preachers."

"The big preachers," says Pastor Wilkins. "They could get you a job, cleaning sewers or social work. But what if your son was going to jail and you didn't want him getting beat up by the gang when he got there. Who are you going to call? What if your momma got beat up by her man and you wanted him not to come around? Reverend Walters and [the other "big preachers"] didn't have no time for that."

"It was not that they didn't have no *time*," chimed Johnnie Xavier, "but they had no '*know how.*' What were they going to do? They were dealing with people with the Mercedes Benzes. That's a whole different kind of problem."

"So you all grew apart from the [big preachers]?" I asked. "You never worked with them any more?"

"Well," said Pastor Wilkins. "Now, it's not so simple. That's always what you hear, that we went our way, we were not friendly to them, they didn't approve of us. Yes, they had a different way of dealing with people around here, but I could call them and say 'I need a job for Michael; he's getting out of jail and he's a good kid.' Or, 'I need a few hundred dollars for a program.' It was just that you couldn't use them for everything and, to be honest, folks around here didn't really trust them, so you had to make your choices and live with them. Some of us felt moved to respond to the hardest around here, those who needed the Lord and who needed us in more direct way, let us say. I'd say there were about forty of us, folks that were lot more modest in our means, that just decided to do things a little differently. We were called on by the Lord to not turn away from the muddy stuff, the messy things that messed up people's lives all the time."

At times, says Wilkins, the forty preachers planned agendas, but mostly they worked alone or spontaneously in groups of two and three to address a particular issue. They retained a close relationship with the Maquis Park residents, many of whom favored their modest, storefront places of worship over the larger churches. Says Pastor Wilkins, "We just knew who to call, got together when something was wrong, no one ever got credit or asked for nothing. It was just part of our ministry, helping the youth and the people, but also the police. We all knew they had a tough job and needed us."

The second outcome for the clergy was to become police intermediaries. They brokered conflicts between residents and police as well as situations in which aggrieved store owners had been robbed or looted and needed to solicit effective police assistance. Wilkins, Xavier, and others became the first points of contact with law enforcement agencies struggling to find effective ways to maintain order in inner-city communities. In public, black leaders chastised city officials for lack of parity in the allocation of law enforcement services to the Southside and West Side black neighborhoods; the more militant voices criticized the continued use of "control and containment" whereby officers appeared to confine drug trafficking, vice, and heinous crimes to these areas, ensuring that neighboring white and middle-class areas were not threatened. In private, however, there grew a working arrangement in which police turned to religious leaders to resolve conflicts, find perpetrators, disseminate information, and otherwise stay in tune with local matters. The clergy were quickly and quietly becoming the liaison that facilitated this new brand of cooperation between residents and police. Brother Patterson explains:

> "Police don't want to keep putting folks in jail," said Brother Patterson. "Not because they don't like that, but it's not good for them. They need informants on the street and, really, they need to

have the community trust them: jailing people, unless that's what the community wants, is not helpful."

"Why did you [in the clergy] get involved? Why did you think it was your responsibility?" I asked.

"Well, like I was saying, and this is going to sound funny, but, I'll say it anyway: what folks wanted is for some people, you know the rapists and killers, to be jailed, but lot of them didn't think that a kid selling drugs for the first time should get ten years in prison. And the lady stealing bread or clothes? Well, that was due to poverty, trying to get a bite to eat or clothes for their kids. These were problems, but you didn't need to break up families. Jailing was just making things worse.

"We [in the clergy] saw a moral responsibility to help make sure things weren't worse than they needed to be. See, many of us knew these kids, these folks stealing to eat. We just naturally became their advocates. Spoke for them, said that it was better to get them food in other ways than put them in prison."

"That was it? Just kids selling crack and shoplifters? And didn't the police dislike you for this? I don't see how you were helping them."

"We started with little things and then, we were getting stolen cars back for people. Maybe you beat up your old lady and so we worked with police to make sure the kids was okay, the lady was safe. James, he still fixing cars, right? Back then, we worked with police to make sure people paid him. Lot of things. I think this was very useful to the police particularly when fighting broke out, people started shooting and looting. They knew we could help them come into the community and get cooperation. They needed us."

As the clergy and the police learned to utilize each other, the clergy became involved in a growing number of community problems. In years to come, the work of the clergy would attract broader attention, particularly due to their explicit intervention in the organized criminal activities of neighborhood street gangs. This would jeopardize their working relations with some police officers who found their brokerage role suspect and thought they might be facilitating gang activity. But that was some years away. In the mid-1980s and into the next decade, a growing number of police officers seemed to accept, and even appreciate, the clergy's assistance. Sergeant Terry Waters, then a prominent police officer in Chicago's Southside, expressed gratitude for being able to call on the local clergy:

> I worked mostly with Minister Hortons, he helped me when gangs started fighting, helped to make sure they didn't kill everyone around them. It was very valuable. If somebody got robbed, I called on him to help me find out who did it. Lot of times we couldn't get that TV back! But we got the guy [who stole it] to pay for it. Little things, little things, they go a long way to helping police do their job, and those ministers, they helped us get trust in hard times.

Officer Marcellus Harrison met both Johnnie Xavier and Pastor Wilkins in the early eighties. He worked with both of them informally to respond to crime throughout the neighborhood. He says that he extended and deepened some of the work of his own father, Ainsley Harrison, who was a police detective in the late seventies and whom he says worked with preachers in a similar manner.

> Pops and Pastor Wilkins, they just decided that you can't ignore this new thing going on. Someone had to say, "Okay, you dealing [drugs], you pimping. Now, you did this or you killed so-and-so,

so you need to deal with it. But it was all behind closed doors, so you never heard about it, read about it. See, it's easy to ignore it, but there were people killing each other for stupid shit, I mean stealing $5. Pastor Wilkins and my dad, they realized they couldn't stop the dealing, but they could do something about it getting out of control. By the time I came around, it was real easy, because this was going on for years already, and it was keeping the area safe. Pastor wasn't the only one, now. I mean my dad was working with maybe six or seven people, all ministers who had a little church, or a storefront.

Officer Harrison described the many police officers in his father's station who agreed to help local residents solve problems and disputes behind closed doors, and outside of the normal legal channels. His list of the most common problems that involved the officers included pimps beating up prostitutes, domestic violence, gangs fighting for turf, shoplifting and theft of businesses, and drug dealers selling poisoned narcotics. Often local clergy could help the assigned police officer return stolen goods, bridge a disagreement, find compromise, and temporarily restore order.

It was clear that Pastor Wilkins and his colleagues had gained some notoriety, and perhaps even respect, because of their ability to work with both local residents and local police, with gang members and store owners. These men filled a necessary void and, in doing so, they began to command the attention of powerful clergy who thought of themselves as playing a similar role, albeit in relation to institutions in the wider city. Wilkins still could not obtain a municipal job or city contract very easily for a friend or congregant, but his ability to create truces between warring gangs was quietly earning him the loyalty of many local residents and stakeholders.

As the larger churches cemented their relationships with wealthier commuting parishioners from other neighborhoods, the smaller and storefront preachers were equally active in solidifying their social ties with local residents. By the dawn of the nineties, clergy in Maquis Park could be seen working informally with a variety of stakeholders whose capacities and resources were as varied as their livelihoods: pimps, gang leaders, small businessmen, beat cops, precinct captains, homeless and streetcorner persons, block club presidents, public housing tenant leaders, community organizers, school principals, teachers and security personnel, contractors hiring general laborers off the books, gambling kingpins, and security guards who could transport letters, food, and other goods into prisons and jails. These persons all possessed social capital, but their particular abilities were often limited in scope and tied to a few street corners or empty lots. This assembly of the respectable, the charlatan, the down-and-out, and the blue-collar had deep ties to the shady world, whether as traders of illicit goods, perpetrators of heinous crimes, or simply survivalists who needed to put food on the table any way they could. These actors were the lifeblood of the underground economic network that saturated Southside Chicago, and the clergy were intimately connected to many of them.

Not all was rosy in the newfound commitment by Maquis Park's grassroots and storefront preachers to community building. The preachers certainly saw themselves as providing healing, guidance, and practical assistance. But they were also getting something in return, and the exchange could be awkward, especially in the eyes of the public. In March 1992, Pastors Wilkins and Barnes organized a Southside Chicago "Youth Peace" rally at a local high school, with Principal Mark Waters. They brought ex–gang members and older gang leaders on the platform to address the high-school-age crowd. Religious rhetoric and the "scared straight" speech—where gang leaders spoke of the horrors behind prison walls—filled the cool air. In the back of the room sat reporters from all of the major city newspapers, which itself was a strange sight, given that only one Chicago reporter, Ethan Michaeli from the *Chicago Defender* newspaper, had been covering the nascent movement by clergy, school administrators, gang leaders, and community stakeholders to reduce gang-related violence. The reporters in attendance were skeptical about the budding relationship between clergy and the street gangs. One said, "I've seen this before, it's what the El Rukns [a street gang] problem is all about. Wilkins and Barnes have lost all credibility as far as I'm concerned. Taking money from the gangs. That's where it has to stop." Another countered, "It's hard to say no, if there's no other money around. You think the mayor's coming down here? No way."

The reporters were essentially debating the merits and dangers of what criminologists call the "social work approach" to street gangs: namely, using power structures within gangs, such as the influence of older members on younger recruits, to destabilize the organization's capacity to carry out organized criminal activity.[19] If the allegations were true, then Pastor Wilkins and his colleagues not only had failed to adequately embrace the social work strategy, but they had crossed a moral threshold by accepting the gang's donations. By the time of this 1992 rally, rumors had traveled throughout the city that donations to black churches were coming from drug-trafficking gangs. In fact, prosecutors who had leveled racketeering charges against the El Rukns street gang—a historic gang in the nearby Woodlawn and Englewood communities—were actively exploring the links between the gang and churches, businesses, social service agencies, schools, and other organizations that were suspected of laundering drug money, warehousing guns, facilitating drug running, and otherwise aiding and abetting a criminal organization.

The press focused disproportionately on patterns of corruption and street gang influence, but paid little attention to the ties between shady entrepreneurship and political capital. Only in 1995, when ex-gang-leader Wallace "Gator" Bradley ran for Chicago alderman in the Third Ward, and prominent African American ministers (including Reverend Jesse Jackson) lent support to nationwide street-gang-led "peace" initiatives, did public inquiry focus on the new political energy in inner-city Chicago. The involvement of clergy in public rallies was not as surprising as the press made it seem. It was the product of years of struggle and commitment by stakeholders in alienated Southside communities to develop an alternate strategy for repairing a torn social fabric. Thus, the formal political union of gang and church was the logical outcome of more than a decade of highly localized community building between equally marginalized individuals and social groups. In peace rallies and when gang members turned political aspirants, one saw a piece of Chicago's Southside not easily captured in sensationalist stories about corruption and moral failing—although moral licentiousness, questionable relations, and the influence of criminal organizations were all part of the story. For better and worse, there was under way a community-organizing process in which new relationships were being formed and new opportunities were arising for addressing local problems. Things would soon become unstable, however. In the words of Minister Ashland, one of the "big preachers" who criticized the work of the grassroots and storefront clergy, there would be serious "consequences" for those clergy who had chosen to play in the shady world.

The Politics of Donations

When Pastor Wilkins, Brother Patterson, and other Maquis Park clergy discuss their role in the underground economy, hesitation colors their voices. The shift is striking because these are people accustomed to proclamation and assured delivery. They are, after all, motivated by a higher authority. When talking about shady matters, however, an uncertainty creeps in. When asked to reflect on the late eighties and early nineties, when their work in the shady world had fully developed, they will scratch their heads in exasperation and lower their voices. There are questions that follow them: Did they help local residents by policing gang disputes, or did they end up strengthening the gang? Did they make life better for people making money off the books, or did they further alienate young adults from the mainstream economy? Did they compromise their own moral position by accepting money whose source was illegitimate? And did they lose valuable friendships and alliances among other clergy as a result of these activities?

Clergy who are involved in underground matters typically find themselves mediating disputes and playing the role of broker between underground traders and customers. They can be compensated in one or more of the following ways. Most directly, their work yields revenue in the form of increased donations to the church. A minister who helps a store owner find a looter or retrieve expensive stolen equipment might receive a $250 contribution the following Sunday, sometimes anonymously and other times directly. A preacher who convinces the police not to jail a mother's only teenage son might find a check for $500 from the mother's well-to-do brother. Permitting the use of the church for funerals of slain gang members can easily net a struggling storefront several thousand dollars.

In addition, there may also be direct payment for services rendered. Two pimps arguing over the use of an abandoned building might give the preacher $100 for arbitration services. A gang leader will pay a minister $50 to help deter one of the teenage members from shooting a rival gang affiliate. The church facility proves to be attractive for all manner of entrepreneurs needing to rent physical space: hairstylists give preachers 10 percent of daily proceeds for cutting hair inside; women selling homemade foodstuffs and clothing out of the back room will pay a similar fee; and gang members who occasionally use the church office or basement for a lucrative poker game might give $500 to $1,000 to the minister. Finally, pastors receive in-kind support. For example, a police officer asked Pastor Wilkins to help him find a thief; he returned the favor by looking the other way when a gang funeral took place at Pastor Wilkins's church. (Police sometimes will arrest gang members after these memorials.) A preacher who locates two inexpensive day laborers for a grocery store owner may end up with free food for a month.

The prevalence of barter, promissory notes, and in-kind payments make it impossible to provide an accurate accounting of individual remuneration for the clergy. However, there are three general ways that clergy work with the community and are compensated; any clergy member may benefit from more than one means of generating income. Some preachers make themselves a central part of criminal networks. Pastor Wilkins belongs to this small group of six to ten preachers (the number changes over time) who are the first point of contact for breaches of contract and social disputes between shady dealers—street gangs, prostitutes, and burglars among them. These pastors and ministers will retrieve stolen property, mend a broken relationship between pimp and prostitute, and prevent a street gang battle from escalating into a war. One minister estimated that, between 1989 and 1995, he earned approximately $10,000 a year for such services. Pastor Wilkins reported garnering $10,000 to $13,000 annually in that time period—although he says that he received less than $2,000 for such services before that time. Wilkins would not admit a personal role in storing guns, drugs, and stolen property, but he said that some clergy performed these functions and, in doing so, would earn roughly $7,500 per year.

A second set of preachers work more closely with the residential population. They help find off-the-books work for adults and often rent their spaces to individual entrepreneurs who need a place of business, be it for hairstyling, gambling, psychic services, or car repair. These clergy routinely contact their counterparts who work directly with criminal organizations in order to find electronic equipment stolen from a home or an apartment. They earn far less money—two ministers said they make $2,500 per year, on average—but they are more likely to receive in-kind donations and services, such as free car repair, food, clothing, home maintenance, and security from sympathetic police. There were usually fifteen to twenty clergy who played this role.

A final group provides two critical services: brokering police relations and serving as liaison for neighboring communities. In this group one can find clergy with prominent public voices, such as Minister Hortons, Brother Patterson, and Reverend Barnes. Hortons estimates that he could earn $7,500 to $15,000 per year, but that much of the support he receives is in the form of "promises and IOUs." Hortons might help a resident find a job outside of Maquis Park, and in return the individual might pay the minister 10 percent of the salary for the first six months. Barnes earns a finder's fee for sending renters to landlords in nearby communities. And all three men have been paid by law enforcement when they bring in a suspect or help settle a dispute. Hortons describes some other work that falls in these two categories:

> "I was never one for taking the gang's money. Most of us, that's not our thing. But with the work we do, we know the cops watch over our property. We may get the police to respond quickly to a problem and, yes, the person who was helped might make a donation or just give us a check. Or maybe we can get the aldermen to relax on a building inspection. Someone might give us a bigger donation for that. It's a little, well, unsettling. But I would lie if I said it didn't matter or it didn't help."
>
> "But I just don't see how you could make that much money, just doing that," I said.
>
> "Well, it's a lot more than that. Remember, we also help find people jobs, we bring cars over for Johnnie to fix. Brother Patterson can find any stolen car on the Southside! I suppose what I'm saying is it's not about the money. It's about getting things done. I'll never be rich. None of us will be. But when you can bring out a thousand people on a rainy day to protest. You are a wealthy man."
>
> "But how do you get paid for that?" I asked.
>
> "Well, sometimes you don't. You get what I call 'promises and IOUs.' You understand? You help someone, they help you out later. Look, I have a car, right? I'll never pay for it to be repaired because every store around here will fix it, with parts! I have a house. I've never paid for a repair. The bank knows me and helps me out. Everyday somebody fixing me a plate of food, and the restaurants

don't charge me. My wife and I haven't cooked lunch in ten years! So, I've got my costs down and, frankly, I'm grateful to be loved around here."

Although they can quickly summon an audience of a gang leader or pimp, these clergy take care to distance themselves from daily engagement in the netherworld. Typically they help the police work more effectively—for example, by mediating discussions between police and block club presidents or public housing tenant leaders. They are usually older, with strong political connections, and they can mobilize parishioners effectively for mass protests, voter registration, candlelight vigils, and other conventional community organizing activities.

These distinctions are blurred in practice. A minister may personally benefit from his work with gangs at one time, but he may simultaneously help the police find criminals. Some who are working productively with the police may also be deriving compensation from residents for helping them find off-the-books work. The distinctions are important because they differentiate the kinds of compensation that clergy can derive from shady activities. Moreover, the clergy themselves are less disposed to accept donations from criminals than they are to take a finder's fee for helping police or residents in underground matters. In the course of everyday life in the neighborhood, where poverty demands innovation and adaptation, members of the clergy—like the lay population—may gravitate to available opportunities without thinking too much about the consequences of accepting different forms of shady remuneration.

Not everyone in Maquis Park feels that it is appropriate for their clergy to be performing these services. Congregants do not necessarily want their ministers to participate in local dispute resolution, particularly when those disputes involve dangerous, destabilizing activities. A preacher who allows his church to host funerals for slain street gang members and then suddenly purchases a fancy new car may give the impression of impropriety and moral negligence—even if the donations do not originate from involvement in criminal activities. Until the mid-1990s, the various informal social control initiatives that involved clergy were largely backroom efforts; they received minimal publicity, and therefore widespread criticism was not common.[20] Preachers managed to keep much of their work with police, underground entrepreneurs, and pimps out of the public eye. Clergy typically worked by themselves and in limited geographic areas—mostly near their own places of worship. They did not necessarily try to hide their actions from each other, but at the same time they did not have much reason to confront one other about their shared involvement in local social control.

Preachers who worked in the shady world would become more visible in the local community over the course of the nineties. Maquis Park's clergy were part of the rise and fall of the corporate gang in that decade. They were some of the strongest champions of the efforts by gang members to channel rebellious youth energy into electoral politics. They joined with other community activists in publicizing this grassroots campaign as a sincere attempt by marginal inner-city youth to turn their lives around. As they took such stances, not only did they have to answer publicly to their congregants about their involvement with gang-affiliated political campaigns and voter registration drives, but they also debated among themselves the proper role of the church in non-religious community affairs. The atmosphere was emotionally and politically charged. As reports and public speculation increased over ministers accepting donations from disreputable actors, an identifiable split emerged within the clergy: on the one hand, Pastor Wilkins advocated "staying true" to the mission of helping those whom the rest of society had neglected. The grassroots and storefront clergy should withstand the temporary public outcry, Wilkins said: "We had to stay true and not be swayed by people who didn't understand what it means to serve in the name of the Lord."

In slight contrast, Pastor Barnes, Wilkins's longtime friend and associate in the grassroots contingent, wanted reflection and redirection: "We needed to reflect on where we had come from, make some changes, get back to healing and away from these temptations in our faces." Barnes was one of the forty preachers who had historically challenged the elite clergy. But in the early nineties he began airing his views and separating from Wilkins, his collaborator for over a decade. The cleavage sharpened after 1992, when Barnes received an invitation to join the Greater Grand Boulevard Development Group, a prominent economic development agency representing the area that included Maquis Park and several neighboring poor communities. The agency was the publicly recognized spokesperson for economic and real estate development interests, in particular for contracts and resources that came via the Daley administration as well as from government agencies and businesses friendly to the mayor. Barnes spoke loudly of the need for clergy to distance themselves from the gangs, eschew their involvement in underground activities—even as mediators—and build productive alliances with the power base in the area. Not surprisingly, his definition of the power base was now very different from Wilkins's, and included prominent clergy, aldermen whose votes fell in line with the mayor, and real estate developers seeking to rebuild on cheap lots and demolished public housing tracts. By this point, Barnes had ended his involvement in the backroom dealings with street gang leaders. Most importantly, he successfully persuaded a dozen of the forty grassroots preachers to join him in declining questionable donations and shifting their support toward the political mainstream.

Pastor Wilkins was not one of these twelve. He continued to work with Brother Patterson, Minister Hortons, and a few other clergy on mediation and brokerage in the underground arena. Wilkins and his colleagues lent moral backing to Maquis Park's voter registration drive of troubled youth (including known gang members) and the correlate campaigns to elect an ex–gang leader to aldermanic office (he eventually lost the race in a runoff). He also actively defended his taking gang donations and commissions for his services. Despite the indictment of street gangs as organized criminal entities, these preachers continued to speak of gang members as potential community leaders who, in the words of Brother Patterson, "had turned themselves around and wanted to be the future of Maquis Park." These preachers were deeply distrustful of officials in Mayor Daley's administration who dangled grants, loans, and development opportunities in front of their counterparts in return for quiescence and political support. They remained firm in their belief that these offers did not alter the overall indifference displayed by the city's political elite to poor black people.

> If they had tried to help people get a job, get off drugs, yes, yes, yes! I would be right there with them. But trying to build $200,000 condos is not what we needed. Who was that for? All them so-called preachers with their businesses building housing, they were the only ones benefiting. We still didn't see how all this talk about "the new [Mayor] Daley" was helping anybody around here. They

were tearing down housing, stores were closing, people were on hard times. That's why I couldn't join up with them. It just wasn't right.

The disagreements between Pastor Barnes and Pastor Wilkins resulted in diminished collaboration among clergy more generally, in mediation and brokerage activities that, up to this point, had brought them together relatively frequently. Barnes became hesitant to help residents retrieve stolen property. He asked his fellow clergy to remove gambling from their churches and to be more discriminating in taking commissions from underground entrepreneurs. But not surprisingly, street gang activity became the focal point of the debate. Barnes asked his colleagues to refuse to intercede in street gang conflicts. He suggested that they shift their involvement in crime reduction from backroom negotiations with gangs and troubled youth to a supportive role in police investigations. Those in his camp stopped appearing at public protests over inadequate city funding for at-risk youth and at high school rallies intended to show the new, reformed face of the street gang movement. Unlike in the past, Barnes now agreed with critics who said that these events were signs that gangs had made inroads into the legitimate organizations in the community. Even though their involvement in street gang activity was only a small part of the preachers' efforts to deal with local conflicts in the shady world, the gang became the rallying cry in Barnes's campaign to realign the black clergy with the Daley machine. One of the preachers, Reverend Joseph Washburn, expressed this succinctly when he said,

Was Daley buying out the black preachers? Maybe. But if you see money coming into your community and housing being built, you better get on board. Our brother, Pastor Barnes, realized we were only hurting ourselves by placing our hopes in people who had already gone astray and whose lives were in need of healing. We [in the clergy] were being weak when we thought that those who were really hurting—on drugs, strung up, dealing drugs, in and out jail—could really be foundation for our community. No. This was a mistake. We were wrong not to see them as hurting, and so we changed our strategy.

The divide forming within the grassroots-and-storefront clergy stratum was not solely a result of Mayor Richard M. Daley's drive to suppress criticism of his policies and fold black preachers into his political machine. There were other changes taking place in the political economy of inner-city Chicago, transformations that further divided the Pastor Wilkinses of Maquis Park from the Pastor Barneses. As we have seen, the eighties offered few economic resources, outside of the Democratic political machine, to which Southside Chicago's political leaders and spokespersons could turn for community building and economic advancement. Financial institutions and real estate developers were largely unwilling to invest in Maquis Park and surrounding communities. Manufacturing and light industrial companies had eschewed the ghetto for the suburbs and areas overseas, taking valuable blue-collar jobs with them.

At the end of the decade, however, there was blossoming a small but prominent civic and governmental interest that promised to bring considerable resources to Chicago's ghettos. Its profit ventures took shape in Empowerment Zone initiatives that mostly subsidized the efforts of businesspeople outside the neighborhood to start ghetto-based businesses. The other major development initiative was also a government subsidy: starting in

1993, the Chicago Housing Authority began demolishing large, undervalued tracts of public housing and resold the lands to private developers who built homes there for middle- and upper-class families.

The nonprofit face of this increased development activity manifested in foundations, charities, and some governmental agencies that collectively promoted the virtues of "comprehensive community initiatives" (CCIs). This catch-all category included a wide range of grants, fellowships, and investment strategies, all connected by the premise that residents and stakeholders working in collaboration could achieve more good than a single person or organization could. Millions of dollars of charitable funding became available to social service organizations that bought into this vision.

The "CCI movement" altered the conventional funding strategy wherein an individual organization receives a grant and administers a program (such as housing rehabilitation, youth service delivery, or mental health assistance).[21] Philanthropy, so the CCI proponents stated, could better restore the social fabric of American inner cities by creating coalitions, umbrella organizations, and collaborative entities that engaged in joint and cooperative ventures. While cooperation was one part of the CCI ideology, avoiding political activity was another. That is, activists, community organizers, and other rabble-rousers who preferred protest and social movements were usually not welcome in these initiatives. The new mantra of collaborative service delivery eschewed the past thirty years of grassroots political action. The notion of collaboration sponsored by CCI granting agencies was almost always for nonpolitical purposes, like youth programming. Not surprisingly, this tended to anger grassroots leaders who could not obtain CCI support for their community organizing, political empowerment, and other activities that contested the status quo. As a result, the directors of CCIs tended to either ignore local activists or push organizations with political interests into a more sterile "service delivery" profile. So, for example, a church leading protests against the city for affordable housing might be asked by a CCI initiative to lower their cries and instead lend public support to a large nonprofit corporation buying up land tracts in order to build a housing complex for working and middle-class families. In return for their support, the church might receive a large grant to work with other CCI agencies providing services to newly arriving residents.

In theory, within the CCI movement the clergy were a natural resource for external funders like charities and large foundations. Around the country, such initiatives had placed the clergy in prominent positions within CCI efforts. Clergy were well connected to families, and they had a historically proven ability to provide services and offer help in a compassionate, trustworthy way. Participating clergy could also help deflect local criticism of CCI initiatives, as their moral standing legitimized the CCI preference for nonpolitical activities. Around the country, in large urban areas such as Baltimore and Atlanta and smaller cities like Hartford and Memphis, one could find clergy playing an important role in helping CCIs get off the ground. They ensured participation by local families, they helped service providers understand the contours of household need, and they ensured that CCIs had some legitimacy, particularly when external funders unfamiliar with the neighborhood wanted to play a role in families' lives.

In Chicago's Southside, millions of dollars were suddenly being allocated each year by CCI initiatives. But as these coalitions worked to build housing, provide social services, organize youth programming, and improve community–police relations, clergy were all but invisible. In places like Maquis Park, surprisingly few preachers ever participated in CCI initiatives. Their absence was noteworthy because churches had few other sources of material support—the majority hosted poor congregations and did not receive much money from the city and state political machine—and so one would expect them to take advantage of funding opportunities created by CCIs. Ultimately, however, only a small number—mostly the more prominent preachers—were listed as participating members of CCI councils and federations that shepherded the allocation of philanthropic funds. Most inner-city preachers played a minimal role. Many say they were never invited or their political leanings were not accepted. But some are quick to add that their myriad involvements in other forms of community building and grassroots politics left them little time for such initiatives. Even if they had time, most operated out of modest storefronts and small buildings that had little capacity to host programs for youth; this effectively placed them out of reach of funds that were being allocated to local organizations for programming. And it meant that their constituents who might not have strong connections to other churches and to other service providers were also effectively shut out of the benefits of the CCI movement.

What none of the clergy mention, however, is that their ties to street gangs emerged again as a problem and made the leaders of the CCIs hesitant to draw on the clergy. The Greater Grand Boulevard Community Association (GGBCA) is an example of one of many prominent, newly created CCI entities. Community organizations applied to become a part of GGBCA and then became eligible for the money that the Association received from charities, foundations, and government agencies. Membership had many practical benefits, including grant money and social connections to wider funding agencies. However, from 1991 to 1995 a count of the GGBCA members revealed very few churches. The absence of Maquis Park's clergy in GGBCA was a clear loss for many parties, in particular those residents who turned to churches for information about available programs and services. The reasons for their absence were troubling, not only to those setting up such organizations, but for the clergy themselves. Allegations of collusion with gangs and of accepting inappropriate donations had definitely reached a wider public. Preachers found their moral legitimacy threatened, and their absence in such collaborative organizations was a sign of the cost of public stigma. Myra Wilson, one of the early leaders of the GGBCA, describes the challenges of bringing the grassroots and storefront preachers into the fold of her CCI.

> There were obvious reasons they weren't at the table. Lot of them didn't have the capacity to receive money from us, or carry out programs. They were very small. And this is unfortunate because they were really the ones who had ties to the residents, who could get residents on board—which, to be honest, was really the greatest challenge. But there was another problem. They were not trusted by other community leaders. There was suspicion that Brother Patterson and Pastor Barnes, and the others, were too close to the gangs. That they were getting their money illegally. That they could really not be worked with without making our own funders nervous. Maybe there was a solution, but we decided early on that the risk was too great to invite them.

It was against this backdrop that Pastor Barnes joined forces with some of the more powerful clergy in Maquis Park to seek a place in GGBCA and thereby benefit from the new money and status. By 1995, GGBCA and other similar coalitions had succeeded in drawing attention to the needs of black Chicagoans in the Southside community. Residential real estate development had been revived, attracting new black middle- and upper-class families. (News of impending public housing demolition assuaged the fears of many prospective homeowners that they would be moving into a community that was still depressed.) The Daley administration had strengthened its relationships with prominent black preachers, many of whom were benefiting from municipal contracts for affordable housing development and social service provision. And banks, real estate development firms, grocery store chains, and service retailers had a growing commercial interest in some parts of these poor areas. Barnes saw an opportunity to benefit from the newfound interest in a rebirth of Chicago's historic Southside region. As he withdrew from Pastor Wilkins and the other grassroots and storefront preachers, Barnes declared openly his allegiance to the new civic infrastructure, led by GGBCA and the Greater Grand Boulevard Development Board, that was spearheading the drive to gentrify an historically ailing Southside. His efforts proved successful: in 1996, Barnes was made a member of GGBCA, and in less than six months he became an influential member of the organization's steering committee.

The end of the nineties would reveal a split in the ranks of Maquis Park's preachers, with one segment deeply immersed in the underground world and the other trying to reconnect with the political mainstream. It is difficult to gauge whether the mainstream aims of Pastor Barnes and his colleagues had meant that they had fully severed ties with shady types and would no longer provide brokerage-style services in the shady world. But perhaps more important is the public commitment that the Barnes and Wilkins contingents had made. Wilkins and his colleagues were adamant that the clergy attend to marginal families, and if that meant working outside mainstream channels and in secretive ways to restore social order, so be it. The other group had adopted a discourse of redemption by crying out that it was time to mend the wounds in Maquis Park. Pastor Barnes spoke of the mistakes he had made by courting the criminal class: "Even the clergy is not beyond sin. Yes, we tried to help the young people, but when you are helping the criminal be a better criminal, you are not do-ing your duty as a preacher. It's time to admit the error of our ways, it's time for healing."

In addition to an ideological cleavage, there was attrition in the ranks of the clergy. By the year 2000, only nineteen of the forty preachers who had been working at the grassroots level in the mid-1980s still had an active church. (The larger churches were still in operation, and twelve new ministries had come into be-ing). The others listed the inability to pay for rent and upkeep as the main reasons for dissolving their ministries. In this way, they were not unlike urban preachers around the country—grassroots and storefront churches often close and reopen as financial cir-cumstances permit.[22] Yet, while the attrition rate was not far off the norm, the changes could still be hard on families who de-pended on both clergy and congregation for support and fellow-ship.

One cannot underestimate the dependence of many grassroots and storefront preachers on the underground economy for their own livelihood. Even if their receipt of money and services was indirect, in the shady economy many found a potential source of manpower, resources, and funding that enabled clergy to with-stand the twin forces of their community's economic impover-ishment and the political marginalization from the local power elite. In their histories, one sees that the post-civil-rights political economy of Southside Chicago, so often written about in terms of its effects on families and households, had an equally devastating impact on the church, the one long-standing source of moral guidance and social support in black urban America. We would be remiss to think that the church would somehow be sheltered from economic and political alienation.

By 2000 there remained in Maquis Park a small number of clergy who worked actively in local dispute resolution and police–community mediation. But they were a splintered group, and the members had little contact with one another. The infighting had reduced the number of collaborations and the spirit of unity within an historically marginal clergy. Brother Patterson said that by the end of the century, he and his colleagues in the ministry were exhausted. They felt ignored by powerful members of various Chicago circles: philanthropic, political, and spiritual. In particular, they felt the sting of being left to fend for themselves by former colleagues, most of whom were associated with Pastor Barnes, who once worked closely with them. So, Patterson says, they retreated into their own churches.

> I think, to be very honest with you, that all of us feel that we need
> to ask the Lord for direction. We have to find our solace, our
> spirit, our sense of purpose from the Bible, from the teachings,
> from our Church. I don't think we have gone astray, I don't think
> we led anyone else astray, but it is now a very difficult time for us.
> To work so hard to stay together and then to just be discarded, ig-
> nored, left behind by people whom we trusted and whom we
> needed. We all feel a little alone and, like I say, man we are tired.

There were now only a handful of active ministries that espoused the virtues of building community by drawing on the marginalized and downtrodden. Although these churches might appear determined and resilient, in practice the clergy had little energy left to build and sustain a collective movement. There were consequences for residents. Some greatly valued those preachers who remained active in helping calm waters in the shady world. Problems like theft, gang violence, public disorder, inadequate policing, and municipal neglect had not disappeared in Maquis Park at the end of the decade. Big Cat's gang, hoping to compensate for dwindling crack revenue, renewed its drive to control underground activity, and the gang's takeover of public space, fights between store owners and hustlers, and the decreasing safety in parks were some of the thorny issues that would require active intervention by local leaders if the community was going to remain habitable.

Maquis Park's preachers were not strangers to exhaustion. This generation of clergy had been working from their churches since the seventies, sinking into the daily life of the downtrodden, improving solutions, and offering a hand. Of course, in Maquis Park it was impossible to do God's work without having some dealings with the local underground economy. The shady sphere helped bring resources not only into homes and businesses, but also into cathedrals and storefronts. The eighties and nineties showed that the struggling preacher—struggling to make rent as well as to ensure that there were sufficient resources on hand for congregants—was no less vulnerable to the goods, money, and services that might be procured off the books than was the proprietor who could not qualify for a bank loan (and so turned to a loan shark) or the block club president who could not obtain effective policing (and so made secretive deals with a criminal class). The preacher found in the underground economy a place to keep his own livelihood intact—however temporary this stability may have been—and to keep the church moving forward.

Parishioners are understandably uneasy when it comes to clergy taking advantage of off-the-books opportunities. Perhaps the most common (and pithy) response was made by Gloriella Jackson, a sixty-three-year-old member of Pastor Wilkins's congregation. She elegantly described the situation faced by local preachers, one not altogether different from that of the general population:

> [Pastor Wilkins] knows in his heart when something he's doing is not right. We have faith that the Lord speaks to him just as the Lord speaks to us. So, no, I'm not concerned when I see the gang come in here for their funerals. And, truth be told, we are all God's children. All of us need to be tended over, to be told what is right and wrong. Around here, it is not so easy all the time to figure out what is right and what is wrong, who is good and who is bad. We are poor people. And so are our ministers. So, why would you think he acts any different than us? We need him to be our leader, not perfect or without sin.

When confronted with stories of preachers who solved problems in the shady world for a fee, most people shrug and move on, offering little in the way of judgment. They talk about gang leaders, prostitutes, and others in the underground who engaged the clergy, but their judgments tended to fall on the laity, not the preacher.

Certainly, part of the silence may be due to a discomfort people feel about allegations that their spiritual leader not only is fallible but has behaved immorally. In their need to see their leaders (spiritual or secular) as having a higher, morally legitimate authority, they are hardly unique. But it also may be that their evaluations of the clergy are tempered by the shady activities that are more public, namely, the situations in which clergy are solving problems, responding to gang crime, helping settle disputes, and otherwise keeping law and order. The ever-present need to deal with the illegality of the underground economy means there is always a need for those people who try to mediate it and provide some ethical guidance. There is rarely proof that one's minister purchased his brand new car with money he received from his dealings with criminals. But there is usually evidence of the minister's work in the shady sphere. Indeed, in sermons, clergy will mention the ways people stray—including, in Maquis Park, their involvement in illegal moneymaking—and the ways the preacher might have counseled and otherwise provided corrective guidance to such individuals. These narrations are powerful stories because they are the familiar struggles of daily life in Maquis Park; they are the situations facing nearly all of the households who must work and live amid a vibrant local underground economy. And such explicit recounting by clergy emphasizes to parishioners that, however else the ministers may be behaving, they are doing something productive by dealing with problems rather than sweeping them under the rug—or, perhaps worse, by taking the attitude of other political and civic leaders and neglecting them entirely.

The history of clergy involvement in the underground arena shows that this kind of community building is fraught with danger. Clergy were rarely physically abused by virtue of their involvement in shady activities, but they did suffer public criticism, exclusion from certain policies and programs, and the stigma that can sometimes accompany work at the boundaries of shady and legitimate realms. The work of some clergy with gangs in the mid-nineties made others wary of inviting them to participate in philanthropic initiatives that dispensed funds to local organizations; some also suffered the rebuke of the city administration for their explicit support of marginal actors—like youth in gangs—who were leading a key part of their lives in the shady realm. The exuberance of some clergy for the needs of the dispossessed did not subside after 2000. In fact, Big Cat and the Maquis Park Kings street gang had caused a stir locally and were providing more than enough opportunities for the clergy to resume their role as mediator and healer. Pastor Wilkins had already responded to the local need in his work with Marlene Matteson and some of the shopkeepers on West Street. But after the hustler Babycake Jackson died in 2002, he would try a more impressive strategy to monitor and regulate those working on the shady side of economic life. And just as in the past, he and others who joined him would be taking on great risks in their interventions to keep Maquis Park safe and habitable.

Chapter Six
Our Gang

Big Cat turned the pages of a dusty and worn book and read out loud passages of a bygone era. "A Black King is a Black King for life. He is a man who protects his family and children. He places the life of other Black Kings ahead of his. He never forgets the community." He stopped, cleared his throat, and with more than a hint of emotion in his voice, he read the last sentence another time, emphasizing "community." In a book entitled *Literature of Black Kings Nation*—the primer for an aspiring member of the street gang—the powerful gang leader pointed to expectations of chivalry and to the exhortations to sacrifice for one's fellow gang members, one's family, and one's community. The rules and regulations for membership in the Black Kings organization said little about how to manage a criminal organization or what the protocols were for the use of violence. Instead, these pages described a utopian vision: one day, all black street gang members in the United States would join together to wrest control of their communities from white colonizers. Before this day came, the manual instructed, all Black Kings members must learn the secret handshakes, hand signs, and codes of conduct. They were trying to prepare themselves, to make themselves ready.

Big Cat was proud of this book. Often in Black Kings meetings, he would read aloud and preach the gospel of gangland—a place with eerie resemblances to the solidaristic ideals of college fraternities and divisions of the armed forces. "We have several hundred members," he would say. "We are a nation, a nation within a city." Two of his brothers, three of his uncles, and many of his cousins were also Black Kings members. "I have never had a family," he would say, describing a life in poverty in which he was shuttled from apartment to apartment, as first his mother, then an aunt, then a friend of the family fell on hard times and was unable to care for him. "These guys [the Black Kings] are my family."

And alongside his men, Maquis Park was his community. "I was born and raised here, and I'll die here," he promised. "Don't know how or when I'll pass. But I *will* die here." He frequently would refer to residents of Maquis Park as "his people" or "my extended family," and he indicated that his charity in local matters knew no bounds. "Ask anybody around here," he liked to say. "I am a man of the community, a community man. I give money, my boys clean up the parks, we help old ladies cross the street. Anything to help people get what they need." Close your eyes, and you would think Big Cat either held elected office or was landed gentry.

But ask residents, and a different opinion emerges regarding Big Cat and the Black Kings organization. It is less positive, less consistent. The men and women of Maquis Park have been living with street gangs for decades. The boasts of Big Cat are nothing new to them. Many could recall gang-affiliated youth who sat on corners and sang, who participated in civil rights struggles, and who provided manpower for black machine politicians eager to intimidate residents into voting for one candidate or another. They saw in the Black Kings a different gang. One of the most popular maxims one could hear on the streets referred to the sixties and early seventies: "Back then, there were gangs; today, it's a business." By the early part of 2000, the gang was no longer an informal ensemble of youth; it was a more serious organization whose members would do whatever it took to make money. And most recently they saw a gang that was branching out from its shady profile as drug dealer and impinging on the (arguably) less-shady labors that involved—and sustained—the wider community. Big Cat and his gang members were no longer happy to rest with a monopoly on crack cocaine and heroin sales, in part because that economy was no longer so lucrative. As they set out to extort businesses, take over the illicit rackets long held by non-gang-affiliated residents, and tax shady traders working in parks and alleyways and on the streets, their impact on the community grew.

Because Big Cat had enlarged his shady profile, it became harder and harder for Maquis Park's residents to ignore the outlaw organization. And just as important, they could not rest their hopes on the police to come to their aid in these changing times. Though life on the street was changing in many worrying ways, one thing remained consistent. For nearly a century, black Chicagoans had never been able to rely on law enforcement, be it for gang- or non-gang-related problems. Thus,

Maquis Park's residents understood that alternate means would be required to combat these new threats to their safety and security.

But in Maquis Park, as in so many American ghettos, confronting the local gang requires wading through some very murky waters. This community is in many ways held together by a pervasive underground economy, and here, in the gray areas of ethics and legality, gang members and residents are inextricably linked. In practice, many residents might have no direct involvement in shady trading. However, as we have seen, the underground economy manages to touch all households, whether as a direct source of income, as a place to acquire cheap goods and services, or as a part of the public theater. Thus, it is not so easy to separate the innocent from the perpetrator. The same person who despises the gang's drug trading may depend on a member of the household to bring money into the home by fixing cars off the books. Fixing cars is not equivalent to dealing drugs, but as Chicago's working poor entered the year 2000, the gang's advances were making very blurry the lines that divided shady traders from one another. When *good* and *bad* have become very relative terms, how do you solve your problems?

Since the early twentieth century, kids growing up in cities have been tempted to join their local street gang. Until relatively recently, whether in white, black, Latino, or Asian neighborhoods, most gang members were adolescents and teens. They looked to the gang primarily for peer support. And their socially destructive behavior consisted primarily of petty delinquency, such as hanging out on street corners, gambling, and shoplifting; violent crime, drug trafficking, assault, and more serious forms of theft were rare. Notably, economic gain was neither a primary motive nor much of an option—one heard occasionally of ward political organizations paying gangs either to turn out the vote or to harass the opposition's supporters, but there were few other money-making activities. The gang's limited economic attraction was clear, and as members became young adults they would graduate out of their adolescent boredom or become disillusioned with the easy thrills of gang life, or they would realize the need to work and tend to family responsibilities. They were assisted by a battery of parole and probation officers, employers, and social workers who implemented a "rehabilitative" model of youth delinquency that aimed to integrate these young people back into family, school, and workplace.[1]

Around the late seventies in Chicago's Southside, as in the ghettos of most large American cities, the street gang became a prominent economic force—scholars noted the shift as the birth of the "corporate" gang. At a time when most Americans still pictured gangs in the singsongy hues of *West Side Story*, suddenly the gang had fully developed commercial interests, primarily in the sale of narcotics and, to a lesser degree, commercial extortion. Far from brotherhood or bonding, its primary mission was to further illicit gain. While gangs always had individuals who earned off the books, the organizations as a whole historically were not oriented toward economic pursuits; now the dollar became almighty.[2] The gang's corporate turn was part and parcel of the broader decimation of American inner cities after the Second World War. The hundreds of thousands of youth who joined Chicago's gangs during and after the civil rights era faced social conditions similar to those of their counterparts across urban America: there were no jobs in their neighborhoods; unions and city governments discriminated against them, and hired mostly whites instead; a growing middle-class leadership fought their working-poor counterparts to win the meager political and economic crumbs that city leaders threw black urbanites. In other words, sociologist William Julius Wilson's late-1980s work on "socially isolated" urban poor aptly described those young people; they turned to the gang as a means of supplanting the utter lack of mainstream work opportunities.[3]

To be sure, as in the past, some teens continued to join the gang for social support; but these young people were now modeling themselves after a contingent a few years older who had broken their teeth on the emerging drug trade. Big Cat, a young man in the eighties, was one of these many acolytes. With his adolescent strut, he modeled himself after the then-ascendant leaders of the Black Kings—celebrated men like Babyboy Matteson and Butternut Watkins—and dreamed of someday living in glamour like these older men, some of whom were barely of legal drinking age, who boasted high illegal incomes and manifested their power in flashy clothing, jewelry, and sports cars. The bulk of revenue for the gang came from drug distribution; additional monies could be derived from organizing prostitution and gun-trading rackets, extortion, and, much less often, investments in legitimate businesses. There is no consensus as to the precise reasons why gangs suddenly grew to successfully direct large-scale illegal economic activities and began to experiment with various entrepreneurial schemes. Some point to the departure of the Italian Mafia (which opened the door for black hustlers of various stripes to take over gambling and drug trafficking); others point to the lack of police protection in the ghetto (which enabled gangs to extort businesses, steal, and otherwise run their shady dealings); and there is some truth to the argument that twenty- and thirty-somethings, being at a different point in their lives than teenagers, will give higher priority to finding an organized means of earning income. These and other factors were probably all at play.

Regardless of the exact origin of corporate gang activity, law enforcement throughout urban America quickly understood the impact of this historically novel street gang presence. In 1978 Chicago's law enforcement agencies merged their street gang and narcotics divisions because of the overwhelming involvement of gang members in drug trafficking.[4] Other cities soon followed suit. In the late eighties and early nineties, as a confirmation of street gangs' success in dominating the drug economy in Chicago, the federal government would utilize powers granted by the 1970 Racketeer Influenced and Corrupt Organizations Act (RICO) to try to dismantle the organized criminal networks of gangs throughout urban ghetto neighborhoods. Eventually, several hundred senior gang members and their sympathizers ended up in jail for their roles in drug sales, commercial extortion, tax evasion, and other crimes tied to gangs' criminal enterprises. Five of the highest-ranking members of the Maquis Park Black Kings outfit were convicted and sent to prison, leaving a gaping hole in the leadership that Big Cat and his peers eagerly filled.

As the indictments rolled in, law enforcement officials painted a picture of corporate gangs that showed their firm rooting in the inner-city community soil. Millions of dollars had flowed into the gangs' coffers from the community, and out of them right back to their neighbors and associates. Only then did the American public begin to understand not only the extent to which the street gang had had changed but also the new kinds of relationships that gangs had developed with residents, police, local organizations, and others in the community.

In this time period, roughly 1985 to 1997, the corporate gang had become a vital institution in black (and, to a lesser degree,

Latino) neighborhoods, one that could not be easily rebuffed by law enforcement interdiction or social work intervention. Collaborations between residents and gang members were not confined to neighborhoods of dire poverty. Even in middle-class areas that were predominantly black, gang members worked with local stakeholders to organize recreational leagues, keep drug dealing away from schools and public parks, and otherwise address public safety problems (that they themselves may have created).[5] It would be foolish to infer that black Chicago decided to embrace its local gangs with open arms. But it be equally silly to claim that the gang's relationship with other local actors in the community was an entirely novel phenomenon. Although the nineties might have witnessed the spread of *economic* ties between gang members and the wider populations, over the past one hundred years where there was extortion, corruption in city politics, and the need to bring out the vote, one could find a gang milling about and working with other politicos. What changed, and what residents of Maquis Park and other Chicago communities had to contend with, was the extent to which the gangs had insinuated themselves—and their drug money—into the deepest reaches of the community. And this aspect of the gang's corporate turn is as important as the aging membership or any preference among its membership to eschew social activities in favor of economic ones.

In fact, during the eighties and nineties, people throughout the community became implicated in what became known, in a phrase popularized in that era, as Chicago's "gang and drug problem." Car dealerships, dry cleaners, and real estate companies that laundered money were found to be directly complicit in gangs' illegal activities.[6] In one case a company offering tours of significant African American historical sites in Chicago was found to be laundering drug revenue.[7] But blame was not reserved for companies alone. The law reached deep into the community and under the RICO banner indicted local organizations and individuals: clergy who accepted donations to host slain gang member funerals; principals who employed gang members as hall monitors to patrol other gang members; police officers willing to exchange information on crimes for leniency with respect to patrols and arrest; and social service agencies willing to admit the gangs into their facilities.[8] These were just some of those who faced police investigation and public criticism.[9]

The eighties also witnessed a surge of grassroots activity as organizations in poor and working-class neighborhoods registered gang members to vote, hoping to turn wayward youth into engaged citizens. Former gang leaders sponsored political candidates, many of whom also were former gang leaders. An older gang leadership, in their thirties and forties, saw the general cooperation between grassroots groups and gangs as an opportunity to translate shady economic power into political capital. Those with gang affiliations worked with members of churches, community development corporations, mainstream political organizations, youth agencies, and activist groups to turn rank-and-file gang members into potential voters.[10] Many high-ranking gang leaders stated to inquiring ethnographers and to the media that they hoped that political power would eventually help them invest in property and otherwise become legitimate economic agents. A small percentage, including Maquis Park's Big Cat, hoped to be recognized as political leaders in their respective communities. One prominent gang leader who was eventually jailed for his role in distributing crack cocaine said to me, "You [are] not going to be remembered for making addicts, but you will be for making change . . . lot of us now feel like we need to give back a little to the community. Maybe this is how we do it, getting young kids to realize [being in a gang] is not about violence, it's about standing by other niggers like you who's down and out."

But the new hopes of entrepreneurial gangs remained ideals, however vibrant and exciting they were. The final burst of federal indictments, around 1995, would fracture Chicago's gangland well before any gang's aspirations—for political power, for a presence in the legitimate economic arena, for mainstream political capital—could be realized. Ultimately the trafficking of crack cocaine proved an unreliable infrastructure for a gang's dreams of social and political mobility.[11] The leadership of many gang organizations were eventually incarcerated, and gang hierarchies were destabilized. Just as important, the demand for crack cocaine diminished during the nineties, leading to a significant drop in potential underground revenue for these inner-city street gangs. So, on city streets, the coordinated drug-dealing operations of the Black Kings and others were in tatters. There were still plenty of addicts who bought illegal drugs from the gang, but younger gang members did not know where the next supply of cocaine, heroin, or marijuana would come from, and they were less proficient at selling it. Nevertheless, the young adults in the gang still depended on illegitimate income to pay rent, help spouses, and support children. Most had no other work experience that could help them obtain meaningful, well-paying jobs.[12] So the gang's many members fought for whatever was to be made—they fought with members of their own gang over reliable drug supply connections, and with neighboring gangs as everyone struggled to expand their territorial boundaries.

In the Black Kings gang, Big Cat used his powers of persuasion to wrest power away from four other senior members who wanted to assume the mantle of leadership after their predecessors had been arrested. Unlike other neighborhood outfits in which infighting among rank-and-file members determined the new leadership class—sometimes, quite literally the last one standing in a violent physical fight would then rule—Big Cat met with the aspirants in his gang and convinced them that the was the right person for the job. Those whom he superseded attest to his diplomatic victory and his successful campaign. He succeeded by emphasizing the economic prerogatives of modern-day gang activity. Carlton Prentiss, a senior Black Kings officer at the time and one of those moved by Big Cat's politicking, recalled fondly, "Man, that was the time when you joined the BKs [Black Kings] because you had something in your heart. You could see Big Cat had heart. He would tell us that making money was more than just about making money, but it was about a love for yourself, for your family. No one else knew how to speak like that. Man, the nigger was deep. Still is."

From law enforcement's lofty perch, there was great fanfare made of the beheading of Chicago's large gang coalitions. To their credit, the brain trusts of the city's largest street gang organizations were now incarcerated, killed, or sent on the run with little chance of returning to their old ways. However, there was little evidence that the number of gang members in Chicago declined significantly as a result of the federal sweeps and the decreased demand for crack cocaine. The Black Kings, for example, suffered neither substantial attrition in their ranks, nor any diminishing interest among Maquis Park's teens to join their group. And, when one includes the neighborhoods immediately adjacent to Maquis Park, my study of local gangs showed, on average, a 20 percent *increase* in active rank-and-file members from 1995 to 2000. Nor, for that matter, did it really appear that gangs were no longer economically oriented. Crack may have yielded less revenue, but across Chicago's Southside neighborhoods, the gangs were in many respects more visible than ever before. With many of the gangs' top leaders incarcerated, adolescents and youth who previously could only dream of becoming gang leaders now faced the real possibility of directing fifty or one hundred other such young people, as well as drawing on the income that this office yielded.[13] And these "shorties" would fight well into the next century for control of neighborhoods, of their own organization, and for any and all prospects of illegal revenue that their locale held.

For a community like Maquis Park, the public record fails to capture the effects of this period of gang destabilization on daily life. Arrests of gang leaders did not mean that the scourge of corporate street gangs had been wiped away. These kinds of assessments—and their eager reception by the city and the press—proceeded from incorrect assumptions, namely, that the gang and the community were wholly separate entities, and that the latter was searching for any means to rid itself of the former. In contrast, for residents in Maquis Park and other such communities, the gang leader had a name, a recognizable face, and in many instances a personal relationship to family and friends. The gang leader did not come out of nowhere, but was once a child, a student, and a neighbor, and might still be a close relative or part of a local peer group.

As a result, we must rewrite the public record. We must begin by acknowledging that the gang cannot be adequately understood outside the context of its relationships with everyone around it, from family members and neighbors, to shopkeepers, clergy, and law enforcement personnel. Similarly, the economic profile of the gang must be understood in the context of the underground activities in place in the wider community. A gang does not simply run its own shady affairs. The organization competes with others so laboring. There may be other residents, say, who are selling narcotics or taxing street hustlers for the right to occupy a corner. At times the gang can make deals with nongang competitors like gun traders or pimps based on mutual interest. At other times, conflict is inevitable. And at all times, one of the gang's most basic challenges is to ensure a steady supply of goods and services. Thus, the gang is continually trying to find drug and weapons wholesalers, legitimate businesses that will launder its money, and block club presidents and landlords who will store their caches of drugs and guns. Finally, the gang inescapably occupies public space—it meets in parks, and moves about the street—and thus its members come in contact with nearly everyone in the neighborhood who is trying to supplement their income by making money off the books. For the underground economy to function, everyone involved must connect with everyone else; Big Cat's leadership of the Black Kings would reveal the depth of these connections throughout Maquis Park and the peril that this web of connections could bring.

As the country was gripped with the now-quaint fears of Y2K and pondered the coming of the third millennium, on the Southside of Chicago, on streets largely ignored, Big Cat had more practical problems. For the last six years he had been the leader of the Black Kings, assuming leadership after the arrest of the former leader, Cornelius Desmond, who died in jail and had not appointed his successor. The Black Kings was one of Chicago's feared gangs, and now it was a gang in trouble. Big Cat had anywhere from 150 to 200 gang members who answered to him, but he also had to answer to them. He had to keep them happy, keep them paid, and keep them in line. But all this took money, and the money was not coming in as easily as it had just a few years ago, when crack users saturated the area and supported the gang's drug-trafficking enterprise. Unlike the past, when the gang was a social center and its leaders sponsored parties, gambling, basketball tournaments, and other nondelinquent activities for its members, Big Cat's men expected gang membership to deliver the benefits of a corporate position: namely, a steady income and a mobility path to greater fortune down the road.

Big Cat knew that the gang had to alter its entrepreneurial mien if he was to deliver on the organization's promise to its rank and file. Although the Black Kings had a monopoly over crack cocaine (and secondarily, heroin sales) in the community, this was a faltering economic sector. So Big Cat decided to spread out the gang's entrepreneurial presence into other shady waters. There was already an underground economy in place through which residents bartered, traded, earned income, and otherwise made ends meet. The gang threatened not only the community's safety and welfare—because after all, any kind of shady activity, whether sales of socks or drugs, held potential for danger—but the gang also emerged as a competitor to local underground traders, thereby threatening people's livelihoods. In the process, the organization impacted the wider community in new and unexpected ways.

Big Cat's thrust outward, from the sphere of drug distribution into other hidden economic arenas, took on greater force in 2000, when the gang began taking over Homans Park. As described in Chapter 2, Marlene Matteson, president of the 1700 South Maryland Avenue Block Club, and her neighbors saw in Big Cat's advances several threats to their welfare. Their children could lose a place to play in relative safety because the gang wanted to turn Homans Park into a bazaar filled with prostitutes, car mechanics, food and candy sellers, and other illicit traders whom they would tax. Parents feared that the gang's presence would threaten the safety of children and their guardians who had to walk by on their way to school and work. Increased economic activity also meant increased foot and car traffic. And both the gang and the new shady traders it was recruiting posed competition for their own use of the park for moneymaking.

Marlene and her neighbors were stuck, unsure how to respond. Historically, they had little success enlisting the police, so while they thought of calling on law enforcement, they almost by instinct sought other opportunities. In addition, they recognized that poor people using public space for entrepreneurial schemes was a defining feature of their community. Most of Marlene's neighbors themselves worked off the books to supplement household income. Believing they could never entirely eradicate underground economies outside their homes, they had to find a rapprochement with the shady traders arriving in Homans Park.

In the spring of 2000, when the gang's takeover of Homans Park appeared imminent, the residents on Marlene's block adopted a self-described "realist" position in dealing with Big Cat. Marlene's neighbors permitted her to explore deals with the gang, such as permitting certain kinds of illegal activities (food sales) but not others (sex work). Some gave quiet assent to Marlene as she negotiated arrangements whereby Big Cat would not impose a tax on local residents who sold food or clothing, solicited clients for their gypsy cabs, and otherwise used the park for economic purposes. Others wanted Marlene to plead with Big Cat to keep drug sales and prostitutes out of the park, at least during those times when children were playing. The only issue upon which there was consensus was that the residents should not act by themselves. In addition to working with police, they decided to enlist the services of Pastor Wilkins.

Despite their agreement to employ the pastor in their efforts, there were deep rifts forming between residents who were willing to solve problems off the books, and those who felt it was dangerous to take over enforcement functions normally reserved for the police. These differences of opinion expressed themselves often in debates over the need to create a temporary truce versus a more permanent solution. Marlene and her neighbors argued continually—in casual conversations on the street and in block club meetings—about the merits of bringing about immediate changes in the gang's behavior or focusing their energies on creating a lasting security. These debates are revealing and demonstrate the constantly shifting nature of collective, informal social control in the ghetto.

The spring of 2000 began a new era in Big Cat's reign as local gang leader. He and Marlene accepted Pastor Wilkins's invitation to his church, where they deliberated for several days. In a damp basement, surrounded by religious objects, Bibles, and musical instruments that had not made their way upstairs into the fellowship hall, they sat at a large table and discussed their respective concerns. Even Big Cat's presence was remarkable, but such was the clergy's power in Maquis Park. And such was Big Cat's involvement in the well-being of his community; an unapologetic criminal, he nevertheless knew that he couldn't afford to be insensitive to his neighbors. He had an underground enterprise to run, and he could not completely antagonize the community if he was to be successful. Big Cat's and Marlene's need for a cigarette enabled frequent breaks, which were especially welcome when the discussion grew heated and a stalemate loomed on the horizon. Big Cat initially resisted attempts to curb drug sales. Some of the older members of his gang were frustrated at the lack of moneymaking opportunities. There were grumblings of leaving the gang for good. So, whereas in the past Big Cat had acceded to residents' desire that he curb drug sales before and after school, now he was intolerant of such requests. The following interchange occurred at the second meeting that Wilkins mediated:

"What worries me," said Marlene, "is that there's about seventy children on my block who use that park—and that's not counting the ones who live on the other side. Can't have them around your boys."

"You all are something else," Big Cat said shaking his head. "I been cooperating with you all for years now, never complaining that I'm losing money. Shit, I don't get no respect for that? Keeping the violence down. Ain't been a shooting around here for the longest, you know that."

"If you're in our park, we can't be. It's as simple as that," Marlene replied. "I'll give you the nighttime. Maybe I can convince folks that you all need to work at night, but that's going to be tough. But, bottom line, baby, is we can't have you all there during the day."

"I don't even know why I come to these things, shit." Big Cat slouched in his chair.

"Okay," interjected Wilkins. "Now, you have to stop for the summer Big Cat. We're not asking for a two-year thing, or nothing like that. Just when the kids are outside."

"I guess I could work it on 59th, but that Arab keeps telling us he don't want us around, keeps calling the cops. Last time, nigger started firing that bullhorn at us until we left."

"If I get him to leave you alone during the day, and you can hang out in that parking lot on the other side of the store, you'll leave the park for the summer."

"Yeah," Big Cat replied, dejected at the compromise. "Okay, we'll be gone."

"Good," replied Wilkins. "Now, that's enough for now. This was good. Marlene, I need you to go back and let people know Big Cat is cooperating. Don't call a group meeting or nothing, just let them know that the kids are going to be okay. Then, call [Officer] Marcellus [Harrison] and tell him he's got to go easy on Big Cat's boys in the new spot. See if he agrees."

"Okay," Marlene said, reaching over and tossing Big Cat's hair as if he were her nephew. "See you Big Cat, see you tomorrow and we'll figure out the rest."

"Crazy," said Big Cat, smiling. "I can't figure out who's crazier, me or you niggers."

After several more meetings, Wilkins had managed to foster an immediate détente, one that he hoped would last until late August, when children returned to school. Marlene and her neighbors would no longer publicly chastise the prostitutes and scare away their customers, and they ended their phone calls to the police. For the summer, Big Cat agreed to limit his drug trafficking to late-night hours, and the pimp would move his sex workers into the abandoned buildings farthest away from the park. Big Cat also agreed to residents in Marlene's block selling their own underground goods in the park; they would have priority over any other trader, and they would receive protection from the gang for the same price that others paid.

Big Cat's capitulation to their demands was somewhat surprising even to Wilkins and Marlene. They knew that they had some leverage over the gang because the organization's opportunities to make illegal money were drying up. They also knew that Big Cat wanted local residents to look at him as a community stakeholder rather than a criminal. Big Cat's aspirations were larger than running a street gang, and although neither Marlene nor Wilkins wanted to help him gain political capital in local affairs, they did feel it was better for the negotiations to acknowledge his right to be a part of the community. But they were still taken aback when Big Cat acceded to their demands without much fuss. As Marlene said after the meetings between the three persons had concluded, "I'm not holding my breath. Let's see how Big Cat behaves. You watch: things could change at any time, that's just how life is in general around here."

For his part, Big Cat understood that he had little choice but to enter into the negotiations. As he said at the time, "Folks like [Marlene and Pastor Wilkins] can make my life hell if they want, bringing the police down on me, and I have enough to worry about. I don't need their trouble." He was right: he did have enough to worry about. Big Cat was struggling to ensure that his rank and file wanted to remain part of his gang—which meant that for most of them, he had to provide opportunities to make money. Finding new sources of revenue to make up for the drying crack cocaine stream was not easy. He was relatively certain that any new source of revenue for the gang was likely an existing source of revenue for someone else; thus, he would be taking money away from others. And if, in the process, these new moneymaking ventures created new points of contact with local residents, he had to ensure that conflicts were minimal and people did not always contact the police. Many of these options were constrained because his gang was geographically bounded. He could not simply leave the area anytime soon and find a new market in another part of town. He would likely confront another gang. Thus, he was stuck with the Maquis Park and its residents, as much as they were stuck with him.

Not all of Marlene's neighbors were happy with the result of the mediation that the pastor had initiated. Some wanted less gang involvement. A few said tolerating any illegal activity was a harbinger of trouble. They made their feelings known to Pastor Wilkins at a block club meeting about ten days after the negotiations. They met in Wilkins's basement to hear the pastor and Marlene outline the agreement that had been reached.

"Goodness, Pastor Wilkins, you call that safe?" said Sandra, Marlene's next-door neighbor. "I mean we don't want any whores in the park or near it. I can't send my child there if they have to walk by people [having sex]. I mean we want the violence to stop."

"Sandra," Pastor Wilkins said, remaining calm. "I understand your concern. I'm trying to get that young man to calm things down just for a little while until we can find a solution. First, let's get the place ready so you all can use it, then, well, we can take on a better solution that everybody can deal with."

"I agree," said Cotton, one of the local sex workers. "I mean I think if we can show that we can get the gang to stop, we can even go down to the police and say, 'Hey, we shouldn't be the ones that have to do this, you are the police, you get paid to keep drug dealers out.' We been over this before. I don't see why everyone's getting so angry. We know it's never going to stop. Take it from me, [prostitutes] are going to find a way to make our money. One way or another, they'll be back at the park."

"You're crazy," said Timothy. "No one's coming back unless they pay us some money. Like I said, if they come back, they ain't going to be making money while I'm the one who may be shot and killed."

"Okay," Pastor Wilkins chimed in. "Let me say again, you all asked me to get the boys out the park and keep it safe. I'm trying to do that. How you want to deal with it after the summer, that's on you. You can decide all that. I'm just trying to get Big Cat to get out of there right now, not forever. *That's* going to be harder, and we need to think about that."

"I don't want to tell you your job, Pastor," said Arlene. "But we're making a deal with the devil. I just hope you'll be here with us next year, when everything starts happening again and they all start shooting at each other."

"The Lord hasn't left me," said Wilkins. "And I don't plan to leave you. And I *never* make deals with the devil."

Wilkins's insistence throughout the meeting that he was committed to the block club was not only motivated by his need to assuage residents' fears regarding negotiating with a street gang leader. Wilkins had his own aspirations to be a recognized stakeholder. Years ago he had played a central role in the election of local politicians and procuring city resources for Maquis Park, and he made liaisons with various civic and business interests that wanted to establish a local presence. After he fell from this perch in the mid-nineties, he no longer carried so much influence in local affairs and, as a result of a correlate diminution in support from residents, his church's revenues dropped substantially, Thus, his acceptance of Marlene's request for help was not purely selfless. Among other things, there was also the potential increase in donations to his church, from both Big Cat and residents, that could result if his diplomacy proved successful.

Beyond financial motivations, Wilkins did have faith in Big Cat. For one thing, he did not see the gang leader—or the rank-

and-file members—as evil persons who needed to be expelled from the community. They were youth in need of healing, and the Pastor had seen examples of the clergy helping troubled men and women turn their lives around. For his part, Big Cat was familiar with the pastor's work over the past two decades. Older members of the Black Kings spoke admiringly of the pastor, and Big Cat appreciated the pastor's willingness to open up his church's doors when a gang member was slain—only a few churches in the community would host funerals for members of the Black Kings.

As the summer wore on, the residents rested their hopes on Pastor Wilkins to ensure that their access to the park would be secure and that the shady trading would not jeopardize public safety. They also preferred not to meet, unless it was for purely social gatherings intended to provide food and recreation for their children. Discussions of shady trading and gang mediation now took place in private conversations with Marlene, rather than in public group settings. In this way, the Homans Park incident proved useful; residents of the block identified several people to whom they could turn for support. They now knew that, through Marlene and Wilkins, they could call upon other community actors to respond to problems in their immediate area. And they could make their calls without having to suffer public admission of their own support for illegal income generation, for collaborations with the gang, and for supplementing negligent law enforcement with other forms of mediation and policing.

But the disagreements and differing views held by those on Marlene's block could have been working in Big Cat's favor. Although the gang leader was isolated from the discussions among residents, he nevertheless benefited from the lack of consensus, even if only indirectly. If residents were busy debating with each other, it could make it more difficult for them to agree on a collective response to his gang's behavior. Big Cat understood this basic dynamic. In the past, he used a divide-and-conquer strategy to his favor in running a drug-trafficking operation. For example, he would often pit people in the community against one another by paying off some people to keep silent; he would give some local residents money to ensure that they didn't call the police or work with others in an anti-gang prevention effort. These were sporadic and highly secretive efforts, and because Big Cat would not talk about them in great detail and residents often did not admit to receipt of gang payments, it is difficult to know how pervasive these arrangements had been. And he would not admit to employing the same tactics in the Homans Park incident. All he would say about it was, "If something worked before, why not try it again."

Whether speaking collectively or in private, nearly everyone on Marlene's block expressed gratitude for Pastor Wilkins's mediation services. Wilkins worked with Marlene closely over the summer of 2000 to ensure that Big Cat kept his promises. He had the two stakeholders meet at his church each week to address any complaints about the gang or other shady entrepreneurs. Residents brought up incidents where either party was reneging on its promises. Wilkins would then try to mediate by pushing Big Cat to reduce drug trafficking in Homans Park. He repeatedly told car mechanics to pick up their tools and not leave sharp metal car parts lying around. And midnight would find the pastor telling prostitutes to leave the streets—for the church, if they were so inclined.

Perhaps most middle-class neighborhoods, black or white, are not so intimately involved in the law and order of their streets. But Maquis Park operates by different rules, and the self-initiated policing puts into sharp relief the temporal dimension of social control for urban poor residents. Working with intermediaries and directly with those involved in socially destabilizing behaviors has the distinct advantage of facilitating a quick response: conflicts can be mediated before they get out of hand, subsequent prevention is enhanced because residents can try to pressure offenders not to commit the acts in the future, and cooperation may also occur as individuals come together, building trust and collective efficacy. Long-term stability, however, might not be achieved. Working by themselves does not necessarily help residents create more productive relationships with the police—who may feel that the community is tolerating crime rather than working to stop it. Particularly when a situation involves dangerous elements, like gangs and pimps, who might resort to violence, direct negotiations also carry a risk of assault or verbal threats. Luckily, Marlene and her neighbors went through the summer of 2000 without suffering these.

These varying costs and benefits would begin to surface after that summer, as Big Cat and his gang made even more attempts to supplement their illegal revenue in the community. The park, as some residents feared, was just their first foray into usable public spaces in the neighborhood. There were signs that the gang was interested in finding other such places to congregate and anchor their drug trafficking. Moreover, rumors were circulating that Big Cat was expanding his shady interests by going around the community and finding stores to extort and entrepreneurs to tax. People feared not only gang reprisal but also that their own underground attempts to support their households were going to be threatened. They would have to find efficacious ways to stave off the gang and maintain social order, and all the while preserving their own livelihoods.

The Death of Babycake Jackson

As residents feared, after summer 2000, Big Cat's efforts to enrich the gang's coffers did not rest with his colonization of public areas like Homans Park and his harassment of the street hustlers and independent underground traders. He made another move to solidify his position in the local underground economy. For about a year, Big Cat had been considering an offer by Ellis Clearwater, the leader of a neighboring street gang, the Centurions, to merge the two outfits. Ellis's gang was based in several public housing communities—the Robert Taylor Homes, Stateway Gardens, and the Dearborn Homes—that were being torn down. He once controlled nearly a thousand gang members and possessed a fleet of sports cars and homes around the Chicago area. Ellis also had strong contacts with the city's police force, particularly those officers assigned to the "tactical unit," the small subgroup ostensibly responsible for responding to gang violence and organized criminal activity in public housing. Ellis tried to limit gang wars in public housing, and he cooperated in police investigations by providing information about perpetrators of violent crimes. In return, there was minimal police disruption of his round-the-clock drug trafficking inside the high-rise "project" buildings. It is worth noting that Ellis had never been arrested and had few problems amassing his large, illegally obtained fortune. (There was considerable speculation by local residents that Ellis did not go to jail in the federal RICO indictments because of his connections to police officers who might have persuaded federal prosecutors to grant him a reprieve.) However, as each housing development high-rise was torn down, he lost both gang members and drug purchasers. His economic standing, as well as his stature as a gang leader, were weakening.

Big Cat accepted Ellis's offer to merge, and around March 2000 he welcomed Ellis's rank and file into his own Black Kings organization. From Big Cat's perspective, Ellis offered an opening to several underground markets in which Big Cat himself had limited power. Ellis had reliable connections to heroin suppliers who could help Big Cat meet the rising demand for the product from the white customers who drove to Maquis Park from surrounding neighborhoods and outlying suburbs. Ellis also had control over most of the gun suppliers and traders around the housing developments, including in Big Cat's neighborhood. Gun sales were not as lucrative as drug sales, but they provided Ellis a steady revenue stream. And Ellis had built these economic operations in physical spaces—namely, public housing—that were at the crossroads of black, white, and Latino working-class communities. The proximity of several Chicago Housing Authority developments to exits on the Dan Ryan Expressway had transformed these concrete high-rises into contiguous red-light districts, with not only prostitution but also drugs, weapons, and gambling. Ellis had a strong base of customers, and he could redirect them to Big Cat. To top it all off, Ellis knew how to extort store owners so that they deemed it in their interest to pay the gang a street tax. A police officer who had observed Ellis's extortion of stores in and around public housing marveled at Ellis's "Mafia" tactics:

> He would walk into a store, using a Mafia style. He would tell them, "You are making money, you are in a neighborhood where there's no police, no one in the area likes you because you are for-

eign or because you don't hire residents. What security do you have?" Ellis would tell them this and say, "I wouldn't like to be in your shoes." And then he'd leave. Then he'd send over people in the area to start doing things, silly things: throwing up in the store, urinating there. Maybe sticking them up. And you know, he was right, we [in the police force] didn't always help [the shopkeeper]. We responded, always. But we always didn't think it was a good use of our time to go out and find the guy who vomited in the store. Ellis could find them, so after a few weeks, the store owner found him, or he came back to the store and said, "I can help you, and this is how much it will cost." Amazing, this guy.

With the merger, Ellis agreed to have Big Cat as his superior. (This was one of the clearest signs of Ellis's desperation to find a new source of income.) Ellis told his own rank and file to spread the word among their client base that they could now purchase drugs in one of several new venues in Maquis Park. So dozens of ex-Centurions—who were now officially affiliated with Big Cat's gang—brought clients to the Black Kings, who sold drugs on corners, in crack dens, and in abandoned buildings. They set up lucrative gambling contests, but it was Big Cat, not Ellis, who received the taxes from hosting these parties. Ellis showed his enterprising spirit by borrowing Big Cat's men to spruce up several abandoned buildings in Maquis Park: he changed the locks on doors, and he pirated electricity and water; in one building, he placed several couches in the basement and threw parties, replete with alcohol, prostitutes, and drugs; in another, he traded guns and drugs.

Ellis convinced Big Cat that they could earn considerable revenue by taxing other people in the neighborhood who were making money. This included people who earned *legally* and *illegally*.

The two leaders began by moving up and down West Street notifying stores that they may soon have to pay the gang a fee for security. As in the past, Ellis did not immediately extort the shopkeepers if they did not accede to his wishes, but he tried to instill fear in them. He told them if they did not agree to the gang's demands, their stores would be inundated with homeless persons, gang members would loiter inside and around the entrances, and the store might be vandalized in the coming months.

Ellis and Big Cat had differing motivations, however, for their work. Ellis needed to make rent and mortgage payments, pay for his legal retainer, and help meet child support obligations for ten children, divided among six mothers. Big Cat had grander aspirations. He believed that the black urban poor must use the underground to amass the necessary political and economic capital to improve their social standing and become influential actors in the wider city. "Each time black folk start making money and then thinking about running for office," he said, "taking over the community, buying property, that's when Johnnie Law comes down on us. We're okay, as long as we know our place." Big Cat sought ascension as a successful shady boss, which he believed would then catapult him and the other entrepreneurs into such a high social position that the wider world would have to recognize and incorporate them into mainstream social and political institutions. With Big Cat's grandiose aspirations, you could hear Booker T. Washington rolling over in his grave.

Not surprisingly, Big Cat and Ellis were not consistent in their application of commercial extortion. To some degree this was Ellis's intended effect, as it created an atmosphere of arbitrary mercy and threat, sowing fear in a business environment that already was unstable. Some stores were not approached, others refused to pay and escaped the gang's wrath, and still others were repeatedly vandalized. Big Cat's men sometimes robbed the staff of certain stores, taking their money and clothing and sending back a warning to the store manager that payment had better be sent. But even those who agreed to pay, like Mason who owned a convenience store, said that the gangs often forgot to pick up their money. "I was really scared, so, yes, I said I'd give them $100. But they haven't been here in about a month. I don't understand Big Cat. Should I stop paying?"

The gang's inconsistency added to the West Street shopkeepers' fears. In December 2000 only about 20 percent of the stores reported that Big Cat and Ellis had extorted them. Although Big Cat generally did not shy away from telling me about his dealings with proprietors, he would say little more than to confirm that the 20 percent figure was nearly accurate.

> Let's just say we're beginning this shit. So, yeah, maybe about a third of them, about that much is paying us. But, you know we got time and like I said, I ain't telling you all that shit, Sudhir. You on a need-to-know basis [laughing]. I mean there's a lot of ways we work with the stores, not just money. They hire our boys, they know we're part of this community, so it's a lot of cooperation too, not just them paying us. See, if I knew you were going to put the positive shit in the book, I'd tell you more. But you still haven't made me no guarantees, so, for now, I ain't telling you shit.

After the gang had broken the window of a West Street hardware store for the third time in December and nearly set fire to the place, Autry Vincent worried that the gang was going to move eastward, targeting his dollar store next. Sitting at a local bar, with fellow shopkeepers Marlon DeBreaux, Ola Sanders, and Leroy Patterson, Autry anticipated the gang's next move.

"I think he's a bunch of wind," said Leroy. "I know Ellis, I fix his car for free. That nigger ain't going to do nothing. Just causing a lot of fuss."

"Yeah, well, ain't taking that chance," said Ola. "Boy is crazy, just like his father. Both been raised in jail more than around here."

"Naw, brother ain't crazy," said Marlon, "just pissed cause he can't make no more money [selling crack cocaine]. I think setting fire to the place, now that's just taking shit too far."

"Too far?" yelled Autry. "Shit, the boy could be coming after you next, I mean you acting like he's done doing what he wants to do. Hell no, I seen this shit before with them Italians. They used to run my poppa's place. Start coming around, asking for a few dollars, next thing you know, they take over the business. They want to see who's scared. Just don't show no fear."

"Well, I ain't scared of that nigger," said Leroy. "I mean, ain't like anyone's paying him. I mean who's paying? Are you giving him money [Ola]? Are you [Marlon]? Only ones paying are the Arabs and that Kim [the Korean American liquor store owner]."

"He's coming after all of us. Whether or not you paying, that's on you, but the brother is going to make a move and ask all of you for some change. I say pay the boy. Shit, he probably do better than the police keeping them whores out of my alley. Shit, if he wants to beat the shit out of them niggers [sleeping outside my store], let the brother get it on. I been complaining about that for months, ain't nobody hearing me."

"Yeah, and right after he beats them up," said Autry, "he's coming after you."

Most shopkeepers waited to see how the gang would act in the coming months, but some took matters into their own hands. For example, fearing the gang's demand for cash, Marlon DeBreaux struck a bargain on his own with Ellis and Big Cat: any gang *leader* could eat lunch at his restaurant for free, two days a week. Ellis would sometimes appoint a rank-and-file member as a temporary "leader" just to anger Marlon and increase the number of free diners. Typically Marlon was feeding six to ten gang members per week. The in-kind payments were a big savings, he says, compared to paying cash.

In time Big Cat and Ellis would be extorting merchants not only on West Street, but on all of the local commercial thoroughfares in the community. The fee they charged varied. From foreign-born shopkeepers they would demand several hundred dollars or more each month. They levied the highest fees on stores selling liquor and sporting goods. For black-owned stores, they were slightly more forgiving: some of these stores reported having to pay $50 or $100 a month, although the amounts could change and for no discernible reason. Eventually Big Cat would demand that stores hire his rank-and-file members and launder his money, but that was still down the road. For all of the stores, Big Cat promised to find stolen goods, prevent vandalism, and monitor the homeless persons and squatters who sometimes harassed customers and urinated in the shops.

Before the gang's extortion expanded, other problems arose. Sometime around February 2001, Big Cat's gang began to colonize new public areas for drug trafficking. Some members camped in public parks, where they furtively dealt drugs and threatened passersby who tried to inhabit the secluded spots. Others trafficked in busy commercial thoroughfares, like West Street, where residents shopped or sent their children on errands. This repositioning of drug dealing brought about waves of complaints from families and local stakeholders. The objections did not always reach Big Cat directly. Sometimes his rank-and-file members reported being chased away by angry parents. On other occasions, police officers, clergy, and precinct captains told Big Cat that he needed to stop antagonizing families. Big Cat was in a pinch. He needed some measure of tolerance from local residents to traffic drugs publicly; he wanted to show local stakeholders that he was (in his words) a "community man." But while Big Cat could not provoke residents excessively, he also could not entirely give into residents' demands and risk a sharp loss in underground income.

The merchants continued to pursue a third party who might help them with the new threat from the Black Kings. It was not an easy task because few people had the trust of both the business community and the gang. Merchants had been previously able to call on local stakeholders, like Pastor Wilkins, Alderman Carson, and various precinct captains, police officers, and block club presidents, to deal with the Black Kings. But these persons were now having greater trouble as the local Maquis Park gang moved well beyond its historic guise. The new behavior of the gang dictated that the community had to use new interventions and strategies, but no one knew yet what these should be.

As merchants continued to worry about threats to their legal enterprises, police began to notice an increase in fights between street gangs and other organized criminal entities in the area. From their reports, it appeared that the gangs were taxing not only legitimate businesses, but, as winter moved forward, illegitimate ones as well. Although the Black Kings gang was probably the largest and most visible organized criminal entity in the neighborhood, they were far from the only outfit seeking out illegal income. Maquis Park was and still is inhabited by individuals who rob houses, sell stolen cars, deal narcotics, organize gambling and prostitution, coordinate gypsy cab and delivery services off the books, and engage in other shady dealings. A complete accounting of these criminal networks may be impossible, not only because the individuals are working secretively, but also because those involved might associate to carry out a particular criminal activity and then disband—never working together again. The Black Kings gang is formal, with rules and codes of conduct, and has been around for decades, but most associations are ragtag and operate well under the radar.

Once in a while, however, local talk is colored by news of a criminal organization that is carrying out highly organized and successful heists and illegal ventures. When Big Cat and Ellis expanded their shady interests, they took stock of other groups who were laying claim to underground revenue in the community. They came upon the Braziers, two brothers who stole cars in the neighborhood, took them apart, and sold the parts for profit. If the Braziers were simply stealing cars, that would have been a problem but it would not have directly jeopardized the Black Kings. However, it appeared that the Braziers were actually trying to steal from the gang, not just threatening them with competition. Big Cat's response was swift and aggressive. Clearly, the gang's capacity to manage a viable underground enterprise depends on their ability not only to evade law enforcement but also to navigate—with force, if necessary—the rough-and-tumble waters of the shady economy.

Between January and April 2001, police responded to approximately a dozen shooting matches between Black Kings and the car theft ring. One detective described the competition between the two outfits:

> "I have to tell you, this is the strangest thing I've seen in a long time, and you see everything around here. I guess what's going on

is that you got the Braziers, the two brothers who steal cars around here, starting to rob Big Cat's boys."

"Car thieves robbing drug dealers?" I asked in disbelief.

"Yes, can you believe it?" Officer Blue replied. "They're taking them for all they got. Coming up to the boys on the corner, taking their money, guns, drugs, jewelry. I guess they robbed one of the leaders and Big Cat got upset and they retaliated and shot this guy. That's why he's in the hospital."

"Has this been happening for a while?" I asked.

"Well, it's funny because we know about this ring [of car thieves]. They work mostly over in South Shore, Hyde Park, some of the nicer areas where you got better cars. I guess they ran out of cars to rob or they had trouble with the cops over there, I don't know. Then, someone told me that Big Cat and Ellis were paying some people to rob cars and get parts, so maybe it's competition."

By hiring car thieves to work for them, Big Cat and Ellis were competing with the Braziers. To exact revenge, the Braziers were robbing Big Cat's rank-and-file drug sellers late at night. This led to months of shootings and reprisals between the two bands of thieves.

Toward the end of autumn, Big Cat and Ellis tried to prevent the robbings by hiring some of the local street hustlers to serve as undercover lookouts. Hustlers could not necessarily provide the gang any meaningful security—gang members were armed, and theoretically were better able to defend themselves from a pimp or a sock vendor. But few would suspect that these small-time hustlers were working for the gang, and their continuous public presence, Big Cat hoped, might provide details as to who exactly was a threat to his gang. He asked James Arleander and the brothers Babycake and Bill Jackson to watch over his gang members who were selling drugs along West Street, in case they were robbed. He was also anxious about losing the large amounts of cash that his dealers held. He offered to pay any hustler $50 a night to keep an eye on not only West Street but four or five other nearby locations where the gang sold drugs. At first Big Cat asked the hustlers to look out for the Braziers (and others in their criminal ring). But a week later his demands grew, and he asked them to alert the drug sellers when police were nearby. He then asked the hustlers to snitch on merchants who called the police and who complained about gang behavior. Knowing that James and Artie were friends with some of the local cops, Big Cat demanded that they find out information about upcoming police busts. Then he forced some hustlers to carry guns and drugs, which distributed some of the risk assumed by the gang members on the street corners. For all of this, Big Cat continued to pay $50 a week.

For a street hustler $50 was a good week's revenue, so there was no shortage of persons willing to work for the gang. But this does not mean that the choice was easy for James, Artie, the Jackson Brothers, and the others who hustled on West Street. On the one hand, they certainly needed the money and they did not want to suffer the consequences of declining Big Cat's request. But working with Big Cat could compromise their own dealings with locals who were invaluable in helping them to work on the street and make ends meet. Many of the established hustlers on the street enjoyed good relations with police officers, who looked the other way when a hustle was taking place or who found them shelter and sent customers their way. James and his counterparts, in truth, routinely gave police information about crime in the area. Now they were being asked to betray those relationships and share information with the gang. In addition, if a merchant discovered that a hustler had a material stake in the gang's drug trafficking, that might be enough reason to terminate the relationship and find another vagabond soul to work with them. As a result, the street trader would lose not only income, but perhaps more importantly a place to eat, use a washroom, and sleep on a cold winter night.

From September 2001 until January 2002, Big Cat employed several hustlers on West Street, including Carla Henderson, James Arleander, the Jackson brothers, and Tony Terrell, to counter any attack by the Braziers' criminal ring and to look out for police. Artie Calvert, perhaps the best-known hustler on the corner, declined the opportunity because he felt it would compromise his own moral position on the street. "I'm not doing criminal things. I help people, I provide good for people around here. I don't want them confusing me with a bunch of thugs," Artie said. For his part, Big Cat respected Artie's longtime presence in the area and his general influence over others in the community, and he did not respond to Artie's refusal with any threats.

Big Cat quickly benefited from putting the hustlers on his payroll. He received word from them about activities of the police; a few hustlers had expertise rooting out undercover police officers and they would tell Big Cat if they spotted any that were close to Big Cat's dealers. A few told him when they spotted enemy gang members in the area. And several other hustlers brought customers to his rank-and-file drug dealers, and some even offered to take drugs to customers in other neighborhoods. The hustlers' labors did not substantially increase Big Cat's revenues, but the gang leader felt that he now had one additional means by which to find out what was happening on the streets, particularly newsworthy information that might help him to avoid arrest by police or intrusions by other organized criminals.

These benefits did not necessarily accrue to the hustlers, however. As expected, both police and merchants began questioning these hustlers about their work with the gang. The hustler Artie Calvert felt that the police were arresting the hustlers with greater frequency as a result, and he pressured James and others to end their work with the gang. These conversations sometimes caused public fights.

The tensions were spilling over and affecting interactions between hustlers and the gang members they watched over. On one occasion, some of Big Cat's men beat up Carla Henderson because, in their opinion, she had failed to alert them of two undercover cops in a nearby car. The officers then chased Big Cat's men; two managed to escape, but two others were caught and sent to jail. Carla went to the hospital with several broken bones in her face.

Another altercation took place when Big Cat beat up the manager of a local currency exchange for snitching on the gang's efforts to launder money through the neighboring dollar store. Big Cat told the store manager that a local hustler had told him about his snitching. This was actually a lie, said James Arleander. "Big Cat walked over there with a baseball bat, broke the man's legs, then took a gun and shot up the place. Told the [store owner] that Tony [the local hustler] told him about . . . calling the cops. Now Tony can't come around no more because nobody trusts him. It was all a lie, but now Tony lost his job." Before the incident, the currency store manager would pay Tony $10 to clean up the store after hours. After the gang beating, the manager asked that all of the other merchants on West Street not hire Tony anymore.

In February 2002, fearing that the local cops would be upset at his own collaboration, the West Street hustler Babycake Jackson decided to terminate his relationship with Big Cat. Babycake was the first of the collaborating West Street hustlers to do this (Artie had refused outright to collaborate with Big Cat). Babycake refused to accept more money from the gang and said he would no-longer serve as a lookout. Big Cat would have to find somebody else. The decision may have cost Babycake his life. Early one morning in mid-February, two people walked into the abandoned building where Babycake and his brother Bill slept. They shot Babycake twenty-two times and, according to Bill, they then said to Bill, "Don't ever think you bigger than us, 'cause you're next." The perpetrators were never found, and Babycake's death remains unsolved. The ripples from his death were palpable, and surged through the community. Street hustlers feared that Babycake paid for vocally resisting the gang's takeover and for refusing to pay the gang a "tax" on his illegal activity. And with Babycake's death, the residents feared that Big Cat was now indiscriminately trying to control nearly all underground economic activity in the area. If the Maquis Park Kings gang leader had killed an enemy gang member, that would have been a serious problem, but the community had ways of coping with such feuds. Taking a home-less man's life was quite another matter. Big Cat now seemed to be developing a depravity that made him almost unknowable and unreachable.

The community's fears that Big Cat was becoming vicious were quickly supplanted by other problems. Big Cat's imperialist practices had generated new antagonisms where once there were only minimal disagreements between gangs, street hustlers, and residents. In any given area of Maquis Park, the parties involved may not have known that their dramas were being played out on other blocks and in other alleys. But the hustlers knew: as nomads who migrated to several spaces to work or sleep, they routinely met fellow hustlers in other parts of the community. As they roamed, they discovered a shared and growing dislike of Big Cat, Ellis, and the other members of the gang. James Arleander explains:

> I could take you to probably four or five people right now dealing with these cats, like we are. Having to pay [the gang], getting beaten up by them, it's just not right and a man can't earn a living. Hard enough for brothers—and for sisters—to make their nut, find a place to stay. Now you got Big Cat and them niggers bothering us. I mean I heard that they robbed that boy, Marion. You know the one who don't see too good. They took his money. In James Park, you heard what's going on? Big Cat told Tony he couldn't sell his socks and T-shirts unless he watched out for the police. Told him that he had to give him a few bucks to sleep in the park. Shit, Tony has been in that park for the longest. This just ain't right.

The situation continued to worsen. People were becoming more and more fed up with the gang's behavior, Marlene Matteson said to me, after she had finished mediating her third dispute in two days between a gang member and a resident who was kicked out of a local park for getting in the way of Big Cat's drug trafficking.

> "I always support [Big Cat]," said Marlene. "I know that sounds funny, but what I'm saying is these so-called gang members are our kids. Now I'm seeing that they getting too big for themselves and we have to do something, but I still will defend them and say that they are part of our community."
>
> "How can you say that?" I asked. "I'm confused. You just said all these people, all over Maquis Park, not just on your block, are calling you now asking for help. You and [Officer] Blue just spent a week running all over the damn place trying to put out fires."

"Think about the family you grew up in, Sudhir. What was it like? When something really bad happened, did you leave the family? Did you say you were no longer a member of the Venkateshes? No, you didn't tell nobody that momma shot daddy, or daddy slept with momma's best friend. You just figured out what to do. Same here."

"You have a family of thirty thousand people?"

"More than that. And yes, everyone in Maquis Park could be in my family. But right now, I know that Big Cat is. And at least I can get him to behave once in a while. Think if someone new took over. Who knows what kind of killing would be going on?"

But Marlene's theory of the gang—that the devil you know is always better than the one you don't—did not stop her from eventually organizing a response to Big Cat's behavior. In March 2002 she turned, as she had done in the past, to the clergy. She called several other block club presidents and two police officers whom she trusted, Officer Blue and Officer Harrison, and asked if they would meet with Pastor Wilkins to discuss some of the gang's recent behavior. Pastor Wilkins, whose church was only a few blocks from West Street, had already gained Big Cat's trust that previous summer in the negotiations with Marlene and the 1700 South Maryland Avenue Block Club around the use of Homans Park.

The gang does not exist in isolation. And the corporate gang never operates outside the broader ensemble of persons, groups, and organizations making money in the area. The situation on West Street, where both legitimate businesses and street hustlers operated, brought into relief the overlap between gangs and other economic actors. The social dynamics in Maquis Park make evident that there is a partly symbiotic relationship between the formal and the informal economy, where legitimate and shady traders work with one another in their respective efforts to make money. The gang must be viewed as a part of this interchange, albeit one that can exert a stronger effect than most other players. Big Cat's gang exemplified the power that a criminal organization can accumulate in the underground arena. Through their colonization of hitherto unexplored underground arenas, more and more people in the community found their lives affected by the gang's activities. Even if legitimate businesses were not being extorted by the gang and did not draw on shady goods and services, they were indirectly affected by the growing climate of fear, by the gang's escalating violence and indiscriminate harassment, and by the daily reports from friends and business associates that commerce in Maquis Park was, unbelievably, becoming even more difficult. "What to do?" everyone wondered. With people like Babycake Jackson paying with their lives, this question weighed heavily on their minds.

Preaching in the Community's Court

There was no legal proof that Big Cat had killed Babycake—either directly or by taking a contract out on his life. But police investigations and court proceedings were never the final word in Maquis Park, and the government was not a third-party arbiter in the underground economy. So, regardless of the outside world, most residents believed that Big Cat was guilty. When I asked Brother Patterson if he believed that Big Cat killed Babycake, he replied, "If I say yes, you'll ask me how do I know. If I say no, you'll ask me how do I know. That's why you're not black and dirt poor. You ask those questions. *I* know, *we* know, the *community* knows." Judging by his reply, the community's answer was yes.

For his part, Big Cat was reclusive and agitated after Babycake's murder. It had thrown a wrench into the gang leader's overall plan to increase the gang's social and economic stature. At a time when the organization was moving into uncharted waters, the last thing Big Cat wanted was swelling resident hostility or, even worse, increased resident cooperation with the police. But he now realized that those around him believed as fact that he had killed a local hustler for not cooperating with the gang.

Big Cat drank more and started earlier in the day. He began snorting cocaine, which he had not used in five years. He yelled at his rank and file and physically beat them, sometimes for no discernible reason. Ellis, junior to Big Cat in the gang's hierarchy, had now assumed control over much of the gang's operations in order to keep things running. Ellis did this quietly, with little notice by residents, because Big Cat conceded authority to Ellis over internal affairs but retained control over the gang's dealings with the public. Big Cat felt it was still his responsibility to direct extortion, money laundering, and general negotiations with local stakeholders.

Big Cat wanted to act before local contempt turned to retaliation. To manage the rising chorus of disapproval, Big Cat turned to Pastor Wilkins, with whom he had already worked successfully on several occasions to quell resident unrest. On a blustery autumn day about two months after Babycake was killed, Wilkins brought Big Cat and several local stakeholders together, including block club president Marlene Matteson, barbershop owner James Carter, and Ola Sanders, the owner of a local beauty salon. The group met at Wilkins's Maquis Park Prayer and Revival Center.

Their six-hour conversation was straightforward and business-like. Residents made no mention of Babycake's death, and there was no discussion of overall problems caused by gang activity, only specific, concrete instances of conflicts between residents and the gang. For example, Ola did not complain about gang extortion and harassment *per se*. Instead, she said the liquor store owner had been promised a set of security services by Ellis, but the gang had not yet delivered on them: "You all," Ola said pointing to Big Cat, "you all were supposed to stop them boys from stealing chips and things from Clay's [store]. How come that didn't happen? Isn't that what you said you'd do?" Ola then mentioned Big Cat's pledge to pay her a fee for the use of her beauty salon for nightly parties—she claimed Big Cat owed her $500. Similarly, Marlene could have told Big Cat that her neighbors were tired of the gang's unrelenting appropriation of public space—which is exactly what she had been hearing in her recent visits to local neighborhood associations, block clubs, and churches. Instead, she listed specific problems in specific places: "Missy Wilson!" she shouted at Big Cat. "Did your boys tell her that for $100 they would find the guy that beat up her son? She said she paid, but ain't nothing happened yet."

Big Cat never once alluded to the fact that his organization sold drugs, extorted merchants, or needed to maintain a revenue stream. He was careful not to publicly admit that he was managing illegal economic activity. And like the others in the room, he did not discuss Babycake's death. Instead, he addressed each specific accusation: "I'll tell Johnnie to pay that man back his money unless he does what he's supposed to do." "Billy and his friends shouldn't have taken the money until they found the boy that beat up Missy's son. I'll talk with them." In his retorts one found a combination of stonewalling, politicking, and diplomacy.

That the residents did not point to general problems associated with Big Cat's gang was not surprising, because they were hesitant to take over the work of the police. Residents had to walk a fine line between solving problems that police would not respond to while still hoping (and lobbying) for improved law enforcement services. Their protestations to police officials would be diluted if police could claim that they were trying to solve problems outside the law. Confronting Big Cat about particular problems was easier—because it offered a short term, immediate solution—than saying that they wanted to change how the gang operated or provide an overarching regulatory presence. For his part, Big Cat knew better than to publicly admit his role as a criminal; even though he was depressed and dismayed at the residents' hostility toward him, he still wanted to be considered a community spokesperson in their eyes. And of course, admitting to coordinating organized criminal activity in front of potential court witnesses was also not in his interest.

Pastor Wilkins suggested a rapprochement, one that might build on the kind of exchange occurring between Big Cat and others around the table. In the past, Wilkins would mediate disputes by bringing people together and establishing a compromise or offering a ruling. But now he offered a somewhat novel idea: meet for the sake of coming together, even if there was not a particular problem or dispute.

"Looks like you all just needed to get together," Wilkins said toward the end of their meeting. "Now, Big Cat, I'm not happy that we have to be dealing with these things and that people can't walk around safely, but I suppose we can at least try and get these things out in the open. What would you say to meeting like this, maybe every week, same time? Saturday. Just us."

"I don't get it," interrupted Ola. "I don't understand what you're saying. What are we meeting *for?*"

"You and me and anybody else who comes here," Marlene said,

bending over the table so that Ola would not mistake what she was about to say. "We're going to figure out what to do about what's going on. You got a problem with Big Cat. You just said you had one, right? So, what happened, Big Cat said he's going to pay you. Now what if I was to tell you, he had to pay you half up front and then half later on. That way you know you're getting something from him using your place."

"I suppose," said Ola.

"That Arab got a problem with Big Cat's boys messing with his customers," Marlene continued, this time looking at Ola but addressing everyone in the room. "Fine, tell him you'll help him. Don't tell him what you're going to do, but just bring it here. We'll deal with it."

"I don't know," said Ola. "I ain't trying to be the police or nothing. I mean it sounds a little crazy like we sitting here helping everyone. I mean I got my own problems, I ain't got time to be messing in nobody's business."

"She's right," said Wilkins. "This is not about being the police. All I'm saying is that you all know what's happening in this community and we need a way to solve things sometimes. I mean ain't no way police is going to help with the kinds of things you need, so let's just keep communicating."

"Go ahead," Big Cat interrupted. "I'll come, I'll be here every week if it will show you all that I mean it when I say I'm here to help."

Pastor Wilkins's notion of meeting weekly at his church was innovative because it created another forum for discussion. Over the next few weeks, he worked not only with Big Cat but with several other clergy and local stakeholders to devise a system akin to community policing, but adapted for the shady side of life.

Here, residents could assemble, register their problems, and receive help. Law enforcement would not play the chief mediating or juridical role, although empathetic officers would sometimes be in attendance. As he explained, "If you want to shut down drug dealing, well, I'm all for it. But I can't help you. I mean these boys got guns, they got power, they'll kill you. Now, the other stuff is *quick time*, you understand. Someone's got to help Marlene deal with the angry mommas, angry 'cause Big Cat's boys have been recruiting their kids to join the gang. And someone has to see if Big Cat will take his [gang members] out the park on the weekend. See, all the police in the world can't make a momma safe unless you got that going on. Police never done that around here."

For his part, Big Cat was skeptical about the weekly forum, though he reserved his opinion and stayed silent as the forum coalesced. Even though he had worked with many residents, shopkeepers, and clergy over the past few years to address their concerns, he did not feel that residents would actually bring incidents to the new forum and negotiate in good faith. He also felt uncomfortable creating a quasi-public venue where they could put him on the defensive. "Look around, it's going to be me and ten of them. They can say what they want all day long and I just have to sit there and take it. It don't feel right."

The gang leader did not resent the fact that Wilkins set the rules—indeed, he appreciated that a third party was taking the reins and intervening. But he did have to deal with the resentment of other senior members of his gang, like high-ranking officer Ellis Clearwater. Many of the leaders were older than Big Cat, and they felt that it was dangerous for the gang to speak with residents in such a setting. They encouraged him to meet with Wilkins alone, so that others did not find out information about the gang. As Ellis told me a few days after learning of the new forum, "We will support Big Cat, but you have to understand that you can't just talk to folks because they'll use what you say against you. I learned this the hard way in the projects [where his former gang had been based]. We can't stop them from going to the police. And you never know what they'll find out. I don't want them knowing how we operate, how we do our thing. That's secret stuff." Just as he had to work intimately with Marlene and Pastor Wilkins to set up the forum, Big Cat had to spend time allaying the fears of his senior leadership who were entirely distrustful of the new proposal for mediating disputes in gangland.

Despite his reservations, Big Cat realized that he had little choice but to join with Wilkins and others in this new community court. He faced pressures from all sides. He was branching out into new underground economic waters and creating new kinds of animosities with residents as a result; his own membership wanted a stable revenue stream, like the one they managed years ago when the crack economy was in full swing. Big Cat also knew that there was always a danger that Ellis and other Black Kings senior officers could exercise a coup, particularly if they felt that he was putting their lives in jeopardy. He knew they would use any means necessary to avoid being arrested. If he did not show a capacity to provide leadership, which meant both quelling resident outcries and convincing his own membership that he was not airing gang secrets, he could suffer dire consequences. So he began showing up at the weekend meetings and negotiating with the assembled jury, but along the way he assured his own membership that the gang's organizational secrets would never be discussed at the meeting. To allay his men's concerns, he allowed Ellis to join him in some of the meetings.

Pastor Wilkins decided that gang-related activity was the most pressing concern, and so to keep things relatively simple, he limited the weekly meetings to discussions of local gang members' behavior. He said he wanted the group to address only those incidents in which the gang and a resident had a problem with one another—although he anticipated that people in attendance would ignore his instructions and list general concerns about life in the community. Big Cat generally followed Wilkins's lead in the conduct of these meetings. He also wanted a focused discussion, and he told Wilkins that he would be willing to discuss only particular problems. He did not want to be pulled into general discussions about crime and safety in the neighborhood.

Over the next two months, Pastor Wilkins and Marlene Matteson brought together a small group of people to talk with Big Cat and discuss specific gang-related activities. Marlene, James Carter, Ola Sanders, Gary Davis (director of a youth outreach center), and Big Cat attended every meeting for the next six months. Once in a while another resident or an empathetic member of the clergy or a social service agency came to air a grievance or listen to the discussions. These individuals always had the approval of Big Cat and Pastor Wilkins. The group remained small, but grew as large as a dozen people over the six months.

In the first three months, during the summer of 2002, the group met fifteen times—once each weekend and several times impromptu to address crises after Big Cat's men shot members of a rival gang. The number of problems aired grew in each successive month, an expected result given that the group was showing some success in helping to settle disputes between gangs and residents: in the first month, two dozen incidents were brought to the group's attention over four meetings. In the next month, in six meetings, the group addressed approximately sixty problems. And in the third month, the group heard fifty-five complaints over five meetings.

During the fall, the incidents continued to grow in number. And at the end of 2002, at the six-month anniversary meeting, the group heard four reports of gang members who kicked teenagers out of the park for interfering with drug trafficking; three complaints by a gypsy cab driver who said the gang forced him to run errands for free; an accusation by a restaurant owner that the gang failed to pay a "rental fee" for a large poker game; two reports of teenage gang members chasing down prostitutes and stealing their money; and an unseemly complaint that two Black Kings rank and file had defecated on the front step of a man who had been yelling at them to stop selling drugs on the corner.

Though only a select few participated, other Maquis Park stakeholders, and even members of storefront churches whose preachers were associates of Pastor Wilkins, came to know about the meetings. Some were plainly excited that the church was working to reduce violence and crime. Others were less enthused, still suspicious of any gang involvement with Pastor Wilkins, or perhaps frustrated that their own concerns were not being addressed. However, in general, individuals still preferred to resolve many gang-related disputes themselves, rather than bring them to the group's attention. For example, shopkeepers who had troubles with street gangs usually approached Wilkins or another member of the clergy privately, and Wilkins, Brother Patterson, and their associates would attend to the matter discreetly and outside the context of the larger meetings. When asked why shopkeepers preferred a more secretive approach, Patterson replied that the proprietors did not want others to know about their use of non-law-enforcement actors to settle disputes. Similarly, Marlene preferred to handle problems in private, stating that if the aggrieved party wanted to maintain complete confidentiality, she would not bring the matter to the attention of the larger group.

But the mediation that Wilkins initiated was not insignificant. The police had no capacity to address these issues, and no one in the community thought that the gang—or their threats to public safety—would disappear. So Wilkins's creation, as imperfect and temporary as it was, was also unique and innovative. Word of the weekend meetings had not spread widely, so there was no chorus of approval or dissent. Other residents, aware that the meetings were taking place, tended to make comments like that of Melinda, a thirty-five-year-old mother of three who lives next to an empty lot where prostitutes and gang members had been battling for the right to distribute their respective goods:

> I like the fact that someone is doing *something,* I mean it's better than just having these damn fools [the police] drive by and never get out of the car! I just worry about it, that's all. Brother Patterson got that prostitute out of my backyard as soon as I told him. He told me he had this group of people working with them gangbangers and that he could help me. So, I like that, but I don't know that I like the police not being involved. I mean, it's supposed to be the police who keeping us safe. I don't want that to change, you know? I want them to fight for better police around here.

Melinda's comment alluded to a sense of comfort that some residents received knowing that there was a visible means of gang intervention. However, her statement also shows the tone of skepticism that colored residents' views. Particularly for those who had grown up in the area, there was a sense of déjà vu. Gangs always seemed to be around, as did ineffective police and the need to supplement poor law enforcement services with creative and sometimes clandestine attempts to ensure public safety and security. This history probably mitigated both an immediate celebration of the new meetings as well as widespread hostility. Thus, it is not surprising that residents were cautiously guarded in their approval of the service Wilkins and others were providing—most were not even aware that the meetings were occurring.

Residents' views also pointed to the dangerous road that Pastor Wilkins, Marlene Matteson, and other organizers of the community court were walking. The pastor and his colleagues downplayed their omission of mainstream law enforcement. Police were ineffective, they argued, and so it made little sense to call on them or expect that they would respond in a timely manner to the problems at hand. But their criticisms of police officials and local officers could not hide the fact that these neighborhood leaders were now taking the law into their own hands and collaborating with a criminal organization. Ironically, these same leaders had been in Maquis Park a decade ago—and some were participants—during a failed attempt to turn gangs around with voter registration and other approaches that did not involve law enforcement or social services. These initiatives had resulted in critical press and police scrutiny: both alleged that the community was colluding with gangs and facilitating drug trafficking. Now, in 2002, it appeared that many of these spokespersons and grassroots organizers were willing to undertake a similarly risky initiative in their drive to respond to public safety issues. When reminded of this parallel, those involved said little more than to claim that desperate times called for desperate measures. They could not sit idly by while crime threatened families and a wider world paid little, if any, attention. Their determination betrayed a disturbing truth—beneath the superficial historical parallels, Maquis Park was confronting a gang unlike any they had seen in the past. The times were desperate indeed.

At the end of 2002, the times were also growing desperate for Big Cat. Neither his senior officers nor his rank and file had any experience with an external entity adjudicating their disputes—although many of them were used to one-on-one backroom negotiations with a community leader. That is, in the past Big Cat or a senior officer, like Ellis Clearwater, would hear about a conflict and then proffer a ruling and levy punishments or fines. Either one might engage in discussion with a school principal, police officer, or block club president, but these conversations always had an air of secrecy and mystery. Now, even though Big Cat was part of the meetings and he could probably resist any ruling that the pastor and the others devised, many Black Kings felt that the community was openly directing the gang. To many rank-and-file members, it appeared that the gang was losing control over its affairs; most were not paying attention to the benefits of the community court for dampening conflicts and facilitating underground economic activity. It was not necessarily surprising to hear senior gang members criticize Big Cat—"He's losing his mind, and going over to the other side," Mason Morandis, one high-ranking officer, liked to say—because they were his peers and some definitely had an interest in ousting him as leader. But now even the rank-and-file teenagers in the Black Kings looked askance at the new happenings. Most would not criticize Big Cat in public—insubordination carried hefty punishments including beatings and monetary fines. Instead, they directed their disgust at residents whom they confronted in public and whom they felt were now taking a brazen attitude toward the gang. As one nineteen-year-old member of Big Cat's organization said, "I got these little mommas telling me to get off the corner. Man, who do they think they are? No one pushes me around, nigger, or I push back. She's going to be sorry if she keeps pushing me, that's all I got to say. I mean something's got to change, this shit can't be happening."

It was doubtful that the community court was actually pushing residents to confront the gang more directly. Most still feared Black Kings who had guns and who were willing to use violence. Instead, the rank and file were most probably reacting to the expansion of their underground economic operations, which was generating increased local opposition. When the gang members confronted outspoken critics, it was easy for them to believe that these residents were being energized by the new community court.

By the spring of 2003, as the community court approached the nine-month mark, its members met at several places in the community. Participants continued to gather at Wilkins's church, but they also used other places where the gang was welcome. The list of such places was growing. Dr. D. J. Watkins asked that the group come over to Paths Ahead, his social service center, about a mile away from Wilkins's church. It was no secret that Big Cat had paid for the complete renovation of the gymnasium inside Paths Ahead—it now hosted a Southside intergang basketball tournament and weekend dances, for which Watkins received several thousand dollars per month in rent. Similarly, Gary Davis, leader of All God's Children, a small organization of social workers and youth counselors who ministered to local troubled youth, hosted several weekend meetings. Davis did not deny that he, too, received money from Big Cat: All God's Children used some of the gang's largesse to build a small storefront office in the nearby Englewood community, where they provided social services to ex-offenders and street gang members trying to find jobs and vocational training.

Although Davis refused to cite figures, Big Cat said he paid Davis $2,000 per month to help find legal jobs for his rank and file—which enabled them to open bank accounts, which in turn helped the gang store its illegally obtained cash. These were relatively small expenditures for Big Cat; and he sought out these payments for many reasons, some pragmatic some symbolic. On the one hand, he needed places to meet, and large gymnasiums and rooms inside youth centers could accommodate his gang. In addition, the gang also had always benefited from some of its members being employed. Many who had legitimate paychecks opened bank accounts and stored the gang's cash—otherwise, Big Cat had to hide money in mattresses, television sets, and other places inside his apartment. Big Cat liked to cite examples of Black Kings in the workforce to build up his "community man" image: he would tell local residents like Marlene that he was more than a drug dealer and that he was genuinely interested in the developmental paths of his rank and file; on occasion, he would cite passages from the street gang's bible, *Literature of Black Kings Nation*, which said that high school graduation and a "legit job" only helped the gang in its overall mission. All of this may have been true, but Big Cat could not deny that he actually devoted fairly little attention and few resources to helping his rank and file obtain their high school diplomas and find mainstream work. Even in less hostile times, if ever there were such moments, Big Cat's orientation was toward monetary gain; now, with a community breathing down his back and his men growing restless to maintain their economic standing, his charitable gestures were negligible at best.

The organizations led by Watkins, Wilkins, and Davis were only a few of the ones on Big Cat's payroll. Marlene counted about a dozen who received money from the gang to permit the rank and file to use their space to congregate. Many individuals and organizations tried to find the gang members jobs; some offered services to female gang members associated with Big Cat's gang and resolved domestic disputes between male gang members and their female partners; in rare cases, a few organizations allowed the gang to store its cash and weapons in their buildings. Marlene placed the decisions of these organizations to accept Big Cat's money in the context of their historic neglect by local philanthropies and the Greater Grand Boulevard Community Association, the main conduit for government and philanthropic support in the area—and one that had actively shunned the grassroots sector in the community. By 2003, as these arrangements grew more elaborate, she became disturbed. In the past she had seen such pairings "slip out of control"—her words to describe how the gang could grow greedy if their power was not checked:

> I'm never going to stop people from taking [Big Cat's] money. I mean we're poor people, poorest of the poor. You got the Association and they never give us shit: we have to fill out forms, have bank accounts. Shit, most of us don't have a dime to our name. Now what I'm a little concerned about is that we don't have a way to tell Big Cat enough is enough, especially the way he's acting now, just doing as he please. It will all slip out of control, just like that [*snapping her fingers*]. He's going crazy and I don't know why.

Maybe he killed Babycake and he thinks he's going to be caught for drugs or something. I don't care. I'm just worried about the fact that you got these people taking his money and they're good people. They may get hurt if they don't behave, and I don't want to see that.

Pastor Wilkins shared Marlene's concerns about Big Cat's erratic behavior and the private relationships the gang leader was building with organizations via his shady philanthropy. He worried that Big Cat's work with the organizations would decrease the spirit of unity among the grassroots stakeholders, effectively dividing them and forcing them to give higher priority to their need for personal remuneration than to collective initiatives to maintain law and order. He knew that Big Cat might ask some of the people who received his money not to cooperate with Marlene and him. But with so many gang-related problems coming their way, Marlene and the pastor had little time to reflect on these potential drawbacks or Big Cat's recalcitrance. So they made note of their concern and moved on.

For his part, Big Cat said little outside of the Saturday meetings. He continued to be hard to read. But his clandestine ties with organizations in the community were growing. By means of his donations, he pushed ahead ferociously to buy the allegiance of cash-strapped organization directors who had few other potential sources of funding. Rumors circulated that he co-opted several grassroots activists by paying them to store the gang's receipts; a police raid on a transitional housing facility showed hidden caches of guns, which many residents believed to be the property of the gang. A block club president in Maquis Park told Marlene that the gang was paying her husband—and other security guards at a local high school—to turn off the metal detector and look the other way when Big Cat's rank and file stored guns, drugs, and cash inside school lockers. Big Cat would not admit to any of these payoffs, but he did say that he wanted to make sure that the community court did not threaten his private ties with local residents and stakeholders. "Let me put it this way, I'll go to these meetings and listen, but I got a business to run and I'm not letting nobody get in the way of that. That always comes first."

We cannot underestimate the diplomatic work entailed in bringing together the community, dispossessed and often disgruntled, around a common cause. The public's moral outrage over a gang and its violent ways only increases the burdens of such diplomacy. Working with a gang has never been popular, and accusations of impropriety are likely to follow even it if brings benefits, like violence reduction and conflict resolution. Perhaps it was only a matter of time, but as the summer of 2003 dawned, despite the commitment of Wilkins and his colleagues to obtaining justice and some semblance of safety, the practical limits of their juridical voyage became manifest.

By the beginning of summer, 90 percent of the cases brought to the group's attention involved two problems: First, to no one's surprise, the gang's increased drug trafficking meant more rank-and-file members in public space to harass residents and intimidate passersby. Residents now feared sending their children outside, either alone or in the company of adults, and they wanted to restore safe public passage. The second set of issues was unforeseen. By canvassing areas like parks, street corners, and alleyways, the gang was in growing contact with Maquis Park's underground traders, including hairstylists who did business in the park, pimps and prostitutes who worked in abandoned buildings, street hustlers who fixed cars or shined shoes on streets and alleyways, and mothers who sold food and clothing on sidewalks. The dozen or so senior leaders in Big Cat's gang had made themselves a part of these transactions. In the gang's desperate need to make money, to squeeze it out wherever they could, they were now stepping into the tiniest puddles of the underground economy. Big Cat had taken his strategy to the extreme. During one meeting in July, James Carter complained to Big Cat about Fay, one of Big Cat's senior officers:

> "Your boy, what's his name, Fay? Mabel said she was selling soul food and Fay told her that she couldn't sell to the stores on 44th [St.] because Eunice is selling over there. [Fay] said she had to leave."
>
> "Yeah, that's right," said Big Cat. "Eunice has been over there, that's her spot. Fay was doing what I said."
>
> "Now, listen here boy. First, if you gonna make that work, you got to make sure you out there when Mabel is complaining, because she's angry. Fay said she needed to pay him $50 a week, even though she wasn't selling nothing!"
>
> "No, no, no!" Big Cat shook his head. "Fay ain't supposed to do that. He ain't supposed to take money from Mabel. He knows that. The brother is getting some change from Eunice, but not from Mabel, no, no, that's not right. I'll talk with him."
>
> "Okay," said James, who then leaned over in his chair and wagged his finger at Big Cat. "Fine, talk with him. But brother, I'll tell you something else. You better stay off my street, because I find you been charging people, I will kill you. You dig?"
>
> "All right," interrupted Pastor Wilkins. "Let's bring this down a bit."
>
> "No, sir." James Carter shook his head. "Big Cat charges people

on my street and I'm losing money. There's no way that's happening."

"Hold up," said Big Cat. "Old man, you got your thing going on, good. Just tell me. I'm not looking to take you out or nothing. You weren't on 44th to begin with, shit. So, calm down. I ain't coming over to West [Street], okay?"

The incident James described involved Mabel and Eunice (Marlene's neighbor), two women who prepared soul food lunches in their homes and sold them under the table in Maquis Park. Mabel tried to advertise her lunches to staff at a clinic on 44th Street, historically one of the areas where Eunice conducted business. On Big Cat's orders, Fay had been extorting $50 a month from Eunice by promising to rid 44th Street of other lunch sellers. Attending to his duties, he told Mabel not to come to the street to sell her goods. But he continued by demanding that she pay him $50 for no apparent reason. Mabel became upset and vowed to call the police. Fay then retaliated by breaking into Mabel's house and physically threatening her. Feeling that the police could not help, Mabel called her friend James Carter, who then reported the case to Big Cat and the entire group. The resolution, formed out of a consensus by those in attendance, was that Fay should pay back all the money he had collected from Mabel plus an apology and a 5 percent cash penalty. Grudgingly, Fay made the payment, although he said he would never apologize.

The lunch dispute was one example of the gang slowly taking over the regulation of everyday business, a role that had been long fulfilled by an older generation not in the gang—community leaders, preachers, business owners. James Carter, for example, had worked for two decades to help people iron out disputes and find customers for their goods and services. He was one of many people who not only directly managed underground economic exchanges but more generally addressed conflicts and helped restore social order. And like other mediators, he received money from the entrepreneurs he assisted. He helped local women sell homemade jewelry and clothing to white-collar employees in downtown office buildings where he worked; he found clients for several people who used their cars as gypsy cabs; he brought Medicaid recipients to a local doctor who paid him $10 for each client. Even though the gang did not threaten all of these shady dealings, James saw Fay and the gang's actions as a potential threat to his own revenue stream—he had been receiving payments from people like Mabel, who sold food and clothing and who now made their payments to Fay. He wanted some reassurance that Big Cat did not intend to usurp this role that he had held in Maquis Park. Big Cat, however, would offer no such guarantee, as he explained to Pastor Wilkins after the meeting.

"That nigger [James Carter] wants to get his piece of the pie," said Big Cat, chagrined at James's rebuke.

"So? I mean don't you think it's a big deal, taking over other people's gigs?" I said. "The man has to eat, after all."

"Eat? The man ain't starving," Big Cat replied. "Anyway, like I said, I ain't stepping up and doing what he says. I'm not taking over what he's got. But I can't sit here and tell you that this ain't happening or that it's not going to happen. I mean we can offer people protection. James can't give you shit. So why pay him? I told you I'm a businessman, I'm going to make my money."

"Now, you need to realize what you're doing," cautioned Wilkins. "Lot of people—and me, I'm one of them—we all have something going on. Everyone has to make their money, Big Cat, you know that. So you come into what we got, well, a dog will bark if it's being attacked! Just don't get greedy, Big Cat, that's all I'm saying, just be careful and don't get greedy."

Wilkins's warning was indicative of the deeper issues at play. James Carter was a little upset about the gang's policing of lunch sellers and other petty traders like gypsy car drivers and alleyway car mechanics. But what really provoked his ire was unspoken and far more serious: the gang's intrusion into his primary source of underground revenue, namely, gun trading, which could net him several thousand dollars per year—a substantial supplement to his low-wage income. Carter was one of several local brokers who charged a fee to gun traders for placing them in contact with potential customers. Carter had been finding gun purchases for local brokers for nearly ten years. As an intermediary, however, Carter and others provided more than simply a liaison between buyer and seller; they often mediated disputes that arose over, say, the price or quality of the weapon sold. Moreover, because they knew who was purchasing weapons, they were valuable for helping to settle gun-related conflicts and incidents of violence. Thus, they also earned money by settling disputes. (On occasion, the police department turned to them for information about a violent crime.) The gang's ever-expanding underground role made gun trading the next business frontier; and the threat to Carter and the other gun brokers was obvious.[14]

Big Cat laughed at Carter's view that the gang was trying to take over his own brokerage role. "It was the guys [with the weapons] that came to me! Carter and them weren't able to sell nothing, so they asked us [in the gang] to take over. People think I'm trying to close up their shop, but it ain't like that." Big Cat countered Carter's accusation by saying that the market for guns had grown inefficient and that the gun traders were growing restless in their dealings with locals—like Carter—who were unable to find customers for them. The gang leader was correct that gun markets are not as smooth as many other shady economies, such as gypsy cabs or drugs or homemade lunches, in which buyers and sellers have relatively little difficulty finding one another. But Big Cat was incorrect to say that this was the fault of brokers like Carter or that he was not trying to take business away from other gun brokers. The supply of guns waxes and wanes and is always unstable. Traders have difficulty finding guns to sell, so they cannot easily and immediately reply to a request on the streets. The sale of a gun can net several hundred dollars, but guns are not addictive, like drugs, nor are they inexpensive, like home-cooked meals, so transactions do not occur all that often. Moreover, many weapons are not in working order, so there are always disputes between customers, brokers, and traders, which can lead to delays and distrust. Brokers, no matter effective they may be, cannot realistically change these conditions. The gun traders may have approached Big Cat's gang—and in so doing, they took some of their business away from the established brokers like Carter—but Big Cat had to admit that he was actively trying to usurp these brokers' roles. He couldn't lay the fault in the brokers' hands for losing business.

The disputes between Carter and Big Cat's gang were set off toward the end of May by an incident involving a prominent local gun trader, Milton Morton, who worked with both Carter and the gang. For all gun traders, securing a storage site for weapons was a persistent challenge. Big Cat and Ellis thought they could be of help by paying a small fee—usually around $250 per month—to a slumlord who owned three broken-down brownstones. Ellis then promised Morton that for $500 per month he could keep his weapons in the basement of one of the brownstones. The gang would protect the cache, and for each gun sale that Ellis managed to facilitate, the gang would charge a small tax. (Over the next three months, approximately a hundred guns would be sold from that basement, netting the gang several thousand dollars.)

Intrigued by Ellis's offer, Morton decided to take his gun-trading business away from James Carter and other brokers and give it all to the gang. He also promised the gang that he would help them recruit other gun traders—thereby further decreasing the revenue for James Carter and other gun brokers who weren't affiliated with the gang. Of course, Carter and two other brokers saw this as a threat to their livelihood. Not only were they losing money from the diminishment of their opportunities to act as a liaison, but they also discovered that they were no longer being sought out as independent mediators when gun-related conflicts erupted. More often than not, the mediation was being conducted under the auspices of Big Cat's gang.

Sensing a precipitous drop in their income, Carter and his colleagues who brokered gun sales in Maquis Park asked Marlene Matteson to intervene on their behalf. Marlene felt the issue was too difficult for her to handle, so she brought it to the attention of Pastor Wilkins. The pastor was concerned about the availability of guns in the community, particularly the capacity of young people to acquire guns. Those gun brokers, like James Carter, who were not affiliated with the gang generally acquiesced when Wilkins and other stakeholders asked them not to broker gun sales to teenage and adolescent customers. The pastor felt that this was an important form of social control, one that he was loath to relinquish to Big Cat. Realistically, he could not keep all guns out of the neighborhood on his own, but he felt that his ties to gun brokers enabled him to reduce the number of sales to the very young members of the community. If Big Cat took over gun trading, Wilkins believed, local youth would be able to obtain guns with relative ease. A second concern was simply Big Cat's growing desire to extract cash anywhere he could, even if it meant encroaching on the right of all people in the area to make money:

> This is something I really don't want to see. Big Cat and them starting to get a little greedy. Not sure where this is coming from, but they are starting to act like one of them old-time bosses. You know, the kind that, whenever he sees money being made, he wants some of it. I mean, I hear that the brother and his boys are trying to find small gambling, you know, dice games where he can charge a few bucks. This is getting ridiculous. I mean I don't know what's worse: that these brothers are peddling that disgusting [drugs] to the community or getting in the way of everyone's live-lihood, harassing folks, not letting up.

During the summer of 2003, Wilkins did not tell the others at the weekly meetings that he was concerned that Big Cat might sell guns to local youth. Instead he began to suggest that Big Cat's usurpation of other shady traders' earnings was much bigger than the few incidents that had been reported to their assembled group. Wilkins and Marlene knew that Big Cat and his officers were now frantically trying to regulate the gamut of underground economic activity in the community, upsetting all sorts of people who were making small amounts of money settling disputes, finding customers for sellers of goods and services, brokering deals, offering credit, and so on. The gang tried to extort burglars and stolen car rings—essentially networks of adult criminals who placed stolen contraband and car parts on the underground mar-ket—by charging a fee to operate in Maquis Park. They told bar-tenders to send them anyone who was looking for a prostitute, thereby taking over the business of some local pimps. Big Cat found late-night poker games and offered the players low-interest loans in hopes that they would go into debt and be forced to borrow additional money. On occasion he set up dice and poker games, charging a $20 entrance fee to play. Big Cat's men combed public housing for people selling candy out of their homes. These petty capitalists—earning about $20–$40 in profit per week—already paid the tenant leader in their building a 15 percent fee, and now they were forced to pay Big Cat's gang.

Marlene and Wilkins knew that their own group could not adjudicate each such shady dispute, for many reasons, including not only the impracticality of ascertaining all illegal activity occurring in the community but also the fact that residents would fear retaliation if they spoke about gang extortion. Similarly, it was doubtful that Big Cat could regulate all underground activity in Maquis Park, even in a delimited sphere like gun trading, which involved only a dozen traders. Shady traders tended to resolve their conflicts informally and spontaneously, even if they chose to enlist a third-party mediator in their dispute. The rules constantly changed. As a result, there was no single system in place that the gang could identify, challenge, and usurp. It was not as if Big Cat was forcibly taking over an established criminal justice institution, with courts, procedures of punishment and redress, facilities for incarceration, and so on.

Wilkins was not worried that the gang would become a parallel governmental entity, overseeing the shady side of the economic fence. Instead, he saw that Big Cat's efforts to expand his sources of underground revenue meant that the gang was increasing its presence in shady entrepreneurial spaces and, in so doing, escalating the likelihood of conflict with the wider residential population. Gang members could be found throughout Maquis Park, along major thoroughfares, in small and large parks, and in empty lots. They sometimes challenged other shady traders for access to areas of high pedestrian traffic, or places where cars parked, with doors opened and merchandise on display. While the rank-and-file gang members argued and fought with their counterparts at these hot spots, the gang's officers—particularly Big Cat and Ellis—extorted the shady traders and demanded payment in return for gang protection. And as we have seen, Big Cat and Ellis found themselves regulating various aspects of underground commerce, sometimes directly by facilitating transactions and at other times unintentionally by mediating disputes among local traders. By the middle of the summer of 2003, it seemed that no illicit activity was too small for Big Cat: there were reports that he jumped out of his car to demand payoffs from local "squeegee men" washing windows; others claimed that he raided chess games in the park where very small bets were placed.

From June to September 2003, several problems for those participating in the community court became paramount. Only one of these was Big Cat's intrusion into underground economies that once had been controlled by other residents in the community. There was growing criticism by people like James Carter—still stinging from the loss of his gun-trading revenue—who felt that the weekly meetings at Pastor Wilkins's church only enhanced Big Cat's power in local shady economies. After one meeting in which Big Cat was dismissive of resident requests to stop capricious harassment of local merchants, Carter waited for the gang leader to leave and then stood up and spoke to the group:

> What are we doing? We need to ask the question. We lost our control over these boys. We were supposed to be trying to get them to

stop killing each other and killing us. Not helping them make money. Look, [Big Cat] ain't even listening to us. It's noon and the brother's drunk. He left because he was too sick to hear us. You know it's over, he don't feel like we can do nothing to him. Pastor Wilkins, we need to change the tune. We need to bring the police in here.

Carter was not alone. Others involved in or familiar with the weekly meetings in Wilkins's church had started to worry that the group was effectively lending its approval to—if not facilitating— certain kinds of criminal behavior in the community. At its inception the previous fall, Ola Sanders forcefully made the case that the group should deal only with "big shit, not little shit," by which she meant that the attendees should not try to play police officer and adjudicate every little matter. Instead, they should simply act as a standing body that could deal with crises when they arose. Now, with the end of summer nearing, she suggested that the group model themselves after the Greater Grand Boulevard Community Association, an entity that responded to pressing problems, like unemployment or lack of social services, by lobbying external actors, like the mayor's administration, for money or support. Because the GGBCA in Ola's eyes had no interest in dealing with troubled youth or other marginalized and neglected constituencies, she felt that her peers could operate as an alternate spokesperson, bringing the needs of the grassroots to the attention of the city.

Big Cat did not hear these complaints in the public meetings, and no one admitted that they told him in private of their concerns. He benefited from the residents' dissension because it diminished the likelihood that they would confront him in a unified way. One August day, he reflected on the expanding economic base of the gang, much of which seemed to be at the expense of other underground traders. "If you are asking me whether we are making money in new ways, well, yes, I guess I'll admit that. And like all businesses, there is competition and those who are losers will always be pissed off. But, fuck 'em. I can't be worried if I'm better than them at their own game. Shit, maybe this will be what they say is a wake-up call." Notwithstanding his self-laudatory comments, he was hearing complaints from his own senior gang members, who did not believe that the rising income was sufficient to meet their own demand. In private meetings, senior gang officers complained to Big Cat that they wanted to consider other options, including expanding their drug trafficking, forcefully taking over neighboring gangs, and extorting additional businesses. From Big Cat's perspective, all of these activities could potentially lead to further violence and jeopardize the gang's existing economic operations, which were already unstable because of resident opposition. So he did not lend his support to the proposed ventures. He said everyone in the organization needed to focus on the task at hand, namely, maintaining somewhat stable ties with the local stakeholders. But from the perspective of his subordinates, more ambitious initiatives were necessary to ensure the gang's material viability. More lucrative schemes needed to be developed, most felt, if the gang was going to have adequate opportunities to get income.

While Big Cat managed his relationships with other leaders in the Black Kings, Pastor Wilkins and others persisted in their efforts to develop the community court. And Ola and James grew fearful not only that the group was giving license to criminal activity, but that it might jeopardize the few relationships the community had with certain police officers. Both Ola and James suggested that any of their attempts to provide redress might offend the officers who had been cooperative with them when public safety required secretive, backroom negotiations. They worried that the police would no longer tolerate their creation of a "star chamber," where issues ostensibly under the domain of government were being handled outside the law. Not inconsequentially, they also worried that empathetic officers who tolerated their own underground economic activity might no longer look the other way—they sensed a threat to their own livelihoods. So they began to argue that the group should reach out to police officers and alert them about the weekly meetings. All of the people around the table had the capacity to work with police informally and attend to issues off the books—a power never underestimated in an area lacking in law enforcement. They worried that officers who once had been friendly would grow angry when they discovered the degree to which local residents were taking matters into their own hands. This might worsen the already strained relations between police and community residents. They also worried, though, that if other residents found out about the meetings, the participants might be accused of extortion, bribery, and complicity in gang violence and the police might react by refusing to work with them. So the challenge for group members was to find a way to deal with local problems without advertising their forum too widely, thereby attracting too many requests for help and too many admonishments. Not everyone believed that this tightrope could be walked.

Over the course of the summer and into the autumn, these various problems and tensions would play themselves out, not always in productive or pleasing ways. The summer began with Pastor Wilkins's acknowledgment of the cautionary opinions of Ola and others around the table. But by autumn, Wilkins, Marlene, Big Cat, and many other supportive stakeholders attending the weekly forum effectively ignored Ola's advice that they not practice community justice by trying to enforce underground economic contracts, or settle petty disputes, or otherwise act as a separate enforcement body. Into the fall of 2003, Pastor Wilkins continued to sponsor the weekly get-togethers; his primary justification was the need to prevent fatalities, like what had happened to Babycake Jackson. He found himself defending the meetings as the most useful way to prevent gang-related problems from escalating and as the only opportunity to keep law and order in the shady world. The problems in the shady arena and in gangland, however, continued to grow. The pastor's interventions may have successfully lowered the flame on certain conflicts, but group participants could not legitimately claim that they were reducing the total number of incidents, disputes, threats, and problems in the community that stemmed from the behavior of the Black Kings.

By autumn Big Cat had isolated himself from the community court. During his irregular appearances, he responded to reports of his gang members' bad behavior with distracted nods, drifting off, saying little. Sometimes, in the middle of a negotiation, he jumped out of his seat, stretched as if there was an official break, and walked outside to smoke a cigarette. Many of the promises that he made to people were not fulfilled. "I can't be bothered with all that," he claimed on a blustery September afternoon, at the end of one community court gathering. "It's just getting to be more of a pain than it's worth. It all sounds good when you're sitting around the table, but I got a lot of other things on my mind and, you know, I just can't be worried if somebody got some problem with us." His rank and file had now expanded so far out of their purview—they had moved far beyond drug dealing—that he was trying to manage all sorts of challenges, from appeasing gang members' need for income to stabilizing new kinds of underground activity. His energies were now almost fully taken up by the need to deal with economic exigencies. Although he knew that appeasing the locals was instrumental for his own success as a shady merchant, he seemed to increasingly view the task of attending to relations between the gang and the community as a burden.

At the end of September, Pastor Wilkins and Marlene Matteson decided that they must enlist the police in their community mediation. By this point, many of the attendees had privately told friends on the police force about the community court, but no one spoke publicly about the police officers' reactions. And no one was sure exactly how to involve officers who had been sympathetic to their backroom strategies. Should they invite police to join? Should they disclose all of the cases to the police? Or should they simply offer to keep lines of communication open by maintaining some kind of diplomatic stance? As they struggled to devise a strategy, they reasoned that it would be good to first establish the support of some of the more prominent residents in Maquis Park who, up to that point, had not been participating in their weekly community court. They hoped that by widening their base, they could show police and other skeptical parties that their alternate forum was valuable and worthy of support. They knew Big Cat would not approve of these efforts, so they did not inform him.

Wilkins turned to other storefront clergy with whom he had worked in the past—though there were not many to chose from since Pastor Barnes had pulled some away from street diplomacy and into the established political camp. Brother Patterson was invited to a meeting because a complaint about Big Cat's henchman involved the extortion of a shady trader who attended Patterson's storefront church. Wilkins also called Minister Hortons, and both tried to work with the gang members hanging out in the two parks near Horton's church. To complement Wilkins's outreach, Marlene and her neighbor Eunice brought some nearby public housing tenant leaders to the meetings at Wilkins's church. These leaders faced similar gang-related problems, particularly because many gang members lived in public housing. Marlene capitalized on the historic lack of any human services for public housing, whether law enforcement, sanitation, or youth programs, to convince the tenant leaders to declare their backing for the weekend forum. In this way, Marlene and Pastor Wilkins expanded their networks and created a small group of committed stakeholders who, as in the past, decided to dedicate themselves to confronting local problems that the police and the more prominent community spokespersons neglected. They hoped that with this diverse set of community leaders on board, they could begin the more difficult process of telling police about the forum they had developed. They reasoned that police might work with them once they saw that support for the forum extended beyond simply Wilkins and his immediate circle of friends.

In this way the demands of the gang pushed the community leaders in unforeseen directions and unintentionally positioned them to take on other battles. As these community leaders responded to Big Cat's advances, many found a newfound atmosphere of activism and solidarity; it was easy to tell that they had hoped that the energy would spill over into other areas, outside of gangland. One heard shouts of "It's so nice to be working together again!" and "I knew I wasn't the only one in the community dealing with these problems, I'm glad we're in this together!" For the moment, however, few said anything more concrete than to exclaim their relief at having others share their burden and their desire for change. It had been more than a decade since one had seen grassroots activism and community organizing in these neighborhoods, and so the emergence of hope among these stakeholders was not difficult to understand.

Expanding the forum raised another problem, however. Although the group did not want to attract too much attention from other local residents—preferring instead to deal with conflicts behind the scenes—they knew that, as their support increased, word would spread across the community. It seemed almost certain to many of them that there would be speculation that grassroots leaders were now in cahoots with local criminals. Throughout July, in private conversations with other forum participants, Wilkins would broach this issue, but he said that the conversations were usually short because no one knew how to handle the problem. So he just pushed onward, continuing to meet weekly, expanding the base of participants, and hoping that rumor and innuendo would not ultimately lead to their downfall.

Alas, while the residents seemed able to organize themselves, Big Cat and the gang were ill-prepared to work in a productive capacity with residents. Big Cat and his senior officer, Ellis, had moved very quickly in their attempts to extort shady traders over the last year. Everyone was complaining. Underground traders tried to guard their own interests against gang encroachment; brokers and mediators whose income was threatened by Big Cat similarly tried to resist the gang's efforts; and residents frustrated at their inability to walk safely about their neighborhood either yelled at the gang or shouted at Wilkins and his colleagues to put an end to the gang's practices.

Looking weary, and still faced with public recrimination over the death of the street hustler Babycake Jackson, by mid-July

Big Cat was missing most of the Saturday meetings. Sometimes weeks would pass and no one could get hold of him. A lover of gambling, he would leave for junkets to Las Vegas without informing his own leadership. Rumors circulated that Big Cat actually never left Chicago and instead holed up inside his apartment where he drank, snorted cocaine, and hid from others in the gang.

On the last weekend of July the gang leader went to Florida, and it was left to his second in command, Ellis, to attend Wilkins's church meetings. Allowing Ellis to attend the meetings in his place signaled an important shift in the gang's internal workings and, in turn, its relationships with other people in the community. Ellis had neither the authority nor the legitimacy to speak for the gang. He attended the meetings and said relatively little when incidents were discussed or when prodded by members of the community court to give the official gang response. "I'm just here to listen," he would usually mutter, "I'll get word back to Big Cat and get back to you all." On those rare occasions when Ellis acted, Big Cat would usually return from his trip (or his apartment) and summarily overturn all of the compromises Ellis had reached with Wilkins and others around the table. "He thinks I'm the enemy," said Ellis, referring to Big Cat, "but the boy's paranoid and better get his act together." If Big Cat had sent any other officer to represent him at the meetings, people would not have thought much of it. But they knew that Ellis had been a powerful gang leader in his own right—in fact, he had managed a gang four times the size of Big Cat's—and most laypeople and rank-and-file Black Kings speculated that he was interested in overthrowing Big Cat. Ellis never admitted to these aspirations and would usually just shrug his shoulders when asked about them. One sensed, however, that he was smart enough to see that an opening was presenting itself and all he had to do was let Big Cat dig his own grave.

Big Cat's unpredictable behavior and poor rule had serious consequences. One important result was a decreased monitoring of the gang's rank and file. Many of the younger members sensed that their leader had been preoccupied and had grown less interested in working out compromises with local residents, so they grew more callous in their harassment of underground traders and they were less cooperative when residents asked them to move from public areas or limit their drug trafficking. Even the senior leadership seemed to take advantage of Big Cat's unreliable oversight. They increased their wanton extortion and, with little rhyme or reason, doubled or tripled their monetary demands on the locals. In fact, sometimes two or three different senior gang officers approached the same business and asked for a weekly payoff. And worst of all, Big Cat received increasing reports that neither the senior officers nor the rank and file were adhering to the rules that mandated that they turn over most of their revenue to the gang's coffers. This was particularly worrisome to the gang leader because it meant that all of his efforts to increase underground economic opportunities were not leading to benefits for the organization as a whole. On one occasion, in October, he severely punished a twenty-five-year-old Black Kings member for taxing a store owner without permission; Big Cat beat up the young man, broke both of his hands, and sent him to the hospital—all as a sign that he would not tolerate insubordination. More people than Ellis wondered if Big Cat was "losing his mind."

By the end of the autumn, the weekend community court meetings grew less frequent and fewer people attended. A number of factors were at play. First, Big Cat and the gang seemed to make fewer and fewer concessions to local stakeholders—although they had never been fully cooperative. Gang recruitment and storage of drugs and weapons, especially in high schools, had increased the determined work of the group; in the past, school-based recruitment had not been such a serious problem. And whereas in the past they felt some control over the gang's usurpation of parks, sidewalks, and open areas, Wilkins and his colleagues now felt impotent to curb these intrusions. Finally, the local gang activity was reaching a point where the police acted with greater speed and force. Faced with mounting criticism about school-based recruitment and gang trafficking in public space, police officers arrested Big Cat's men with greater frequency instead of waiting for Marlene and others to intercede.

Simultaneously, the gang and its leadership were becoming unpredictable. Big Cat now suspected everyone of being a police informant and would assault residents and shopkeepers on a whim. Unlike in the past, he let teenage Black Kings carry guns and perform public displays of bravado, like shooting off their weapons outside of nightclubs, robbing prostitutes, and assaulting women on dates. (Such actions had previously carried stiff penalties because they violated the organization's rules and they tended to attract police). Black Kings even began threatening the very organizations that had offered services and social support to the gang. In one of the worst incidents, on a cold October weekend Ellis beat up a youth counselor at the Paths Ahead center, where the gang had a strong relationship with staff members. The assault was followed by vandalism and looting, as Big Cat's rank and file allegedly broke into the place and stole computers, a large-screen television, and a pool table.

At the same time there were troubles in the shady world that had little to do with the gang. The demolition of approximately five thousand units of public housing, which had started in 1996 and eventually brought Ellis into Big Cat's fold, was still continuing. Scores of underground traders continued to leave the demolished high-rise buildings and parking lots that had once been their sales spots. They migrated east into Maquis Park, where they set up shop on the street corners and in the alleyways along West Street and began to compete with the hustlers already there. Increased competition, for physical space and for business, caused greater conflicts among underground traders. In the words of James Arleander, who ran his car mechanic business from the alleys near West Street, "We never had nobody competing with us like this before. Now with these [public housing] buildings coming down, you got cats who think they have the right to push you aside and take over what you're doing." James found himself contending with several newly arrived hustlers who were also car mechanics and who tried to recruit customers away from him. Other longtime hustlers on West Street experienced similar threats to their livelihoods, and many began approaching Pastor Wilkins and Marlene Matteson for help settling disputes.

To those stakeholders who had spent years monitoring underground activity and devised solutions for the myriad situations birthed by the shady world, times were growing tough. They measured the pulse of their neighborhood by their own capacity to be useful in the underground arena. They all acknowledged that such tenuous vital signs inevitably wax and wane. But this recent downturn was difficult to stomach. Community leaders were faced with a triptych of problems: the neighborhood's equivocating support for their formal backroom diplomacy; the escalating and highly volatile behavior of the local gang; and the growing public conflicts of underground traders. Less than a year ago, one had sensed optimism among stakeholders. In the face of police neglect, they were confident, perhaps naively, that they might still be able to control shady activities in the neighborhood. They had never expected to eliminate delinquency and criminal behavior, but that had never been their goal to begin with. They simply wanted an effective means to respond to specific incidents and maintain social order.

As one of the residents with an interest in stabilizing underground economic activity, Big Cat was also facing hard times. Although many of his difficulties arose from within his own gang, he grew pessimistic about his ability to work with other residents to deal with problems between gang and community. Not surprisingly, he placed much of the blame on locals who did not understand the pressures he faced. When he said, "I need them to see what I'm dealing with and appreciate it," he was in effect asking that they help him stabilize an organized criminal operation. He expressed surprise and disgust when residents and stakeholders did not accede to his demands—by this point, however, he had grown so detached from the community court that no one really had a sense of what Big Cat wanted from them.

Importantly, there was no consensus among all parties, including Big Cat, as to the value of their community court. Indeed, participants who were not affiliated with the gang had some fear that their success would bring about retaliation, in the form of resident outcries and police hostility. They wondered whether neighbors and local law enforcement would see their efforts to resolve conflicts as taking the law into their own hands. Their concerns were not speculative: Ola and others said, both in private and to the whole group, that some police officers were not happy that the group was aiding and abetting gangs and other criminal activities. This was not welcome news.

Pastor Wilkins and Marlene Matteson arranged a meeting with two police officers who had worked with residents informally over shady dealings in the past, but who were now rumored to be critical of the community court. Officers Marcellus Harrison and Thomas Blue were assigned to patrol Maquis Park. They appreciated the assistance with gang intervention, but they were concerned about community leaders cozying up to the street gang and taking the law into their own hands. They came to Wilkins's church, where they had coffee with the pastor, Marlene, Ola, Gary Davis, and James Arleander. Afterward, the two officers commented:

> "Most people I work with think you can just lock [gang members] up, put them away for life," said Officer Harrison. "Like that's really going to do anything when you have five hundred more of these people waiting right behind them. We have, now, in Maquis Park a long history of reaching out and doing things a little differently because we have to. I grew up here, all over the Southside. Ain't no different. The most important persons you will find are in the church, they're working with kids, and they are in the block clubs, barbershops. That hasn't changed. And I'm glad they are working problems out by themselves. We help when we can, but the community is really in the lead."
>
> "So, what do you think Wilkins and them can really do by working with Big Cat?"
>
> "I told them *not* to work with Big Cat," said Blue. "Don't even invite him to the meetings. Just meet among themselves and then always, always approach Big Cat collectively with a problem and let [police] know what you are doing. That way, you are never an accessory to crime and you are just trying to do intervention. And that way, we can help you."

"See," said Harrison, "If you sit in a meeting and say, 'Okay, Big Cat, you can sell drugs here but not there,' that's not good. I mean, it's not legal! But it's not good for other reasons, which is that Big Cat thinks he can control you. And remember, he'll kill you. I mean it, he will. You have to be very careful. If you have to work with him, then do it like we've done it all along. Get him alone, get him to the side. That way, he can't divide you."

"Divide you? What do you mean?" I asked.

"Look, we all know he's paying off people. Wilkins too," said Harrison. "That money is there so that people will be shy about confronting him. So we can't really stop that. But you're only helping him become a pain in your ass if you invite him to the table."

"Lot of these little arguments are just stupid, and it's okay to help people so they don't kill one another over $5." said Blue. "But you can't meet like this. You are not a judge. You are not the police. We said they have to stop and go back to just doing what they were doing. And again, work with us. We're not going to tell them to stop solving problems, but it's just that they can't act like they own the whole place."

Both of the officers wanted group members to return to their work as brokers and regulators who could control underground economic activity, but they preferred that social control occur in a decentralized manner and with at least some involvement of local police. They pointed out that they were working individually with each person who attended the community court—even with Big Cat. For example, Marlene would call and notify one of them of problems, particularly for shady activity that took place in public areas and that could be disruptive for residents. Usually Marlene met Officer Harrison in a bar or in her house once a month or so and casually told him what was happening around the neighborhood. The two would not jointly intervene. Instead, Harrison would act on his own and supplement the work of Pastor Wilkins, Marlene, and the others if it was necessary. For organizations that were receiving donations from the gang, Marlene says the officers provided a recourse in case the gang leaders grew violent or made exorbitant demands. She and Officer Blue described an incident in which they prevented Big Cat from trafficking marijuana from a local youth center.

"I told him I'd put him in jail right away if he didn't stop what he was doing," said Officer Blue.

"What was he doing?" I asked.

"Oh, just being stupid about things," chimed Marlene. "Carter Fallows [a director of the Maquis Park Social Outreach Organization] sometimes did Big Cat a favor by tutoring some of the kids who weren't doing so well in school. And he probably got a little change. I think a couple of hundred bucks or something like that. He's a good man, said that he wasn't going to let the boys deal dope from inside."

"Did Big Cat pressure him?" I asked.

"Big Cat *demanded*," said Officer Blue. "Said if Carter didn't cooperate, he'd get beaten up. So we told Ellis that Big Cat needed to cut that shit out."

"See," said Marlene. "That kind of thing helps us, when Blue gets involved in the mix. Then we all see that we don't have to be scared about Big Cat. No matter what he does or no matter if we trying to work with him and take care of messes."

"Well," Officer Blue said to Marlene, obviously aware that I would be taking notes about the conversation. "Let's be careful about the words we're using. I am not condoning you and Pastor Wilkins trying to punish people yourself. The best thing you can do is to call us. Carter's a good man. Now, he shouldn't be taking any money, but he is. We can't do nothing about that, really, to be honest. But I am glad that you all are starting to see that these niggers [in the gang] ain't playing! Be careful, be very careful, that's all I'm saying."

The position of Officers Blue and Harrison affirmed that the underground economy held everyone in the neighborhood in its grip. From the vantage point of these two policemen, it was impossible to eliminate illegal economic activity. So, like the residents, they too must have a realistic attitude, which in this case meant that they needed to ensure that lines of communication were open to all parties in the shady world. This included Big Cat, whom they worked with to keep the gang under control. Of course, what constituted an out-of-control gang was always relative, and depended in some measure on the strength of local clamor for effective policing and the type of toll that gang activity exacted on the populace.

Stated differently, the police in inner cities are another type of broker, intervening in an underground sphere and motivated by a particular set of interests. Their interests, however, are not necessarily the same as those of officers working in middle-class communities where residents have political capital and therefore do not have to tolerate illegal activity. In such places, there may not be any tolerance for officers who work in stealthy ways with gang leaders and other notorious types. In Maquis Park and other ghettos, however, this kind of backroom negotiation is typical. Most residents are probably aware of, and support to some degree, the work of those officers who can put out a fire in gangland before it threatens others. They may not want to know all the details, but I have rarely heard a disparaging comment from a resident regarding the informal work of police to monitor gang activity and deal with gang-related conflicts before they escalate.

By the end of 2003, the cracks in this indigenous, self-help strategy were clearly showing. Even though Maquis Park's community court was led by the church—the unquestioned source of moral legitimacy in the black community—it was only partly effective in ameliorating the problems of a poor people immersed in the underground. It was clear that, in response to local crises that stemmed from the need to regulate illegal economic activity, the community had responded. But it was not clear that the response was altogether appropriate or ultimately beneficial for the security and welfare of those who lived in Maquis Park.

Whether one assigned credit or blame to the pastor and his colleagues for their work with the gang, it was becoming fairly clear that the community court could not be the appropriate place to realize the goal of social order maintenance in Maquis Park. It was too limited and modest in scope to be an effective tool of crime prevention throughout the community. With no public legitimacy from the residents or the police, it was always in danger of being cast in an unfavorable light, with its duplicitous character outweighing any success it had in solving local problems.

The community court was not in regular session from late September until mid-November. Pastor Wilkins decided that there were too many internal problems—people not participating, disagreements over the scope of the court's jurisdiction—and there was mounting criticism from the police and, increasingly, from residents who began asking grassroots clergy about the origins of the court. Wilkins felt that other stakeholders, particularly clergy members who were so important in the lives of the marginalized, should not be hurt in the long run. He also did not want to jeopardize the assistance, however spotty and informal, the police provided in helping keep law and order. So he said that the court was officially dissolved—at least temporarily. He told Big Cat and Marlene, Ola, James Carter, and others that they should all continue to work informally as they had done in the past. They could still use his church as a meeting place, but it had to be done spontaneously and not under the auspices of a juridical setting like the court.

Residents seemed grateful that their relationships with the police did not suffer tremendously and that the court ended before there was widespread rumor that the criminal and the law-abiding classes were growing too intimate with one another. But they were upset that they had lost what seemed to be a tool in the struggle to preserve social order in a place where few resources were available to help residents fight crime and keep the community habitable. Perhaps James Arleander summed up these conflicting feelings best when he said, "This happened before and it will happen again. It's what life is about when you are poor. You never give up, but never giving up means taking risks. And risks mean failing, you know? So maybe we failed, but we'll try again. We're a little depressed now, but we'll all go back to our work. We'll work alone, but we'll come together again, like we always do. And I'm sure Pastor Wilkins will be right there with us. We never doubt that he's with us all the way." For his part, Big Cat did not say much about the dissolution of the court. By the end of 2003 he had little contact with most of the stakeholders, except for Pastor Wilkins and Marlene, whom he spoke with on occasion.

It is by working off the books, in back rooms and behind the scenes, that the local residents come up against the limits of their collectively efficacious practice. In the short term, local leaders can come together and put out a fire and bring about peace for the time being. But because they have done this surreptitiously, sometimes taking the law away from the police and putting it into their own hands, they risk further alienating themselves from the wider world. Because they are implicated in the very dangerous and destabilizing activities they are trying to address, they can never really show themselves to those in the social mainstream—philanthropists, advocates, employers, and so on—who would otherwise find their work courageous and worthy of acknowledgment and reward. It is nearly impossible for the press and political leaders to recognize their work as anything other than aiding and abetting, accessory to crime and contributor to the social pathology afflicting the community. Thus, in the long run their success as mediators does little to help them advance personally. Their grinding labor does not create more productive relationships with those outside the borders of their community who have the resources, influence, and capacity to help them turn things around. Their blessing becomes their curse.

Similarly, when Big Cat and other gang members dream of attaining social recognition, respectability, they seem destined to fail. They are, at root, managing an organized criminal operation that preys upon residents. No matter how philanthropic the gang leaders may be or how accommodating their rank and file are to parents who need their children to be able to play in parks and walk down streets, their need to make money only diminishes public safety and exacerbates the problems of an already poor and struggling community.

If the residents faced only petty, nuisance problems, it would not be so alarming to hear them make compromises and strike quid pro quo deals with those involved in the shady world. Helping a car mechanic and a client solve a pricing dispute before things get out of hand not only is eminently reasonable, but this kind of diplomacy is likely to be found in all American communities. Indeed, it would be fair to say that we expect most, if not all, citizens to try to intervene in local affairs that jeopardize public safety. The problems for Maquis Park and other inner-city communities stem from both the type and the scale of the issues that threaten their daily security and welfare. No one should have to respond to a criminal organization earning thousands of dollars per day peddling narcotics; extortion of shopkeepers should not be an expected part of the business climate; street hustling born of impoverishment need not be a time-honored tradition. Maquis Park is flooded with these shady activities, as it has been for decades. The combined presence of poverty, desperation, and crime makes the shady world more than a fly on the back that can be ignored or swatted away. It pervades. It seeps into the homes of even those who struggle mightily to keep it at bay.

What is perhaps most surprising about this thicket of underground negotiations is that Big Cat was so willing to participate. He and his Black Kings created—or at least exacerbated—many of the issues that caused Marlene and others so much agony. Why did Big Cat offer to help squelch problems he profited from? The answer, it seems, lies in the unique relationships created by the underground economy. Although leading a marginal and outlaw group, Big Cat was inextricably intertwined in the lives of others outside the gang. His own material welfare depended to a large degree on his capacity to work with others in the community. With some, he needed to work directly in shady ventures or pay off with donations; with others, he needed to continuously make promises to keep his gang in line. He could not completely antagonize residents, even while he wreaked havoc in their lives with his wanton disregard for much of their needs for safety and security.

But as the Black Kings became ever more corporate, and then ever more arbitrary, they continually upset the underground economy's delicate balance. Each time they threw the dynamics of a life in urban poverty in sharp relief. This entrepreneurially oriented criminal organization, composed of adults as well as teenagers, is an imposition not only because it fights with other gangs, competes with other drug sellers, and otherwise runs amok in gangland. By virtue of its public behavior, it becomes a very real presence for all people, in and out of the gang, who live in the area. After 2000, when the crack cocaine economy diminished, the Black Kings gang decided to shed its skin and look elsewhere for revenue. It may seem bizarre to hear that residents were less worried when the gang simply managed its own affairs, running drugs and competing with other gangs. But it must be remembered that safety is a relative issue. Things can—and sometimes do—get worse. When Big Cat moved beyond drug trafficking and wanted to become a "community man," people who could have otherwise escaped the gang's wrath found themselves caught up in the gang's net. Misery compounded daily as gang members voraciously sought opportunities to make income. Perversely, some residents wished for a return to the halcyon days when the gang was interested only in drugs—a time when those who weren't interested in either the gang or drugs could manage to avoid getting caught in the thug's path.

Whether one agrees with the type of response that was ultimately made to the corporate gang, it is important to acknowledge that Maquis Park's residents and their leadership did make a concerted effort to improve their lot. Some shied away, to be sure, and they probably were in the majority. But a few did plead with the gang, call on police for help, and work together to come up with solutions when all else failed them. These efforts did not always produce the hoped-for results, but their initiative must certainly invalidate the breezy interpretation so often found in popular discourse that poor communities tolerate crime and poor people lack the motivation and skills to deal with the complexities of their lives. I doubt that many would contest the notion that the natural response to an organization with the capacity to easily retaliate and inflict harm would be to stay at home and call the police. Maquis Park's residents did that and they did not receive much help. So some banded together and explored alternative strategies; though their actions would certainly offend the ethos of the American middle class—black and white—their other options seemed few and far between.

As 2003 came to an end, and the community court had safely receded into people's memory, few residents of Maquis Park had the time to sit back and opine on their achievements and failings. Their lives were busy and there were always other problems to confront. Big Cat and his gang were still moving about, spreading their tentacles wider and showing no real signs of diminished ambition. Despite erratic behavior and arbitrary violence—or perhaps because of it—the Black Kings were still a feared force; but just as a corporation fears managerial instability, a corporate gang is vulnerable to sudden changes at the top. Almost daily, one heard speculations on the streets that Big Cat would not last long as leader. There were reports that he had basically lost hold of the reins and that few other senior officers were adhering to his demands. People did not take this news lightly, because Big Cat was never known to give up without a fight. They knew he would never voluntarily turn over control over his gang to another person. What they did not know, however, was whether in the course of the struggle, Big Cat would direct the fight at other members of the gang or at the wider public in Maquis Park—both of whom controlled his fate.

Chapter Seven
As the Shady World Turns

Big Cat's funeral was held at Pastor Wilkins's Maquis Park Prayer and Revival Center. On one side of the aisle, the Maquis Park Kings gang members sat, their young faces alternatively blank and mournful. None spoke on Big Cat's behalf. Most sat quietly, fidgeting and looking across the aisle at the more visibly expressive mourners. This group included Big Cat's extended family and his girlfriends and their children. Hundreds of people would visit his body that day. They too seemed to fall in two groups: those who knew Big Cat as a gang leader hugged and shook hands with the rank and file; those who knew him as a friend, relative, or child of the neighborhood went immediately to the family and offered condolences.

Big Cat died in a vengeance killing. An enemy gang caught him unawares, on a street corner where a few of his gang members were peddling drugs. The corner marked the boundary between territories controlled by two different gangs. Both street organizations had wanted to use the corner for drug sales, but each leader felt that it was too dangerous for their members to stand outside with drugs and cash. At the border, it was easy to be fired upon or robbed. So neither group marketed their goods from that spot. In late autumn of 2003, however, Big Cat boldly placed his gang members on one side of the street, in a small park, where they could sell crack cocaine to passersby. His rivals drove by one night, shooting at the assembled Black Kings. Big Cat was there. Several eyewitnesses report that he was clearly the target. Three shots fired from a car entered his back. Big Cat died instantly. An investigation soon followed, but no one has been arrested.

In the weeks after Big Cat's death, Pastor Wilkins, Marlene Matteson, and other Maquis Park residents met frequently to deal with the consequences. His death left a general uncertainty in the shady world because the local underground economy had just lost an active player. Big Cat had brought together residents, businesspersons, and other civic activists who in the past had little reason to work with one another. In their response to and involvement in Big Cat's shady dealings, these local actors formed new relationships—both out of a common interest to resist the gang and out of selfish desires to make underground profits. The gang leader's aspirations to regulate underground economic activity had put into place arrangements between people that were now in limbo. Ola Sanders did not know whether the gang would continue to rent her space for parties—this off-the-books rental fee was a significant part of her monthly earnings. Street hustlers wondered if they could save money by not paying the gang's imposed street tax. Others, like James Carter, smiled because they might now reclaim their positions as brokers in the shady world—positions that Big Cat had usurped in his effort to find new sources of shady revenue. Numerous service providers wondered whether Ellis Clearwater, Big Cat's successor, would continue making donations to their organizations in the quid pro quo exchange that gave gang members the right to congregate in relatively safe shelter, shielded from the eye of residents and police. Many shopkeepers came to depend on arrangements with street hustlers who provided them with cheap labor and brought customers to their stores. A gang killing always meant potential retaliation, decreased public safety, and so street-based hustlers might not be around as often. Many store owners and managers now wondered who they could hire cheaply and under the table for menial work. Similarly, Marlene had set up deals with underground entrepreneurs to make sure that shady behavior in parks would be regulated so that children could play there. Some of her deals involved Big Cat, who agreed to limit drug selling or keep his gang out of the park entirely. Like other residents who had reached such arrangements with the gang, she wondered whether she could still count on cooperation from the Black Kings to keep public spaces safe.

Big Cat's death also affected relationships in Maquis Park that did not center on the gang. Consider the community court. Despite the bickering and differences of opinion, Pastor Wilkins felt that the monthly resident meetings showed that Maquis Park had a vibrant grassroots. He knew others shared his enthusiasm, and he wondered whether the passing of Big Cat might diminish their spirit. Although they may have been working together on matters that did not always involve the gang, residents' incentive to collaborate had partly disappeared when Big Cat passed away. It was uncertain whether Wilkins, Marlene Matteson, and their associates would continue to use their community court to adjudicate problems in gangland and the underground economy. At the least, they would have to wait until Ellis had made some decisions as to the gang's future orientation. Pastor Wilkins feared that "waiting may mean we all go our separate ways instead of staying together and keeping in touch and, praying and working on things together."

Big Cat's death had revealed the degree to which his presence anchored much of the ebb and flow in the underground. He played a more critical role in Maquis Park's underground economy than nearly anyone else. Many of the events in the local shady world were influenced by his gang's activities, even when the participants had no affiliation to the Black Kings. But his presence—as well as his passing—revealed more than simply how powerfully a charismatic figure can influence the exchange of goods and services when there is no third party, like the government, that regulates exchange. Notwithstanding his willingness to use violence or to cajole and bribe nearly everyone he came across, Big Cat could not monopolize the use of force and assume control of each and every off-the-books trade. His thirst for rule could not be quenched, because many underground transactions are hard to detect and, as just important, the dynamics of the shady world are contingent on personalities and events that are often unpredictable in their occurrence and unforeseeable in their consequences. So it is always possible that leaders like Big Cat will fall as quickly as they rise, no matter how much diplomacy, guile, and power they wield.

For those in Maquis Park, the spontaneity of the shady world and the serendipity of its movement are not all that revelatory. People like Marlene Matteson, Pastor Wilkins, and the restaurant owner Marlon DeBreaux may have marveled at the capacity of an outlaw figure to strike out from gangland, but they nevertheless saw Big Cat as part of a long-standing tradition of disreputable and pious figures aspiring in an alternative sphere of personal gain. As a gang leader, Big Cat may seem quite different from an elected ward politician, member of the clergy, or block club president, all of whom may be managing underground moneymaking schemes. But from the vantage point of those who have long been living and laboring in the underground sector, Big Cat is just one of many individuals who were brought down seeking power and prestige in the shady world.

As much as Big Cat's death points to the unique circumstances in Maquis Park, a time where the street gang played a more important role than in the past, it also shows us the degree to which the underground economy is a web in which many different people, from the criminal to the pious, from the down-and-out to the bourgeois, are inextricably intertwined. Residents, shopkeepers, police, homeless persons, and block club presidents live within a structure of trading and regulation that dictates a great part of their daily life, and they are caught up attending to the chores that ensure that trading does not get out of hand. And any stability they manage to achieve in the short term is precisely that: short-term.

The gang leader's death shows not only the fragility of this network of illegal exchange—how susceptible it is to the twists and turns of circumstance and individual aspirations—but also how instrumental the shady economy has become for the working poor in the ghetto. Inner-city households are as dependent on underground work as they are fearful of the dangers associated with it.

An economy is at its core the exchange of goods and services among people. Any such exchange involves some level of trust and assurance, so that actors are willing to enter into a relationship, and a minimal understanding of how to act in the event of a conflict, dispute, or disagreement. The types of trust and the options for addressing grievances in underground exchanges are highly varied and probably innumerable. Returning to an example from our opening pages, selling lemonade on a suburban lawn and selling crack on a ghetto street corner are both off-the-books trading, but a customer aggrieved over poor quality of lemonade will probably act differently than a customer aggrieved over low quantity in a bag of crack. Both might act differently than a car-repair customer who felt that James Arleander's $10 increase in his fee was unfair without prior notice. And all of these examples likely differ from Maquis Park at the end of the nineties, where there was a powerful gang leader, Big Cat, willing to deploy violence. Many clients in the community altered their behavior to avoid punishment or retribution of the kind that the gang member might deploy.

While it is possible to construct likely scenarios for various kinds of off-the-books transactions, what transpires will depend on the local context. If traders and customers tend to see one another every day, decisions to pursue one or another course of action may take shape accordingly. In particular, if your adversary runs in the same shady circles, then you may want to reduce enmity. Why confront James about a $10 discrepancy and run the risk of having to confront Big Cat, who supports him, when suffering the immediate monetary loss enables one to continue to use James's services, and possibly his gang-related contacts, at a future date?

Behavior can also differ according to the presence of a third party broker who has legitimacy to settle disputes. Knowing that Pastor Wilkins successfully mediates conflicts involving shopkeepers and hustlers, an aggrieved merchant may find it prudent to enlist the pastor's services for a fee rather than approach the hustler directly. As we have seen, these intermediaries can themselves be planted firmly in the underground economy, dealing with disputes while they are themselves hawking goods off the books. Pastor Wilkins accepted the street gang's money as a church donation, which made him directly complicit in the shady world; nevertheless, he continued to be viewed by many residents as a legitimate, albeit interested, broker of disputes. In this way, in practice one finds that car mechanics, shopkeepers, pimps, gang members, and gun traders can employ each other to provide arbitration, whether this means determining fair prices or providing a ruling on an exchange gone awry. In general, in a community void of these intermediaries, underground exchanges might involve more direct confrontation and, depending on the types of clandestine trading, an increased likelihood of violent altercations.

Not all intermediaries are equivalent. In Maquis Park, few people prefer to use the street gang for mediation rather than a pastor or a block club president. Even local police officers who are known figures in the community will be enlisted before the gang is. But at the end of the nineties, the Black Kings gang sought to alter these patterns by forcing people to draw on them, not only for goods and services, but also for third-party arbitration. Big Cat wanted to be a "community man," and in his desire to gain legitimacy, he sought out opportunities to participate in various affairs that brought people together in the shady world. He wanted to control how public space was occupied, the amount of money people could earn, and the ways in which they solved their disputes. This was something that shocked most residents, even those who had knowledge of the past and the many storied figures who managed Maquis Park's shady world in previous eras.

In a fundamental way, the dynamics of the underground economy, including how people behaved toward the Black Kings gang, was shaped by the history of off-the-books trading in the community. In Maquis Park, there are institutionalized and at times predictable ways of acting in the underground, even though this is a social arena that is highly unstable and subject to change. To see history in action, consider again the decision by Pastor Wilkins and some residents to create a community court where the problems of shady trading could be managed. Such a venue was really only a more formal case of an established local practice whereby community-based stakeholders came together to deal with neighborhood affairs. In bygone eras, the ward boss, bootlegger, and shady politician may have sat around the table, dispensing patronage and dealing with problems that arose in local gambling, illegal liquor sales, underground credit and lending, and gang activity. We know about these backroom practices from the many histories that document African American life in Chicago's Southside.[1] But this history is also visible in the practices of those living in Maquis Park and the surrounding neighborhoods that make up the contemporary Black Metropolis.

The past is not lost on people like Eunice Williams, who works to keep order in Maquis Park. Her status, both as a shady trader and as someone who intervenes in pricing disputes among street traders, is reminiscent of her grandfather's role as a preacher who held powerful positions in the black political organizations of Chicago in the sixties. Her remembrances draw out some of the historical continuities between black leaders working in the mid-twentieth-century political machine and her contemporary grassroots colleagues who operate secretively in back rooms and church basements:

> "Papa Joe [her grandfather] would know every little thing that was happening around here. If you had a little under-the-table

thing, what we called in them days 'shady,' you had to get permission from Papa and from people like the local alderman, or maybe you had to talk with Junebug Wilson who ran the only bank in town. And you know, of course, the police had to say yes . . . They met at Wilma's [café]. They ate lunch and then just took care of business."

"What kind of business?"

"Well, all kinds. But mostly when someone wanted to make money or when something went wrong and people got hurt, or they were going to get hurt. You know, like I remember when Papa had to stop this man from killing another man who slept with his wife. This guy had slept with the lady and then stole her jewels and sold them to a pawnshop. Papa got the jewels back from the pawnshop, made sure that the guy who slept with the man's wife was beat up. I mean that's just what you did. Police weren't around. I mean they were around, but they mostly wanted us to take care of our business, which we did."

"Didn't you ask the police for help?"

"Well, you had to *find* them to ask for help! And they were never around. Usually, you go to the station and no one hears you. But they were never, I mean they were *never* on the street, unless they were coming for you. Usually, they'd just come by the house, talk with Papa and whoever else was around, and then leave."

There are some factors that distinguish Eunice, Pastor Wilkins, and other modern-day underground regulators. Eunice's grandfather and the other old ward bosses and politicos tended to have material resources at their disposal. Hundreds of patronage jobs, in both illegal and legal economic sectors, were at their fingertips. They disbursed these to residents in a way that elevated their own status and respect. Some of these bosses sought only a promise of a favorable vote on election day, which they could use to gain further patronage from the city's political leaders, while others received monetary rewards for their dispensation. Few of the grassroots intermediaries today have access to people and organizations in the wider world that provide them with jobs, money, cash for underground loans, or any other significant resource. They cannot curry the favor of underground traders—or anyone else, for that matter—with their shady dispensation; nor can they threaten the traders in any significant way by taking away resources. On occasion, Marlene Matteson can call a friend on the police force to arrest a pimp or car mechanic who is not cooperative, but this sort of thing is rare.

The leaders of the past who intervened in the shady world were often widely recognized spokespersons who brokered between black communities and the wider city. For some, their shady activities actually served as a badge of honor—the activities in question may have been questionable, but these persons were, after all, highly successful African Americans in a racist society. Those who work in contemporary Maquis Park do so largely at the grassroots level and behind the scenes, out of the public eye. And they risk public scorn. Police and media are quick to publicize their intimate work with criminal types and rarely acknowledge the benefits. Similarly, local residents may express their support privately, but they share the view of more elite organizations in the community that policing the underground is a job best left to the police.

These comparisons do not exhaust the ways to see history in action in Maquis Park. In everyday life, it is possible to see how the past shapes contemporary behavior—and why this past differentiates the ghetto's underground economy from that of other communities. For example, the transient hustler enters the neighborhood mindful of the fact that local hustlers have already appropriated space, formed economic dealings with merchants, and found ways to earn money. Whether or not the newcomer chooses to respect the extant relationships and ways of doing things, she or he will likely strike up hostile reactions by infringing on other entrepreneurs. In this case, the past informs the action of parties in several ways. The transient hustler will more than likely have to deal with people, like merchants and other hustlers, who have their own underground activities and who want to protect their investments. History will certainly enter into the claims by all of these parties to sit at a street corner and drum up business: those with seniority will try to use their tenure as a defense against a newcomer's encroachments.

Moreover, those with seniority would probably receive the support of other local actors, some of whom may come to their aid in settling the dispute. Thus, the means by which people respond to problems and develop solutions—enforcing contracts, settling pricing disagreements, mediating conflicts, and so on—is also conditioned by what took place before. There are codes of conduct in place in the shady world. People arrive at a situation predisposed to act in a particular way. Shopkeepers decided not to support Marlon, the restaurant owner, because he violated an unstated rule specifying that opportunities to make money illegally had to be distributed among the group. In their decision making, many explicitly stated that Marlon's behavior did not respect regulations that had existed for decades, regulations that forbade merchants from monopolizing shady earnings. In addition, police officers and political officials likely are aware of the off-the-books agreements in place. The police rely on stable connections with the local hustling population to gain information about life on the street and in the alleys. For this reason, even in shady matters, if a new hustler arrives and creates problems, the police may rule in favor of the established hustlers. Similarly, a resident may view James Arleander, a hustler who has been a member of the community for decades, in a much different light than a newly arrived street mechanic who offers to fix cars in an alleyway. The former may be seen by residents as a trusted soul, as someone who is down on his luck but is nevertheless part of the local social fabric, while the latter, as an unknown, might be viewed as a threat to safety and household security.

Whether we are talking about street merchants and hustlers dealing with life on the street, or block club leaders and police dealing with problems in the park, there are time-honored traditions in the shady world that come into play in organizing daily life. Of course, with no law on the books, there will be breaches and disagreements, but the main point is that in situations ostensibly criminal and often threatening to personal security, there is still a structure in place that shapes how people make decisions and engage one another. This structure provides some measure of comfort in an otherwise highly unstable environment where households are unsure what tomorrow may bring. But that structure is also a limitation. On the one hand, knowledge of the past can depress the search for new solutions to old problems. Knowing that one's predecessors fought the same struggles, life seems unchanging—a recognition that consequently produces diminished expectations and lessening optimism that things will turn for the better. On the other hand, few people feel the need for heroics because they have seen what unbridled creativity can bring about in the context of a shady world in which violence and physical retaliation are all too common. Few feel the need to be a hero. This does not mean people in Maquis Park lack courage to end their misery, only that a pragmatic attitude based on previous personal encounters and on local historical knowledge may shape their approach to a given situation. Indeed, in such circumstances the very decision to act may be the best sign that people have not given up fighting for their community.

One wonders to what degree Maquis Park is unique in terms of the type of underground activity present, or its scope and effect on those living there. A simple survey of urban neighborhoods— or a cursory reading of the many federal government reports on the subject—will quickly reveal that there are plenty of places where people are working off the books to earn money, keep their businesses running, support their families, and so on. The distinctiveness of Maquis Park proceeds from both the types of off-the-books activities one finds there and the ubiquity of illegal income generation in most households. Simply put, it is nearly impossible for residents in Maquis Park to avoid underground economic activity: it is an ever-present threat on the streets, in parks, and other public places; and for the working and poor families, it is always a temptation, given the hardships of living near the poverty line. Recall that, at any point in time, nearly half of the community is out of the labor force, so poverty by itself will force people to seek work outside the mainstream.

Not every American community will be similar to Maquis Park, with its decades of shady dealings. But, disregarding for the moment the newly built suburban tract or another such planned development, most neighborhoods will contain local actors with requisite political capacities to attend to local matters. Particularly in the northern urban ghettos, where black Americans have lived for over a century, much of this local fare is shaped by people who have themselves obtained status by living and working underground. The history of this shady activity can enter into decision making in very complex ways, and therefore, to make sense of how people actually behave in the underground economy, it is important to have some grasp of the past and its link to the future.

Yet, as we have seen, not all is rosy and beneficial when people have to respond to shady ways of living and working that have been part of the local social fabric for decades. In their efforts to ensure safety and stability, residents, merchants, hustlers, police, and other actors orient their actions to both short-term and long-term futures. "Short" and "long" can mean different things to different people, and it is important to recognize how this dual temporal outlook shapes the lives of people who live and work underground. In thinking about the future, one should not import too quickly a middle-class perspective in which the experience of time is colored by all manner of planning, including saving and investing, prioritizing rationally, acquiring full information for decision making, and proceeding methodically without fear of impoverishment or physical danger on the horizon. Maquis Park is a community of poor and working-poor households where local businesses hover on the same economic precipice as families. In the ghetto, the meaning of time is organized around impermanence and the lack of material resources, so for many of life's matters, it may not only be a luxury, but a fool's way of thinking, to sit back and opine reflectively.

This does mean that people fail to plan, but that there are separate temporal horizons, one in the immediate future and the other a longer way off. Here the shady world becomes critical in people's perceptions and actions. An entrepreneur needs to pay a bill and so will rent out his store for a few dollars to other hustlers in order to make money quickly. There may be no time to strategize about more effective advertising or ways to expand the customer base. The community is broke and getting poorer by the day, the payment is due in a few weeks, and so money must be earned in whatever way possible, even illegally and with an unstable street population. Any potentially harmful long-term consequences will have to be ignored or tolerated. Similarly, a block club leader may need to kick drug dealers out of a park. Because the police typically are slow to act, striking up a compromise with the gang leader is the best route to bringing about park safety for the next few months—a longer-term strategy that seeks to obtain effective policing may have to be tabled until immediate security needs are met.

In both of these cases, the actors know that they cannot act in a way that greatly differs from how shopkeepers and block club leaders acted before them when facing such situations. Store owners have watched others face the same dilemma and have seen the decisions that have been made to ensure business solvency. They have heard stories in the more distant past, in the narratives of failed businesses and courageous entrepreneurs who managed to stay afloat. So too the block club president knows how parents acted in the old days and is keenly aware of the kind of help black Americans can realistically expect from the police.

People in Maquis Park turn to the underground economy to bring goods, services, and resources into the home. The underground may offer these commodities on a cheaper basis, there may be opportunities to pay in-kind when cash is not at hand, and the shady arena might be the only place to obtain certain items—not only illicit services like sexual favors, but even short-term cash loans and household items that are not available in local stores. In other words, the underground economy may be viewed from above as a vestigial space of exchange, one defined largely by its evasive posture with respect to the legitimate realm, but in a poor ghetto it is often the primary (or preferred) economy. Because shady money can be key for heads of households, they cannot shrug off the problems associated with it. They must strike a balance between its immediate utility and the dangers that lie ahead. Keeping children fed and maintaining a roof over one's head are no small tasks for poor households. If the underground helps, then at some level it must be considered useful and supportive.

But there are serious questions about the long-term consequences of survival through shady means. Many of these questions arise because the underground arena is not simply a place to buy goods and services. It also is a field of social relationships that enable off-the-books trading to occur in an ordered and predictable manner. That is, it necessarily involves social regulation, such as self-policing, dispute resolution, and conflict mediation. Surely one can buy a pair of socks on the street or sell one's labor on the cheap without ever having to deal with gangs that impose a street tax or clergy who act as intermediaries. But things do not always proceed smoothly—in any economic exchange—and so some kind of structure must be in place that enables people to respond to problems and obtain redress. Importantly, the regulation and management of the underground is itself taking place outside the context of the state. In this arena, the government apparatus of courts, lawyers, and police does not provide the primary forum for enforcing contracts and adjudicating claims of impropriety. Residents must find other ways to monitor and direct shady activity while at the same time participating and benefiting from hidden earnings. There is no legitimate third-party arbiter—more accurately, at any one time several parties may be fighting for the right to oversee and tax exchange.

We cannot say enough about this basic fact, namely, that the manner of earning income and the ways of regulating it are both outside the societal mainstream. Imagine not only facing the burden of keeping a business solvent, but also inventing the means by which to obtain redress should something go wrong. It is difficult enough to advertise, find customers, keep up with local tastes, and attend to the normal demands of commerce. The added task of having to mete out the law when, for example, a customer steals or does not pay, is no small endeavor for the underground trader or for the legitimate businessperson dealing off the books. These are added encumbrances that consume time, energy, money, and manpower. In the shady world, attending to these exigencies can mean dealing with people who are not afraid to use violence or physical retaliation to reach their objectives. It should not be surprising, then, that people may find it preferable to pay a third-party entity, even a criminal organization like a street gang, instead of addressing issues directly. Not only do shady entrepreneurs patronize these kinds of third-party enforcers and mediators, but even a legitimate shopkeeper, facing lax police services and the ever-present threat to store safety, will work with the gang or another third-party enforcer. (Obviously, in cases of extortion, the merchant may not have much of a choice.) While this does not excuse illegitimate behavior, such practices do not occur in vacuum or, more importantly, in a middle-class context. One can only complain to the police or lobby for better government services so often without results before acting on one's own to keep commerce flowing.

In Maquis Park, the management of the underground economy emerges from the local organization of collectively efficacious practice. That is, underground regulation is really rooted in the myriad ways that people have organized—through block clubs, gangs, churches, social service agencies, networks of human service agencies, and so on—to act on local issues that may not necessarily be economic in nature. By establishing some level of collective energy within these formal and informal organizations, local actors then transfer their social capital to the underground. Not all choose to do so, of course, but it is telling that some of the most important people who police and monitor the underground have another identity in the community, one that is more specific than simply that of "resident." They own or manage stores, they represent social clubs, they have congregations and constituencies, and they speak on behalf of issues that affect their neighbors, like sanitation and the condition of the parks and schools. For many of these people, their concern for the welfare of households and the health of the community means that they must deal with the underground economy in a direct way. Some certainly enjoy the status and prestige they derive from being a mediator or an economically powerful agent in a particular sphere of shady trading. But many also feel they have little choice but to make the gang member, street hustler, shopkeeper, and client work things out and get along. The security of the community may depend on it.

Thus, asking about the short- and long-term consequences of the underground means considering the impact of shady trading not only on the individual participants and their households, but also on local groups, organizations, and institutions.[2] For example, the neighborhood block club suffers the impact of a local underground economy in a slightly different way than the parent who lives on that block. The organization as a whole may expend much of its energy on shady matters, such as kicking hustlers and prostitutes out of the park, which leaves little time for organizing social events for its constituents. Responding to the shady side of life may be its most pressing short-term issue. In the short term, individual parents may look elsewhere beyond their street block to find activities for their children. And in the long run, by not offering these services and by having to be somewhat circumspect about its dealings with local shady types, the block club may lose contact with, and support from, the local parents who do not see its value. Over time, individuals grow less connected with each other, quality of life is adversely affected, and an organization that could do much to bolster the spirit of a community withers due to lack of local backing.

We have already seen that individual hustlers, business owners, members of the clergy, and youth can suffer dire and sometimes fatal outcomes by working underground. But even when things generally are proceeding smoothly, the participants are not actively creating the foundations for human capital and skills enhancement. They cannot use accumulated money to spur investment or to build a line of credit. They are exposed to unsafe work conditions, and in general there is little of the foundation for upward social mobility that is at the core of the American way of life. Organizations also rarely derive great benefit in the long term from involvement in underground activities. Marlene Matteson and her colleagues who direct community-based organizations and who deal directly with shady types are constantly facing criticism from their neighbors. The rebuke and stigma they suffer means that their block clubs and neighborhood associations can be overlooked by institutions in the wider city who want to channel resources into Maquis Park. Ultimately, the local residents are the ones that suffer from lack of funding—while, in the short term, they may be benefiting from the safety that these very organizations promote.

This kind of effect receives very little attention from scholars and policymakers, most of whom prefer to focus on the effects of poverty on individuals and households.[3] But in any community, the civic and organizational sector plays a key role in keeping the social fabric intact. Even in a depleted ghetto, there will be collective actors in place who attend to neighborhood affairs, and it is important to seek them out in our assessments of how the poor are living. It is equally critical to note that their time and energy are taken up by matters that do not always make it onto the radar of the wider world. They may be working in the immediate present to make sure that children can walk safely on the sidewalk or through the park to enter their organization. To do so, they may have to find the pimp, car mechanic, or other hustler and iron out the problem themselves. Doing this repeatedly can mean reduced time to prepare funding proposals, train staff, develop new programming, and work effectively with police to develop law enforcement strategies. The unfortunate consequence is that many of these civic actors suffer in the wider world the stigma of dysfunctional organizational capacity, when in reality they have not had the freedom to develop any transferable human capital—skills that help them act locally as well as with the institutions in the surrounding city. Unlike their suburban counterparts who are more likely to have decent city services and far fewer shady types roaming about, they do not have the time to luxuriate and plan for the future.

In this way, the underground enables poor communities to survive but can lead to their alienation from the wider world. For groups and organizations, as well as individuals, surviving in the ghetto via shady means can result in their overall remove from the city. It is a pernicious cycle. On the one hand, the underground economy is a space forged by exclusion from the social mainstream. Much of the reason for lending to one another, hiring off the books, and solving crimes without the aid of the police is that banks discriminate against the poor, mainstream employers and unions do not do effective outreach to the poor and minorities, and law enforcement does not provide adequate service to the inner city. On the other hand, however meaningful and satisfactory it may be for those involved, this kind of adjustment does little over time to bring about improvement in credit availability, labor force participation, and policing. It does little to leverage more stable and productive relationships with the institutions of the wider world.[4]

There are many reasons why this partly adaptive, partly efficacious behavior does not lead to social integration in the mainstream through improved relationships with institutional actors. For people in ghetto communities, living underground largely means creating ties of dependency to other actors who are equally hard up. Poor people sharing with other poor people has its limits. Their resources run out at some point. The economy becomes predatory, and hustling shows its ugly side, not as creative and explorative, but as exploitative and punishing. And around them, businesses shut down, households run out of ways to bring money into the home, parents cannot support their children, and service organizations find it impossible to meet the demand for support and care. Additionally, it is hard to translate the short-term achievements of working off the books into socially legitimate arenas. Paying off a loan shark on time does little to improve one's credit rating, providing excellent car repair on the street does not bolster one's résumé, and establishing a détente with pimps and drug dealers so that children can walk to school will not help one obtain a job in diplomatic circles. On a more literal level, unless laundering rules are overturned, money made in the shady world does not enable one to open a savings account, invest, buy property, refinance a mortgage, and otherwise catapult into mainstream commercial theaters.

One should not come away from these examples solely with the impression that toiling in the shady world is a mistaken long-term investment on the part of poor people. To the degree that people are making choices, we should hold them partly responsi ble for bad decisions. However, underground economies make it clear that the vulnerability of ghetto communities is a product of the relationships that weave these areas into the social fabric. Without a change in the kinds of resources that make their way into places like Maquis Park, there will never be much in the way of meaningful opportunities for inner-city inhabitants to experience economic stability—let alone upward social mobility. And without an adjustment in the relationship of the ghetto to the wider world, residents will continue living underground.

Notes

One: Living Underground

I am required by guidelines developed at Columbia University to ensure that the risks to human subjects in my work are minimized and that I do not endanger them either directly or indirectly. In an effort to adhere to these requirements, I have changed the names of locations in this book. *Maquis Park,* for example, is a pseudonym for the very real, and otherwise unaltered, neighborhood where I spent my time conducting fieldwork. Names of people and organizations have also been altered, unless the account is addressing public officials whose activities are a matter of public record.

1. Sociologists St. Clair Drake and Horace Cayton coined the phrase *shady world* to deal with these blurred boundaries and deep interrelations of legitimate and illegitimate economies. They provided the seminal account of Maquis Park and the surrounding Black Metropolis in the thirties, when black migration to, and settlement in, Chicago's Southside made the region one of the most important centers of black American social and cultural life in the twentieth century. In their work, *shady* referred to both underground earnings and the specific individuals who gained local power, prestige, and respect by laboring illegally, settling disputes, dispensing off-the-books patronage, and otherwise directing resources to a segregated black population See St. Clair Drake and Horace Cayton, *Black Metropolis: A Study of Negro Life in a Northern City* (1945; Chicago: University of Chicago Press, 1993).

2. The study of underground economic activity in American inner cities was not well established until the seventies, when Louis Ferman published a pathbreaking paper on "informal economies." (See L. Ferman and P. Ferman, "The Structural Underpinning of the Irregular Economy," *Poverty and Human Resources Abstracts* 8 [1978]: 3–17.) Until that time, studies of unreported income could be found in histories of early twentieth-century prohibition, biographies of mafia leaders, anthropological studies of vice and hustling, and sociological inquiries into family life and public behavior generally.

3. The variation in definitions of the underground may be found in L. Ferman, S. Henry, and M. Hoyman, "Issues and Prospects for the Study

of Informal Economies: Concepts, Research Strategies, and Policy," *Annals of the Academy of Political Science* 493 (1987): 154–172.

4. See Alejandro Portes, Manuel Castells, and Lauren A. Benton, eds., *The Informal Economy: Studies in Advanced and Less Developed Countries* (Baltimore: Johns Hopkins University Press, 1989). Two prominent U.S. government studies also observes this distinction. See U.S. Department of Labor, *The Underground Economy in the United States*, Occasional Paper Series on the Informal Sector, no. 2 (Washington, DC: U.S. Government Printing Office, (1992); U.S. Department of Labor, *Estimating Underground Activity* (Washington, DC: U.S. Government Printing Office, 1992).

5. In scholarship, the most common example is research on immigrant sweatshops—a hallmark informal economic practice. Employing immigrant laborers breaks the law on two counts: it is illegal to hire foreigners who do not have a permit to work in the United States, and it is illegal to pay them substandard wages. (And in most sweatshops, work conditions usually break other laws stipulating ventilation, safety, and lack of rest and breaks.) Those who study "informalization" processes suggest that this unreported work is not the same as other "criminal" activities, like drug trafficking, yet there is usually no justification for privileging some activities as part of the underground economy but not others. In other words, it is not clear what makes some activities *more* criminal than others. For an example of this ad-hoc conceptualization, see Portes, Castells, and Benton, *The Informal Economy.*

6. For a general survey of the difficulties in estimating unreported earnings, see E. Feige, "How Big Is the Irregular Economy?" *Challenge* 12 (1979): 5–13.

7. Jonathan Caulkins and Daniel McCaffrey, "Drug Sellers in the Household Population" (Santa Monica: Rand Corp., Nov. 11, 1993), based on data from National Institute on Drug Abuse, *National Household Survey on Drug Abuse: Population Estimates, 1991*, DHHS Pub. ADM-92-1887 (Washington, D.C.: U.S. Government Printing Office, 1991).

8. Larger estimates help justify increasing the resources allocated to monitoring underground behavior. Oppositional voices are few because no one wants to defend illegal criminal activity. However, liberal politicians often caution against heightened government interference because the usual targets are not corporate America or the wealthy, but poor inner-city residents. Thus, opponents charge that calls for regulation amount to regressive taxation.

9. Peddlers may set up shop on sidewalks and disrupt the flow of pedestrian traffic, like the Greenwich Village booksellers featured in Mitchell

Duneier's revealing ethnographic study *Sidewalk* (New York: Farrar, Straus and Giroux, 1999), although at the same time these vendors make a contribution to public safety. Others may walk into the middle of the street and stop cars to offer window-cleaning services or batteries, socks and T-shirts, or electronic equipment. Moreover, people can take matters into their own hands if a disagreement or dispute occurs in the underground. Law enforcement officers, in particular, grow uneasy when confronted with hidden exchange of all sorts, particularly because verbal problems over, say, pricing or quality can lead to physical confrontation that threatens not only those involved but also passersby. Of course, police and government officials are not equally concerned with every type of activity that generates unreported income. (To offer one example, renting out an extra bedroom to a newly arrived immigrant couple may not attract much attention in a suburb. However, in the dense immigrant neighborhoods of New York City, such landlord "conversions" are a principal source of overcrowding. Because they are both a public safety and health hazard, it is reasonable that the city expends significant resources to eliminate this kind of hidden earning.)

10.   For general histories of Chicago's Southside, see James Grossman, *Land of Hope: Chicago, Black Southerners, and the Great Migration* (Chicago: University of Chicago Press, 1991); Nicholas Lemann, *The Promised Land: The Great Black Migration and How It Changed America* (Westminster, Md.: David Mckay, 1992); Allan H. Spear, *Black Chicago: The Making of a Negro Ghetto, 1890–1920* (Chicago: University of Chicago Press, 1979); Kevin Mumford, *Interzones: Black/White Sex Districts in Chicago and New York in the Early Twentieth Century* (New York: Columbia University Press, 1997); St. Clair Drake and Horace Cayton, *Black Metropolis: A Study of Negro Life in a Northern City* (1945; Chicago: University of Chicago Press, 1993); and Sudhir Venkatesh, *American Project: The Rise and Fall of a Modern American Ghetto* (Cambridge, Mass.: Harvard University Press, 2002).

11.   For studies of inner-city economies, see Timothy Bates, *Black Capitalism: A Quantitative Analysis* (New York: Irvington, 1973); Daniel Fusfeld and Timothy Bates, *Political Economy of the Urban Ghetto* (Carbondale: Southern Illinois University Press, 1984); and William Tabb, *Political Economy of the Black Ghetto* (New York: W. W. Norton, 1971).

12.   See Betty Lou Valentine, *Hustling and Other Hard Work* (New York: Free Press, 1978); and Loic Wacquant, "Inside the Zone: The Social Art of the Hustler in the Black American Ghetto," *Theory, Culture, & Society* 15, no. 2 (1998): 1–36.

13.   William Julius Wilson, *The Truly Disadvantaged: The Inner City, the*

> *Underclass and Public Policy* (Chicago: University of Chicago Press, 1987).

Two: Home at Work

1. A general treatment of ghetto prostitution is Alexandra Murphy and Sudhir Venkatesh, "Vice Careers: The Changing Contours of Sex Work in New York City," *Qualitative Sociology* (2006).

2. This seasoned ethnographer begins his argument by (1) stating that these two terms are those of the people he studies (i.e., he does not impose his own moral framework) and (2) arguing that there is tremendous fluidity and people can code-switch between the two moral/legal systems. Yet, curiously, although his informants speak of trying to balance the two value systems, Anderson himself seems intent on using the heuristic more rigidly, placing people in boxes from which there seems to be no existential escape. See Elijah Anderson, *Streetwise: Race, Class, and Change in an Urban Community* (Chicago: University of Chicago Press, 1990).

3. Gerald Suttles, in his study of a multiethnic ghetto, called this a process of "ordered segmentation"; see Suttles, *The Social Order of the Slum* (Chicago: University of Chicago Press, 1969).

4. For a more complete discussion of how distinctions between public sphere and private sphere manifest along gendered lines for African Americans, see Pat Hill Collins, *Black Feminist Thought: Knowledge, Consciousness, and the Politics of Empowerment* (New York: Routledge, 1991).

5. See Carol Stack, *All Our Kin: Strategies for Survival in a Black Community* (New York: Harper Collins, 1974); Sandra Danziger and Sheldon Danziger, "Child Poverty and Public Policy: Toward a Comprehensive Antipoverty Agenda," *Daedalus* 122, no. 1 (1993): 57; Sharon Hays, *Flat Broke with Children: Women in the Age of Welfare Reform* (New York: Oxford University Press, 2004).

6. A review of the scholarship on sex-role differentiation in the family appears in Louise Tilly and Joan Scott, *Women, Work, and Family* (New York: Rinehart and Winston, 1978).

7. Gershuny finds that although men's and women's relative contributions to the household have moved closer to one another nationally, men contribute roughly 50 minutes a day toward household work while women contribute about 220 minutes (Jonathan I. Gershuny, "Economic Development and Change in the Mode of Provision of Services," in *Beyond Employment: Household Gender and Subsistence,* ed. Nanneke Redclift and Enzo Mingione [New York: Basil Blackwell, 1985]). Using

such figures, Hoyman argues that women are driven into the underground economy by their need to attend to these household duties, which are themselves not paid and which often require labor arrangements (e.g., day care, barter) that are not integrated into mainstream institutions. See M. Hoyman, "Female Participation in the Informal Economy: A Neglected Issue," in *The Annals of the American Academy of Political and Social Science: The Informal Economy,* ed. L. Ferman, S. Henry, and M. Hoyman (Newbury Park, Calif.: Sage, 1987), esp. 72.

8. The men in Liebow's study wove various myths, such as being "too manly" for marriage, which not only helped them cope with their inability to be a reliable husband but also provided them with an alternate source of meaning and identity—what Liebow would call a "value stretch." In describing how these men "stretch" the "mainstream" values and behaviors of middle-class Americans, Liebow wrote that the men do not have a normative "future time orientation" and so do not recognize and value long-term social arrangements, such as living with one spouse and taking care of children. They live in a world of immediacy and instability. See Elliot Liebow, *Tally's Corner: A Study of Negro Streetcorner Men* (London: Little, Brown, 1972).

9. The two professional couples both worked full-time in the corporate and government sectors. Although they certainly could have been supplementing their work with off-the-books labor, I could not document any such activity in their home. I am far more confident that their living arrangements were restricted to a nuclear family, however, because neither I nor their nanny ever saw any signs that relatives or friends were boarding with them.

10. Carol Stack has studied these internal family dynamics in poor African American households with great care. See Stack's *All Our Kin.*

11. See Mary Patillo, *Black Picket Fences: Privilege and Peril in the Black Middle Class* (Chicago: University of Chicago Press, 1999).

12. Martin Sanchez Jankowski provides a systematic analysis of how gangs develop relationships with persons and organizations in the wider community. See his *Islands in the Street* (Berkeley: University of California Press, 1991).

13. For the classic rendition, see Jane Jacobs, *The Death and Life of Great American Cities* (New York: Vintage, 1961), 30.

14. Robert Sampson has developed the notion of "collective efficacy"—the "working trust and shared willingness of residents to intervene in sharing social control. The concept of collective efficacy captures the link between cohesion—especially working trust—and shared expectations for action." See Sampson, "Neighborhood and Community: Collective

Efficacy and Community Safety," *The New Economy* 11: 106–113, quote at 108. This inquiry may be seen as an empirical examination of a style of collectively efficacious practice that has emerged in contemporary inner cities.

15. Susan Saegert, "Unlikely Leaders, Extreme Circumstances: Older Black Women Building Community Households," *American Journal of Community Psychology* 17, no. 3 (1989): 295–316.

16. "Since sexism delegates to females the task of creating and sustaining a home environment, it has been primarily the responsibility of black women to construct domestic households as spaces of care and nurturance in the face of the brutal harsh reality of racist oppression, of sexist domination . . . This task of making homeplace was not simply a matter of black women providing service; it was about the construction of a safe place where black people could affirm one another and by so doing heal many of the wounds inflicted by racist domination" (Bell Hooks, *Yearning: Race, Gender, and Cultural Politics* [Boston: South End Press, 1990], 42).

Three: The Entrepreneur

1. See William Julius Wilson, *The Truly Disadvantaged: The Inner City, the Underclass and Public Policy* (Chicago: University of Chicago Press, 1987).

2. Raphael W. Bostic and Breck L. Robinson, "Do CRA Agreements Influence Lending Patterns," *Real Estate Economics* 31, no. 1 (2003): 23–51. For Chicago CRA activity, the Woodstock Institute's *Community Lending Fact Book* is an invaluable resource, as is their report "Community-Bank Partnerships Creating Opportunities for the Unbanked," *Reinvestment Alert* no. 15 (June 2000).

3. Because TIFs are government subsidized (e.g., future tax revenue in the area must be used to offset government loans to development entities), they are a public good. However, certain sectors of the public have received relatively little benefit when their area has been "TIF'd." In Chicago, minority poor constituencies—both businesspersons and residents—have been shut out of development. Thus, practically speaking, the TIF is ending up as a contemporary form of urban renewal in which the government exercises eminent-domain powers or otherwise amasses large parcels of land and for a small fee turns them over to private corporate entities. For an excellent discussion of tax increment financing, see David Ranney, *Global Decisions, Local Collisions: Urban Life in the New World Order* (Philadelphia: University of Temple Press, 2004). For a detailed review of Chicago-based TIFs, see "How TIF

Funds Are Spent in Chicago" by the Neighborhood Capital and Budget Group, in Chicago; and "The Right Tool for the Job? An Analysis of Tax Increment Financing" (2003) by the Developing Neighborhood Alternatives Project, also in Chicago.

4. Richard Dye and David F. Merriam, "The Effect of Tax Increment Financing on Economic Development," *Journal of Urban Economics* 47 (2000): 306–328.

5. A survey can be found in Jeffrey A. Robinson, "An Economic Sociology of Entry Barriers," Ph.D. diss., School of Business, Columbia University, 2004.

6. For a critical review, see Harold E. Aldrich and Roger Waldinger, "Ethnicity and Entrepreneurship," *Annual Review of Sociology* 16 (1990): 111–135. A contemporary study of diverse ethnic entrepreneurs in the inner city may be found in Jennifer Lee, "Retail Niche Domination among African American, Jewish and Korean Entrepreneurs," *American Behavioral Scientist* 42, no. 9 (June/July 1999): 1398–1416.

7. Timothy Bates, *Race, Self-Employment, and Upward Mobility* (Baltimore: Johns Hopkins University Press, 1999), 13.

8. In a somewhat caustic appraisal, Bates attributes ethnic immigrant success to the foreign-born entrepreneur's visionary assessment of the lax rules in place post-1980 that could enforce health and safety, environmental protection, and hiring and worker rights. The argument reads as both an invective against foreign-born merchants and a loosely worded culturalist argument that attributes the capacity for exploitation to "ethnic" types. See ibid., 18–19.

9. There is a body of scholarship on African Americans who conduct business directly in their own concentrated poor neighborhoods—often in the areas where they live—and who must work continuously and creatively in their local environments in order to survive. Some noteworthy articles include Robert L. Boyd, "A Contextual Analysis of Black Self-Employment in Large Metropolitan Areas, 1970–1980," *Social Forces* 70, no. 2 (Dec. 1991): 409–429; Robert L. Boyd, "Black Entrepreneurship in 52 Metropolitan Areas," *Sociology and Social Research* 75, no. 3 (1991): 158–163; Frank Fatoe, "Social Capital of Black Business Owners," *Review of Black Political Economy* 16, no. 4 (Spring 1988): 13–51; Joe R. Feagin and Nikitah Imani, "Racial Barriers to African American Entrepreneurship: An Exploratory Study," *Social Problems* 41, no. 4 (1994): 562–585; Ivan Light and C. Rosenstein, *Race, Ethnicity, and Entrepreneurship in Urban America* (New York: Aldine de Gruyter, 1995).

10. "Research on inner city business development has not proceeded far

enough to serve as a useful guide for policy. Most of the research has been and continues to be on exceptional inner city enclaves; business conditions and outcomes, with inadequate consideration of social and political contexts; and the direct economic and employment benefits of inner city business development, or more specifically the lack thereof." R. Gittel and J. P. Thompson, "Inner-City Business Development and Entrepreneurships," in *Urban Problems and Community Development*, ed. R. Ferguson and W. Dickens (Washington D.C.: Brookings Institution Press, 1999), 473–520, quote at 274.

11. For essays on informalization and immigration, see Alejandro Portes, Manuel Castells, and Lauren Benton, eds., *The Informal Economy: Studies in Advanced and Less Developed Countries* (Baltimore: Johns Hopkins University Press, 2004).

12. About half of startup businesses in general close after four years, so the short tenure rates are not specific to ghetto-based businesses. Also, closure does not necessarily mean failure: businesses may merge, proprietors may find new and better economic opportunities, and so on. See Portes, Castells, and Benton, *The Informal Economy*; Brian Head, *Business Success: Factors Leading to Surviving and Closing Successfully*, Working Paper #CES-WP-01-01 (Washington, D.C.: Center for Economic Studies, U.S. Bureau of the Census, Jan. 2001); Jim Everett and John Watson, "Small Business Failure and External Risk Factors," *Small Business Economics* 11, no. 4 (1998): 1–7.

13. John Sibley Butler, *Entrepreneurship and Self-Help among Black Americans: A Reconsideration of Race and Economics* (Albany: SUNY Press, 1991); John Sibley Butler and Kenneth L. Wilson, "Entrepreneurial Enclaves: An Exposition into the Afro-American Experience," *National Journal of Sociology* 2: 127–166; and Robert L. Boyd, "A Contextual Analysis of Black Self-Employment in Large Metropolitan Areas, 1970–1980," *Social Forces* 70, no. 2: 409–429.

14. The Small Business Administration's definition is based on establishments that have fewer than five hundred employees. In Maquis Park, there are few such businesses. In 2004, Maquis Park had a total of 781 small businesses, and only 10 of those had more than a hundred employees. The criterion is not very helpful for understanding more modest merchants, whose experiences are very different from those of the proprietor who manages dozens or hundreds of employees.

15. Elliot Liebow, *Tally's Corner* (1967; London: Little, Brown, 1972); William H. Whyte, *The Organization Man* (New York: Simon and Schuster, 1956).

16. A lucid contemporary discussion of African American working-class

men is Mitchell Duneier's *Slim's Table: Race, Respectability, and Masculinity* (Chicago: University of Chicago Press, 1992).

17. Liebow, *Tally's Corner,* 63.

18. Liebow's 1960s study finds an interesting counterpart in Young's study of the assessment of life chances by black men in Chicago's inner city. See Alford Young Jr., *The Minds of Marginalized Black Men: Making Sense of Mobility, Opportunity, and Future Life Chances* (Princeton: Princeton University Press, 2003).

19. This view is supported by a study of small business owners in Miami, conducted by Joe R. Feagin and Michael Hodge. After providing many testimonials of black businesspersons who feel as though their white counterparts have numerous personal connections that help them get by, they write, "African American businesspeople are often shut out of the critical social and political networks, making it virtually impossible to run a business successfully . . . It is well recognized [by the businesspeople] that much of the business that is transacted is done at informal, social events. The people who are well connected will reap the greater benefits." Feagin and Hodge, "African-American Entrepreneurship and Racial Discrimination: A Southern Metropolitan Case," in *The Bubbling Cauldron: Race, Ethnicity and the Urban Crisis,* ed. Michael Peter Smith and Joe R. Feagin (Minneapolis: University of Minnesota Press, 1995), 112–113.

20. Duneier, *Slim's Table,* 112.

21. The primary exceptions are the real estate developer who may have a presence in another black or Latino community, or the contractor who might receive the occasional city contract—e.g., a janitorial procurement in which black custodians work in a predominantly white school or clean up after "special events," such as City of Chicago fairs, festivals, and concerts.

22. I interviewed these fifteen men extensively in order to obtain life-history information. They are not by any means the only successful entrepreneurs in Maquis Park. They should be viewed as examples of individuals who have local power in economic development.

23. For a moving account of the relationship between South Asians and African Americans in contemporary U.S. society, see Vijay Prashad, *The Karma of Brown Folk* (Minneapolis: University of Minnesota Press, 2000).

24. See D'Souza Dinesh, "Work and the African American," *American Enterprise* 6, no. 5 (1995): 33–34.

25. For a critical review of comparisons of black Americans with other ethnic groups, see Bates, *Race, Self-Employment, and Upward Mobility.*

26. On their limited relations with financial institutions, see Frank Fratoe, "A Sociological Analysis of Minority Business," *Review of Black Political Economy* 15, no. 2 (1986): 5–29.

27. "People often interpret such statements to mean that nontraditional credit sources (families, friends, revolving credit associations) are the main sources of financing for small businesses created by Asian immigrants. This is incorrect: equity capital is the most important source; loans from financial institutions ranks second" (Bates, *Race, Self-Employment, and Upward Mobility*, 123).

28. See Butler, *Entrepreneurship and Self-Help*.

29. An alderman's power and influence in Chicago is the product of several factors, one of which is the capacity to bring out the vote in her ward. The lack of clout of Alderman Mattie Carson in the Chicago City Council is often attributed to her inability to ensure a large voting bloc in her ward. In part, this is due to voter apathy and the historic antagonism between Chicago's black constituencies and the white-dominated political machine. However, another important factor is the gradual population decline in poor neighborhoods such as Maquis Park. Since the sixties there has been a steady departure of middle- and upper-class residents and a continuous loss of jobs and commerce, not only from Maquis Park but also from the adjoining communities with African American working poor and concentrated poverty. This has resulted in the subsequent departure of working families and the disenfranchisement of the remaining population, who may be apathetic or have little faith in the power of political leaders to address their needs.

30. One could argue that the political dealings alluded to above are "underground economic" practices. But I separate them out of this discussion because they are also part of the routine of doing business. Their relationship with the underground, then, is that they engage in institutionalized activities that support off-the-books income generation.

31. According to economist C. Lowell Harris, "'Redlining' refers to the arbitrary decisions of government and financial institutions not to lend in certain neighborhoods because of general characteristics of the neighborhood rather than of the particular property to be mortgaged" (Harris, *History and Policies of the Home Owners' Loan Corporation* [New York: National Bureau of Economic Research, 1951]). The practice of redlining was initiated in the twenties as a result of an attempt by the Home Owners' Loan Corporation (HOLC) to predict the risk of mortgage financing through the development of a uniform system for appraising a home according to the block on which it was located. Accordingly, a block's rating was based upon both the quality of its housing

stock, including its sales demand, age, and degree of needed repair, as well as the demographics of those living on the block, with specific concern for their occupation, class, and race. There were four grades of ratings. Neighborhoods in which the residents were homogeneous in race and class and where the neighborhood was deemed to be in high demand in good and bad times were given the highest rating. The lowest rating, the fourth grade, denoted by the color red, was given to neighborhoods that were considered to be in a state of decline with no hope for future improvement—neighborhoods that were considered risky investments. Lending to these areas was not advised. In the thirties, research conducted by Homer Hoyt found that housing values declined in accordance with the socioeconomic status of residents and that the movement of blacks into a neighborhood resulted in a drastic decline in housing prices there. HOLC used this study, and others that showed a relationship between falling housing prices and the movement of blacks into neighborhoods, when appraising real estate. Thus, those neighborhoods where blacks either lived or had recently moved in were deemed a risky investment and "redlined." Both public and private financial institutions, as well as the Federal Housing Administration, adopted these appraisals made by HOLC and used them when making their own financial decisions (see Kenneth Jackson, *Crabgrass Frontier: The Suburbanization of the United States* [New York: Oxford University Press, 1985]). The result was massive financial disinvestment in homes and businesses in black residential areas as funds were redirected from redlined areas. Massey argued that the unequal distribution of financial resources between white and black areas that resulted from this practice of redlining not only deepened, but also institutionalized, racial and class segregation in American cities (Douglas Massey and Nancy Denton, *American Apartheid: Segregation and the Making of the Underclass* [Cambridge, Mass.: Harvard University Press, 1993]).

32. In the majority of cases, borrowing among elites was motivated by non-profit-sector opportunities that emerged. These individuals routinely respond to government and philanthropic "requests for proposals" to offer day care, social services, job training, counseling, and affordable housing to the poor in their community. Many have already established nonprofit corporations, and when an opportunity comes about, they shift their energy and resources for a short period of time to win a contract or secure a grant. Just as quickly, they return to their earlier commercial pursuits or move to a new one altogether.

33. There are seventeen active creditors in Maquis Park. As in any community, there are also innumerable individuals there who make small

loans. However, these persons are widely known to be "creditors"—i.e., in the underground economy they are primarily seen as lenders of money. Most of them work in other jobs, and they are all longtime members of the community. Eighty percent of them were born and raised in Maquis Park, and only two have lived outside of Chicago. (One was in the armed forces.) They all have strong political connections to local assemblypersons and city council members, which enables them to ward off police interdiction. In fact, ten obtained their current jobs because of their connections to the local alderman; twelve said that their parents had patronage jobs as well. Six have had parents employed by the Chicago police force at some point in their lives.

34. In addition to a failure to build up relations with financial institutions, there are other negative consequences to internal community lending. In the worst cases, there are reports of physical retaliation by creditors for unpaid loans. In Maquis Park at least a dozen persons were beaten up each year by a creditor for failing to make payments. Most were residents, not local proprietors. Among the merchant class, it was more common for the creditors to demand payment in kind—free meals at restaurants, free groceries, free auto repair, etc.—or to ask that their money be laundered through the establishment. Laundering inevitably places the store owner at risk, not only for apprehension by law enforcement, but to escalating indebtedness to creditors. They must meet weekly payments, which carry steep interest rates and require them to find other sources of cash—which means they may have to use other creditors or, if lucky, draw on the goodwill of friends and relatives who have cash on hand.

35. As Feagin and Hodge argue in their study of the perceptions of black entrepreneurs, "connections" and social supports generally for black merchants are seen as both the ability to rely on those in one's social network as well as utilizing those networks to access resources in the wider society. See Feagin and Hodge, "African-American Entrepreneurship."

36. Manning Marable, *How Capitalism Underdeveloped Black America* (Boston: South End Press, 1983).

37. It is telling that this sentiment has long been a part of black entrepreneurship. St. Clair Drake and Horace Cayton wrote of elite blacks in Chicago's Southside in the mid-twentieth century that a "defensive racialism" shaped their attitudes: that is, these elite blacks emphasized the need to fight segregation and discrimination in economic opportunity, but they simultaneously retreated by privileging the need for blacks to engage in commerce with one another. See St. Clair Drake and Horace

Cayton, *Black Metropolis: A Study of Negro Life in a Northern City* (Chicago: University of Chicago Press, 1996), 554.

38. Abstracting away a set of principles risks lending the appearance that individuals construct or learn these rules *a priori* via scholastic means, rather than by observing one another over time in response to invariant social inequities. The general issue is addressed in Loic J. D. Wacquant, "The Double-Edged Sword of Reason: The Scholar's Predicament and the Sociologist's Mission," *European Journal of Social Theory* 2, no. 3 (Spring 1998): 275–281.

39. For a contrastive case, see the examination of Italian working-poor residents in Chicago in Gerald Suttles's *The Social Order of the Slum* (Chicago: University of Chicago Press, 1969).

Four: The Street Hustler

1. In perhaps his most ambitious underground venture, James hired six other squatters to walk up and down the Dan Ryan Expressway searching for cars that had flat tires or needed other repairs. The men would call James, who would offer to fix the cars at low cost. In the first week one of the men decided to rob a stranded driver, and the police told James that he had to keep those men off of the highway.

2. It is worth mentioning several national trends that altered the physical landscape of central cities and, in so doing, put shelter at a premium for the poorest urbanites. From 1970 until the end of the eighties, more than a million single-room-occupancy units—a primary residential habitat for marginal minority and poor Americans—were demolished. In Chicago all such "cubicle hotels" for housing the poor were totally eliminated. And between 1973 and 1993, 2.2 million low-rent units disappeared from the urban housing market (National Coalition for the Homeless, "Why Are People Homeless?" NCH Fact Sheet #1, Washington, D.C., Sept. 2002). Additionally, Illinois, like other states, eliminated the General Assistance grant program, which funded single poor people and which has long been a means of preventing homelessness. In 1992 the state legislature stopped making payments to sixty thousand Chicagoans ("Aid Down, Homelessness Up," *Chicago Sun-Times*, July 30, 1992).

3. There is not a great deal of scholarly work on hustlers and hustling in the American urban context, particularly the status of hustlers within an urban neighborhood. There is some research on the inner city after the civil rights period, including Dan Rose, *Black American Street Life: South Philadelphia, 1969–1971* (Philadelphia: University of Pennsylva-

nia Press, 1987); Ned Polksy, *Hustlers, Beats, and Others* (Garden City, N.Y.: Lyons Press, 1967); Bettylou Valentine, *Hustling and Other Hard Work: Lifestyles in the Ghetto* (New York: Free Press, 1978); Gail Sheehy, *Hustling: Prostitution in Our Wide Open Society* (New York: Delacorte Press, 1973).

For the period after the eighties, the definitive work on hustling in a wider social context is Mitchell Duneier, *Sidewalk* (New York: Farrar, Straus and Giroux, 1999). Apart from Duneier's work, one has to glean from studies of drug traffickers, street gangs, and organized crime to arrive at some understanding of the relationships between hustling and neighborhood social organization. Given that people with tenuous residential status often practice street hustling, one useful source of information is the research on urban homelessness. A review of the homeless literature appears in J. D. Wright, B. A. Rubin, and J. A. Devine, *Beside the Golden Door: Policy, Politics, and the Homeless* (New York: Aldine de Gruyter, 1998). However, even in this research tradition only minimal attention is given to the wider social context of homelessness. Instead, the research focuses on enumerating homeless persons and understanding their ties to mental health and criminal justice institutions. This is in part due to the removal of traditional "skid row" neighborhoods, which has balkanized urban homelessness in a process Ruddick calls "polynucleation" (S. Ruddick, *Young and Homeless in Hollywood: Mapping Social Identities* [New York: Routledge, 1996]). The dispersion of the homeless in Chicago is confirmed in Barrett Lee and Townsand Price-Spratlen, "The Geography of Homelessness in American Communities: Concentration or Dispersion?" *City and Community* 3, no. 1 (Mar. 2004): 3–27.

4. See Loic Wacquant, "Inside the Zone: The Social Art of the Hustler in the Black American Ghetto," *Theory, Culture, & Society* 15, no. 2 (1998): 1–36.

5. Some cities, like Chicago, limit the access of certain groups to these spaces. Some have laws that prohibit the convening of gang members, homeless encampments, and the like. Even more common are the loitering and public nuisance ordinances that have been around for decades.

6. Several studies have examined social ties among the urban homeless. The results generally suggest that this population has weak social ties to one another and to nonhomeless persons. Snow and Anderson suggest that the homeless are "plagued by contradictory characteristics," such as being simultaneously reliant on each other for support but distrustful of one another and constantly on the watch for exploitation by associ-

ates (D. Snow and L. Anderson, *Down on Their Luck: A Study of Homeless People on the Street* [Berkeley: University of California Press, 1993]). Similarly, Grisby et al. find that impermanence and impoverishment force street-based individuals to rely one another and to develop fewer ties with more stable residents, which they say becomes a "double edged sword" that serves to reinforce their marginal position (C. Grisby, D. Baumann , S. E. Gregorich, and C. Roberts-Gray, "Disaffiliation to Entrenchment: A Model for Understanding Homelessness," *Journal of Social Issues* 46, no. 4: 141–156).

7. See Duneier, *Sidewalk*.

8. Community policing in Chicago was implemented in several police districts throughout the city in 1993 and was expanded to the entire city in 1995. The mission of this law enforcement initiative, officially titled "Chicago Alternative Policing Strategy" (CAPS), was to replace the former "reactive" approach to policing with a model of solving problems ranging from crime, to community concerns, to problems with city services, using the resources and energies of both the police and the community. A central feature of CAPS is cooperation between police and the community in both identifying community problems and working together to address these concerns (Wesley Skogan, Susan Hartnett, Jill DuBois, Jennifer Comey, Marianne Kaiser, and Justine Lovig, *Problem Solving in Practice: Implementing Community Policing in Chicago* [Washington D.C.: National Institute of Justice, 2000]). To achieve this end, the implementation of CAPS required the development of new responsibilities for the Chicago police that were designed to create novel approaches to problem solving. Such changes included a reorganization based on small police beats in which individual police officers were solely committed to their designated turf; providing police with greater access to city services, which was intended to facilitate more effective responses to public concerns; and facilitating cooperation between police officers and their beats through the organization of beat meetings and district advisory committees (DACs), which provided a forum for the community to express their concerns and the police to directly respond (Wesley Skogan, Lynn Steiner, Jill DuBois, J. Erik Gudell, and Aimee Fagan, *Taking Stock: Community Policing in Chicago* (Washington D.C.: National Institute of Justice, 2000). For more information on community policing in Chicago, see also the program evaluation series and community policing working papers published by the Institute for Policy Research at Northwestern University; Wesley Skogan and Susan Hartnett, *Community Policing: Chicago Style* (New York: Oxford Community Press, 1997); Wesley Skogan, "Community Policing in Chicago,"

in *Community Policing,* ed. Geoffrey Alpert and Alex Piquero (Prospect Heights, Ill.: Waveland Press, 1998), 159–174; David Weisburd and Anthony Braga, *Prospects and Problems in an Era of Police Innovation: Contrasting Perspectives* (Cambridge: Cambridge University Press, 2005).

9. Cf. Jane Jacobs, *The Death and Life of Great American Cities* (New York: Random House, 1961).

10. Other sociologists examining public space have taken up Jacobs's writings to highlight the capacity of vibrant streetfare to enable social control. Duneier's study of a middle- to upper-class Manhattan neighborhood documented the contribution made by the local street vendors and sidewalk booksellers to the local sense of public safety. Elijah Anderson's *Streetwise: Race, Class, and Change in an Urban Community* (Chicago: University of Chicago Press, 1990), which is based on a gentrifying neighborhood of Philadelphia, suggests that in periods of urban renewal, established social control procedures are never devised based on abstract citizens, but are always inflected by race and class, such that "public" space is a place where differing social groups effectively fight over the right to appropriate space in different ways.

11. See Anderson, *Streetwise.*

12. See Archon Fung, *Empowered Participation: Reinventing Urban Democracy* (Princeton: Princeton University Press, 2004).

13. For example, the Chicago Police Officer Home Ownership Incentive provides up to $5,000 in home ownership subsidies to police officers who purchase homes in low-income neighborhoods (Greater Chicago Housing and Community Development website). To be eligible, officers may either purchase homes in designated neighborhoods where at least 50 percent of the residents have incomes at least 80 percent below the median area income, or they may purchase homes that are located in a Chicago Housing Authority (CHA) Redevelopment Project, which is a residential or mixed-use development built as part of the CHA Plan for Transformation ("Reports of Committees 45589 Committee on Housing and Real Estate," Apr. 6, 2005, Chicago City Clerk, City Council). The hope is that the incorporation of police officers as residents in such communities will improve neighborhood revitalization efforts in these areas throughout the city (Greater Chicago Housing and Community Development website). This program is similar to the U.S. Department of Housing and Urban Development's national program, Officer Next Door, in which police officers may purchase HUD homes for half price in designated "revitalization areas" in which they patrol (James DeBoth, "Specialty Mortgage Programs for People Who Don't Fit the Mold," *Chicago Tribune,* retrieved from www.chicagotribune .com in 2005.)

Five: The Preacher

1. Sociologist Mary Patillo writes in her study of Chicago's black churches, "The black church has a documented tradition of involvement in extra religious civic and political activities." See Patillo, "Church Culture as a Strategy of Action in the Black Community," *American Sociological Review* 63 (1998): 767–784.

2. Forrest E. Harris Sr., *Ministry for Social Crisis: Theology and Praxis in the Black Church Tradition* (Macon, Ga.: Mercer University Press, 1993), 21. See also Samuel D. Proctor, "Black Protestants and Public Policy," in *Black Religion and Public Policy: Ethical and Historical Perspectives*, ed. Joseph R. Washington Jr. (N.p.: n.p., 1978).

3. James H. Harris, *Black Ministers and Laity in the Urban Church: An Analysis of Political and Social Experience* (New York: University Press of America, 1987), 67. In this respect, black churches are more community focused—that is, more focused on service delivery—than their white counterparts. Stephanie Boddie writes, "Overall, the black church is more involved in providing the following services than is their white or interracial counterparts: basic needs, health, community development, and advocacy" (Boddie, "Faith-Based Organizations and the Sharing of Social Responsibility: Comparing the Community Programs of African American, Interracial, and White Congregations," Center for Social Development Working Paper no. 03-15 [St. Louis: Washington University, 2003]).

4. See Ernest N. Morial, "Black Religion and Civil Rights," in Washington, *Black Religion and Public Policy*.

5. For a discussion of the theological roots of diversity within the black ministry, see Cheryl Townsend Gilkes, "Some Folks Get Happy and Some Folks Don't," in *Courage to Hope: From Black Suffering to Human Redemption*, ed. Quinton Hosford Dixie and Cornel West (Boston: Beacon Press, 1999).

6. For a review of studies on black ministry in contemporary urban environs, see Omar McRoberts, *Streets of Glory: Church and Community in a Black Urban Neighborhood* (Chicago: University of Chicago Press, 2003).

7. In a pathbreaking study of black urban preachers in Detroit, Ronald Johnston sorted black urban clergy into three categories—"militants" who emphasized political engagement, "moderates" who understood the need to adopt an activist orientation but who thought it to be secondary to preaching, and "traditionalists" who remained wedded to the notion that the preacher's responsibility was to translate scripture. See Johnston, "Negro Preachers Take Sides," in *The Black Church in Amer-*

ica, ed. H. M. Nelson (New York: Basic Books, 1971). For a critique of Johnston's taxonomy, see John Brown Childs, *The Political Black Minister: A Study in Afro-American Politics and Religion* (Boston: G. K. Hall, 1980).

8. See James R. Grossman, *Land of Hope: Chicago, Black Southerners, and the Great Migration* (Chicago: University of Chicago Press, 1989), 229–231.

9. St. Clair Drake and Horace Cayton, *Black Metropolis: A Study of Negro Life in a Northern City* (1945; Chicago: University of Chicago Press, 1993), 428.

10. "As the primary social and cultural institution, the black church tradition is deeply embedded in black culture in general so that the sphere of politics in the African American community cannot be easily separated from [it]." C. Eric Lincoln and Lawrence H. Mamiya, *The Black Church in the African-American Experience,* (Durham, N.C.: Duke University Press, 1990), 234.

11. Evidence for this is not readily available. However, years later the *Chicago Reporter* would confirm that a small number of churches held a monopoly over resources in Chicago's Southside because of their influence in Mayor Daley's administration. See "Black Ministers Put Faith in Daley," *Chicago Reporter,* Sept. 2000.

12. In Chicago, the period roughly from the height of Richard J. Daley's administration in the mid-1950s to the beginning of his son's (Richard M. Daley's) administration in 1989 marked a key transition in black Chicago's political landscape. Until the middle of the 1960s, the first Mayor Daley depended on black leaders—religious and secular—to bring out the "black vote." While it is debatable whether the black community received anything resembling a fair exchange in return, the most powerful African American stakeholders were loyal to the Daley regime. After the civil rights era, the traditional support base for Daley waned, not only because of black Chicagoans' widespread frustration with the white political machine, but also because Daley managed to shift his base of support to the city's white wards. Black voter turnout was no longer imperative for reelection (Paul Kleppner, *Chicago Divided: The Making of a Black Mayor* [De Kalb: Northern Illinois University Press, 1985]).

13. Abdul Alkalimat and Doug Gills, *Harold Washington and the Crisis of Black Power in Chicago* (Chicago: Twenty-First Century Books, 1989), 27.

14. William J. Grimshaw, *Bitter Fruit: Black Politics and the Chicago Machine: 1931–1991* (Chicago: University of Chicago Press, 1992), 195–196.

15. See William Julius Wilson, *The Truly Disadvantaged: The Inner City, the Underclass and Public Policy* (Chicago: University of Chicago Press, 1987).

16. See Sudhir Venkatesh and Steven Levitt, "Are We a Family or a Business? History and Disjuncture in the Urban American Street Gang," *Theory and Society* 29, no. 4 (2000): 427–467.

17. See, for example, Wilson, *The Truly Disadvantaged.*

18. For a similar discussion on Italian American working-class churches in postwar Chicago, see the chapter titled "Institutions" in Gerald Suttles's *The Social Order of the Slum* (Chicago: University of Chicago Press, 1969).

19. I. A. Spergel, *The Youth Gang Problem: A Community Approach* (New York: Oxford University Press, 1995).

20. There are, of course, exceptions. In the 1960s, black storefront and grassroots churches—and sympathetic white churches—were in the public eye because of their alleged support for Chicago's militant black youth movements. The Woodlawn community's First Church, like many other churches in the Southside, were repeatedly chastised for storing illegally obtained weapons and cash for gang members, for sponsoring meetings of the Illinois Black Panther Party, and for otherwise obstructing justice by failing to cooperate with police in investigations of local activist organizations. See, for example, John R. Fry's memoir, *Locked-Out Americans* (New York: Harper and Row, 1973).

21. For a critical discussion of CCIs, see Robert Chaskin, Prudence Brown, Sudhir Venkatesh, and Avis Vidal, *Building Community Capacity* (New York: Aldine de Gruyter, 2001). For a historical analysis of neighborhood-based initiatives in urban America, see Robert Halpern, *Rebuilding the Inner City: A History of Neighborhood Initiatives to Address Poverty in the United States* (New York: Columbia University Press, 1995).

22. See C. Eric Lincoln and Lawrence H. Mamiya, *The Black Church in the African American Experience* (Durham: Duke University Press, 1990), for a discussion of tenure of urban preachers.

Six: Our Gang

1. See Irving A. Spergel, *The Youth Gang Problem: A Community Approach* (New York: Oxford University Press, 1995).

2. Latino gangs in Chicago did not necessarily follow the path to "corporatization" at the same time, in the same manner. See Ruth Horowitz's *Honor and the American Dream: Culture and Identity in a Chicano Community* (New Brunswick: Rutgers University Press, 1983) for an excel-

lent study of the relationships of young Latino youth to their communities. For a general survey of post-civil-rights gang activity, see Brenda Coughlin and Sudhir Venkatesh, "The Urban Street Gang after 1970," *Annual Review of Sociology* 29 (2003): 41–64.

3. See William Julius Wilson, *The Truly Disadvantaged: The Inner City, the Underclass and Public Policy* (Chicago: University of Chicago Press, 1987).

4. Some accounts point to waves of African American adults leaving the criminal justice system; they could no longer find jobs in the industrial labor force and so joined gangs and turned them into economic actors. On the demand side, crack cocaine and heroin, the principal commodities traded by corporate gangs in the seventies and eighties, lent themselves to mass production; the exponential rise in demand for these highly addictive drugs pushed gangs to develop connections across neighborhoods, work in large groups, and otherwise develop the organizational capacity to direct underground economies that not only spanned neighborhoods but often traversed the city. For an analysis of this period of change as well as a description of the realignment of the Chicago police force, see Felix Padilla, *The Gang as an American Enterprise* (New Brunswick: Rutgers University Press, 1992).

5. Mary Pattillo-McCoy, *Black Picket Fences: Privilege and Peril among the Black Middle Class* (Chicago: University of Chicago Press, 1999).

6. See *Chicago Tribune*, June 19, 1988, and *New York Times*, Dec. 27, 1985.

7. See *Chicago Sun-Times*, Apr. 7, 2002, and *Los Angeles Times*, Mar. 24, 1997.

8. The principal of Englewood High School awarded plaques and awards to one jailed gang leader and his associate for their help in forming a truce between warring gangs inside the school. See *Chicago Sun Times*, Oct. 30, 1993.

9. See *Chicago Sun-Times*, Mar. 20, 1997; *Chicago Sun-Times* Special Section, Apr. 8, 2002.

10. At one point, each drug dealer in the Gangster Disciples gang had to pay $5 weekly to a common fund for political activities (*Los Angeles Times*, Mar. 24, 1997). In October 1993 there were ten gang members on the ballot for local school council elections (*Chicago Sun Times*, Oct. 22, 1993). Inner-city black Chicagoans faced an unpleasant choice: they could continue voting for the status quo, which effectively meant the elected alderpersons who had done little to challenge the mayor's visible disinterest in poor people, or they could seek gains in power through new elected officials who sported questionable histories but who seemed at least partly sincere in their desire to increase the power of the

grassroots. This movement attracted prominent Chicago leaders, including the Reverend Jesse Jackson and former Chicago mayor Eugene Sawyer (see *Chicago Sun-Times,* Aug. 31, 1992). Thus, residents saw gatherings where gang members were surrounded by clergy, merchants, prominent black elected officials, schoolteachers and administrators, activists, and members of community-based organizations (see *Chicago Sun-Times* Mar. 21, 1995, and *Chicago Sun-Times,* Aug. 30, 1994). A resident could join with the wider civic community in its skepticism of the intentions of candidates who were, or formerly had been, members of gangs, but unlike their neighbors across the city, they had to decide whether they would be part of a social movement in which the gang was playing a major role.

11. There are several explanations for the diminishing presence of crack, none adequately substantiated and most built around speculations about the deaths of crack users, shifts in the global narcotics trade resulting from the federal government's war on drugs, and improved policing at the neighborhood level in most major cities. Whatever the cause, by the late nineties there did appear to be fewer new users of crack cocaine.

12. See Sudhir Alladi Venkatesh and Steven D. Levitt, "Are We a Family or a Business? History and Ideology in Chicago's Street Gang," *Theory and Society* 29, no. 4 (2000): 427–467.

13. Steven D. Levitt and Sudhir Venkatesh, "The Financial Activities of an Urban Street Gang," *Quarterly Journal of Economics* 115, no. 3 (2000): 755–789.

14. See Philip J. Cook, Jens Ludwig, Sudhir A. Venkatesh, and Anthony A. Braga, "Underground Gun Markets," NBER Working Paper no. 11737 (Cambridge, Mass.: National Bureau of Economic Research, 2005).

Seven: As the Shady World Turns

1. See Kevin Mumford, *Interzones: Black/White Sex Districts in Chicago and New York in the Early Twentieth Century* (New York: Columbia University Press, 1997); and St. Clair Drake and Horace Cayton, *Black Metropolis: A Study of Negro Life in a Northern City* (1945; Chicago: University of Chicago Press, 1993).

2. We could extend this line of thinking further by considering the impact on cities, regions, and nation-states, as a number of scholars have done. See Saskia Sassen, *The Global City: New York, London, Tokyo* (Princeton: Princeton University Press, 2000); Barbara Ehrenreich and Arlie Hochschild, eds., *Global Woman: Nannies, Maids, and Sex Workers in the New Economy* (New York: Henry Holt, 2003); Bruno Dallago, *The Irreg-*

ular Economy: The "Underground" Economy and the "Black" Labour Market (Brookfield, Vt.: Dartmouth Publishing Co., 1990); J. J. Thomas, *Informal Economic Activity* (London: Harvester Wheatsheaf, 1992); Alejandro Portes, Manuel Castells, and Lauren Benton, "Conclusion: The Policy Implications of Informality," in *The Informal Economy: Studies in Advances and Less Developed Countries,* ed. A. Portes, M. Castells, and L. Benton (Baltimore: Johns Hopkins University Press, 1989); Vito Tanzi, "The Underground Economy: The Causes and Consequences of This Worldwide Phenomenon," *Finance and Development* 20 (1983): 10–13D; Robert McGee and Edgar Feige, "Policy Illusion, Macroeconomic Instability, and the Unrecorded Economy," in *The Underground Economies,* ed. Edgar Feige (New York: Cambridge University Press, 1989); Alejandro Portes and Saskia Sassan-Koob, "Making It Underground: Comparative Material on the Urban Informal Sector in Western Market Economies," *American Journal of Sociology* 93 (1987): 30–61.

3. A notable exception is Nicole Marwell's study of nonprofit organizations in New York City. See Marwell, "Privatizing the Welfare State: Nonprofit Community-Based Organizations as Political Actors," *American Sociological Review* 69, no. 2 (2004): 265.

4. For a discussion of the ways in which urban poor residents navigate areas outside their neighborhoods, see Mario Small, *Villa Victoria: The Transformation of Social Capital in a Boston Barrio* (Chicago: University of Chicago Press, 2004).

Acknowledgments

A grant from the National Science Foundation's Faculty Early Career Development (CAREER) program enabled me to complete this book. The Department of Sociology and the Institute for Research in African-American Studies at Columbia University and the Institute for Scholars at Reid Hall, in Paris, provided support throughout the writing period. My companions at Harvard University's Society of Fellows suffered quietly my endless excursions outside social science.

My friends and colleagues, too many to mention, read drafts patiently. Alford Young, Jr., Dan Cook, Nicole Marwell, Ethan Michaeli, Peter Bearman, Baron Pineda, Omar McRoberts, Matthew McGuire, Benjamin Mintz, Sunil Garg, and Steven Levitt offered encouragement and constructive feedback. On all my projects, I turn to Nathaniel Deutsch for clarity when the road is muddy. Daniel Brown gave me the love of Chicago; he is the city's greatest intellect. And, from a faraway place, Mike and the Mad Dog helped me get through days and chapters; it was from their voices that I learned to love the process.

This is the second book that I have completed under the guidance of Joyce Seltzer at Harvard University Press, and I continue to learn from her wisdom and intellect. David Lobenstine helped to craft this book with just the right mix of criticism and editorial insight. Alexandra Murphy gave much of her time, perhaps too much—thank you.

Autry Harrison and Dorothy Battie helped me navigate the waters of Chicago's Southside: thanks for watching my back.

I am grateful to Katchen Locke's love, ideas, and support at every turn. She will always be a part of my life and work.

Last but not least, to my mother, father, and Urmila: by my side at every turn.

Index

Advertising, 129–130, 131, 165, 171, 198

African Americans: "decent" values vs. "street" values among, 37–38, 60–61, 392n2; collective action of women among, 88–90; as small business owners, 97–107, 109–113, 117–118, 130, 149; vs. immigrants as entrepreneurs, 97–98, 114–117, 130; vs. whites as entrepreneurs, 117–118, 149; white churches vs. churches of, 215–216; migration from South, 222, 230–231, 389n1; imprisonment of, 242. *See also* Clergy; Households; Racial discrimination

African Methodist Episcopal Church, 227

Agnes (Maquis Park resident), 164

Ajay (Maquis Park resident), 160

Alcoholism, 131, 242

All God's Children, 330–331

Allison, Orlando, 112, 138–139, 148

Anderson, Elijah: on "decent" values vs. "street" values, 37–38, 60–61, 392n2; on control of public space, 404n10

Anderson, L., 402n6

Arleander, James, 211–212, 356; on gang activity, 3, 4; car repair by, 3, 4, 6, 128, 133–134, 153, 156, 166–168, 175–176, 185, 212, 213, 251, 260, 354, 371, 377, 401n1; relations with "Big Cat" Williams, 4, 311–312, 313, 314, 316; on relationship with other hustlers, 187, 194, 211; on getting a place, 198–199; on poverty, 361

Artistic products, 33

Ashland, Kevin, 236, 239–240, 256–257

Assault, 80, 89, 124, 281

Attitudes of Maquis Park residents: toward gangs, 1–4, 6, 22, 48–49, 58, 60, 62–90, 124, 156–157, 159, 161, 237, 239–240, 245–246, 252–253, 257–259, 261–263, 264, 265–266, 279–281, 285, 291–302, 306–308, 311–318, 319–339, 343–344, 367–370, 371; toward drug trafficking, 2, 4, 6, 26, 37, 39, 45, 47, 54–55, 56, 73–75, 76, 80, 82, 86–87, 124, 163, 208, 211, 252–253, 281, 312–313; toward public safety, 2, 4–5, 8, 13, 23, 39, 61–64, 71–75, 79–80, 81, 84, 124, 227–228, 244–245, 274, 291–292, 328–329, 334, 370; toward police, 2, 22, 72, 76, 77–80, 81, 84, 88, 106, 109, 126, 163–165, 167, 175, 183, 198, 200–204, 206, 213, 239–240, 250–251, 280–281, 292, 293, 297, 299, 307, 320–321, 322, 324, 327–328, 336, 344, 345–346, 349, 364, 365, 372, 374, 375, 380, 382, 385–386; toward ethical issues, 8, 24, 37–39, 48–51, 60–62, 73–76, 80–81, 82–84, 88–89, 106–107, 124–125, 216–217, 256, 257, 261–262, 275–276, 281; toward work, 19, 100–102, 115, 116; toward friends and relatives, 22, 25, 45–53; toward religion, 22, 39, 56–57; toward the future, 22, 39–42, 51, 53–59, 100–102, 293, 298, 301, 379 381, 393n8; toward public officials, 22, 72, 81–82, 106, 121–123, 125, 135, 158, 175, 235–241, 244–245, 248, 260, 264–266, 271, 370, 398n29; toward social mobility, 38, 40, 101, 103–104, 149–150; toward prostitution, 49–51, 52–53, 56–57, 73, 74–75, 76, 80, 81, 82–83, 163, 164, 208, 211, 225, 239, 243, 275, 295, 297, 327; toward helping others, 60; toward the past, 101–102, 373–374, 377–379, 380; toward financial institutions, 121, 135–136, 143–144; toward clergy, 219–220, 261–262, 275–277, 370

Auletta, Ken: *The Underclass,* 19

Automobile repair. *See* Car repair